Diaspora 4

ANTONIO D'ALFONSO

I Could Have Been a Contender

(On Five Films)

Bread and Chocolate
A Pain in the Ass
Queen of Hearts
The Mediterranean Forever
Raging Bull

CASA LAGO PRESS

Diaspora
Volume 4

As "diaspora" is the dispersion or spread of people from their original homeland, this book series takes its name in the intellectual spirit of willful dispersion of subject matter and thought. It is dedicated to publishing those studies that in various and sundry ways either speak to or offer new methods of analysis of the Italian diaspora.

The publication of this book has bene made possible through a generous grant from an anonymous donor who wishes not to be identified but urges others to donate to historical and cultural studies.

COVER IMAGE: An image from *Raging Bull* when Jake LaMotta looks for the gold ball that Vickie hit, which disappeared under the church.

ISBN 978-1-955995-09-2
Library of Congress Control Number: 2024943641

© 2024 Antonio D'Alfonso

All rights reserved.
Printed in the United States of America

CASA LAGO PRESS
New Fairfield, CT

TABLE OF CONTENTS

Acknowledgements	7
Note	9
Introduction	11
1. *Bread and Chocolate* (1974) by Franco Brusati	45
2. *A Pain in the Ass* (1973) by Édouard Molinaro	104
3. *Queen of Hearts* (1989) by Jon Amiel	143
4. *The Mediterranean Forever* (2000) by Nicola Zavaglia	215
5. *Raging Bull* (1980) by Martin Scorsese	270
6. Conclusion	330
Films Cited	340
Works Cited	345
Index of Names and Titles	355
About the Author	361

Cinema is a weird profession. They discover you once you are dead. So, Manfredi, don't worry. Just wait and see all the films they'll want you to do when you're dead and gone. Every director will be asking for you.

Totò to Nino Manfredi,
Jean A. Gili, Le cinéma italien

What we emphatically do not want is that these distinctive qualities should be washed out into a tasteless, colorless fluid of uniformity.

Randolph Bourne,
"Trans-national America"

Acknowledgements

Film, one could surmise, is about a scene that either stays put and makes us feel as though we are watching a play, or it can extend itself in a variety of ways, aggluntinating with other scenes to create a sentence of sorts, a sequence.

It would be impossible to mention all the friends and colleagues I watched movies with through the decades. It began when I was a teenager, and it continues today. To each one thank you for sharing your thoughts with me, helping me understand the pleasure of film.

Elisabeth Pouyfaucon has been sitting beside me in cinemas and in living rooms for almost two decades; thank you too for reading the first drafts of this work. I must thank Rocco Capozzi, at the University of Toronto (Italian Department), who mentored me for three years while I wrote these analyses. I thank Sylvie Leblond for proof-reading the manuscript. And most of all I am grateful to Anthony Julian Tamburri, without whom you would not be holding this book in your hands.

Note

Written between 2011 and 2012, these analyses propose an in-depth inquiry of five films (*Bread and Chocolate*, *A Pain in the Ass*, *Queen of Hearts*, *The Mediterranean Forever*, and *Raging Bull*), which deal with the Italian reality outside of Italy. The segment-by-segment examination of these works discloses parameters that can be used to define a deterritorialized culture which I name the Italic culture. This sort of synchronous and chronological segmentation of a film can assist scholars and students to better understand what constitutes the cinematographic narrative of ethnic films or, if the reader prefers, films on ethnicity, though one does not necessarily mean the other.

The title of this work is "I could have been a contender", which derives from a monologue spoken by Jake LaMotta (Robert De Niro) in *Raging Bull* by Martin Scorsese, which is a paraphrase of another monologue said by Terry Malloy (Marlon Brando) in *On the Waterfront* by Elia Kazan. Albeit idiomatically similar, the words of the soliloquies unchain different meanings. What for Malloy is a craving for success becomes for LaMotta a criticism of this very success. It's as though one was ready to sell his soul to the Devil, but the Devil refusing to buy that lost soul. Norman Mailer suggests in his conversation with Michael Lennon, *On God*, that at times some souls lose their desire to exist.

Presented as a study of forms and a survey of cultural connotations, our investigation proposes a journey into the representation created by immigrants and children of immigrants who, by refusing to disappear into sameness, question the substance of contemporary identity.

Introduction

The grouping of five disparate films directed by five unrelated artists, produced in five different countries, at various times, can, in many ways, be questionable on the artistic, social, and political levels. As we attempt to demonstrate, despite the dissimilarities, there are thematic, stylistic, semantic blocks that overlap, both on the specific as well as on the global planes. What is vague on the individualistic sphere often, when viewed collectively, reveals synonymity, parallelism, and kinship.

Cinema has never been a precise art form. Filmmakers can have no preconceptions of any kind when embarking on a project. What is genre, what is fiction, what is nonfiction, what distinguishes one technical instrument from another are, as Christian Metz warns, *formules de cinéma* (cinematic formulae).

Films insist on remaining "evanescent and uncertain about their own boundaries" (*Le signifiant*, 53). Again, according to Metz, film belongs essentially to a "mixed space *(lieu mixte)* where specific codes (that more or less make up the proper of cinema) converge and blend with the non-specific codes (more or less 'shared' by different 'languages' and by cultural systems)" (*Le signifiant*, 50).

The films which we propose to analyze — *A Pain in the Ass* (*L'Emmerdeur*, Édouard Molinaro, 1973), *Bread and Chocolate* (*Pane e cioccolata*, Franco Brusati, 1974), *Raging Bull* (Martin Scorsese, 1981), *Queen of Hearts* (Jon Amiel, 1989), and *The Mediterranean Forever* (Nicola Zavaglia, 2000) — belong to distinct moments in the history of cinema and are not part of a single, well-defined, stylistic tradition. To dare place these disparate films one beside the other, we are aware, might be somewhat contrary to the practice of discussing films grouped together by dominant artistic canons. Still, there is no mention of Molinaro, Scorsese, Zavaglia, Amiel, or Tony Grisoni in her book on Italian film by Millicent Marcus, *After Fellini*, a monograph which offers itself as a witness to the Italian "national story" (*After Fellini*, 6).[1]

Why would they be? Except for Brusati, the rest are not Italian filmmakers. At least, not legally speaking. And yet they are somehow "Italian". They are Italian outside Italy filmmakers. What does that make them? Let's call them *Italic*.

Truth be said, these five films are brazenly, indomitably, defiantly singular, and resemble the fingerprints of their creators. The filmmakers reach out beyond their national and territorial confines.

If we choose to label these artists by their ethnicity, it is in order to step outside national borders by, paradoxically, digging into the skies of their real or imagined origins. A *what if?* proposition. Let's wager on this hypothesis and see what happens.

These filmmakers and their films, as diverse as they are from one another, might perhaps form a category that is more cultural than generic, more sociological than psychological, more communal than individualistic. There has always been talk of minorities in film treatises, why not push the research in a pre-established direction, and see if, by any chance, there is something similar, a common denominator, that binds them in some mysterious (or not so mysterious) manner.

Viewing films such as *Green Pastures* (Marc Connelly and William Keighley, 1936), *Le Casque d'or* (Jacques Becker, 1952), Marty (Delbert Mann, 1955), *The Garden of the Finzi-Contini* (Vittorio De Sica, 1971), *The Godfather Trilogy* (Francis Ford Coppola, 1972, 1974, 1990), *Italianamerican* (Martin Scorsese, 1974-1975), *Rabbi Jacob* (Gérard Oury, 1973), *Concrete Angels* (Carlo Liconti, 1987), or *La Sarrasine* (Paul Tana, 1992), even if one is not a movie fanatic, one can notice that, despite the diverging technologies, styles, narrative plots, these films share something. We will call this common thread the *Italic*.

The trait entails a non-territorial pursuit for men and women interested in the Italian peoples scattered across the Western world. This telltale sign, like the stain left by a soiled finger, is an indelible mark, not only on the spectator's mind but also on the canvas of national culture. It screams for recognition. This seal, often "unnoticed" by the newspaper film reviewer, has become more and more visible. Because it is not a popular token, it is silenced by politicians. This badge of the psychological, moral, social, and cultural is pinned onto the fabric of society wherever. Its presence cannot be removed, it is a threat to many, even to those who carry it on their forehead. This signpost, this artistic buoy, this inescapable colophon, is expressive enough for us to assign it a name: the ethnic. The ethnic is nationless and, though it feeds off the territory, it is without a territory of its own.

In his indispensable book, *Beyond Ethnicity*, Werner Sollors explores the origins of this most controversial concept. Ethnicity — sadly, Sollors has since reneged on the ideas he promoted in this outstanding work. Sollors mentions W. Lloyd Warner who, in a study dedicated to cultural communities in Newburyport, Massachusetts, first advanced the possibility of dissociating ethnicity and territory and freeing ethnicity from one's place "of birth". One could be, say, Polish, without being born in Poland.

David Reisman pushes the concept of ethnicity further still from territory in a 1953 essay entitled "Some Observations on Intellectual Freedom". For Reisman, ethnicity includes class struggle. Peter Kropotkin speaks of the Kabyle's *çof* as being

> a widely-spread form of association... for mutual protection and for various purposes — intellectual, political, and emotional — which cannot be satisfied by the territorial organization of the village, the clan, and the confederation. The *çof* knows no territorial limits; it recruits its members in various villages, even among strangers... supplementing the territorial grouping by an extra-territorial grouping intended to give an expression to mutual affinities of all kinds across the frontiers (*Mutual Aid*, 145-16)

The term "ethnic" gradually includes connotations of pluralism. The possibility of placing ethnicity alongside pluralism had already been intelligently developed throughout the early twentieth century by radical United Statian pluralists, such as Horace Kallen, Randolph Bourne, and W.E.B. DuBois. These thinkers proposed an anti-assimilationist world view which they opposed to the prevalent assumptions based on the "melting pot". In the 1970s, Sollors defended "cultural pluralism" (Kallen's concept) that stood against a unified Anglo-Saxon country. Interestingly enough, such radical perspectives, for the most part, have been dismissed in Europe. Cultural identity, there, rises inside national borders, and takes root in the principles of *jus solis* and *jus sanguinis*. We propose to move away from these legal concepts, whereby identity is based on either territory and blood links, and step toward the cultural realm of what we call conscience identity.[2]

Etymologically, "ethnic" is a noun derived from the Ecclesiastical Latin (of the thirteen century) noun *ethnici* and adjective *ethnicus*, meaning, "heathen", "pagan", "Gentile" (as opposed to the people of the Jewish faith). The Latin term is itself derived from the Greek words *ethnikos* and *ethnos*, meaning "group", "nation", and "people".

An interesting point to mention is that terms "ethnic" and "enthic" (mores, character, manner of being on a daily basis) share the same Indo-European root: *swedh-, swe, se* (referring to "self" (selfhood) as in the Italian *se* and *sui*). The use of the adjective, according to the *Dictionnaire historique de la langue française*, came into usage in the nineteenth century and always with a reference to a "peuple" ("people"). Around 1896 the term meant "a people having the same origin and lifestyle".

For decades the terms "ethnic" and "race" were used interchangeably until scholars, like Sollors and Michael Walzer, preferred to use the term "ethnicity" over "race":

> ethnicity included dominant groups and in which race, while sometimes facilitating external identification, is merely one aspect of ethnicity (*Beyond Ethnicity*, 36).

In *Race et histoire*, Claude Lévi-Strauss stresses the notion that "race", as presented by Arthur de Gobineau (1816-1882) — whose theories were later appropriated by the Nazi — could easily be vilified because Gobineau linked diversity to biology. Diversity, Lévi-Strauss explains, has nothing to do with anatomy or physiology, and everything to do with "geographical, historical and sociological circumstances" (*Race*, 8). Culture is the result of people separating from one another according to their "sociological and psychological creations". These differences are always distinct, and often unequal. Without these cultural inequalities one would be hard pressed to understand why, for example, "white" man's society can create advanced technology, while other societies seem fixed in a lifestyle frozen in time.

Notwithstanding Gobineau's shortcomings, Lévi-Strauss admitted that Gobineau foretold the ever-growing tendency to *métissage* (intermarriage) and how such exogamy would eventually complicate human matters in an irreversible way. They have, and in a positive way.

Should we then concede immediately that the films we will be discussing are the natural by-products of cultural *métissage*? The mixing of cultures, however, does not help us understand the choices artists inevitably make. The mixing of cultures never cancels whatever cultures are being mixed.

If *métissage* entails the obliteration of the ingredients being mixed, then *métissage* becomes an unfortunate synonym of the melting pot. Cultural mixture does not annul what constituents are mixed but marbles them. What *métissage* should produce is not a "monotone", but a "poly-tone" person, not a new "monoculture", but a "pluriculture". Pluriculturalism is not a national "monoculture". This is not the predominant point of view that is being promoted in the Western part of the world. Culture does not present itself as a secluded, homogenous, and compact bloc; culture is a construct built following the rules of fixed parameters. If anything, culture looks like a juxtaposition of "social presences" (Lévi-Strauss's metaphor) in constant movement. Culture can be recorded.

Thanks to the written word, some peoples have recorded their specific histories and customs. These literate cultures stand in sharp contrast to the multifarious cultures that were not able to chronicle through writing their own histories and customs, in manners understandable to us. To achieve a balance between history and memory, a people have to master a formal language codified in a written alphabet.

Lévi-Strauss reminded us that "ancient" cultures will forever remain a source of mystery to the contemporary student of anthropology simply because most peoples did not transmit their experiences and knowledge in written form. Culture, anthropologists claim, grows directly from agriculture; the peasant counting his livestock gradually led to the written word. Had these illiterate men and women possessed the visual and sound technology to "narrate" (historify?) their everyday reality, we would probably be living in a different world today.

One can only fantasize about the databanks that would have been at our disposal had prehistoric men and women recorded "visually" (via film) their everyday activities which today still remain inexplicable. More than a literate culture, the Italians have recorded their customs visually, cinematographically.

Film was born in 1895. In Italy, on November 11, 1895, Filoteo Alberini applied for a patent for an instrument that could produce moving pictures. Thanks to film Italian have provided us with a vast array of fictionalized and realistic documents on the way Italians spoke and continue to speak as they go about their quotidian activities. More than the written word, film has safeguarded much of the tangible reality that makes up Italian culture.

Few writers capture the complexities and variegation of dialects as well as Roberto Rossellini in *Paisà* (1946) or Matteo Garrone in *Gomorrah* (2008). The written word, let alone the onomatopoeic one, can never fully reveal the medley of colors in the voices of a people. Dialectical writing attempts to imitate the sound of the voice, but the alphabet will never free itself of its abstract signs. Unlike analog or digital recorders, writing does not exactly duplicate sound as it is produced. To use a philological notion, recorded sound functions as the autograph of the person speaking. The relationship between reality and the reproduction of reality is almost one to one — "almost", because the sound on tape is not the real thing, but a copy of the real object, its double, its mirror image, its analogue representation. Charles Sanders Pierce would have called it an *icon*, and Charles W. Morris *pleroma*. There again semioticians do not agree on whether sounds can be studied as signs at all.

Linguists have demonstrated how words and their functions can be dissected to a great degree (*monene* and *phoneme*), but this is not the case with film, though many scholars have struggled hard to come up with the codes it must surely have. But film has neither monene, nor phoneme; there is no *langue* (rule). Film is primarily a *parole* (a performance, an invention). Furthermore, as Christian Metz warns us, an image cannot be broken down to smaller units.

Roland Barthes dedicated a number of essays on the analysis of the photogram and photography, but these personal exercises, as fascinating and revealing as they are, cannot be imitated or repeated with much success: breaking down an image into codes and laws — the studium, the punctum, the noeme, the third sense — is no easy task. Besides, a photogram is not a photograph. The film image, the shot, is an ambiguous unit. It belongs to a larger sequence to be fully understood.

Words on a page are visual representations of the spoken word; yet words contain a mysterious self-referential component that leads us away from reality. As Paul Valéry explained it, the moment a person's eyes started to compare the written word to a landscape, that is when obsession with imitation of spoken language ceased. The written word is — who can deny it? — also and mostly about writing. No word can be taken for granted.

> Longtemps, longtemps, la voix humaine fut la base et condition de la littérature. La présence de la voix explique la littérature première... Un jour vint où l'on sut lire des yeux sans épeler, sans entendre, et la littérature en fut tout altérée (549).

Break away from the voice, and one stumbles on the written word. Break away from the national canon, and we can begin to appreciate the art of difference. The art of capturing reality on film is also the art of revealing the culture in that reality. The culture in some films is national; the culture in other films is ethnic.

What is ethnicity? Ethnicity moves at the opposite end of nationalism; ethnicity is not to nationalism as *langue* is to *parole*. Ethnicity stands on a higher plane than nationalism. Ethnicity might spring from a place, but, unlike nationalism, it is not limited by territory. Incredible resistance has appeared in nations across the globe when dealing with people within its borders who do not fully comply with its view of a unified "melting pot". This "foreign" voice rising from within is not a backward genetically based view of the world. It is a total re-mapping (de-mapping) deterritorialized societies and cultures of tomorrow.

An ethnic community is made up of autonomous individuals who share, to quote Nathan Glazer, "a common history and experience and defined by descent, real or mythical" (74). At once diachronic and synchronic, the ethnic adventure requires the mastering of two active centers in a single person. Only once s/he has mastered his/her "marbled" being can s/he fully grasp the conjectural model s/he has chosen to abide to. To be an ethnic is more a matter of private choice than any sort of natural or, worse, biological, outcome of being-hood.

One is not born an ethnic, one chooses to become an ethnic. In other words, by becoming an ethnic one becomes a non-nationalist, a trans-national. The ethnic de-nationalizes herself. However, writers and artists prefer to let go of the ethnic and hyphenated identity, and choose to adhere to the national side of their being. This passing over, we should be able to see at work in the five films analyzed. To be a "trans-national", to use Randolph Bourne's concept, is a social program that goes contrary to the ideologies of assimilation and the melting-pot.[3] Non-melted identities are ethnic, as Michael Walzer and Cornell West would elaborate on these issues in their different works.

The individuals who detach themselves from their national community do so at their own expense. Passing for someone one is not, giving up one's parental culture, forgetting one's ancestral language is not always easier than walking the least path taken. Rebecca Hall delves into the complicated experience in her film *Passing* (2021). Often financial retribution facilitates the "passing" artist to make it in the mainstream. Many intellectuals and politicians repeat that acculturation and assimilation, surrendering to the dominant cultural group, are prerequisites to membership and success.

By promoting stereotypes and typecast actors, as Paul S. Cowen advanced, movie producers are able to represent different cultural communities via "visible characteristics or appearances rather than in terms of abstract concepts or underlying traits" (quoted in Friedman, 355). Yet, at the opposite end of the spectrum, there are exceptions, to varying degrees, to the norm. But whenever an exception does arise, it is viciously criticized for being a miscue, a *lapsus linguae*, an oversight, a fault. One could almost consider this sort of "mis-performance" a cultural Freudian slip, an artistic parapraxis, the result of a conflict between the individual unconscious and the social conscious intention.

What if we were to view these singular outbursts from a totally different perspective, beyond the horizontal spread of a single country? What if we pushed them upright — vertically? Would we then be able to consider these artistic forays no longer as individual bedlam but as collective (conscious and unconscious) artistic happenings? What on the diachronic level seems transient becomes permanent when pulled onto the synchronic plane. What on the horizontal plane sounds like a monologue resonates, when pushed vertically, as baroque polyphony.

From the start, film proposes ethnicity solely as a topic of conflict. Ethnicity consists in depicting an individual belonging to a minority group as a weirdo; the person is usually presented from the outside, as a foreigner, as an alien. "Look at her", the camera seems to whisper. "Do you want to have such a person as a neighbor?"

The camera pans over unfamiliar sites and ultimately zooms in on the national flag. The lens captures the outsider and pushes him into a bottle which is then cast in the river of Lethe. No matter how muddy the waters, all rivers lead to the sea, and it is on the shores of today's sea that we notice the bottles of cultural oddities floating back to our feet.

Films that basically reduce cultural parameters to what the audience expects of certain minority groups are on the wane. Less powerful is the need for the individual to convert to the majority's religion. Less powerful is the call for the ethnic to embrace the lifestyles of the dominant group. Cultural coercion, nevertheless, leaves its scars on artists. Rare are philosophers and thinkers, such as Randolph Bourne, who, in the early 1900s, tilt the balance to the other side of what is expected of them:

> We are not dealing with individuals who are to "evolve". We are dealing with their children, who, with that education we are about to have, will start level with all of us. Let us cease to think of ideals like democracy as magical qualities inherent in certain peoples. Let us speak, not of inferior races, but of inferior civilizations. We are all to educate and to be educated (250).

What many films reveal are mostly the relics that dried up decades ago. Unfortunately, scarce are authentic ethnic creations, such as defined by Werner Sollers: "works written by, about, or for persons who perceived themselves, or were perceived by others, as members of ethnic groups, including even nationally and internationally popular writings by 'major' authors and formally intricate and modernist texts" (243).

No artist — critics of pluralism remind us — wishes to be identified to what the mainstream ridicules as being reactionary, counterproductive, conservative, at the margins of the official canon. We agree with Lee Lourdeaux who, in his book *Italian and Irish Filmmakers in America*, wonders if a student of film were to analyze ethnic works, how he would deal with "the strong undercurrent of positive ethnic values beneath surface assimilation" (5)?

Ethnic identities offer positive values (tolerance, for example) that are not always encouraged in films promoting the ideology of the melting pot. One can count on the fingers on one hand the men and women who dare tread the vast horizon of creativity with the certainty of producing a body of work that promotes an idea larger than the call for the disappearance of cultural and religious difference. The majority are converts and, what Randolph Bourne called, "cultural half-breeds" (Bourne, 254).

We strap ethnic "we-ness", to use an image by Lawrence H. Fuchs (2), in civic duty, and any glitter of non-integration is attacked for developing a threat to national security and patriotic responsibility. Yet the trend is on the wane, even though the ethnic artist is an exception, not the rule.

When cultural institutions from varied nations fiercely proclaim their financial support of cultural diversity, they are not always honest. There is a defensive overemphasis on sameness. How many instances of a film spoken in Persian and produced independently, in the U.S.A., can one find today? *The Suitors* (1988), by Ghasem Ebrahimian, is one such invaluable film. Beyond the limits of plot and stereotypes, and into the heart of what one names without a moment of hesitation the ownership of one's means of production — this is the exemplification of the free ethnic filmmaker. An oxymoron: aloneness amongst the mass, and a loner with a collective mind. The separation from the majority and the creation of the community of cultural allegiances.

Imagine five such filmmakers working across the globe, alone, confirming what no single nation can ever do as a group: on the horizontal plane, a solitary; and on the vertical axis, the appearance of a new brand of social and cultural illustrators. What used to be one now breaks into a multitude of vanishing points. The straight line curves and twirls into a spiral: this is the birth of heterogeneity. From this baroque aesthetic of the multiple, diversity propagates all its facets. Still from this supposedly mosaic dissonance rises a melody which, when applied to artists of Italian descent, can be named the Italic song, the experience of borderlessness.[4]

By thrusting the linear continuum of ethnic works out of the confines of a nation's art mainstream, one gets a glimpse of these works *sui generis* from a viewpoint, unique and free of repetitive national simulation, to use Jean Baudrillard's term.[5] Nevertheless, many scholars who have explored the ethnic consciousness (as rare as these have been) end up comparing a brilliant piece of work to the "genuine" (national) thing, and conclude that the real tradition will stress a point of view that amounts nothing less to the defense of the melting pot.

Thomas J. Ferraro, for example, begins his brilliant *Ethnic Passages* on immigration and mobility with elegant ideas but soon finds himself comparing a master novel such as *The Godfather*, by Mario Puzo, to works that squish ethnic consciousness down to a content bordering on the ridicule. If tokenism might be an appropriate designation for instances of passing-over, acculturation, and assimilation, how are we to label intolerable work that promotes inauthenticity and appropriation of voice? We do not want to place ourselves in a position of antagonism, whereby we justify (or refute) a theory by comparing an ethnic film to a "national" film made in the same country. Such drudgery would be deceptive on our part; we would be comparing dissimilar objects that should not be compared at all. What good would it serve anyone if we were to correlate, in our case, *Bread and Chocolate (Pane e cioccolata)* by Franco Brusati with *Amarcord* by Federico Fellini, or *A Pain in the Ass (L'Emmerdeur)* by Édouard Molinaro with *La maman et la putain* by Jean Eustache, four excellent films produced in 1973 and released in 1974?

There is nothing to compare except the fact that two films were produced in Italy, and the other two in France. We are not trying to classify films according to their place of origin. And we especially do not want to compare films made in Italy to films about Italian made outside Italy, nor do we want to establish a tag for films made outside Italy that promote or demote Italy for that matter.

The five films analyzed herein have very little to do with Italy, though that country's shadow falls on the sidewalks on which the characters of these films walk. We are not out to tag the centimeters or degrees that separate these films with the Italian peninsula.

Establishing, however, the type of interrelationship *L'Emmerdeur* has with *Pane e cioccolata* might very well reveal fascinating, unexpected programs for semantic analysis.

Correlating works issuing from common ethnic origins but situated in different localities, yes, the wager is worth the while, is promising. Comparing *The Godfather* (1972) by Francis Ford Coppola and *Goodfellas* (1990) by Martin Scorsese might motivate a scholar to deduce a theoretic framework founded on the complementarity of ethnic solidarity and corporate capitalism, but is this sort of analysis that persons interested in ethnicity wish to read? Yes, such studies might abound, yet we expect a little more from scholars struggling within such an historical conjecture.

Artists of Italian origin are working everywhere, across the globe, away from Italy, in, about, and beyond Little Italies, in, about, and beyond the countries they inhabit. I am interested to see what is being done and what deductions analysing these works might arise.

Franco Brusati is included in this study because the protagonist of his film foreshadows in every aspect the experiences often left unsaid in films made by or dealing with first-, second-, and third-generation Italian emigrants. Brusati's film is a natural point of departure for what I call the Italic culture: an intellectual jump-start.

Lodging epexegesis on linear divisions, according to national boundaries, does not reduce the need for interpretation and appreciation of the works that move beyond territorial borders. I did not want to produce a sociological study of all the Canadian films on or by filmmakers of Italian origin. Such a book would be welcomed, I am sure. But wouldn't such a work end up repeating in its own way territorial obsession?

By disconnecting "ethnic" works from their geographical confines, and by transposing these detached works on to a higher epistemological emplacement frees them from their physical constrictions. What we are curious to discover is not only what Italian-U.S. filmmakers are about, but what filmmakers with some connection to Italy are, consciously or unconsciously, expressing both, specifically and collectively, about culture.

By paradoxically needling our way into the fabric of these five films I should be able to bring forth a broader analysis that goes above and beyond the simple paraphrasing of ethnic narratives. Whatever meanings these films develop respectively should, I imagine, be altered when relocated.

I admit the fact that neither formal and stylistic parameters, nor plot deployment, of each separate film will ever produce a unified stamp. *Bread and Chocolate*, *A Pain in the Ass*, *Queen of Hearts*, *The Mediterranean Forever*, and *Raging Bull* are distinct and very different films; nevertheless, these films, produced in different countries, and directed or written by artists of Italian background, might very well disclose subtle associations, a commonality, some generic marking that we could consider as being an Italic variable. This quality might not be precise in any way, yet symbolically whatever glue binding these five works together could be used to study films not included in this study.

What, if any, is the constant variable in this root sign? Is it Italy? Perhaps, but not necessarily. Does an Italic film automatically steer the viewer back to Italy? The drive is long, the turns convoluted: three of the films chosen lead us out of Italy (*Pane e cioccolata*, *Queen of Hearts*, and *Mediterraneo sempre*); one film escorts us momentarily back to Italy *(Mediterraneo sempre)*; another hints at Italy *(L'Emmerdeur)*; and one film does not even once show an image of Italy in the rearview mirror to the Italian peninsula *(Raging Bull)*.

Why call this common denominator "Italic"?

Though things Italian remain a constant in these films, I did not feel at any one time the need to refer back to Italy the country. Italy is a reference; but the feature I point to is an element smaller than the State and, at the same time, larger than the country. The dilemma of naming this association or structure is a serious one. How to conjure Italian culture without stirring up nationalist and patriotic lore?

So we made our way back to pre-Roman history and came across the "Italic", the name of an ethnolinguistic group, descended from the Indo-

European peoples, who did not limit itself to a single camp. On one hand there is the Nomad, and on the other the Sedentary. Already there is emigration, and there is tribalism. But the word "Italic" is more than just a slanted typeface. Italic encompasses a notion that is larger than the title "Italian" which contemporary instruction has tagged onto an imaginary single people residing on the European peninsula. Italic does not mean Italian. The notion, the noun, and the adjective "Italian" has to be pushed aside here, because it inescapably leads us to a conglomeration of fronts established in a precise territory. Italians come from Italy.

I needed an expression that designated something larger than one place, than one language, than one group of people. This does not suppose that there is a single Italian language spoken in Italian by a single group of people. No common language, no common ancestor, no common diet: these men and women don't practice the same rituals for the same gods. Some have no gods at all. Italy is a complex ecosystem, and so the Italic concept had to be an even more complex ecosystem.

Throughout its complicated history, the country that eventually became known as Italy hosted a variety of peoples who spoke a variety of languages: Greek, Etruscan, Oscan, Latin, Gallic, Albanian, Slavic, Arabic, Hebrew, and no doubt many other idioms that gradually are not spoken anymore. A multifold of individuals and collectivities reaped the right to exist as Italians on the peninsula. This multiplicity of voices gave rise to a unique cultural and political phenomenon which today we call Italian.

Emigration prolonged this polyphony of peoples, languages, and rituals which continues to broaden the "Italian" experience, and deepens the definition of who is or who is not Italian in Italy. For clarity's sake, we will retain the term "Italian" for people and things that come from Italy. However, massive emigration put a dent to this prim and proper definition.

Gratefully no human wants to ever feel obliged to stay in his or her place of birth. To leave one's place of residence and country in order to live elsewhere is a more common and ancient practice than we care to believe. To emigrate, to immigrate, to migrate, willingly, unwillingly, temporarily, permanently affects every dimension of an individual. Communities, cities, neighborhoods, countries change on a daily basis. Italic peoples, such as the Samnites, practiced the *Ver sacrum* ("sacred spring"): a ritual that required young persons of twenty and twenty-one to leave their communities, often led by an animal protected by a god, in order to find another location to inhabit. This ancient practice survives metaphorically, even when the apparel might seem different. From generation to generation Italian emigrants established themselves in various parts of the globe. Today their off-spring, close to 60 million people strong, has not been an easy topic for political leaders and scholars. Italians, Italian culture, foreigners, and the derogatory wops: who are they and what do they want?

To use the term "Italian" when speaking of these peoples would be, for the most part, incorrect. A person born in Canada is Canadian. There is no legal status in Canada that allows this Canadian to claim his or her Italian heritage. In most cases, hailing yourself Italian is nothing more than a private whim, a wink, a desktop flag, a lapel pin.

In the United States of America, the Immigration Act of 1924 prevented peoples of Italian origin to enter the U.S.A. This sort of ostracization can be found in a number of countries, Italian immigrants were and continue to be victims of xenophobia. The films we will be watching touch directly or indirectly this rather unpleasant problem.

To speak of Italians outside Italy is a controversial issue. Ultimately, asking "Who are these people?" is a political question. Both for Italy and the host country, both countries wondering why these emigrants-immigrants insist on consider themselves Italian? Implicit in the query is the firm belief that emigration becomes immigration becomes disappearance.

One of the first components for measuring the success of assimilation of an immigrant is the loss of one's mother-tongue. Implied in this belief is that language equals nationality. Though there are countries that define their status according to an idiom, this reclamation is beginning to require some adjustments. The Italian woman, born in southwest France, who emigrates to Montreal, possesses a network of identities that troubles the worldly mind. This is the sort of complication no nationalist wishes to face. The statement "An Italian speaks Italian" barely conceals the unilingual nationalist prejudice.

If all Italians could be aggregated in one spoken language, it would make definitions simpler. Thankfully, no individual can be classified according to a spoken idiom. The language parameter is not applicable to Italians. Many Italians inside Italy speak a language other than Italian. Many Italians outside Italy speak a language other than Italian. Unlike other countries, the official idiom spoken at the center does not encompass the peoples found abroad. The same is true for the religious parameter; not all Italians follow the same faith.

Beside the geographical bias, I had to avoid the tapered appellations such as "Italian" and "Italophone" when speaking of the Italics. I had to come up with a fairly neutral nomenclature that would not automatically conjure Italy or the Tuscan dialect. The vocable "Italic" pulls the definition of identity an epistemological notch higher. Not only does the Italic comprise peoples from Italy as well as the peoples of Italian cultures outside Italy, it encompasses the Italic dialects and languages of Italy and all other idioms spoken by the Italian emigrants and their offspring.

By sidestepping the highly politicized concepts of nationalism, the Italic offers a pluricultural and plurilingual worldview. The Italic cannot be absorbed by the melting pot, nor can it be wiped out by the nostalgic perceptions of nationalism. Because the Italic is not tangible, it must be considered a virtual space that is willed: a sort of No-Land — an Atopia. One chooses to be Italic.

This conscious identity should be something a person wants to express. It is not betterment, not belittlement. This quest for ethnic visibility is not exclusive to artists of Italian origin. Without this spark for disclosure, the sentiment of coming-out cannot exist. Removing this longing, this manifestation, this discourse often translates into the desire to be someone else. Passing will always continue, yet running alongside this convention there is a growing urgency for many individuals to present themselves as *someone else* or their works as *something else*. What is proposed herein is study how this ethnic curtain-raiser is achieved.

Detaching each one of these films from their "social" contexts erases the prerequisite of having to spell out a national allegiance. What on the horizontal plane requires attention becomes less important when viewed on the vertical plane. For instance, in the compound X/Y (figure 1) — where X is the artistic work and Y the notation for national allegiance — what would happen if the compound were to lose the Y factor? As soon as an artwork is removed from its geographical confinements it acquires a new non-geographical attribute which we name Z, the Italic factor (figure 2):

Figure 1

Figure 2

By repeating this process for each film, one comes to the conclusion that Z could never be "Italy" since that particular parameter does not appear in all five films. (Z could be the World but that would lead us to another type of comparative study.) By bringing our research to a more realistic level it seems obvious the Italic is the sole characteristic found in the five films. The Italic is the hypothetical quality that bridges entities possessing at least the single one trait sharing "a common [Italian] history and experience and defined by descent, real or mythical." Italians might be Italics, but not all Italics are Italian. The Italic is to the Italian what the *francophonie* is to France, or the *lusophonia* to Portugal.

Normally we would use the term *Italofonia* (Italophone) to explain the supra-national experience proposed by artists of men and women of Italian origin, but such an image would be misleading. The term *Italofonia* encompasses all peoples who speak Italian.

Fearing to repeat ourselves, the handicap of using such a term is that we stress the importance of language in identity. Some Italians speak Italian, but not all Italians speak the Tuscan dialect. And not all Italics speak Italian (as is noticeable with these five films).

Lifestyle, worldview, point of view, a *sentire italico* (but certainly not a *sentirsi italiano*) are more adequate concepts that capture in part the complexities and subtleties of whatever denominators unite people of Italian descent.

Though Italian language cannot be our primary concern here, we will notice that idiom does play role. In some instances, a character will use the official Italian; other times, dialect is used; in most instances, code-switching and code-mixing is prevalent. The characters in the films usually speak in the official language of the country in which these films take place.

Borders are crossed, bridges lowered, the crossing is linguistic as much as cultural. These trans-nationals are plurilingual. But an ethnic is not necessarily a trans-national. When an individual is born in a country but proclaims the cultural heritage of another, adequate definitions fail to capture that identity.

To use the term "Italian" would be erroneous to define that individual. Italians abroad do not unequivocally embrace the Italian identity. Some Italians have an Italian passport; others have exchanged it for the passport of the country they live in. Some Italians like being part of a community; others might not even want to be associated to an Italian community outside of his native country. Italian trans-nationals might even possess dual, triple, quadruple passports.

Some of the characters of the films might not even possess the legal document called a passport. Not all artists of Italian origin are Italians in the true sense of the word: Martin Marcantonio Luciano Scorsese (17 November 1942), of Sicilian heritage, is an American citizen by birth; Édouard Molinaro (13 May 1928), French born, might be second or third generation Italian, if Italian at all (no mention of his Italian background is found in his autobiography[6]; Nicola Zavaglia (30 August 1954), born in Calabria, is considered a filmmaker from Quebec; the only Italian-born filmmaker is Franco Brusati (4 August 1922-28 February 1993); Jon Amiel (20 May 1948), born in London, is not Italian at all (though the script-writer Tony Grisoni is of Italian extraction). Despite of the legal status of these directors, all five participate willingly (and at times unintentionally) in the expression of the Italic adventure.

The Italic should be viewed as a parallel manifestation that encompasses and surpasses the Italian reality. It is not meant to supplant the Italian culture, nor does it replace whatever culture that constitutes the host country. The Italic might have come into being with the first Italian immigrants to have settled abroad; but it might not have come to the fore only with the following generations. One can only speculate what Giuseppe Garibaldi would have thought of this radical, deterritorialized awareness of identity in the making.

Men and women might speak of their past lives, but *nostalgia (passatista)* will not dominate their discourse. Very much like nomads these protagonists move from one place to another. Some might even be ready to sell their souls for a home and financial stability. Traffic will be at once chaotic and orderly. No one on this journey walks on straight planks. This balancing act brings about ascent and success, or descent and failure. There will be much negotiation going on. Every character is willing to exchange official documents and foreign currency for some sort of well-being.

Some of these meanderings might seem predicable, quantifiable, at least on the linearly plane, diachronically speaking, but, as a deterritorialized phenomenon, the migrant's journey appears less fragmented, less monochromatic, less solitary than expected. A gestalt switch alters forever our perception of identity: stereotypes turn to archetypes. Expect no flag waving of any kind from these migrants. Micro-nationalisms (*micro-enracinement* is the word used by Guy Scarpetta (*Éloge,* 19)) are feared as much as nationalism.

So why did I choose to study these particular films? The choice was not random. In general, few films are produced or written by filmmakers of Italian descent outside Italy. The U.S.A. undoubtedly provides the largest range of filmmakers, taking us way back to the early years of Hollywood: Frank Capra is an unavoidable monument. However, camping this study exclusively in the U.S.A. would have ultimately brought us to position the entire Italic experience on the diachronic (historical) plane on a single territory — precisely what we wish to avoid.

In so doing, we would have found ourselves struggling to justify one position against the other: pluralism versus assimilation, ethnicity versus nationalism, identity bound to a single territory. Some trans-nationals possess dual, triple, quadruple passports. We preferred films dealing with Italians, made by "Italians" in one form or another, and produced in different territories. An Italic culture exists in the world today (albeit not always by design).

From the U.S.A., *Raging Bull* was an immediate and personal choice. The title of this study is taken from Jack LaMotta's monologue, which encapsulates the metaphor of brothers divided and conquered. Perhaps *The Godfather* Saga could have served at the task, but to spend so much time on the trilogy would have plunged us deep into the politics of the film auteur. Andrew Sarris's version of the auteur theory is not our purpose here.[7]

Film after film, Francis Ford Coppola has proven that he is unequivocally one of the great (Italian-American) filmmakers; an artist of his caliber is not soon to appear in the horizon, as his latest film, *Tetro* (2009), clearly demonstrates. My vote finally went to Martin Scorsese, whose early works showed the influenced of the unequalled John Cassavetes, who could be considered the Godfather of ethnic filmmaking.

Raging Bull is Scorsese's finest film, starring actor Robert De Niro at his best, based on a script co-written by Paul Schrader, one of the finest scriptwriters and a personal favorite filmmaker. *Raging Bull* is an imperative choice for anyone interested in the Italian experience in the U.S.A.

From England, the choice was more difficult. The Italian presence has not yet truly come to the foreground. Perhaps, Byron, Shelley and Browning monopolized the poetic imaginary to such an extent that it made it more difficult for great Italian-British poets Dante Gabriele Rossetti and his sister Christina Rossetti to spread their ethnic influence adequately. The Rossetti certainly contributed to the understanding of Italian culture and literature, thanks to their original works and translations. The fact that these children of immigrants actually wrote is a statement in itself. These two poets whose parents were born in Vasto, in the Abruzzo-Molise region of Italy, where my family comes from, lived on parallel cultural planes. Let us not forget that it is in a room in London, England, that most of the nationalist writings of Giuseppe Mazzini were written.

The relationship between England and Italy remains special, heavily one-sided perhaps, favoring the Northern country, at the expense of the Southern one which naturally sinks into the quicksand of stereotypical bivouac. The English left the cold for the warmer climes of the Mediterranean; Italians rushed out of that waterless quasi-island, and out of the painful sun, often never to return. *Queen of Hearts* is one of the few films to impose itself to us; we had to submit to scriptwriter, Tony Grisoni, who has worked with Terry Gilliam on a number of films, *Fear and Loathing in Las Vegas* (1998) and *The Brothers Grimm* (2005). Anthony Minghella was a strong contender, however none of his films except perhaps *The Talented Mr. Ripley* dealt openly with anything Italian. Yet both *Ripley* and *Truly, Madly, Deeply* (1990) raise the ominous issue of identity and loss of identity.

Temptation was strong, but the Amiel-Grisoni's film turned up winner. France created the most serious problem. Though Jean Cocteau joked about the fact that the French being "angry Italians", the presence of the "ritals" (the equivalent of *wop* or *dago*) in France is blurry. Besides the famous autobiography, *Les Ritals* (1978) by François Cavanna and the thrillers by Jean-Claude Izzo, Marie-Claude Blanc-Chaléard edited in 2003 the first major anthology of essays entitled, *Les Italiens en France depuis 1945.*

Italians and Italian surnames crop up everywhere in the arts modern France, but the manifestation of the Italian ethnic feature is difficult to grasp fully. It is in France, with its harsh immigration policies and its nearness to Italy, that the Italian ethnic is the most elusive. The presence of famous Italians individuals in France can be seen, yet they seldomly come out as an ethnic collectivity.

Neapolitan Baroque poet Giambattista Marino spent twelve years in Paris in the seventeenth century, Alessandro Manzoni, F.T. Marinetti lived in France. The list grows: the Italian Émile Zola, an Italian born in Paris, became a French citizen in his twenties; two famous artists from Sète, Paul Valéry and Georges Brassens, were born of Italian mothers; in 1935, Jean Renoir released a film on an Italian criminal, *Toni*; there are singers, Yves Montand, Serge Reggiani, Georges Moustaki, Adamo, Dalida, Francis Cabrel, Fred Chichin (Les Rita Mitsouko), Calogero, and others; finally, it is the writings of Sébastien Jasprisot (an anagram for Jean-Batispte Rossi), a major voice in French literature and, the scriptwriter of numerous box-office success thrillers, that led me to consider Lino Ventura as a plausible man of the match. Why Jasprisot made me think of Ventura is beyond my understanding, but he did.

Of the film stars — Serge Reggiani, Yves Montand (Ivo Livi), Lino Ventura, Jean-Paul Belmondo, Fabrice Luchini, it is Ventura, with his stout body, bold countenance, and round virile face, stingy of its sentimental expressions, who imposed himself as being the most classic Italian in France. Yes, Serge Reggiani is masterful in *Le Casque d'or* (1952). It is in *Borsalino* (1970) that Jean-Paul Belmondo established his French-style Italianità. Coming back to Lino Ventura, *L'Emmerdeur* by Édouard Molinaro is a comedy about murder, suicide, and male friendship, wherein organized crime is not the main vehicle for identity. The wager was too tempting; the tandem Lino Ventura and Jacques Brel, inescapable. Murder, suicide, madness, undiscussed questions of identity: too laudable to let go. The cards were played. (Are we not over-saturated with the over-exploited equation Italian=Mafia?)

Choosing a Canadian film was difficult. If there are excellent actors of Italian background in the country, working on both sides of the linguistic wall, a film from Quebec had to figure in the list. Nick Mancuso, Tony Nardi, and Vittorio Rossi reign supreme in the field. Having worked in a variety of languages, Nardi rightfully deserved the awards bestowed on him by the cinematographic milieu. Actresses such as Jennifer Dale, Cynthia Dale, Toni Ellwand, and others deserve more roles on topic. Carlo Liconti directs and produces excellent films since his feature *Concrete Angels* (1987). *Brown Bread Sandwiches* (1989) is a film I seriously considered for this study. Tony Nardi acts captivatingly in both these films. Frank Caruso, another prolific actor, director, and producer, proffers daring scenes shot with impudent gentilly (*Wild at Heart*, 1990). Frank D'Angelo, an entrepreneur in the food and restaurant industry, ventures in the world of entertainment with a feature (*Real Gangster*, 2013), in which an impressive line-up of actors deliver their ware on organized crime.

A fascinating short documentary, *Enigmatico* (1993), directed by Patricia Fogliato and David Mortin, features the lives and works of a handful of Italian-Canadian artists. Engaging Italian stories permeate the Canadian screen, and Toronto stands as the center of the Italic presence in the country. And east of this major metropolis lies Montreal where Italians speak Italian, dialects, English, and French, one of the official languages of Canada. Pluriculturalism and plurilingualism maintain ineluctable appeal to the Italian presence in every city. Yet few filmmakers have tackled this plurality of cultures and languages. Films do not handle this matter openly, either in a positive or negative way. Montreal Italians have no choice but pick at the contention. Most Montreal Italians are tetrahedrons living quadruple lives, each one on its distinct linguistic plane — dialect, Italian, English, French, and Spanish.

Cultural pluralism, to use a concept introduced in 1924 by Horace M. Kallen in the essay "Culture and the Klan", should, therefore, be alive and well in Montreal, with its unique situation on the American continents. It isn't. If before 2022 there might have been ambiguities on the controversy, this is no longer the case. The Premier of the province has officially announced its political agenda. Create uncompromising policies to reinforce unilingualism and nationalism. To paraphrase politicians, the province is categorically against multiculturalism.

La Sarrasine (1992) and *La déroute* (1998) by Paul Tana (both scripts written by Tana, Bruno Ramirez, and Tony Nardi), and *Mambo italiano* (2003), written by Steve Galluccio, had to be considered. If there were not chosen, the reasons can be found in the final scenes of Anita Aloisio's documentary *Calliari, QC* (2022). Singer and composer Marco Calliari cannot smother sniffles and wipe tears dropping on the crushed aspirations of an entire community. There is no place for otherness, there is no cultural pluralism.

And then there are the documentaries by Nicola Zavaglia. The documentary, a genre seldom analyzed alongside fiction, usually serves as an ancillary for the grit and fodder for sociologists' battles With *The Mediterranean Forever*, released in 2000, Zavaglia steps forward, lifts his hand, and whispers, *Sono qui*. I am here. Present.

Paradoxically, of the five films, only Zavaglia's documentary can be considered what Pier Paolo Pasolini called a *cinema di poesia* (a cinema of poetry); the other four are what could be called *cinema di prosa* (straight-forward prose narrative films). A poetic documentary, a poetic reality — an oxymoron? If it was Robert Flaherty who actually invented the documentary film genre with *Nanook of the North* (1922), it was John Grierson who coined the term "documentary" when he first watched *Moana* (Flaherty, 1926) — a neologism derived from the French word *documentaire*, mainly applicable to travel films. Grierson described Flaherty's film as "a visual account of events in the daily life of a Polynesian youth ... [having] documentary value". Years later, he expanded his definition of the documentary to include "the creative treatment of actuality."[8]

In his book *Film and Reality*, Roy Armes dedicated a few pages on the difference between fiction and documentary. He pointed out that for the documentary filmmaker "...drama came out of the physical facts of the existence of his character. In this way he is very different from most directors of fiction films who begin with a situation and then try to locate it appropriately" (37). "Unstaged reality" were the terms used by Armes to describe Cesare Zavattini's neo-realism (a filmmaker Zavaglia studied with in the 1970s, during his stay in Rome), a form Zavaglia, who does not work with fiction, explored to the maximum in his films where form and content is pure realism — a camera positioned in front of a real person, *cinéma vérité*, at its best, as practiced in Canada in the 1960 by Pierre Perreault and other directors.

We wonder, though, how far this realism is from the *realismo poetico* (poetic realism), as Sandro Bernardi coined it, which dominated French cinema after the surrealistic invasion: a poetic form showing not only what is presented but also the emotional state of the character,[9] this double level view of filmed reality being, in fact, "poetic".

In *Empirismo eretico* Pasolini explored how the reality code and the cinematographic code are one and the same. A person shot in reality is an iconic symbol of him/herself like parole, and the person in the abstract is the iconic symbol as langue.[10] Zavaglia uses footage imbued with this double articulated realism and lifts them to another level of significance: the cultural code, and this code to another level: the symbolic codes. One level of activity opens up to a second level of activity, and so forth. What we get is a new baroque performance: multi-levelled and simultaneous symbolic realities. *Pane e cioccolata* (1973) directed by Franco Brusati was written by Brusati, Jaja Fiastri and Nino Manfredi, the latter also acting in the role of the Neapolitan worker gone to Switzerland in search of a better life. In an interview Nino Manfredi admitted that

> To leave enables others to treat you like a dark-skinned person. Emigration is a dreadful problem, because it affects a person's dignity (Gili, 260).

This prize-winning comedy which touched the hearts of millions of spectators is our point of departure. What constitutes a "dreadful social problem" paves the way to new cultural horizons. Our enterprise mirrors the voyage most immigrants undertake: we travel abroad, away from the national center (Italy), embark on a journey which will take us to five different countries, each one being its own cultural and national center (Switzerland, France, England, U.S.A., Canada); we stay over a while, before we finally take the transit back to the original center (now emptied of its original meanings), to the place it all began: Italy. The circumference comes full circle.

What are we to expect from such a journey? Do these films reveal shifting allegiances already at work in these social centers? Will they reveal common attitudes, references, ambitions, fears, goals? As LeRoi Jones reminded us in *Blues People:* "There is no one way of thinking, since reference (hence value) is as scattered and dissimilar as men themselves" (153). By associating music (jazz) and the ethnic origins of musicians, Jones demonstrated how jazz in the U.S.A. emerged from specific "cultural circumstances". He makes it a point to assert that appropriation of voice is a "learned art".

Men and women not belonging to a specific ethnic community are disconnected from the culture to be able to authentically work in art forms that the culture produced. Regardless of this lack of authenticity, many talented artists have "spoken" in the place of others who did not speak, and have been applauded for their success. We wanted to avoid as much as possible having to revert to such works. Lexis, stronger, pushes Logos, weaker, off its feet. The issue becomes annoying for all. We are right to ask whether Lexis needs to copy Logos because Lexis has no Logos of his own, or should we accept Logos's own Lexis even though this one might not be considered as good as the Lexis copy.

French writer, Jean Paulhan back in the 1930s remarked that there was a danger when words and virtuosity gained more importance than facts and events:

> In short, the point is not whether an opinion is true or false, but that it exists (*Les fleurs de Tarbes*, 103).

In one chapter of his book about literature and clichés, Paulhan tells the story of a talkative Calabrian monk in a monastery in Northern Italy. Every time the Calabrian with a heavy dialect opened his mouth, his fellow brothers broke down in laughter. The situation was so bad that the Calabrian at first kept quiet, but then spoke only to predict disasters, and since these happened rarely the monk decided to invent disasters so as to satisfy his need to talk. Will the five films deal with such debatable and delectable discrepancies? If so, they will be discussed; if not, the study will yield some secret, a treasure, or a helpful principle on film or ethnic art. Cinema is a complex art form, and its textual matter integrates multiple layers of filmic and non-filmic elements. Perspective, for example, is not a filmic element per se; *perspectiva artificialis* (monocular perspective) is the direct descendant of humanist painting.[11]

In *Le champ aveugle* Pascal Bonitzer asserts that André Bazin was right in correcting a popular misunderstanding whereby perspective in film was a by-product of *mise-en-scène* and not simply the "passive reception of reality"

(102). Metaphorically speaking, film is a plurivalent organism orchestrated by one person (the director, at times; the scriptwriter, other times; the producer, oftentimes). There is no absolute manner to delimit the assortment of messages being simultaneously bombarded at the spectator. We had to decide which peephole we were going to sit in front of, looking for the cultural code.

This study is divided into five chapters, followed by a conclusion. Each film is dissected in depth. The films in this study were made in countries where we find an Italian community. We want to study how Italians evolve in the country they chose to live in, and how this existential experience is being depicted by filmmakers in their works of fiction or documentaries.

To label a filmmaker is an Italian Canadian, for example, is a dangerous proposition. Only a handful of Italian-Canadian filmmakers hold two passports. Most so-called Italian-Canadian filmmakers are so considered only because they have filmed something dealing with the Italian culture. To the Logos and its Lexis corresponds the Lexis with an authentic Logos. This is a rare occurrence because filmmakers in Canada depend almost exclusively on grants to be able to produce their movies. By extension, we can conclude that films that present some aspect of Italian culture will be classified as an Italian-Canadian work. Which is not necessarily true. But in art what is true or false?

Replace that Italian content with another content, and nothing of the Italian remains. The films chosen had to possess at least one consciously Italian element — so obvious had this parameter to be that if it were removed, the Italian tag would become meaningless. We cannot imagine examining film without considering the kind of phrases a filmmaker uses to articulate his or her own images. Film is closer to poetry than one imagines. In total agreement with Pier Paolo Pasolini, we use the "sequence" as our starting point. However, the sequence itself has been an often poorly defined substance. The manner in which shots are organized in a filmic phrase are detrimental to our understanding of the sequence.

For every film we proceed according to a fixed methodology. In the 1970s many film scholars pursued a scientific notion of semiology and semiotics at times to the point of sounding absurd and ridiculous. In their book, *L'Analyse du film*, Jacques Aumont and Michel Marie caution the film scholar to be cautious, no matter how rigorous his/her methodology might seem.

Film analysis is not a science. The end result of any film analysis should be elucidation and appreciation. These few analytical instruments chosen are used repeatedly, for each film, with alterations and adaptations. There is no single method of revealing meaning in film, even when perceived as a text or, to quote Julia Kristeva, "a translinguistic apparatus". We hope to device a method to film analysis that can be used adequately and repeatedly when needed.

In one of his essays, Christian Metz hints at the idea of sur-segmentation (which he called episodes) in a footnote in his masterful essay "Problèmes de dénotation dans le film de fiction" (*Essais I,* 122). Lino Miccichè speaks of "macrosequenza" in *Filmologia e filologia (*49); in an article, "Segmenter, analyser", Raymond Bellour speaks of "parts" and "super-segments".[12] These "episodes", these large narrative segments, limited in number, we call mega-sequences. Each mega-sequence is made up of the smaller segments *(syntagma)* which are based on Metz's syntagmatic categories. Finally, a mega-sequence can add itself to another mega-sequence to form what we call a chapter. In brief, any one film is made up shots, syntagmas, and mega-sequences (or mega-syntagmas), which are grouped into larger narrative chapters (or macro-sequences). Every act can be made up of one or more chapters that embody an actual, clearly delimited, narrative manifestation, distinct from what precedes and what follows it. Our chart (figure 3), we hope, should clarify the physical make-up of a film, as we view it.

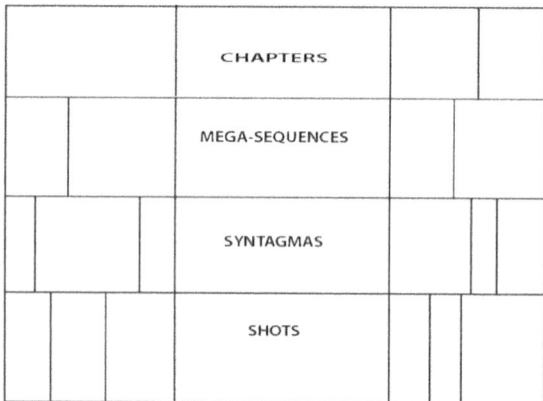

Figure 3

We will not spend any time on individual shots, the smallest filmic atom. This would lead us far from the purpose of our thesis. We have chosen to work with groups of shots grouped according to Metz's "large syntagmatic category of the image track" (*Essais I,* 121-46) (figure 4):

1. Autonomous shot
    (sequence shot, and four types of isolated inserts)

X. Non-autonomous shots
    • Achronological segments
        2. Parallel syntagma   or   3. Bracket syntagma.

    • Chronological narrative segments:
        4. Descriptive syntagma
        or X. Narrative syntagma (Alternate or Non-alternate)

            5. Alternate syntagma (and simultaneous) or
            X. Non-Alternate segments (Scene or sequences)

                    6. Scene.
                    X. Sequence (two kinds)
                        7. Episodic sequence.
                        (Discontinuous)
                        8. Ordinary sequence
                        (Continuous)

                (English terms translated by Michael Taylor.)

                                                Figure 4

These marked segments — clearly limited to the denotative level — are founded mostly on diegetic maneuvers which gives, as Roland Barthes pointed out in *S/Z* (a book that greatly has influenced the *raison d'être* of this study), the illusion of an easy reading:

> Denotation is not the first meaning, but pretends to be so; under this illusion, it is ultimately no more than the last of the connotations (the one which seems both to establish and to close the reading (*S/Z*, 9).

These films conform to the classical narrative pattern. Basing ourselves on Metz's syntagmatic model developed in his study of *Adieu Philippine* by Jacques Rozier, we will stress filmic punctuation marks in the following manner:

- when two segments are joined by an ordinary cut, we will use the equation 1-2=0;
- when two segments are joined by an optical effect, we will use 1-2=dissolve;
- when two segments are joined by a deliberate shock effect, we will use 1-2=montage with effect.

Each film is divided into chapters. Interconnected visual segments (or syntagmas), in turn, yield corresponding soundtrack variations. Strictly speaking, the six combinations Victor Bachy described in his unpublished notes *Esthétique du cinéma et de la télévision*,[13] in appearance limited and non-exhaustive, enable us to come up with a solid description of the soundtrack which instruct us on how the chapters and their respective individual visual and aural components signify throughout a film. Here are the six possible combinations Bachy came up with:

1. Synchronism; diegetical justification; authentic to sound source;
2. Synchronism; diegetical justification; inauthentic to sound source;
3. Asynchronism; diegetical justification; authentic to sound source;
4. Asynchronism; diegetical nonjustification; authentic to sound source;
5. Asynchronism; diegetical justification; inauthentic to sound source;
6. Asynchronism, diegetical nonjustification; inauthentic to sound source.

Each combination can be either subjective or objective when redirected to a character's point of view (focalization). With these elements (chapters, mega-sequences, segments/syntagma, punctuation, sound disposition), as well as the usual script slug line and the minute of the clock, we tackle the films, segment by segment, with the hope of unravelling some of the connotations signified by these textual surfaces, complete onto themselves, hermetic and open, at the same time. The formal description will contain the following information:

Chapter One: Ma che cosa dici?
1. Sequence. People, musicians, protagonist. Sunday.
Exterior. Park with lake. Daytime.
0-1=Fade-in. 0:00-2:15.
Synchronism; diegetical justification;inauthentic to sound source.

Syd Field, best known as a theoretician of screenplays, developed a paradigm model for screenwriters that can assist the analyst of film in capturing semantic shifts in narrative fiction films. More and more European film analysts applaud the merits of Field's paradigm, developed patiently in a couple of handy books, *Screenplay* and *The Screenwriter's Workbook*. Following Aristotle's system, Field divides a film's storyline into three acts:

- Act 1 (the setup),
- Act 2 (the confrontation), and
- Act 3 (the resolution),
- with two major "plot points":
    the first between 25 and 27 minutes;
    and the second between 85 and 90 minutes (figure 5).

The diagram of the Paradigm is by Syd Field.

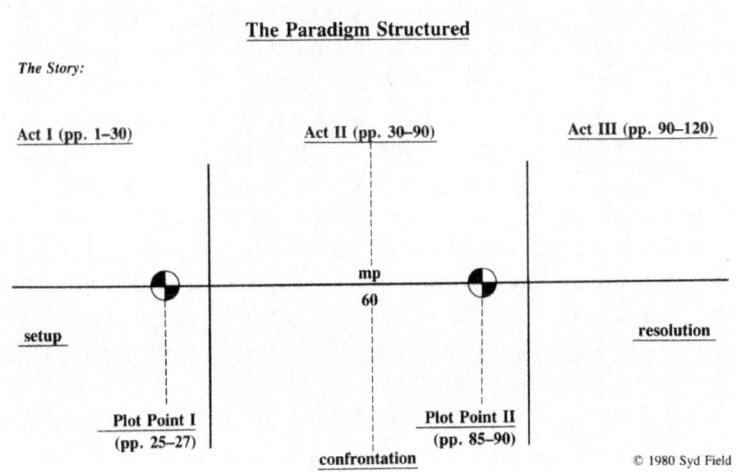

Figure 5

Such a paradigm, although criticized by some scholars,[14] enables us to detect without too much difficulty the narrative blocks that make up a film. In the beginning of his teachings, Field had not noticed the weight that his paradigm was exercising on Act 2.

The confrontation took more than sixty minutes of complicated plot action. It involved an exaggerated number of functions in too large a narrative field. As a "single narrative unit", this was simply too demanding for the writer. It was during a conversation with Paul Schrader (scriptwriter of many of Martin Scorsese films, and a fine filmmaker in his own right, *American Gigolo, Light Sleeper, Mishima, The Comfort of Strangers*), Field realized that he had to divide that portion of the plot into two distinct parts: the middle act and two "pinch points" (at 45 and 75 minutes). The second act, much too long, lacked an important Turning Point that would provide better understanding of what was truly at stake. With a new plot point at the midpoint, the second act altered drastically and, thus, the long one act, that originally contained no specified confrontation, was made to encompass two essential diegetic moments.

Act II is divided essentially in two different acts. During these acts, the protagonist, endowed with antagonistic powers, unravels himself by turning the negative forces into positive ones, and the positive forces into negative ones. We believe that if a character is to be sympathized with at the end, he must be made to seem "evil" or "bad" at the first Turning Point, and vice versa if he is to be "hated" or "pitied" at the end of a film he must be made to seem "good" between 24 and 30 minutes. This major switch from good to evil or from evil to good usually occurs at the midpoint (60 minutes). An example of the first kind of narrative we have *American Beauty* (1999) by Sam Mendes, and for the second kind, *The Talented Mr. Ripley* (1999) by Anthony Minghella (the remake of René Clément's *Plein soleil* (1960)).

This diegetic flip, this transitional instant, when what is shutting down opens up, and what is descending ascends, permits the "negative" subject suddenly to attract the spectator's empathy. Field's Act II, now neatly divided into two separate acts, brings about actions that in many ways contradict whatever was announced in the first half of the film. And so, we believe that most films contain not three acts but four acts: Act I (0-30 minutes), Act II (31-60), Act III (61-90), Act IV (91-120).

We also supply two more plot points (at 10 and 20 minutes): one is dedicated to the protagonist who, during the first ten minutes of a film, is introduced to the spectator and then faces a Turning Point (Inciting Incident); and a second, no less important moment, which presents a second character (the Sender) who opens a new narrative door that ultimately introduces an object of desire. This systematic division of an entire film into disparate macro-sequences — plot points at 10-20-30-45-60-75-90-105-120 minutes — correspond to readily identifiable narrative functions, which help us register explicit displacements in the narration (figure 6). These diegetic switches, occurring at regular intervals, dislodge the most significant elements of the storyline.

By expanding Field's paradigm and by transforming it into a W-shape paradigm, we are able visually to represent how these semantic deviations surface at precise moments. The main question remains: what do these functions in our W method mean?

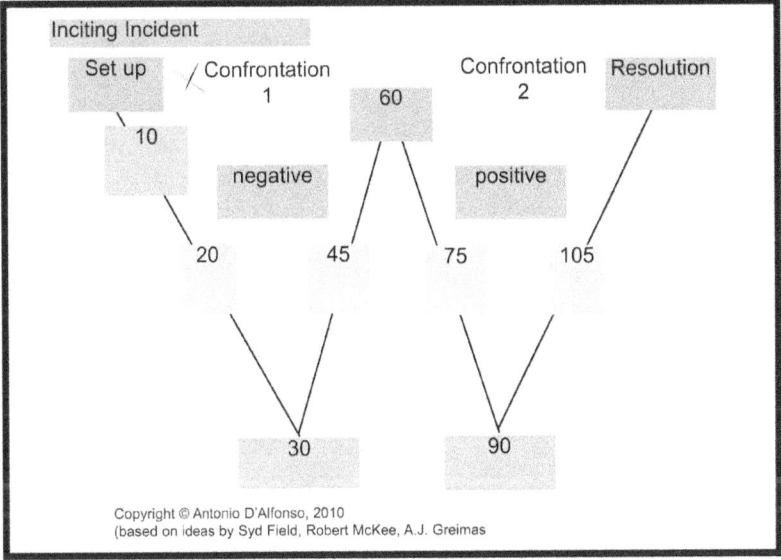

Figure 6

In the same way Will Wright performed in *Six Guns and Society*, with his cognitive analysis of the Western as myth, we too would like to elaborate the narrative functions that express the cultural structures of these ethnic films. Here are the functions we believe exist in these films:

> 1. – 10 minutes: The protagonist is introduced to us during the first macro-sequence (1-10 minutes); ending with the eleven minute Turning Point, which Robert McKee terms the "Inciting Incident".
>
> 2. – 20: The protagonist encounters an adjuvant who has a connection to a first object of desire (10-20). This is the Sender, to use a term used by both Vladimir Propp and A. J. Greimas.

3. – 30: The adjuvant becomes the Sender of this first false object of desire (20-30) and it is here the subject commits an act of actual ferocity or symbolic harshness (for a happy ending) or graciousness and generosity (for the unhappy ending). This object of desire must bother the spectator, or else bring about joy, whatever its significance it most probably symbolizes the opposite position found at the ending of the film.

4. – 45. The quarrel between the first false object of desire and the Sender.

5. – 60. From the quarrel a second object of desire appears.

6. – 75. The quarrel between the second false object of desire and the first object of desire.

7. – 90. From this quarrel a third object of desire appears.

8. – 105. This is the denouement which leads to the end, that is, the subject with the real object of desire.

9. – 120. The ending which is the exact opposite of what happened at the 30-minute point.

The timetable might vary, but the variation in the narrative functions is minimal; these nine plot points recur nonetheless at precise narrative moments in the diegetic entity. Beneath this surface structure we display A.J. Greimas's actant model which enables us to pull out from the narrative semantic blocks which should fit well on our modified paradigm (figure 7). The actant model diagram is by A.J. Greimas.

In a simplified way we would like to advance the hypothesis that the Inciting Incident, the midpoint plot point and the end point are the backbone of all film narratives. Narratives, however, are not about getting as fast as possible to the object of desire, to the end of its story. As Propp has pointed out, story plots are delays, distractions, about getting to the endpoint by the longest way possible. This is the entertainment factor of the storytelling. The subject looks for an object of desire, and is able to get it with the help of adjuvants, but along the way he finds obstacles (opponents).

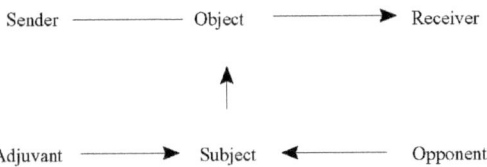

Figure 7

At the end of the film, if the protagonist gets what he wants, it is thanks to the Sender. The subject gets his true object of desire, but also something more. To get what he wants, the subject must first "lose" himself and then find a revelation. This is the pleasure of the text, to quote Roland Barthes. The greatest enjoyment to be had happens when a storyteller "postpones" the finale. Postponement is what film is all about; the subject gets the true object of his desire but only after losing his way there.

By applying Christian Metz's large syntagmatic category of the image track on the narrative functions, we are able to freeze critical segments and analyze these segments as though we were dealing with enlarged photograms. We detail what these disparate and parallel streams of sounds and images have to reveal, by a *pas à pas* (a step-by-step, analytical moments.

Roland Barthes called these segments *lexias* (*S/Z,* 13): some, admittedly, larger and more complex than others, from which symbolic significance can be extracted.

According to Winfried Nöth, there are two historical meanings of the term "code": the institutional code refers to a "set of rules prescribing forms of social behavior"; and the cryptographic code branches out in two directions: 1. cryptography which deals with the task of "developing secret codes" (encoding, enciphering messages); and 2. cryptanalysis which are developed methods of breaking down codes.

Nöth admits that a "code is no longer a rule for the transformation of signs, but a sign system in its own right" (206-209). A code, according to

Jacques Aumont and his fellow film analysts, is basically a principle that governs the relationship between signifier and signified (*Analyse*, 71).

What sort of relationship do images and sounds entertain with reality? In film there are a number of "codes". Thierry Kuntzel in his study on *M* (1931), by Fritz Lang, came up with a set of such codes, some which had been already mentioned by Roland Barthes:

1. Narrative code;
2. Hermeneutic code;
3. Symbolic code;
4. Visual code;
5. Montage code;
6. Semantic code;
7. Proairectic code;
8. Referential code;
9. Composition code;
10. Camera movement code;
11. Setting code;
12. Gaze code... [15]

Filmic codes are too numerous to elucidate here; it would be vain at this point to attempt giving an exhaustive analytical list of every single aspect in a film. What concerns us here are the syntagmas, used as lexias, and how these reveal the proairectic and hermeneutic codes. We will navigate slowly, coasting along, and drawing out the symbolic, referential and other codes that command our immediate attention.

What interests us is how these narrative sequences bring to light the cultural elements that will help us define the Italic. At the conclusion of this voyage we hope to open the doors to a long awaited "cosmopolitan enterprise" (to quote Randolph Bourne), "a trans-nationality, a weaving back and forth, with the other lands, of many threads of all sizes and colors".[16] The title of the study derives from a monologue spoken by Jake LaMotta in *Raging Bull*, which is a paraphrase of another monologue said by Terry Malloy in *On the Waterfront* by Elia Kazan. Though the words of the speeches are similar, their meaning is different. What for Malloy was a need for success becomes for LaMotta a criticism of this success. Perhaps the five filmmakers we will study are heralding the death of the Italian and Italic cultures; maybe they are extolling the merits of assimilation and nationalism. Maybe, on the contrary, they are singing the permanence of emigrant culture. It is too early to pronounce ourselves on what lies ahead. We begin this research with no certitude except the wish to see how the Italic diaspora of filmmakers no longer need a social and political territorial base to continue to exist culturally. It is our secret wish to validate a deterritorialized ethnic identity which resists the great bulldozer of sameness.

Notes

1. Our study, as will become obvious, stands at the opposite end of what Millicent Marcus considers national. We hope to show how Italic films are linked culturally but separated by territory.
2. In *In Italics* and *Gambling with Failure,* I advanced the idea that cultural identity of the Italic writer, if he so embraced such a concept, would be based not on territorial nor blood ties but on conscience identity. In other words, it is up to the writer to decide if he or she wished to belong to this cultural group. Of course, many writers seem unable to let go of the fact that language is not a binding factor to identity. Because languages embrace many cultures in different territories, and territories can often carry many cultures within its boundaries, we should not conclude that a language or a territory possesses the ultimate parameter to identity. The British citizen who speaks English does not have the same culture as the Texan who speaks the same language. The Walloon and the Flemish who live on the same strip of land do not belong to the same cultural group. From such considerations, I surmised that the writer alone was the only one who could identify his/her culture. If a writer or an artist of Italian origin decides that he or she does not want to embrace the Italic culture, it is his or her prerogative. A cultural entity exists for those who wish it. It is possible that a culture comes to an end when its members decide to put an end to their culture. For the time being, I believe the Italic culture is very much alive, regardless of individual dissension.
3. "The effect of the melting-pot ideal is either to influence [the] Anglicizing, or to obliterate the distinctive racial and cultural qualities, and work the American population into a colorless, tasteless, homogeneous mass... Both effects of the melting-pot idealism, I believe, are highly undesirable." These sentences were published in 1916 by Randolph S. Bourne and collected in *War and the Intellectuals: Collected Essays: 1915-1919,* "The Jew and Trans-National America", New York: Harper and Row Publishers, 1964, 124-145.
4. Why use the term "Italic" and not "Italian"? Italian is a term widely recognized as being identified to the peninsula. The Italic is something that includes the connotations within "Italian" and goes beyond whatever is Italian. Italian refers to a political entity; Italic does not. Italian, even when equated to outside Italy realities, connotes the country called Italy. Italic does not reduce itself neither to Italy nor to Italians inside and outside Italy. The Italic is whatever cultural appreciation that can be found when adding Italians/Italy and Italians/Italians outside Italy. Italian reveals a subtractive notion; Italic, an addition. The Italic is a wider concept than Italian can ever be.

5. Jean Baudrillard, *Simulations,* New York: Semiotext(e), 1983, 4: "It is no longer a question of imitation, nor of reduplication, nor even of parody. It is rather a question of substituting signs of the real for the real itself, that is, an operation to deter every real process by its operational double, a metastable, programmatic, perfect descriptive machine which provides all the signs of the real and shortcircuits all its vicissitudes."
6. Édouard Molinaro, *Intérieur soir,* Paris, Éditions Anne Carrière, 2009.
7. Andrew Sarris, "Notes on the Auteur Theory in 1962", in *Film Theory and Criticism,* edited by Gerald Mast and Marshall Cohen, Oxford: Oxford University Press, Inc., 1974. In this essay Andrew Sarris makes his famous comment: "Am I implying that the weakest [John] Ford is superior to the strongest [Henry] King? Yes!" My study will purposely avoid any reference to signatures and deal primarily with what Giles Gunn called "culture": "that is, as a more or less systematically organized and experienceable way of life", quoted in Lee Lourdeaux's *Italian and Irish Filmmakers in America,* Philadelphia: Temple University Press, 1990, 9.
8. John Grierson, *Grierson on Documentary,* London: Faber, 1966, 13.
9. Sandro Bernardi, *L'avventura del cinematografo: Storia di un'arte e di un linguaggio,* Venezia: Marsilio, 2007, 110-111. This sentence is a paraphrase of Bernardi's original: "I francesi ne fanno invece una forma poetica, per mostrare, oltre alla cosa vista, anche lo stato d'animo di un personaggio (soggettiva stilistica)."
10. Vide Pier Paolo Pasolini's "Il codice dei codici" in *Empirismo eretico* (1972) , Milano: Garzanti, 2010, 277.
11. Jacques Aumont, Alain Bergala, Michel Marie, Marc Vernet, *Esthétique du film,* Paris: Éditions Fernand Nathan, 1983, 20.
12. Raymond Bellour, described in Jacques Aumont and Michel Maire, *L'analyse des films,* 2nd ed., Paris: Armand Colin, 2004, 51-53.
13. Victor Bachy, *Notes de cours d'Esthétique du cinéma et de la télévision,* at the Centre des techniques de diffusion, Université Catholique de Louvain. Used by Rogerio Luz in *Analyse structurale du récit filmique.* Michel Chion offers in his books on film sound other methodologies to grasping the relationship between the visual and the aural components in film.
14. Syd Field's structural paradigm has borne the brunt (unjustly in our opinion) of many teachers of scriptwriting: John Truby, *The Anatomy of Story,* New York: Faber and Faber, 2007, and Robert McKee, *Story: Substance, Structure, Style,* and *The Principles of Screenwriting,* ItBooks-HarperCollins Publishers, 1977.
15. Quoted in Jacques Aumont et al., *L'analyse des films,* 72.
16. I am purposely using Randolph Bourne's definition of America in *The Radical Will: Selected Writings: 1911-1918,* Berkeley: University of California, 1977, 262.

1

BREAD AND CHOCOLATE (PANE E CIOCCOLATA)

Synopsis

Bread and Chocolate (Pane e cioccolata) was directed by Franco Brusati in 1973, released in 1974. The screenplay was written by Franco Brusati, Nino Manfredi and Jaja Fiastri. The main actors are Nino Manfredi and Anna Karina.

In the 1970s, an Italian emigrant works part-time in a Swiss restaurant. After being wrongly accused of the death of a child, Giovanni (Nino) Garofoli loses his work permit for urinating in a public place. Nino becomes a clandestine, living with Elena, a Greek neighbor, and her son. Nino eventually finds work with a rich dishonest Italian industrial who, gone bankrupt, commits suicide. Nino's only hope, Elena, marries a Swiss immigration officer who will grant her son the much needed landed-immigrant papers. Finding himself alone, Nino visits the barracks where he once worked. He then finds work with Southern Italian chicken breeders. This experience turns out to be more nightmarish than the barracks had been. Nino dyes his hair blond wanting to pass for a German Swiss. However, during a soccer game between Switzerland and Italy, broadcasted in a bar, Nino's patriotism gets the better of his emotions, and his true identity is unmasked. He must leave the country. At the train station, Elena hands Nino legal work papers, but Nino prefers to jump on the train carrying him back to Italy. Running back to his Italian family is impossible, and so Nino gets off the train. The last image of Nino is him with a suitcase walking out of a train gallery. By the early 1970s, directors looked beyond the 1960s stylistic and intellectual radicalness and delved into new social issues. Here is a list of a few of the major films released in 1974.

Alice Doesn't Live Here Anymore, Martin Scorsese
Amarcord, Federico Fellini
Blazing Saddles, Mel Brooks
Chinatown, Roman Polanski
The Conversation, Francis Ford Coppola
Dersu Uzala, Akira Kurosawa
F for Fake, Orson Welles
The Godfather (Part II), Francis Ford Coppola
Lancelot du Lac, Robert Bresson
Les Ordres, Michel Brault
Profumo di donna, Dino Risi
Stavisky, Alain Resnais
The Texas Chainsaw Massacre, Tobe Hooper
A Woman Under the Influence, John Cassavetes
Young Frankenstein, Mel Brooks

Structure of the film

In his essay "Problems of Denotation in the Fiction Film", Christian Metz writes that a film is a large syntagma made up of smaller codified units (*Essais I*, 122n). In essence, a film is one large mega-syntagma divided up into smaller stacking units — chapters, mega-sequences, syntagms, shots — designed to fit inside one another, much like matryoshka dolls. For example, the first eight syntagmas in *Pane* constitute a single mega-sequence. Pier Paolo Pasolini in *Empirismo eretico* called such a narrative block the long temporal leash ("la grande lassa temporale").[1]

At the bottom of the pyramid we have single shots which, combined, make up a syntagma. These "scenettes", however, once glued one to another, constitute the mega-sequence, which offers a temporal and, in many cases, spatial entity. Mega-sequences make up a large unit we call chapter. At the beginning of our research, we had mistaken the mega-sequence for the chapter.

As the study progressed, we noticed many occurrences where a chapter included more than a single mega-sequence. It is possible for a chapter to be made up of a single mega-sequence, but more often than not a chapter consists of a number of mega-sequences. Chapters interconnect and comprise the entire film. In *Bread and Chocolate*, we have marked fourteen chapters. Our use of the chapter does not correspond to the scene-chapters found on DVDs introduced technically to facilitate film browsing. If it were possible, one could present the action depicted in these syntagmas on a theater stage. Though the codified syntagmas of completely developed actions unfolding in different locations, the story unfolds linearly. For *Pane e cioccolata*, we have come up with fourteen chapters.

1. Chapter One. "Ma che cosa dici?" 0.00-11.08
2. Chapter Two. "Piece you back together with a sewing machine." 11:09-22:00
3. Chapter Three. Going home. 22:01-29:17
4. Chapter Four. Becoming Illegal. 29:18-33:56
5. Chapter Five. Elena. 33:57-42:37
6. Chapter Six. Encounter with the rich. 42:38-51:59
7. Chapter Seven. The New Family. 52:00-59:16
8. Chapter Eight. First Day at Work. 59:17-65:22
9. Chapter Nine. Paper Airplane. 65:23-66:17
10. Chapter Ten. The Show. 66:18-75:49
11. Chapter Eleven. Leaving. 75:50-76:43
12. Chapter Twelve. Chicken. 76:44-88:51
13. Chapter Thirteen. Assimilating. 88:52-98:32
14. Chapter Fourteen. The End-Dream. 98:33-108:43

These distantly related moments are united in the spectator's mind as a single temporal and spatial entity. They are not. We cannot assume that filmic time corresponds to real time. The relation between film and reality might be and might not be contemporaneous, which would have turned this syntagma into a sequence shot. This equivocalness justifies our decision to separate the chapters into smaller units.

These chapters are made of scenes (43), sequences (8), sequence shots (4), Alternating syntagma (3), Bracket syntagma (2), and Descriptive syntagma (1). Formally speaking, Franco Brusati has chosen the scene as his principal unity: one action, one time, one location. Eight sequences are used to link together shifting locations; eight sequence shots to remind us that Brusati is relatively still under the illusion of being under the neo-realist influence. He often shoots an entire scene in a single take. The other six syntagms are used primarily for symbolic narrative effect. This film relies heavily on the one-location theatrical setting. Let us begin with the step-by-step reading.

Chapter 1: "Ma che cosa dici?"
0.00-11.08

1. Sequence. The Introduction. Ext. Park with lake. Daytime.
0-1=Fade-in. 0:00-2.12

The first chapter begins with a man strolling in a park. We do not know the name of this man yet. It is, we will soon find out, Giovanni (Nino) Garofoli. This sequence unites interlocking scenettes with the use of one continuous musical score. Classical music, *Andante Cantabile* by Roman Hofstetter, a serenade that for many years had been attributed to Joseph Hayden (in fact, in the film credited to Hayden), unfolds over mute images: a serenade, a wooing song, usually performed outside, in the evening, below a lover's window.

The film credits roll over short scenes depicting an idyllic summer afternoon. On a lake, a young couple with long fair hair are rowing in a canoe. As welcoming as it might be, this music is not justified: why would Franco Brusati choose this music for such a scene? This ambient film music is inauthentic, non-synchronic, non-diegetically justified, and highly subjective (both from the perspective of the couple in the canoe, and from that of the filmmaker who is making a point). Wouldn't the "realistic" sounds of birds chirping or wind blowing have been more appropriate? In choosing a romantic introduction, Brusati places the spectator in a blissful setting. We are in Northern Europe. Paradise for the Southern immigrant who is wooing.

The camera zooms back and reveals a photographer behind a Rolleiflex, getting ready for a shot. Cut to a family posing for him. Satisfied, the photographer presses the shutter button and runs to join his family. Happiness. Here, Brusati reminds us that he is presenting the filmic images of a happy family. Happy, maybe; a family, certainly.

This initial reference to the family opens the window on one of the main parameters that appear in this journey toward ethnic self-knowledge. The family thematic reappears in the other four films. Not a haphazard image, this picture of the family unit — father, mother, children, grand-parents — brought to the foreground stresses the importance its plays in the emigrant-immigrant's life. Without the family the foreigner-individual loses a part of his identity. Though *Pane e cioccolata* embodies many meanings, the family unit becomes a condition to which the spectator must necessarily refer to throughout the viewing of the film.

It is probably Sunday afternoon. Parents leisurely spend quality time with their children. A grandfather, grandmother, father, mother, wife, children bask in the sunlight for the quintessential family portrait. In the background, on horses, two women discreetly cross the screen from right to the left. Brusati subtly uses these unobtrusive background elements (women on horses) to cut to the next scenette. These two women become a linking device holding various scenettes together in order to form what Christian Metz labelled the "ordinary sequence" (the enlarged scene that covers a wider expanse than the normal "chamber scene", limited to one space).

From the sunlight we cut to the deep darkness of the wooden part of the park. First, a pan to the right with a light zooming out on the two horseback riders gently trotting out of this dark, and then a zooming-in on four musicians performing in a semi-circle. Suddenly the music that was so blatantly screaming its presence finds its source. Here is the quartet responsible for the music we hear. Brusati is playing with the spectator, lying to us, making us believe that it is he who invests so much extraneous meaning onto a sequence.

There is an ambiguity, nonetheless, in this investment. The director lies to us, by postponing the truth, and when the truth is finally told, the meaning is not different from the lie. This "doubleness" of meaning is not something that will go away. Ambivalence, dual personality (more than split personality), "duplexity" will pounce on the spectator over and over again. In an interview with Jean A. Gili, Brusati admitted that *Pane e cioccolata* was riddled with contradictions. He wanted to make it very clear to everyone that he loved northern Europe, and, more precisely, mittel-european culture influenced by Austrian culture; it is in that part of the world that the past is felt with more intensity (*Cinéma*, 196-202).

From the right, from the shadows, a man enters, his back to the camera. An unusual 180-degree cut to the front of the man. With black hair slicked back and neatly trimmed moustache, the man sports a blue suit, a pink shirt with paisley designs, and a blue tie. He stands before the musicians, serious looking, in spite of his outlandish clothes. He carefully scrutinizes each member of the quartet. In close-up, the musicians, one by one, are presented to the spectator. When we cut back to our protagonist, two women stop behind him; they too stop to listen to the music. Our protagonist smiles, impressed, slowly exits to the right. He disappears as he appeared. He is one of the many persons enjoying this Sunday stroll in the park.

2. Descriptive Syntagma. The Park. Ext. Park with lake. Daytime. 1-2=dry cut with effect. 2:13-2:32

The classical music, in the foreground, is non-justified, non-synchronized, non-authentic: the musicians not present, only metonymically through the music they are producing with their instruments, suddenly become the creators of film music, at once, for this film and for this scene. This double intent gives a particular significance to the soundtrack. Forgetting momentarily the source of the music, we come to believe that what we are listening to is "natural" music. Under the spell of realism we come to believe in this paradise while the credits come to an end.

What follows could be viewed as belonging to the previous sequence but the abrupt cut calls forth, on the contrary, a new scene. Instead of following the protagonist strolling in the park, we are given short descriptive clips of people (happy families) carrying baskets filled to the brim with food; a shot of a dog carrying a basket of food as well; a tablecloth being spread on the grass; a cake lifted for us to view.

Synchronic/diatopic: different shots related by a single theme. The spectator savors the happiness of this festive moment. This "conjunctive scene" naturally links Sequence 1 to Scene 3.

>   3. Scene. Man eating a chocolate bar sandwich. Ext. Park.
>   Daytime. 2-3=zero. 2:33-3:48

This syntagma could have been a sequence shot had it not been for the inserts that transform this single shot into a scene. One man eats his sandwich, surrounded by a myriad of nameless characters picnicking. Hofstetter's Andante cantabile accompanies the images. Our protagonist (a solitary man) walks in from the right, smiling at all these joyful families basking in the summer-day sunlight in the park.

He sits at the foot of a tree, and pulls out from his jacket pocket a sandwich clumsily wrapped in napkin. He absentmindedly throws the paper on the grass, but before he takes a bite into his sandwich becomes aware that he has done a misdemeanor. He hastily picks up the napkin, feeling guilty.

The camera dollies forward in on the protagonist who takes a bite of his sandwich, a chocolate bar sandwich. This is where the title comes from. We could translate the title more succinctly: chocolate sandwich. The chocolate bar sandwich equals, metonymically, to the man eating it. "I am what I eat." Chocolate and bread. Possibly we can stretch the metaphor a little more and fall into stereotypes: chocolate for Switzerland, bread for Italy. Chocolate for Northern Europe and bread for Southern Europe. There is confrontation. The man is eating his antonyms, his antithesis, his own contradiction.

Barely perceptible above the music, we hear the sound of mastication, then suddenly a tapping of the baton and the music stops: birds sing. What is it about his eating a chocolate sandwich that troubles the peace in the park? Or so it appears that everyone stops to live the moment this man begins to eat.

A second misdemeanor. A guilt-ridden Nino looks about, conscious that his eating disturbs these people, that the sound he makes while eating is an offense to this perfect society. We can almost hear his thoughts: "What have I done wrong? Worse. What have I done wrong again?" Nino is a collection of misdemeanors.

An insert: a woman, the leader of the quartet stares at the camera (at him? at the spectator?): are we, the spectators, creating a scandal, as much as the protagonist who now eagerly turns his eyes on his sandwich? He shifts his eyes to the left: a second insert: a second woman with sunglasses stares at him. Overhead, a blackbird: even nature is against him? The protagonist looks up, in defiance. A third insert: a blackbird on a branch singing. A rapid cut to a man bringing in a folding table to the woman with sunglasses who breaks into smiles. What seems so ominous becomes relaxed, peaceful, even the musician regains her composure. This outsider is innocent after all. A second gaze at the bird, and everything is back to normal. The music starts anew; a sign of relief on the protagonist's face.

4. Scene. Soccer. Ext. Park lake. Daytime.
3-4=zero. 3:49-5:52

A pan down a tree trunk. A sign reads No smoking, yet there is smoke circling up in the air. Another misdemeanor under the gracious Hofstetter's music. Natural sounds are justified, synchronized, authentic. A soccer ball rolls toward the tree. Nino jumps to his feet and kicks the ball back to a boy with long blond hair who kicks the ball on the green grass in the other direction. Interpreting this action as an invitation to play, the protagonist rushes to the ball, cigarette hanging from his lips, and dribbles the ball before kicking it back to the boy. Like a skilful soccer player, the man handles elegantly the ball with his feet.

This is a European man who voices not words, but sounds, gibberish, grunts, like a dog grunting. Second allusion to the animal kingdom: first the bird, now the dog. This man belongs more to the "animal" kingdom than to the sophisticated people in the park. Interestingly, the beat of this first megasequence (dedicated the park) is about soccer which will be the very thing that will later on reveal Nino's true identity. Soccer is another trait of Nino's identity.

Our protagonist, a foreigner, an accumulation of misdeeds isolates him from the families that color this Nordic world. Once he kicks the ball to the boy words pour out of him: "*Là... Voilà, eccola...* here it is... the ball." The boy looks on, disgruntled, at this stranger smoking, speaking to him in a language he does not understand. "*Tira...,*" orders Nino. "Kick back the ball..." But the boy runs away, kicking the ball to himself.

Nino looks off screen, concludes: "Independent, eh?" Who is he speaking to? He walks toward the camera, speaking in Italian, the boy in the background. The camera dollies back and reveals a park bench where a woman, the mother of the child, is knitting.

The man continues: "He doesn't need anybody to play a game. Not even an opponent. I like that. Do you speak Italian?"

The lady answers: *"Nein."*

The man: "Why should you? Nobody speaks it here. Just me, because I don't know another language."

This moment "off-screen" places the viewer on equal footing with the mother. The spectator stares at this foreigner speaking Italian, cigarette in hand, asking the Swiss woman sitting on the bench beside him if she speaks Italian. No, she does not speak Italian. She speaks German. Yet there is an act of communication, as André Martinet would say; there is a need of "making oneself understood" (*Éléments,* 18). The man is a speaker; the woman, a listener. Or is she just a "hearer", that is, someone who says "no" to everything she hears without listening, shutting herself up, like window blind shut on a landscape? Her "no" is uttered not only to this foreigner's words but his existence.

Yet knitting signifies openness of sorts. Perhaps she is knitting a sweater for the boy playing soccer. The spectator stubbornly asks himself at this point, What is she saying "no" to? This German-speaking woman's response to a question asked in Italian indicates that she does understand the foreign words the foreigner has spoken. She even retaliates in Italian, *"No, grazie",* but refuses to converse with this foreigner.

On one level, we have a confrontation: Italian/German. Adversity. There against here; Nino against her; Italian-speaking versus German-speaking. On the second level, we have formal irony. To make this film comprehensible to an Italian-speaking public it had to be dubbed. Brusati's primary audience is the Italian public that speaks only Italian or some dialect; never did he consider the use of German alone. Had he done so he would have had no choice but to use subtitles for his Italian-speaking spectators.

What we have here is a linguistic situation that will never be resolved in the film. Are the Swiss characters speaking German which Nino understands? Or are they actually capable of speaking Italian and are actually conversing in Italian with Nino?

This plurilinguistic reality, though, never fully explored here — it is taken for granted — is another parameter of the Italic experience. Characters in the five films analyzed here all converse in various languages. Their identity is never stationed in one language alone. Nino speaks Neapolitan, Italian, French, Spanish, German.

Before the spectator comes to grips with this many-language reality, the red and white ball strikes Nino who immediately jumps up and kicks the ball back to the boy in a purposely exaggerated way, like a clown, a mime... reminiscent of Charlie Chaplin and Jacques Tati. Nino Manfredi explains his admiration for Charles Chaplin:

> I must admit that the person who moved me and most influenced me is Chaplin. When I was a child, I would accept measly jobs just so that I could make enough money to see a Chaplin film. Chaplin was responsible for the crisis that overtook me after years of working in serious theater... I decided to dedicate myself exclusively to variety theater and comedies. (*Gili*, 248-249)

Nino Manfredi will perform a number of these Chaplinesque, highly formalized gags. The chocolate sandwich, the blackbird confrontation, and now this exaggerated soccer kick. Charles Chaplin explains in his *My Autobiography:*

> [Humor] is the subtle discrepancy we discern in what appears to be normal behavior... through humor we see in what seems rational, the irrational; in what seems important, the unimportant (210).

A portrait slowly gets formed. Chocolate bread sandwich, cigarette, an Italian-speaking foreigner: this man is not from "here". Henri Bergson says of laughter:

> However, spontaneous it seems, laughter always implies a kind of secret freemasonry, or even complicity, with other laughers, real or imaginary (64).

We, the willing, sympathetic spectators laugh at this stranger, at this *guer* (Hebrew for "stranger"). Nino might smile but he knows very well that he does not belong to this collectivity.

The Italian offers his personal appreciation of this other collectivity: "Oh yes, I like Switzerland. And why, you'll ask? Because it's clean. The air, the grass. [He fillips his cigarette to the ground.] People mind their own business. You say they're cold? No, they're civilized." Civility, cleanliness, discretion: three characteristics that attract him, that will haunt him throughout this film. It is not the Swiss who change, but our nervous foreigner. This "Don Quixote of the Southern Italian unemployed," to quote Piero Scaruffi,[2] does not please critics. Vincent Canby, for instance, does not find Manfredi funny.

The script is not great. It wants to have several characters for the price of one. When it suits the convenience of the authors, Nino assumes a sort of bargain-basement, Chaplinesque innocence. At other times he must behave as one who is basically dim-witted. Then, too, he's a fellow who can question the gods.[3]

Exactly ten years before *Bread and Chocolate* is released, Sergio Leone launches the European Western with *A Fistful of Dollars* (1964). What has *Pane e cioccolata*, a film on emigration to do with the western? Contrary to what one thinks, quite a bit. Both deal with the individual against society; both sing the values of individualism, even though their endings might differ. To paraphrase Kenneth Mackinnon who produced a remarkable study, *Greek Tragedy into Film*, in one film, the hero rides into the sunset after cleaning up the town and, in the other, after destroying its streets, the town kicks the hero out of its gates.[4]

From the start one could compare Brusati's film to what Will Wright defines as the "classical plot" in his structural study of westerns, *Six Guns and Society*. Let us list the first five functions that Wright proposes:

1. The hero enters a social group.
2. The hero is unknown to the society.
3. The hero is revealed to have an exceptional ability.
4. The society recognized a difference between themselves and the hero; the hero is given a special status.
5. The society does not completely accept the hero.

(142-43)

The anonymous "hero-stranger" of *Pane e cioccolata* follows a trajectory similar to the one the western hero does. He will never deal with villains a western hero would have to confront in his context, nevertheless a foreigner, no matter what he does, will never be accepted by the society he tries to enter. The differences between the stranger and the nation are too great to ever be completely replaced by whatever "success" is needed to bridge the gap.

Why will the boy kick the ball toward this Italian man? Red and white, the colors of the Swiss flag. As a metonym, the father/son paradigm is raised alongside the outsider/insider paradigm. If this elegant, indirect reference to fatherhood does not go unnoticed, it is because the-alien-versus-the-native couplet cannot be erased. The foreigner is being invited to become a surrogate father? Or a father tout court?

The spectator is justified in asking: "Where is this boy's father? At work? On a Sunday? Does the boy have a father at all?" With a light blue trenchcoat wrapped on her shoulders and navy blue skirt, this mother sits knitting, alone in the park, a basket of pink and white wool balls by her side, without her husband. Does the husband exist?

The father figure will be raised at various times during the film, though Nino, himself, might be without his family. The drama in this film, but also in the other four films, is that a father without a family is pushed into a situation where he is no longer considered a father.

This "de-fathering" entails a number of consequences which will be dealt with as we move along in this analysis. Perhaps this is where the clown comes into play.

In *Fare un film*, Federico Fellini distinguishes two types of clowns: the white clown and the August clown (*Fare*, 227). The white clown, Fellini writes, possesses "intelligence, grace, harmony, intelligence, lucidity" who inescapably reveals the negative sides of his personality. What seemed open becomes a fault condemned by the authoritative father, mother, teacher, artist and handsome tyrant.

Walking at the opposite side of the road is the August clown who revolts against everything whenever he can:

> È il bambino che si caca sotto, si ribella...; si ubriaca, si rotola per terra e anima, perciò, una contestazione perpetua.
> [He is the boy who pees in his pants, rebels, gets drunk, rolls on the ground and swirls in circles, in a gesture of non-stop defiance.]

In other words, *Bread and Chocolate* is the story of an Italian white clown who along the way switches into an August clown in exile.

The boy's kick expresses defiance. He personally does not like this white clown dressed in dark clothes accosting his mother. Something more than defiance, however, is at stake. The signifier is ambiguous; the child acts as the protector of his mother. By pushing this defiance a little deeper into the metaphorical, the affront manifests paradoxically the boy's willingness to play with Nino who, strangely, is unable to accept the invitation.

There is a hint at Oedipal triangle in the making. The absence of a real father leads us to the adoptive father, but can this clownlike stranger become a father figure at all, let alone his father? (And the lover of his mother?)

Our protagonist, a Southern Italian in the German-speaking region of Switzerland, indulges in small talk with a member of the host country. But Nino the outsider can only speak Italian. Is he a tourist?

Protagonist: "Do you want to know something?"
German mother *(in Italian)*: "No, grazie."

This German-speaking woman does speak Italian. If she is bilingual, why did she lie to our protagonist about her not speaking Italian? There is parody at work here, a duality message (once again). No communication possible if the receiver refuses to receive. The monologue comes to a halt, Hofstetter's serenade fades in. The red ball with white circles once again strikes Nino who looks at the mother who finally scolds her son who, in protest, angrily throws the ball into the woods. Nino runs in the dark patch of trees and, as the father he thinks he is, invites the boy to follow him. In his voice we detect more than just the Italian language — a hint of dialect.

The linguistic registers have altered. If, on the first register, the spectator perceived the confrontation between Italian and German; on the second, it is now Italian and the regional dialect. This shifting of linguistic registers acts as a reminder that Brusati has deliberately chosen to pit individualism *(parole)* against collectivism *(langue)*.

The Italian man stands alone, away from society, at the dark entrance of a woody patch, asking a young boy to follow him. The sexual connotation in this situation is obvious. Sitting on a park bench, too concentrated on knitting, the mother does not notice that a foreigner has just invited her child to take a walk in the dark: the boy refuses to follow Nino.

> 5. Scene: A little girl. Ext. Park: Wooded Area. Daytime.
> 4-5=zero. 5:53-6:55

This scene, a direct outcome of the previous scene, has natural sounds that are justified, synchronized, authentic, except for Hofstetter spicing the background with its twist of sardonic social commentary.

This quiet park where families gather for Sunday lunch also houses unspeakable acts of horror. The camera, like a voyeur's eyes, highly mobile, pans from one side to the other, zooming in and out, tilting up and down, revealing Nino walking into the woods.

Just as he picks up the ball, Nino stops cold, horror on his face, as we glimpse a corpse, leaves on this child's white dress, one leg bent inward under the other. There are traces of blood on her left thigh. Her right arm folded over her bosom, she has her head turned to the left, long wavy brown hair barely distinguishable from the earth; a sunbeam blesses her dead body. Ball in hand, visibly upset, Nino stops by a tree, breathing deeply, staring back to the body of the child in disbelief, unaware that on the other side of the tree trunk stands a priest staring into the void, holding a yellow skipping rope... the color of the girl's sock. Any aspect of the clown vanishes.

The first chapter is divided into two parts, two mega-sequences, each ending with an "Inciting Incident", a term coined by Robert McKee in his book *Story:* "The Inciting Incident radically upsets the balance of the forces in the protagonist's life" (181-207).

In this case, barely seven minutes into the first mega-sequence, a major event occurs, disrupting not only the "balance of the protagonist" but also the entire structure of the plot. This foreigner is faced with a corpse in his hands. The spectator knows the man is blameless. But does society think he is innocent?

If we push the formal analysis a little further we notice that Syd Field's paradigm can very well accommodate the wealth of action that has so far unfolded.

1. Nino is introduced (the subject).
2. A boy playing with a ball appears (the Sender).
3. The corpse of the dead girl is found (the object of desire).

These elements bring about a narrative unit, the story advancing in a logical manner, much like any agglutinative language, the new unit attaches itself to what preceded and alters the initial meaning of the sequence. Nino, the outsider, is in danger.

6. Scene. "Der ball." Ext. Highway. Day.
5-6=zero. 6:57-7:43

In desperation, the protagonist climbs out of the wooden area of the park, near a highway, calling for help. An unmarked police car stops, three officers stare directly at the man with a child's ball in his hands. Nino tries to speak, but all he can do is mutter nonsensical sounds. At last, *"Der ball"* is uttered. Nino knows a little German. The sounds, rising from the road, are justified, synchronized, authentic.

7. Scene. Giovanni Garofoli: Innocent. Int. Police Station. Day.
6-7=zero. 7:44-10:28

The next mega-sequence unfolds in the police station. Through an open window, a washed-out scenery, from which the camera zooms back over flowerpots outside the open window to reveal, in a two-shot at the waist, a police commissioner behind a desk, sitting, and our Italian on the right, standing.

> Commissioner *(voice over):* "Passport."
> Protagonist: "Right away, sir."

Except for these two lines, the soundtrack is composed of incidental noise and dialogue: justified, synchronized, authentic. Interestingly the entire dialogue of this scene is in Italian, not in German. Brusati has made the police offer knowledgeable of the Italian language.

Is this the natural outcome of being an Italian-language film? All films have their own language, chiefly monolingual. Actors simulate accents, use foreign idioms, refuse to speak another language.

This "doubling" of the language spoken by the film occurred during the mother and boy scene; it happened again in the highway scene; it is being demonstrated one more time in this scene. Language is an issue in *Bread and Chocolate*.

> Commissioner *(in Italian):* "Your work permit."
> Man: "I gave it to you with my passport."

An outsider in Switzerland, who does not necessarily speak the language of the country, and who is being asked to produce his work permit. Nino is not a tourist, but a *Gastarbeiter*. Nino says: "I'm Giovanni Garofoli: innocent."

The identity of this stranger is revealed. Giovanni Garofoli: an obvious Italian surname to which our protagonist has tagged a title: Innocent — as one would call a person in authority "doctor" or a lord "sir". Here the name is Innocent Garofoli. The spectator knows Nino is innocent, and is by no means "a man of authority", but does the police know this? A little suspense adds spice to the scene.

> Commissioner: "You're Italian."
> Giovanni: "Nobody's perfect, commissioner."

Giovanni admits that he is not perfect because he is Italian. A *Gastarbeiter* is accused of one more ill. Nino insists he is innocent. Presented as an uncut monologue these introduces Nino not only to a character in the film, but to the spectator.

> I'm a waiter. I'm only temporary. The restaurant is trying me out. I did everything. Construction, carpentry... I slept two years in the workers'

barracks. I even had a bed there. What else did I need? What else does one need after a full day's work. I should have reported the crime. But I didn't, partly out of tact. After all, it's your crime. I'm only a foreigner... I don't know, keep questioning me and you'll believe I'm the killer. I'll confess, and the Turk will get the job... The restaurant only has one opening for a permanent waiter. There are two of us trying out. Me and the Turk... It means everything to me. It could change my life.

Contrary to what one might think the Turning Point ("Ten-Minute Pinch Point", the "Inciting Incident", is not the corpse of the child, although, at first, one might rashly conclude that it is, for the plot swerves into a totally different direction. But this film being neither a who-done-it, nor a thriller rapidly puts an end to the suspense. The culprit, a priest, is immediately accused of killing the child (the symbol, evocative, becomes a metaphor for the Church that kills children?).

In *Rolling Stone Magazine* (the 15 September 2011), the title "The Catholic Church's Secret Sex-Crime Files" reminds us that this topic is not a passing fad. A "father" hurts his child. What is being revealed is that, in this family-oriented Switzerland basking in the sweet melodies of classical music, acts of horror are being committed, and *Gastarbeiters* are not to be blamed for such atrocities.

The real Turning Point comes moments later, in the upcoming scene, precisely when all appears bright for our protagonist.

> Commissioner: "All right, you can go."
> Giovanni: "Go where?"
> Commissioner: "Go home. Didn't you say you were innocent?" [...]
> Giovanni: "You believed me?... I'm proud to work in a country where you believe a man just because he is a man..."

Éric Rohmer writes in *Le goût de la beauté*: "*On ne ment pas assez souvent au cinéma, sauf peut-être dans les comédies*" [We do not tell enough lies in films, except maybe in comedies] (39).

A lie is unquestionably what is being offered here. Whatever freedom granted to Giovanni, as we shall soon find out, will be rapidly taken back. Not a word is exchanged between the three policemen and a priest. No language is necessary. A third policeman taps the priest on the shoulder, for him to sit down, his face staring out of the window. Till now, the characters in the scene spoke in Italian, yet, when the second policeman calls in the killer, German is spoken. Why the linguistic switch? It is possible that we find ourselves on the Italian side of Switzerland. No matter the answer, code-switching multiplies the semantic complexity of the film. More than just a multicultural artefact, here are the first signs of pluriculturalism at work; many cultures are permitted to express themselves in their own idioms.

This linguistic multi-levelled fabric reflects the linguistic reality of the director (born in Milano), of the principal actor (born in Castro dei Volsci, near Frosinone), and of Italy as well as Switzerland. This babelism allows for culture to detach itself from the chains of linguistic nationalism. The Italic is born right at this instant. Something raises beyond the limits of territory.

On the soundtrack the serenade we have associated to this day in a Swiss park turns ironic. According to Roland Barthes, "The ironic code is, in principle, an explicit quotation of what someone said; however, irony acts as a signpost" (51). Whatever commentary might have been expressed about the music gets overturned. If the equation (music+park=happiness) seemed idyllic, it no longer is the case. One could elaborate an entire strategy of role-playing — maybe this is not a real priest; can this be a man who is pretending to be a priest? — unfortunately, nothing in the film points to that eventually. No matter how gentle this servant of God seems (a slight air of innocence smears the face of this blue-eyed rapist) – and to quote Vincent Canby in his *New York Times* review again, "Who makes no effort to hide his guilt" — he who sits in front of us intensifies the horror. Behind the glare of social *bonhommie* lurks a monstrous action. Whatever glimmer of innocence depicted at the beginning of *Pane e cioccolata* has come to a sudden halt. In less than ten minutes, the spectator knows that Switzerland is not Utopia. This film is not about the quest for heaven.

8. Scene. Giovanni, photographed. Ext. River. Day.
7-8=zero 10:27-11:08

Giovanni walks by the river, stops, tries to light a cigarette, but can't. His fingers are trembling. He throws the cigarette on the ground and walks out of the screen. He turns to the brick wall facing the river, and urinates. The camera zooming back reveals a woman in Swiss folk attire being photographed by a man.

This couple could be a photographer with a model (a picture to be used for tourism), or it might be (less probable) a man and wife. The photographer stares, open mouthed, over the woman's shoulder, at the river... of urine left behind by Giovanni as he gingerly gambols out of the right screen, unaware of his being captured on film for indecent exposure.

The soundtrack is constituted of both realistic sounds (justified, synchronized, and authentic) and the Hofstetter serenade still in the background, a reminder of the conceptualized paradise as well as the ironic setting not so paradisaical. We hear the squeaking of Nino's shoes.

Sounds are inauthentic because presented at a higher volume than normal. This simple scene includes the first narrative hook which derails the movement of events that will force Giovanni to change his lifestyle. Syd Field speaks of Pivot Points and Pinch Points (which occur later in the story, respectively at thirty and forty-five minutes). Nevertheless, a primary Pinch Point occurs most of the time around the ten-minute mark. In a chance reading I discovered this revealing passage by Ivor Montagu in Film World:

> An interesting consequent note may be made here, that, in the early days of Soviet cinema when scarcity of machinery made single projector exhibition general even for the theater, it was taken for granted that the film dramaturgists should construct story and film so that dramatic interruptions did indeed come after periods of action lasting approximately ten minutes, each reel being equivalent to an act of a play, expected to be succeeded by an interval, and given a separate dramatic title (80-81).

These intervals lasting approximately ten minutes have formed a more or less tacit rule for film narration up to present day (the maximum reel size of standard film reel measuring about 300 meters). It should come as no surprise that Syd Field's Pivotal and Pinch Points appear at ten-minute intervals. Robert McKee calls this the "Inciting Incident". At this Ten-Minute Pinch Point (Inciting Incident) something in the subject cracks. It comprises a specific element on the personal/private, interpersonal or professional layer. On the denotation level this fracture is inevitable (*Bread and Chocolate* is no exception, as is demonstrated by this scene). Whatever has to happen, narratively speaking, happens at this point: from the emigrant experience (self/society) we tip into the immigrant reality (society/ self). On the connotation level what is unravelled? Giovanni Garofoli, acquitted of the crime of rape and murder, pulls off the tag society and the police have wrongly pinned on the immigrant and is let free. Nevertheless, the stereotype sticks. An emigrant/immigrant does not have a Teflon body; like the gum in *Mon oncle* given to monsieur Hulot by the mischievous girl neighbor, misdemeanors remain glued on Giovanni.

The audience laughs, but urinating on the wall is a serious social offense (as we will learn), because it is exposing oneself in public. Giovanni might no longer be a despicable monster, yet he remains very much a lawbreaker. We laugh at the felony that is neither personal nor professional, but interpersonal.

This immigrant guest worker does not know how to behave in a civilized way. His manners make natives cringe. Here ends the second mega-sequence, and the first chapter.

Chapter 2: "Piece you back together
with a sewing machine"
11:09-22:00

9. Sequence. Giovanni at work. Int. Restaurant. Day.
8-9=edit with effect. 11:09-12:13

Normally a visual punctuation — a fade out/fade in or a dissolve — should have been placed here. We consider this "an edit with effect". Brusati often uses such a device to abruptly jump from one mega-sequence to another, from one syntagma to another. Though there is a change of time and day, the filmmaker refuses to call attention to the narrative ellipse. If the park scenes belong to Sunday, then this sequence can logically be associated to the following day, Monday.

In film, every moment is today. Much like reading a diary. Not that this film is structured according to a calendar anymore than other films are. There are events in the filmic nowness that belong to separate temporal blocks. Some action happens before; others after. The suggestion of dividing this film into days, as we have done, is a convenient way of putting order into the seemingly randomness of filmic narration.

This chapter is made up various mega-sequences associated to the restaurant where Nino works. Brusati concentrates on Nino's professional life now. He is a waiter, and these are some of the daily chores of Nino the waiter.

On the soundtrack, natural sounds of a restaurant, even the pre-recorded canned jazz music, is justified, authentic, and synchronized (most probably, the music comes a radio.) A forward travelling shot on Giovanni who walks across the screen, from right to left, and is joined by a second waiter: a short Semitic-looking man who could very well be the Turk who threatens to take Giovanni's job away. Giovanni and the Turk stand in front of a mirror. This doubling of characters leads us to the thematic of this film. One is oneself, but also someone else. The two men stare straight into one another's beastly eyes; this restaurant hires immigrants who must vie for their survival.

Though he speaks in German with clients, Giovanni is not frightened to interject foreign language phrases (Italian and French). As he is about to slice salmon on a serving platter, an unhappy head-waiter glides behind him and complains about the busboy, Gianni.

The camera dollies in on the two characters speaking in Italian. We cannot help but wonder why is Italian the means of communication. Are these characters actually speaking Italian to one another or are they speaking in German, and this German is presented to the spectator as Italian? Indeed, this film relies heavily on the duality of character and situation.

Made up of scenettes, this sequence begins in the dining room and ends into the exit corridor. Luciano Tovoli's camera floats along effortlessly; Nino Manfredi's choreography is impressively authoritative; Mario Morra's editing masterfully invisible. Moving from one room to another without the least of technical worries, waiters, mostly Italian, perform with a sense of dry humor.

Giovanni rushes through the kitchen doors, screaming: "Where's the son of a bitch?" A fellow waiter jokingly retorts: "Which one? There are so many here!"

Giovanni responds: "I'll kill him. That'll make one less!"

The repartee abounds, the comic gestures are graceful, subtle; we have indisputably entered the realm of comedy.

10. Scene. Giovanni and Gianni. Int. Dressing room. Day.
9-10=zero. 12:14-12:58

Gianni, a young man, runs up a long wide corridor, stops at a wall, hangs his clothes on a hook. Sounds are justified, authentic and synchronized with the visual track; a single word *("Delinquente!")* is heard in voice-over.

Gianni with a black-eye and a band-aid on his right eyebrow turns around. Giovanni screams, *"Disgraziato!"* (Wretched one!).

Gianni expresses himself in a Northern Italian accent. Here are two Italians from opposite ends of the peninsula — Gianni from the North; Giovanni from the South: foreigners in a foreign land. The confrontation is ironic, the southern Giovanni has the upper-hand, a fact that contradicts the stereotypes of what in reality is known about the North-South conflict. Italians are disliked by others, nor are Italians liked by Italians. Ethnic abuse is two-way: from outside and from within, from the stranger and from the brother (the 'I could have been a contender' syndrome which will be explored in detail in *Raging Bull*).

Gianni: "I was in the hospital... They were insulting Italians. I got mad and grabbed one of them..."
Giovanni: "...and he threw you in the hospital... you're playing the patriot..."
Gianni: "I had three stitches."
Giovanni: "Three stitches in three hours? An hour a stitch?... If the Turk

gets the job, I'll send you to the hospital myself. They'll have to piece you back together with a sewing machine."

Patriotism can't assuage the emigrant's need to work. It is more important than identity, more vital than comradeship, more elemental than social security. Giovanni will hurt anyone who meddles with his job. Gianni's role in this chapter seems to be metaphorical; that is, Gianni, whose name recalls Giovanni's, is a mirror reflection of Giovanni. With the excuse of depicting a day at work, what in fact occurs here is the demonstration of the need for female companionship for the immigrant. Gianni is with a Swiss woman, as Giovanni will be with Elena, his Greek neighbor.

With the introduction of the family unit, the writers prolong the father image through various embodiments: Giovanni and the German-speaking Swiss boy playing soccer; Giovanni with the dead girl; Giovanni with his own children left behind in Italy; and Elena's boy Giovanni will later meet in the closet. Giovanni/Nino is a father, a father-figure for others, and a family man.

11. Scene. Giovanni and the Turk. Int. Restaurant. Day.
10-11=edit with effect. 12:59-13:38

The edit cut is abrupt; the sounds are justified, synchronized, authentic. Follow snippets of a workday. Episode after episode, we glimpse into Giovanni's professional life, at how he earns his living. Walking out of the kitchen with a tray, Giovanni is interrupted by the arrival of the Turk carrying a large cushion of tablecloths. Giovanni has no choice but to step aside. Instead of guiding the fellow waiter to the kitchen, Giovanni opens the backdoor that leads to the street. The doors shut. Giovanni delights in the loud screech of a car breaks. This scene is a reference to Chaplin's restaurant swinging-doors scene in *Modern Times* (1936). A diegetically displaced insert: The Turk in the middle of the street, the large padded covering over his face, in front of a red car. Giovanni's trick gives him one up on the Turk. Nino's meanness encourages laughter; the spectator laughs at danger.

12: Scene. Giovanni and the Orange. Int. Restaurant. Day.
11-12=zero. 13:39-15:22

On the soundtrack, muzak, and justified, synchronized, authentic noises. The camera dollies back on a waiter peeling an orange with fork and knife with extreme dexterity, a feat which Nino simply cannot perform. Unable to contain the orange rolling off the plate and onto the floor, Nino asks the white-haired client in Italian if he would not prefer strawberries, but the cigar-smoking client points to the orange. The camera follows Nino behind curtains where, in a medium shot, sinking his teeth deep into the orange, he tears the peel apart. All of this is looked on by the cashier (placed as an insert) who, horrified, stares at Giovanni bringing back the orange on a carefully cut peel that he took from another plate. Giovanni places the plate with the orange in front of the costumer, this time speaking in French: *"Voilà, monsieur."* The client thanks him in German. The comic moment concludes with the restaurant owner, Mr. Boegli, pointing to the orange stains on Giovanni's shirt. The gag comes full circle, proving once again that Nino simply is a collection of misdemeanors.

13. Scene. Giovanni and the toilet chain. Int. Restroom. Day.
12-13=zero. 15.23-15-38

On a soundscape that is synchronized, justified, authentic, Nino is in the rest-room wiping the stains off his shirt with a paper cloth that he discards into the toilet bowl which becomes unanticipatedly clogged. In vain Nino pulls on the chain of the hanging toilet, just like the one used in the toilet scene in Francis Ford Coppola's *The Godfather* (1972).

Films speak to one another; films introduce an on-going dialogue between one films or artworks, a symbolic conversation that enriches the texture of the newer work. Intertextual quotation invests a work with ludic pleasure. In both films the rest room is the setting for the perfect crime. In *Bread and Chocolate*, crime elements are rare, yet they are there nonetheless. A film setting acts very much like a character: its meaningfulness grows on you slowly, subtly, imposingly. The washroom is where one discards waste, where one washes oneself, where one makes him/herself handsome, it is not usually a place where one hides a fish *(Bread)*, a gun *(The Godfather)*. We laugh at what is unexpected, we laugh at the ironic quality of the filmic allusion.

The entire chapter takes on the form of an episodic syntagma. Even at the higher plane, Metz's large syntagmatic category of the image track seems to work. Film develops from the smallest to the largest of its elements is a systematic and logical manner. The global reflects the detail, and the detail contains the global entity.

14. Scene. Burning Plates. Int. Restaurant. Day.
13-14=zero. 15.39-15:54

As Nino repairs the toilet, we are privy to the Turk unhappily picking up two burning-hot plates. In terrible pain, but refusing to break down, the Turk can only allow himself a few tears to swell in his eyes. Indifferent to the pain of the waiter, the Head waiter interjects (unaware of the irony, or worse, meaningly): "Warn the gentlemen that the plates are scorching... Serve them elegantly, please, with style." Style is the last thing this hurting waiter has on his mind. The spectator laughs at his pain.

15. Scene. Giovanni and Michele. Int. Rest room. Day.
14-15=zero. 15.55-16:57

The intertextual filmic allusion to *The Godfather* enables Brusati to symbolically push this comedy up a notch. Giovanni's sinks his hand in the toilet hanging tank, and instead of a gun, he pulls out a fish. The spectator laughs at the crime, here, of another nature. Michele, another waiter, appears. (Brusati baptizes the waiter in honor of Michael Corleone?)

Giovanni says: "This is the second time I have found a fish hidden there." Michele, either Spanish or Portuguese, sighs, *"Ladrones"* (Thieves). For the first time Giovanni is called by his nickname, Nino, who, fish in hand, calls out to Michele who turns around, sausage hanging from his pants. What can an empathetic Nino say when he realizes that the culprit is Michele. "Nothing. Be careful."

The first illusion to crime was sexual: the girl's corpse. Here it is finance, or lack of, that instigates crime. Michele in a lift has a sausage sticking out of his apron: is this not a sexual visual pun linking the ladrones (criminals) to sexuality? Certainly, though sexuality is less important than our realization that the paycheck a waiter brings home from work does not suffice. This immigrant must steal in order to make ends meet. Through these bitter-sweet episodes, Brusati displays the tough quotidian realities of the immigrant worker. Name-calling (Gianni), peer competition (Giovanni and the Turk), violence and discourtesy (Head waiter and the Turk), robbery (Michele), sexuality (Nino first, Michele now): this world of small-time crooks is a few degrees from organized crime.

16. Sequence shot. Int. Restaurant. Later. 15-16=zero.
16:58-17:06

A high-angle shot of the empty restaurant, waiters clean up for the next service. In Europe many restaurants shut down between 3 and 6 pm, clean-up time before the evening service. At the bottom, barely visible, Giovanni in shirtsleeves opens the door and walks out for a cigarette.

17. Scene. The immigrant at rest. Ext. Restaurant patio. Day.
16-17=zero. 16:58-18:26

Relaxing music in the air, a man sings a light melody, unjustified, non-synchronized, inauthentic. The camera pans. Gianni, band-aid on his eyebrow, runs into the frame with *La Gazzetta dello Sport* which he hands over to Nino. "Signor Nino"?

Gianni: "Signor Nino, why do foreigners dislike us Italians so much?"

Giovanni: "Who says? Go see how they treat Southern Italians in Milan. I'd have gotten a life sentence there. There are too many of us here. Two million foreigners in a country of five million. An invasion!"

During the work pause the three waiters (Nino, Gianni and the Turk) contemplate a boat of tourists blowing its horn. Immigration begins as emigration, a travelling away of sorts, a departure, a running away from another reality. Immigration is not tourism. Tourists brings in money to the host country, and immigrants are hired to serve these tourists. Behind the smiles of tourists we find working immigrants. What the emigrant encounters when he becomes an immigrant is a tough world of cruel competition, where racism plays an integral part in this philosophy of, not so much success as much as survival. Man is the wolf of man, Horace words never sounded truer.

18. Scene. The Rich Industrialist. Int. Restaurant. Evening.
17-18=zero. 18:27-22:00

The soundtrack, justified, authentic, is synchronized with the visual track. From a close up of a violinist, the camera dollies back and in so doing fixes the art-deco design of the ceiling of the restaurant. A food tray brings up Jacques Tati's restaurant scene in *Playtime* (1967). There, a fish was prepared a number of times without ever getting served to its rightful patrons. Here, Giovanni might speak in French and Italian and the clients in English and Italian but he is unable to work properly.

After describing what meat is on the platter, Nino realizes the platter is gone. The Turk is pulling the food tray away. The scene turns into sit-com. Nino, not amused, smacks his lips to the Turk, as if calling a dog. The Turk motions vulgarly to Nino by tapping the pit of his arm with his hand.

The gag does not end at this point. In the Turk's hand is a fork. At the tip of the fork is a pig's tongue. The tongue is now thrust away across the room and finally drops into customer's soup. Splash. If the woman evokes Fellini's gruesome characters, this episode specially recalls Blake Edwards' *The Party* (1968). Blake Edwards' stunt itself was inspired by a stunt copied from Jacques Tati's *Playtime*.

In *The Party*, a drunken waiter (played by Steven Franken) first serves salad using his hand instead of cutlery and then accidentally tosses Hrundi V. Bakshi's (played by Peter Sellers) roast Cornish hen onto a woman's tiara. The gag is complete, and out comes laughter. The same happens with this scene. But the gag does not end there. Three elderly clients sitting at the table look to the woman covered with soup in amazement. The gag continues. All turn their eyes up to the ceiling: What is this thing that has dropped from heaven? Is it a tile from the ceiling? A similar situation occurs in Chaplin's *Modern Times*. The tramp in the prison cafeteria sits distracted by fellow inmates at a long table.

Suddenly he finds food in his plate. Where did this meal come from? Where else, but from the sky. Like in *Modern Times,* the victim of the prank looks up to heaven (the ceiling) for an answer. Cinema is very much a conversation between filmmakers: Chaplin, Tati, Edwards, Brusati. A laughter of complicity rises from those who recognize these cinematographic secrets.

Henri Bergson describes the function of laughter as being intimidation by humiliating: "a spark of spitefulness or, at all events, of mischief" (188). Unwillingly the immigrants poke a joke against those who mistreat them. The Turk rushes to clean up the mess on the woman. Nino sneers disapprovingly. The scene comes to an end.

The Head waiter announced the arrival of a man of some importance (Johnny Dorelli) accompanied by a female companion and a couple. Nino leads the guests to a table.

"To what do we owe the honor?" asks Jacques the Head waiter.

"Vacation? Business?"

"Taxes, my friend, taxes," replies sarcastically the industrialist.

"The minute I step foot in Italy, it'll cost me three million."

Illegality once again appears. Immigrants are not to be trusted.

Distracted by the information revealed, Nino forgets to push back the chair he had pulled for Dorelli's partner who immediately collapses to the floor. The upset woman blasphemes in English. This is slapstick, situational comedy. The props: a rich man, his vain companion, a waiter, and a chair. Vanity is about to sit down, but the distracted servant gets distracted. The industrialist looks down at his partner: "Is this a picnic on the grass?"

A wink is made to the world of culture: one to painting history, Edouard Manet's *Déjeuner sur l'herbe* (presented at the Salon des refusés of 1863); the second to film history, Jean Renoir's *Le déjeuner sur l'herbe* (1959). A fine instance of Bergson's dictum: "We look for vanity if only to laugh at it" (173), but also another instance of the "freemasonry' of jokes (64).

Titian's *Pastoral Concert* might well have been Manet's excuse for this jump into modernity, yet what we have in Brusati's film is cruder, less sophisticated. Something about the rich man strikes us as being rude. This is the twenty-minutes mark and something is going to happen to the plot. The owner, Mr. Boegli, appears and inquires if all is alright. The rich Italian interjects by claiming that he is in good hands. Dorelli looks at Nino and says, "We Italians have to help each other. We're both exiles, Garofoli."

The scene ends with the Italian sitting on a chair warning Nino not to pull it away from under him. Not only must immigrants help one another; so must Italians in exile, especially, help one another. At least, on the surface, such is the message.

Exiles they might be, but these two men are not cut from the same fabric. In fact, Giovanni's comment *"tale quale"* ("exactly alike, sir!") sounds more ironic than honest in the context. The meaning of this simple phrase is double: "We are alike, and yet we are not alike": Dorelli is a tax exile; Nino, self-exiled. One is rich; the other poor. When Dorelli speaks of being alike, we ask ourselves in what sense. A question is interjected.

The deracinated man loses a portion of his identity. Does the Italian create a new deterritorialized identity from this loss of identity? Does the Italian who has left Italy create a new sort of identity abroad regardless of his financial situation? The second chapter comes to an end with the introduction of the Sender (the industrialist). As we have remarked, Franco Brusati never ends a scene simply; he always finds a way to link one action to another about to start. With a simple cut, we are led to another dimension of the film.

Chapter 3: Coming Home
22:01-29:17

19. Sequence. Walking home. Ext. Road. Night.
18-19=zero. 22:01-23:37

The sounds, synchronized, authentic and justified, except for the church bell, over Giovanni walking home who notices Gianni smoking a cigarette, waiting.

Giovanni: "What are you doing here? Come, I'll offer you a coffee. Are you upset with me? If I was a little rough on you, don't be hurt. I could be your father. I could be your grandfather. So what if someone doesn't like Italians. Be patient. We often can't stand each other, so imagine how foreigners feel. Feel lonely? Need company? I'm right here. We can work together days, and look for girls at night."

Giovanni notices Gianni looking at a woman standing at the top of the stairs: "If you've got a girl, why have coffee with me? Imbecile. Go, go…"

Giovanni yells to the woman: "Don't make him defend Italy's good name, Miss, or he'll end up in a hospital every day… Some patriot. He talks politics, meaning he's screwing around."

The binary couple German/Italian is not as clear cut as imagined. An interest between cultural communities exists, at least men and women of different cultures can live side by side, and even intermarry. Giovanni is known by the diminutive Nino by acquaintances. Nino is also Manfredi's real name. Saturnino Manfredi was born on 22 March 1921, in Castro dei Volsci, in the province of Frosinone, in Latium, and passed away on 4 June 2004. This switch from fiction to reality immediately pulls in the spectator deeper into the story. That fourth wall keeping reality and fiction divided comes down with this nickname. Suddenly, the actor and the spectator are on familiar ground. As if the spectator, turned voyeur, were permitted to enter the "real" world of Manfredi's real life.

     20. Scene. Home. Int. Apartment Night.
       19-20=zero. 23:38-28:14

An enlarged scene with inserts presents Nino's personal and interpersonal world: inside, there is his wife; outside, there is a female neighbor from Greece. Inside, Nino talks off screen to Maria on a picture of a woman and child; outside, he converses with a stranger. Finally, Nino is talking to himself, an immigrant in lonely reality. "Every six months at least, a man needs his wife." Such is the sex life of the immigrant. "It's different for a woman. A woman is calmer. More sentimental. She doesn't feel certain needs so strongly. Or does she?'

  Are the wife's needs different from the husband's needs? The spectator smiles, but quickly piano music rises off screen — the only sound that is not justified, authentic or synchronized. Beside a window, from where the music emerges, Nino listens to Mozart's *Sonata in Do*, K545, performed by Daniele Patucchi. This music we know is performed by the neighbor's son. The person addressed here both sound-wise and visually is the father image. The father is addressed. The entire scene comes under the sign of Fatherhood.

  A woman's voice interjects: "When I turn off the light at night, I feel alone, too." Letters, as physical as human beings. Stop the film and capture a photogram: the room, dimly lit, small, its walls are covered with photographs of family members. A sense of despair in this landscape intimate, sad, dark.

  A woman voice resounds, in voice over: "Will you really bring us to Switzerland?" A male's voice (the brother-in-law whose hands were blown off by a bomb) interrupts the woman: "He's been there three years. Is he building his own train? A man who's away that long forgets his family." Three years of solitude, three years of exile. Life is difficult: in Italy there are bombs; abroad, there is poverty and insecurity, and loneliness. Nino is a lonely husband separated from his family.

Nino pulls down his trousers, screams to his wife *in absentia*: "Look." What are we to look at? His genitalia? Follows Nino Manfredi's signature stint: he turns around, with pants pulled down to his knees, one hand searching inside, under the back pocket. A ripping sound tears the monologue and out Nino pulls a wallet. "That's just one day's tips." Here are Nino's earnings, more money than one would make in Italy in forty years. Poverty is the reason why Nino has left his country. Unlike the Italian industrialist who escapes Italy's tax police, Nino is escaping unemployment in his homeland. Yet both the rich and the poor suffer. "I want my daughter to marry here, and my son to grow up here."

Nino is not going back to Italy. Unlike Dante in *Paradiso* (*"Tu proverai sì come sa di sale/ lo pane altrui, e come è duro calle / lo scendere e 'l salir per l'altrui scale..."* XVII, 58-60), for Nino emigration is a blessing, even though there are chances children forget their fathers.

Nino rushes to the window and starts a conversation with his neighbor, Elena (Anna Karina), a Greek woman. Voyeurism: he has been gazing at this neighbor for some time; how else would he be able to associate piano music to that particular neighbor? These two have talked to one another before. We are led to believe that she is the piano player. For Nino, she, the piano player, would be a woman he would love to know better. Nino looks, the Greek woman accepts the gaze. More than passive voyeurism, there is a complicity at work. Beginning with voyeurism the relationship has developed into scopophilia, whereby the one watched accepts being looked at. There is no physical contact between these adults, just the exchange of dreams.

Nino with his pants down, looking at his neighbor: is Nino truly a voyeur? His desire more than a symbol is a need to touch her. The woman is aware of this man's desires. Yet she doesn't give in, nor does she shut him out. She obliges, explains how Greeks too had to leave their country... but for political reasons. "True, down there, you were worse off than us."

"Down with the Colonels," Nino shouts. Switzerland is a peaceful haven for exiles of all kinds: rich, poor, political... Nino offers the woman an invitation, which she refuses. The spectator feels Nino's distress call for companionship. The conversation naturally ends, the windows shut... and the apartment door opens.

21. Scene. Silent sharing. Int. Apartment Night.
20-21=zero. 28:15-29:17

The Turk walks in. In the darkness Nino must move out of the way, less the Turk bump into him. Wordlessly the competing waiters walk to their separate beds. The sounds are justified, authentic, synchronized. The Turk cannot be seen, but is heard. He is reduced to a shadow, to a snore. Nino counts one, two, three, and the Turk begins to sleep. Nino's final gesture reveals disappointment; he would even consider communicating with his worse enemy. Irony is deadly. A scriptwriter does not inattentively introduce characters. The Turk, an opponent, and the Greek pianist, an adjuvant, must be kept in sight. These secondary characters will indubitably alter Nino's fate. Especially in the case of the industrialist. Of the three components that make up character's profile (private, inter-personal, professional), it is at the professional level that Nino most needs help. He needs to find a stable job. Like the Turk. Elena the Greek is a political refugee. The rich Italian is a finance escapee. There are many reasons to emigrate.

Chapter 4: Becoming Illegal
29:18-33:56

22. Scene. "Come here." Int. Restaurant. Day.
21-22=edit with effect. 29:18-29.33

This is where Syd Field claims a Turning Point will occur. What happened in Scene 8 at the Ten-Minute Pinch Point (Inciting incident) comes to haunt the Subject. The combination of that event (urinating in public) and this event will bring about a major narrative shift. If the film seemed to move up one particular road, it is here that the story takes a different path. What appears at the end of the first path and at the beginning of the new path is advent of the first Object of desire, that is, a false object of desire. This object is not reducible to a moral value or judgement. This narrative moment is neither good nor bad; whatever it is it is; its existence makes its necessity unsurmountable. If we have been given signs of goodness, this is where total empathy breaks open; if meanness has been growing, it is at this point that evil culminates. This circumstance makes the denouement believable. Transformation begins at this point. Without this blossoming of what had been planted from the start, there can be no reversal of fate. An evil man is at his worse at this point. From here on he ascends to goodness. A good man is at his best here, but descends to evil by the end of the plot. What goes up comes down; what comes down goes up.

Nino's destiny etched as it is will drive him to a dead-end. Mr. Boeglio, smoking a cigar, walks to the center of the screen. The camera, in low angel, points upward. "Nino' is all he says, that is all he has to say. Mr. Boeglio is the boss.

Cut to the high angle shot of Nino, in shirt sleeves, setting the table in the empty restaurant. This is pre-serving time. It must be morning, or the afternoon break, before the first clients come in. The carpet is red, and the tablecloth white. Nino is right off center, Gianni has his back turned to the camera. Nino slips on his dark jacket; Gianni smiles, reassuring him that they have chosen him over the Turk. "Let's hope so."

>   23. Scene. Guilty. Int. Restaurant's office. Day.
>   22-23=zero. 29:34-31:43

Scene 23 follows logically scene 22. They could almost be considered the same scene, but this is not the case. The three parameters that constitute a scene have been altered: change of setting, change of action, time change. The soundtrack, realistic, is justified, authentic, synchronized. Nino, pulling the jacket collar in place, smiles as he steps into Mr. Boegli's office. But the smile soon drops to a frown when he notices the police Commissioner.

> Commissioner: "How are you, Garofoli?"
> Nino: "Still innocent, Commissioner."
> Commissioner: "...What did you do Sunday? ...after our talk."
> [Mr. Boegli, taciturn, smokes in the background, looking out of a window.]
> Commissioner: "You committed obscene acts in public."
> Nino: "It's been months since I thought about obscene acts, even in private."
> Commissioner: "Didn't you pee?"
> Nino: "Why, is it forbidden?"
> Commissioner: "In public, yes."
> Nino: "What pig would do it in public?"
> [The Commissioner hands Nino a photograph in which he recognizes himself.]
> Nino: "Just a couple of drops... you wouldn't kick me out because of this?"

The punch lines are quick to pull laughter from the spectator. Innocent, obscene acts in private, a few drops, the "pig": all these details lead to incrimination. Nino's identity acquires a new trait. His job is at stake. He is not innocent at all. The final decision belongs to Mr. Boegli, silent.

We've reached the Turning Point in the *Pane e cioccolata*. Once kicked out of Switzerland, Nico is filliped down to hell; gone is paradise. From a legal worker he becomes a Worker withOut Papers, a WOP. An illegal immigrant. Whatever identity Nino had up till now collapses. A negative note is tagged on him. Nino becomes what he never dreamt of ever becoming. A *persona non grata.* So begins another film. Up till this point *Pane e cioccolata* was about an immigrant trying to integrate into the culture of the host country. From this moment on, *Pane* tells the story of how an unworthy person finds ways to stay in a country that does not want him.

24. Sequence shot. Suitcase. Ext. Train station. Evening.
23-24=zero. 31:44-31:57

Men and women in bright red and blue ski, talk loudly, laughing loudly, walking toward the camera. Nino, with hat and trench coat, plows his way away from the camera, suitcase in hand, head bent low his back to the spectator, ostracized. Some characters move toward us; others away from us. The denotation here clearly expressing cut and dry connotations of exclusion. Emigration is not for any emigrant.

25. Sequence. Train. Int. Train station. Evening.
24-25=zero. 31:58-33:56

Except for the Italian ("Torna a Surriento") music in the background, the sounds at the station are justified, authentic and synchronized. "They all ice here. No heart," a fat man screams and begins to sing "Torna a Surriento." An insert of the Turk greeting his family. Nino throws his suitcase out the window, and storms out of the train.

A porter, however, lifts the suitcase back into the train. In vain Nino tries to retrieve his suitcase, but the train sails off leaving him straddling behind. The successful Turk and his family glide pass Nino who, from one second to the other, without working papers, turn into an illegal alien, an enemy alien. Nino no longer is an innocent man.

Chapter 5: Elena
38:30-42:37

26. Scene. Elena. Int. Apartment. Evening.
25-26=edit with effect. 33:57-38:30

Elena (Anna Karina) looks at herself in a mirror, pulling her hair back, adjusting an earring. The double image: this splitting into two identities foreshadows her future life. She is the one she is, but she is also someone else. The one she was and the one she will become. The soundtrack is silent, until the doorbell rings. Elena opens the door of her apartment: "What are you doing here? You didn't leave?" Nino, sitting outside her door, on a windowsill, replies: "I can't go back to Italy like this. I'd shoot myself first."

Suitcase in hand, he begs her to let him stay the night. She refuses, telling him that she doesn't live alone, and before she can divulge any information, the doorbell rings again. "It's an immigration policeman." This is the world of the clandestine. "Are there bombs in here?" asks Nino in the middle-shot.

A comparison between two exiles is made. In both cases, the distinction is social. Immigration, political or financial, evidently does not erase class differences. There is light in this house; Elena, the anarchist, and Dorelli, the businessman, have more power than the uneducated; Nino is a subaltern from Southern Italy. Nino runs to hide in a closet; but he is not alone. Haunting blue eyes glow in the obscurity, the gazer's gaze freezes Nino, breaking him like salt. Nino has walked through the "mirror" and stepped on the other side of reality. This crossing over, crossing through, this trans- brings him closer to his ideal. This crossing over the "street" divides his world and Elena's world. It is a crossing over to the symbolic. By allowing Nino to walk into her apartment, Elena is permitting the voyeur to perform, allowing the subject-voyeur to move in closer; he can rub himself against the object of his gaze. But first an obstacle is introduced. Another person. Whose haunting gaze in the dark is the look of power. A struggle ensues; he who wins will be permitted to move on. When finally Elena and her date step out of the house, the closet's door opens, and out comes... not Nino, but a child. The person with the eyes. Grigory does not have his residency documents and both mother and son risk extradition if the boy is caught. Parenthood reappears, the sort of which we had glimpse of earlier on: the images of happy families in the park, the boy with the soccer ball, Gianni, the Turk's family, Nino's own son, and now here is Grigory. The need to leave one's country emerges not from personal, egoistical reasons, but from family reasons. One leaves everything behind for a better future. Professional life reigns over the private and the interpersonal aspects of being.

According to Gianfausto Rosoli, there were about 427,000 Italians living in Switzerland between 1970 and 1986 (5). If Linda Magnusson is right in saying that, at the beginning of the twentieth century, Italian peasants were paying as much as 75% of their salary for food, then reasons to leave one's country become no longer a question of vain aspirations but a necessity (1). One emigrates because one has no choice but to emigrate. Elena says, "My son is called Grigory." Nino looks at Elena and says, "I'm Nino."

She says, "I'm Elena." The family circle is complete: surrogate father, mother and child. This trio should work, but won't. Elena needs to move up if she wishes the best for her son. It is impossible for her to do it on her own, at least in a foreign country. She leaves with the Swiss immigration officer, leaving Nino with her son Grigory.

27. Scene. Grigory. Int. Apartment. Evening.
26-27=zero. 8:31-42:37

Elena's departure brings the previous syntagma to an end. Without a fade out, without a dissolve, the film moves on, as Brusati has accustomed us since the beginning. Grigory is the pianist, not Elena. The soundtrack is realistic: justified, authentic, synchronized. Grigory's card game of solitary is indicative of a new reality; as the boy with the red and white ball, Elena's son needs no one to play with. We will encounter a similar situation in *Queen of Hearts, The Mediterranean Forever,* and *Raging Bull;* children learn to live on their own when their fathers are absent. Independent boys without fathers, there are three fatherless boys in *Bread and Chocolate:* Nino's son, Giacomino; the boy in the park; and now Grigory. Brusati does not draw a pretty picture of fathers; his attack is directed not only against immigrants but persons of all nationalities. In his interview with Jean A. Gili, he draws a negative picture of men: "There is at the beginning of *Bread and Chocolate,* a respectable person. It is a Swiss woman who plays music and hides her skeletons. These skeletons are workers and the dead girl under the trees" (187).

Chapter 6: Encounter with the Rich
42:38-51:59

28. Scene. Morning music. Ext. Yard. Morning.
27-28=zero. 42:38-46:42

In his interview with Gili, Brusati declares that his film is non-realist 5 yet the soundtrack is realistic (justified, authentic, synchronized, except for unjustified foghorn heard midway into the scene). There is no dissolve, no fade-out, no fade-in. Mozart's music ends the previous scene, and now there is a joyful "Buon giorno a te" (Jaja Fiastri and Ugo Calise) that strikes us in all its morning glory. The three musicians step out of the right corner of the screen and stare into the camera. They sing first for us the audience, and then, as the camera pulls back, for the Italian industrialist who becomes the clear receiver of this wake-up song. The visual equivocalness of receiver fashions a semantic equation whereby spectator and character merge. For a moment, we are the rich industrialist who will help Nino in his plight against the Swiss authorities. (Nino on his way to the train station in Scene 25 had his back to the spectator, as if in defiance, as though he wanted to put an end even to the narrative.)

"Well, pisser. Didn't the Swiss throw you out?" The industrialist in his mansion, musicians wake him up, a butler lights his cigarette, he calls a guest *piscione* ("pisser").

"You complain about this country, until it's time to leave... Blame Italy that forces us to emigrate." This supercilious rich man has put his finger on the hurt: it is the country we are born in that kicks us out that is to blame, and not the country that receives us and that we mistake for paradise. Brusati interposes an insert of a naked woman. (It's not the first time we compare Switzerland to a woman.)

>Nino (pointing to the woman): "She's your wife?"
>Industrialist: "She's a whore..."
>Nino (to the woman): "Oh, I didn't notice."
>Woman: "Thank you."

The semantic equation (country=woman) pushed to its limit entitles the spectator to equate this country to a whore. Discourtesy toward others spells misanthropy. "You make money with money, not with work," sneers the rich man who invites Nino to hand over his wallet. Nino pulls down his trousers, repeating for the naked lady, the butler and the industrialist his Chaplinesque dance-gag we were privy to in Scene 21. He hands his money over to the thief of a businessman. "What am I drinking: coffee or tea?" Nino shouts a guess which wins him double the money he has in his possession. This short moment of gambling makes up what Syd Field calls the first Pinch Point. The rich man, who takes Nino's money, owes Nino a debt which at the midpoint will never be paid back. The industrialist disrespectfully orders in Italian his girlfriend to leave; the young woman who answers "yes" in English. In this film, all characters are polyglots and understand Italian.

>29. Scene. The family. Ext. Airport. Day.
>28-29=zero. 46:43-49:34

The rich man warns Nino that she should never purchase a plane. (As if Nino could afford a plane!) "Having a father like you has its advantages," Nino whispers. To which the industrialist snaps: "You're lucky you don't have money."

"Some luck," concludes Nino. The rich man lays his hand on Nino's shoulders, an obvious call for comradely solace: "Here they come." Nino looks at the hand on his shoulder. But there is no woman who steps out of the plane. Only his stiff, genteel, English-speaking boys who walk right by their father without offering the least sign of gratitude. They rush into a Rolls

Royce belonging to a friend of theirs. "They look just like foreigners," says Nino. Be they poor or wealthy, children and parents live in separate worlds in Brusati's world.

30. Scene. Nino gets a job. Ext. Countryside. Day.
29-30=zero. 49:35-51:59

On the soundtrack school-boy's English voices are signing: unjustified, inauthentic, non-synchronized. The voices of the lost children of families broken by emigration. Another gag: the two men share pictures of their wives, the industrialist calling his wife "a piece of shit". In the man's hand a photograph of Nino's wife. Is this rich man is talking about Nino's wife? A moment of hesitation. He isn't.

The gag continues. The industrialist, furious, tears up the photograph. This time it is the picture of Nino's wife. Follow images of Nino, not amused, picking up the scattered pieces of the torn photograph on the grass. Like comic mime, talking to himself, Nino is turning in circles. He learns that this heartless businessman has fired 10,000 workers. The news will come to haunt both men in the next chapter. From a low angle shot (position of inferiority) the rich Italian offers Nino to be his butler ("someone I can trust") who in high angle shot (position of superiority) accepts. Momentarily, Nino reacquires his legal immigrant status. But this is not the midpoint just yet. That moment comes later, as we shall see. This is a narrative lie that keeps the viewer hanging on to the story.

Chapter 7: The New Family
52:00- 59:16

31. Scene. The party. Int. Elena's apartment. Night.
30-31=zero. 52:00-53:27

The absence of visual punctuation between major narrative blocks quickens the pace of the narration. Syntagma after syntagma, mega-sequence after mega-sequence, chapter after chapter, the story drives forward like a train (as François Truffaut calls film in *Day for Night*). Elena carries a grocery bag in her arms, turns on the light switch but the light does not come on. Terrorized, she yells her son's name. There is no answer. Before apprehension sets in sparklers light up in the dark, Nino with Elena's son lights up a candle to celebrate his new job, the new identity of working man with a new family.

32. Scene. Watching TV. Int. Elena's apartment. Night, later.
31-32=zero. 53:27-54:11

No dialogue scene is introduced; a camera pans quickly from a red candle on the set post-dinner table to the television. Rudolf Arnheim: "Television is a relative of motorcar and airplane: it is a means of cultural transportation" (194). What is the "cultural transportation" in this? This world is not reality. If voyeurism is what brought Nino to Elena, it has been supplanted by television, another form of voyeurism: voyeurism of the real turned to voyeurism of the fake. On the soundtrack a joyful jiggle emerges, the music from the TV cartoon program. Grigory sleeps in Nino's arms, Elena smokes a cigarette; both laugh at Yogi Bear in his helicopter. A photo perfect of familyhood: the father, the mother, the child, the TV set? In *The Death of the Family*, David Cooper praised this new sort of family, the "romantic family" (9), one which was founded on a fantasy. Marshall McLuhan explains what this new family might seem:

> The family circle has widened. The world pool of information fathered by electric media... far surpasses any possible influence mom and dad now bring to bear. Character no longer is shaped by only two earnest, fumbling experts (*Medium*, 14).

For Grigory, Nino might not be his biological father but he could become his surrogate father, the adoptive father who can entertain the child on his way out of a fatherless world. Nino throws a paper airplane, which the camera follows before a cut takes us to the next scene. Such a simple gesture (the making of a paper airplane) conveys much about this newly acquired cultural mode of transportation; this symbolic plane will be used later to say "Addio" to Nino.

Chapter Seven has the form of the episodic sequence. It brings together short scenes that are never truly developed into major actions. These visual qualifiers (adjectives and adverbs) modify the main plot action: a man and a woman meet at last. As Cooper writers, "The family is not only an abstraction, that is a false existence, an essence, but also exists as a challenge to go beyond all the conditioning one has undergone in it" (15).

33. Scene. Bedtime. Int. Elena's apartment. Night, later.
32-33=zero. 54:12-55.56

The music cuts off with an edit. Elena's hand pulls bedcovers over her son's body. The soundtrack is realistic: justified, authentic, synchronized. "He's intelligent. I taught him all the bad words my son says..." Nino has plainly taken over the role of father, calling Grigory "Mozart". Grigory mutters as a reply a swear word in Italian. In the background jazz fades in. The mood gradually takes on an erotic tone. Nino would like to divulge a secret to Elena who quiets him. "Tomorrow's a big day for you."

34. Alternating syntagma. Nino and Elena. Int. The rooms. Night. 33-34=edit with effect. 55.56-56:47

With this suite of sequence shots, constructed as an alternating syntagma, Brusati alternates from one character to another with one goal in mind: to unite Nino and Elena. Nino removing his watch reveals via a zoom the picture of his family, the photograph that had been torn by the Italian industrialist earlier during the day. We are in the same apartment, moving along in chronological order. Elena sits on her bed, fixing her reddish image in the circular mirror.

Nino stares at himself covered with shampoo suds in an oval mirror. Why would Brusati keep the sound of applause in a radio show on this scene instead of fading it out? Are we, the spectators (meta-linguistically speaking) applauding Nino's performance? Perhaps.

35. Scene. Nino. Int. Washroom. Later.
34-35=zero. 56:47-59:16

Towel wrapped around his head, Nino carries a carton of bath salts and a pail of water, as his undershirt gets stuck on the handle of the washroom door. Manfredi performs a mime choreography as he frees himself from the door handle, a performance enacted for the spectator as well as for Elena whose shadow in the foreground. A tango-like melody on the radio.

Nino pours bath salts into the pail, sighs in relief when he dips his feet in the water, and finally notices he is being watched by a silent Elena who bursts out laughing. Why should female voyeurism lead to laughter? Nino stands up and, in so doing, accidentally pushes the family photograph into the pail of water. This obvious metaphor, announcing the end of his family life, leaves the spectator wondering if Elena is aware that her laughter is juxtaposed on Nino's family picture sinking in the water.

Nino gently pulls Elena on to the coach – bringing fidelity to an end, kindling a promise of new love which we know will not be fulfilled. "So I make you laugh," whispers Nino to Elena. The spectator continues to laugh as the spectacle comes to an end (the applause is silenced).

Chapter 8: First Day at Work
59:17-65:23

36. Scene. A new job. Int. Kitchen. Day.
35-36=edit with effect. 59:17-60:19

A straight edit where a punctuation should be; a swan in front of a windowpane; the door bell rings; no one answers; Nino in a black suit, suitcase in hand, steps into the house, turns off an espresso coffee pot boiling on the stove, hears a buzzer, looks at number 9 flashing on a metal pane, slips on a white jacket, ready for the task at hand. His first day at work.

37. Scene. Nino as butler. Int. Room. Day.
36-37=zero. 60:20-64:54

Singing, Nino carries breakfast to his new employer, a rose in a glass of water, walks into the bedroom. This is the moment Nino has been waiting for. The industrialist, interestingly enough, left unnamed, is slouched on the side of the bed, in blue pajamas, gets up but collapses to the floor, pushing the breakfast tray of fruits and cup in the air. Nino carries him back to his bed. Looking for some sort of painkiller, Nino notices the photograph of his new boss on the front page of the newspaper, and realizes this crooked businessman has downed sleeping pills and whiskey. Pictures of wives, pictures of family, pictures of millionaires: photographs carry the spectator back to reality. Paradoxically, the more Nino tries to be serious the more a clownlike caricature he becomes. The comedian, as we have seen, works on two levels: on the narrative level (as a character) and on the communicational level (as an actor). Nino Manfredi must continuously switch from one plane to another in order to pull a smile from the spectator. Manfredi masters this double language very well. Regardless of the nature of the scene, there is always a moment for laughter:

- searching for a doctor in the phonebook, Nino falls on columns of bank names: "There's nothing but banks in this country;"
- forcing the businessman to drink coffee will not get his money back;
- pressing on the wrong switch the bed turns into sexual vibrating machine;
- Nino ends up holding a bucket of aquarium water, his face splattered with coffee.

All is vain. The "Dottore" is dead and gone. Nino loses any possibility of finding his hard-earned money; the debt from Pinch Point one (45 minutes) will never be paid back. Dead too is Nino's chance to acquire a legal status. Just as Nino finds himself lost at the foot of the bed, music rises in the background. It is the morning wake-up song, *"Buon giorno a te"*, performed by the musical trio.

We are at the midpoint of the film; it is here that the second object of desire is revealed. The industrialist is the Sender not to a joyful object of desire (financial security), but to a worse peril. Nino must find a new path to travel on, but without money.

Contrary to what we might expect, from here on, the presence of money disappears totally from the narrative. *Bread and Chocolate* is neither about money nor the quest for money. The Italic experience can go sour. "We Italians have to help each other" — an advice that becomes a leitmotiv throughout this study. The paradox is that help among Italians is a rarity, as we will find out.

> The very definition of Italian at the beginning of the great transoceanic emigration is very difficult to give. "Many agree that it is impossible to define the Italian..." "A "unique type" does not exist to define the different races, the different histories, the different climates, and therefore the different customs of our region"; "It would be absurd to combine in a single psychological profile the portrait of a Neapolitan woman with that of a Piemontese, or that of a Sardinian with that of a Venetian, a Marchigian, or a Tuscan." [...] often even belonging to the same class or to the same region is not enough to determine behavior: much depends on the trade or economic order in which it is exercised.[6]

Nino expects a fellow Italian to help him, but that help never materializes. Class difference might be to blame, but the fact remains that there might be nothing cultural that unites Nino to the businessman. All that Nino asked for — the right to an identity as a worker — is refused him. Let alone, the possibility to move up the social ladder. With this ladder breaking, as it obviously is the case, what outcome to expect? As it will be clear in the following macro-sequences, Nino who loses his identity also loses any hope of attaining equality and well-being. From this moment on, it is the descent into the inferno.

38. Autonomous shot. Musicians. Ext. Yard. Day.
37-38=zero. 64:54-65:23

"If not equal in fact, equal in opportunity for every man to become the same as his betters" (119): Horace M. Kallen's wish will be disproved. In one continuous shot the camera pans over the musical instruments and tilts up to the landscape. The green lawn, the Swiss flag, and in the background a ferry boat tooting its horn. The soundtrack is realist; the music rises from a source shown on screen. As so dies the false object of desire (money). Whatever this Sender had to offer vanishes in thin air. It is precisely at this moment that one notices the second object of desire appear. What the businessman had to offer Nino was not a job or financial security. We must not confuse the object of desire with a positive element. Usually quite the contrary, what pushes forth the story is the opposite of what is expected.

Chapter 9: Paper Airplane
65:23-66:17

39. Scene. Solitude. Ext. Bridge. Day.
38-39=edit with effect. 65:23-66:17

This single scene is so important that we gave it the status of a chapter. At times, a syntagma coincides with mega-sequence which coincides with the chapter. The camera follows a red paper airplane crashing to the ground, a paper airplane similar to the one Nino threw in Elena's apartment in Scene 33. On the soundtrack a melody by Mozart (Grigory in mind?) on electric piano, unjustified, whereas the rest of the sounds are authentic, justified, and synchronized.

Grigory runs into the frame and picks up the airplane (which Nino must have taught him to make), followed by Elena dressed in a red sweater and blue jeans and the immigrant officer in a trench coat. The camera pans and zooms on to a pillar where stands a dismal Nino. Before him the newly-formed family prancing away from him — a Swiss flag on the left top corner of the frame. Elena's departure is equivalent to the industrialist's death. Nino smokes a cigarette, a large gold ring on his pinky (the cigarette and pinky will disappear by the end of the film). An insert of what lies ahead of him in a low angle shot: a bus crossing the screen; on the left the Swiss flag blows in the wind. Nino will have to leave Switzerland.

Chapter 10: The Show
66:17-75:49

40. Autonomous shot. Workers. Ext. Work site. Evening.
            39-40=edit with effect. 66:17-66:36

"Fading in and fading out," suggests Arnheim, "is a good means of keeping one scene distinct from the next; for since shots that follow immediately on one another usually appear as part of an unbroken time sequence, it is often not easy to show that an episode has come to an end, and that the scene of action is changing" (119). Fade-ins and fade-out tend to temper the pressure of the story. The soundtrack is realistic: men's voices mumbling as they make their way to their sleeping quarters.

41. Sequence. Gigi. Int. Corridor. Evening.
            40-41=zero. 66:37-68:43

A change of setting qualifies this syntagma more as a sequence than a scene. Different settings are linked by temporal continuity; a corridor, the voices of men in conversation. Another universe opens to us as we step into the underground world of *Fremdarbeiter* (more commonly known today under the title *Gastarbeiter*). The magic of language transforms the foreign worker into a more acceptable noun.

A new character is introduced. Gigi calls out to Nino: "You old bastard... you horse's ass... foolish fat face... old whore's behind..." Upon hearing such (unendearing?) nouns what can Nino say but "Enough with the compliments." The spectator laughs: if these are compliments, what kind of insults could Gigi proliferate? Gigi represents the kind of work Nino did before becoming a waiter. Had he not mentioned this to the police Commissioner earlier on? Something to the effect that he had spent two years in workers' barracks. Not only are we walking into the underworld of workers, we are time travelling into the past. Nino asks his friend if he can stay a couple of nights. Gigi walks with a limp, breaks out in a song: "But if you let me touch you,/I'll never leave your side/Then I'll come a little closer.../And jump right inside." McLuhan reminds us: "You can't go home again" (16). Nino is not home but is asking for a stay over until he finds a door out of his hell. What follows is revealing.

> Gigi: "You'll sleep here in my bed."
> Nino: "Suppose they catch us?"
> Gigi: "They'll think we're gays."

"Gays": the entire scene opens to the revelation of homoeroticism. The film changes tonality from this scene on. Nino Manfredi discusses it in his conversation with Jean A. Gili:

> The problem is solitude. In Switzerland, psychiatric hospitals are filled with immigrants. We decided to be more reconciliatory in the film. On Sunday, workers dress up but end up sitting on their beds, afraid to go out because they will be treated badly; racism in Switzerland is frightening. Immigration is painful because it shakes up a person's dignity (Gili, 260).

More than homosexuals what we are shown in this symbolic portion of the film are men who have lost their dignity. Gigi (Giacomo Rizzo) acts as the guide who accompanies Nino, and ultimately the spectator (Nino is the spectator's guide), across the underworld of a closely-knit society of desperate *Gastarbeiter*. Far from acquiring citizenship of a country, these wretched-faced workers have lost their dignity they need so badly. Perhaps, Gigi, an August clown, to use Fellini's term, can be equated to Charon, the ferryman who carries dead souls across the River Styx, the world of the dead. Dante defines the emotion:

> Caron dimonio, con occhi di bragia,
> loro accennando, tutte le raccoglie;
> batte col remo qualunque s'adagia (*Inferno*, III, 109-111).

> [The demon Charon, with eyes of burning coal, beckons to them and gathers them all in, smiting with the oar any that linger (Inferno 53].

Gigi, whose gaze burns with fire, does not carry an oar, but a guitar. Beneath the musical comedy — the breaking into song when everyday words simply are unable to match the emotion within — there simmer signs of the most troubling kind. What do these barracks with xenos conceal? The opposite of what emigration promises. Not an opening up, but a closing in; not an explosion, but an implosion. The stranger capsizes, inverts, clams up, views not the other, but sameness (the cross-dressing being a momentary, falsified reflection of self). Men living with other men in dangerously closed quarter — a script for individual, professional, interpersonal disaster. Gigi holds an orange-colored dress: "These are our trophies." Male talk, dresses, trophies? The laughter turns yellow. The spectator is twitching in his seat.

42. Scene. The Three Graces. Int. Hall. Evening.
41-42=zero. 68:44-74.99

Acting as the master of ceremony, Nino stands on a table in the eating quarter where dozens of men sit at tables. Gigi, dressed in a black and red corset, wears a red wing, an acoustic guitar in his hand, crucifix hanging onto his/her breasts. The men in the barracks break out in hysteria, laughing, pulling at their faces, throwing kisses to Gigi, touching him/her while he sings to them. But when Renzo, dressed as a young woman, appears, the hysteria dies.

The joking ceases. This is serious. A man, confused, whispers: "Rosa, why don't you write me?"

Abruptly, noticing the desperation in the room, Nino interjects, guitar in hand, with a song, "L'uomo non è di legno" (written by Jaja Fastri and Ugo Calise). With its Chaplinesque *Modern Times* air, this bawdy song recounts the suffering of a lonely immigrant worker who is not made of wood. Nino wears lipstick, and sports a blue woman's hat. Workers are gathered behind a window, gaze in, lonely voyeurs staring at these three Graces crossed-dressed men. This crucial scene ends with Renzo breaking down in tears, running into his room: "I just want to go home."

43. Scene. Tears. Int. Corridor. Evening.
42-43=zero. 75.00-75:49

Nino follows Renzo to his room, but finds the door locked. The sounds are justified, authentic, synchronized.

Nino: "No, he's right. They've screwed us all our lives with a song and a guitar... We've been had. We have to change things, not sing about them." When Renzo comes out, a fellow worker, visibly angry, steps into the corridor, commanding these "whores" to let him sleep in peace. Nino: "Go on, sleep. But it's time to wake up. Look at yourself in the mirror, bitch."

It's time for change, but change cannot come until we look at ourselves in the mirror. By inventing an anti-family, to quote David Cooper,[7] the unhappy ethnic can step out of his self and continue his journey to self-realization. This analytical doubleness launches the process of awareness that never quite settles down: to be part of one reality and simultaneously part of a second reality. Breaking away from one's family the ethnic has to invent a second family, a third family, and so on. Nino exits forever from this family of barrack workers and must find a surrogate family. This breaking away from the workers' past and entering the next family constitutes what Syd Field calls the second Pinch Point.

Bread and Chocolate could very well be described as a non-stop journey taking Nino from one catastrophe (to use an Aristotelean term) to another.

The catastrophes in this film seem to send us back to the family unit. Nino leaves one family and enters another: from his Italian family to the family of waiters; from waiters to the fragile family made up with Elena and Grigory; from Elena to the family of Italian acquaintances (the businessmen); from the business man to the family of barrack workers; from the barracks to the family of chicken breeders; from the chicken breeders to the family of partially-assimilated ethnics (the bar scene); from the ethnics to the family of emigrants returning home; from the emigrants returning home to the family of the No-Land.

If the ethnic is solitary or unsuccessful, there is no family strong or large enough to contain the ethnic. The only family for the ethnic is the virtual space s/he must invent for him/herself.

Chapter 11: Leaving
75:50- 76:43

44. Scene. Leaving. Ext. Train station. Evening.
43-44=edit with effect. 75:50-76:13

A short chapter brings the spectator back to the point of departure. Nino recognizes this corridor leading to the trains; he has been here before. Once again, Nino with suitcase in hand, is about to leave. A train whistle sounds. The soundtrack is realistic. A man stands against the wall under a blue light, his left leg propped up, he clutches a briefcase. McLuhan sees the train as the creator of new families.

> The train radically altered the personal outlooks and patters of social interdependence... It created totally new urban, social, and family worlds. New ways of work. New ways of management. New legislation (72).

The man against the wall offers Nino job opportunities: "Trust a paisan. Outdoor work, no documents needed." This cultural code (Italian acquaintances) reappears, but Nino utters a cold "no" to the offer. Unable to trust fellow Italians, for having been had by Italians more than once — the industrialist, Gigi — Nino bids farewell to the *paisan*. The seventy-five-minute Pinch Point leads the protagonist to a third object of desire. In Nino's universe, Italians are Senders, never object of desires; the way, never the goal.

45. Scene. Leaving again. Ext. Train. Evening.
44-45=zero. 76:14-76:43

As Nino is about to climb on a train, a young man with a guitar begins to sing. Nino can't conceal the disgust on his face. Nino slams the door to the musician and the spectator, for we are sitting in the singer's position.

This refusal of nostalgia, of story telling, this impossibility of ever going back home (home, a concept slowly being erased in Nino's mind) opens up the door to another departure, another arrival. Nino breaks away from one family and entering a new one, once again everything starts in the train station.

Chapter 12: Chicken Madness
76:44-78:51

46. Scene. A new job. Ext. Barn. Day.
45-46=edit with effect. 76:44-77:48

A high angle shot presents Nino in black, his symbolic suitcase in his hands (we never get to see its content). He stands among chickens running free. On the soundtrack, realistic cackling: justified, authentic, synchronized. The soundtrack rarely expands beyond what is expected: what you hear is what you see.

An old man walks out of a barn, Nino on the right, the old man, feathers over his clothes, on the left.

> Man: "Who are you?"
> Nino: "Who are you?"
> Man: "I won't tell you."
> Nino (low angle): "Me neither."
> Man (low angle): "Then we're through."
> Nino: "Our paisan sent me."

The paisan, we are told, is a piemontese, an interesting contrast to the Southerners presented in this chapter. Nino is asked one more time to put his trust in the Italian culture. Not inter-personal, nor professional utterances, though these continue to preoccupy the protagonist, somehow from this unanswered question — "Who are you?" — what to expect if not an off-beat response: "I won't tell you."

The old man calms the tension: "Don't worry, none of us have papers. We're all one big family." One extended, happy family: precisely what Nino does not want. These travels belong to the proairetic code, to use Roland Barthes term. Sequences of empirical actions that need to be named, and confirmed (26).

Actions have been mostly misdemeanors in Nino's case. We are coming close to the end of the story. The future does not seem too bright. Out come two men, feathers covering their entire bodies. One is holding a chicken in his arms; the other shakes Nino's hand. A close-up reveals blood stains on Nino's hands.

"We kill chickens,' explains the old man. Blood pours out from a pipe-tap like water; blood, family blood, *jus sanguinis*. The right to belong, the right to citizenship, according to blood, become meaningless. To be a foreigner in a foreign land is losing one's meaning. Julia Kristeva defines the term "foreigner" in its legal interpretation: the foreigner is "someone who is not a citizen of the country he lives in" (61). Yes, Nino is a foreigner, but more than being an illegal stranger in a foreign country he suddenly realizes that he is becoming a foreigner in his own cultural community. Kristeva continues:

> From now on, the foreigner is neither a race nor a nation. He is neither marvellous and secretive as the Volkgeist, nor can he be dismissed as the heckler in the urban forum of rationalism. Become a source of trouble, the foreigner is within: a stranger to himself, split up in pieces (268).

Without the normal support of the close family Nino is estranged to himself and to extended families. Doubly a stranger (from within and from without), he must tiptoe on the rim of madness. This duality is what Kristeva labels, referring back to Freud, *l'inquiétante étrangeté* (the disquieting estrangement) (269). This disquieting estrangement is present in the five films we are studying. Losing oneself is one of the parameters of the Italic variable to come out of this study.

In this film, the chicken becomes the symbol of this loss. The domestication of this subspecies of the Red Jungle fowl, it is believed, goes back to 10,000 years ago. Primarily a source of meat and eggs, the chicken is also a sign of gods. But there have been no gods so far in *Bread and Chocolate*.

47. Sequence. Chickens. Ext. Barn. Day.
46-47=zero. 77:49-79:13

"At night, you go to sleep with a clear conscience..." mutters the old man. Nino is covered from head to toe with chicken feathers. The pay is peace work: the more you kill, the more you gain. Nino punctuates the man's sentences by adding "Blessed Madonna". The first allusion made to religion, to the Blessed Virgin Mary. What role does religion play in these living quarters? A chicken coop. Feathers seem to have grown on humans. No longer merely metaphors, these men and women have actually turned into chickens. Brusati explains his position:

> *Bread and Chocolate* is not a realist film, in spite of its theme and premise. This wasn't done on purpose. In truth, I would willing make realist films, but for some mysterious reason they change the moment I touch them (185).

More than the shadow of Rossellini of *Rome, Open City* (1945), one senses the presence of the post neo-realistic filmmakers such as the flamboyant Fellini of *Satyricon* (1969) or the magical De Sica in *Miracle in Milan* (1951). The spectator is constantly pushed over the border of normalcy. Fellini and De Sica might be formally very different but their goal is not realism, not even magic realism. They glorify the imagination, the imaginary world. So does Brusati in his own way. We are in the poetic world of symbolism, not the magnifying glass of detailed reality.

48. Scene. Home. Int. Chicken coop. Day.
47-48=zero. 79:14-82:59

This coop-home has a low ceiling. Too low to stand up in. Nino is forced to stoop. "How can you live without women?" asks Nino, bending over. Mimmo answers, "I manage." Cut to an insert of a cackling hen on the boy's bed. Does the spectator dare laugh at the sexual implication? Manfredi quickly opens the door to laughter.

Nino adds in French, *"Pardon, Madame."* The retort is much needed for the gag to work. Respectability is regained.

Men and women are unable to stand straight. They move in the coop bent in two. They sit on chairs with legs sawed off. They eat at a table with legs cut as well. Three short women (daughter, mother, and niece) glide into the coop, carrying food trays.

Nino jokes: "These… you didn't saw in half." Are they not in reality cut in two as well? Dignity is lost. In this descent into paranoia ("being next to one's mind", as Cooper would define it), first through the circle of homosexuality, and now in the circle of bestiality, realistic sounds make this voyage wearier still.

Before a painting of the Madonna di Pompei, Nino whispers, "If I bow any lower it'll seem like adulation." Religion definitely has made it way into the film, but to no purpose.

49. Alternating syntagma. Bathing. Ext. Chicken coop. Day.
48-49=zero. 83:00-83:38

An abrupt cut to one of the young women from coop. With black hair, dressed in black, she is laughing. The camera zooms on her and gradually her expression changes. She is no longer laughing. She has noticed something off-screen. The ideal, what is not present in her world. A desire, a goal.

In this syntagma Brusati compares to worlds: that of the German-Swiss and that of Italian illegal workers. These Swiss speak German. Young blond men and women ride horses by the idyllic river. Fair-haired women versus dark-haired women. Two versions of the "going-back-to-nature" syndrome. One faces the other: the native versus the foreign. The irony is strident. Only the foreign is looking at the native, and not the other way round.

50. Scene. The coop. Int. Chicken coop. Day.
49-50=zero. 83:39-85:29

Nino, in low angle, begins to answer questions asked by the chicken-people: "Who am I? You're Italian. I'm Italian. But is that enough to make us alike? Am I like you?" The insider must face the outsider, the individual is placed against the collectivity. One of the men ventures in advancing the idea that Nino is exactly like the rest of them. And no dissimilarity exists, in fact, between the one and the many. Nino is very much part of this family.

51. Alternating syntagma. The window. Int. Chicken coop. Day.
50-51=zero. 85:30-88:51

Faces pressed against the metal railing, fingers clutching the iron prisoner-like, all with the gaze of admiration, voyeurs all. Classical music fades in: *Symphony No. 1* in C major by Georges Bizet. Realistic sounds are silenced. The addition of music enhances the sadness of the scene. The young Swiss men and women are naked, swimming in the river.

Are they aware of being watched? More than being the passive object of desire, these young people (the late-1960s hippy movement prolonged itself well into the early 1970s) are offering their bodies as spectacle. A tinge of sadism is at play in these images of blonds alternating with images of swarthy men staring through barb wire and dejected women mopping at the table. Nino is certainly part of this new family of voyeurs.

Two separate scenes unfold simultaneously in two fixed locations. By comparing the rich and the poor, Brusati stresses the difference in social status. On one hand, marginalized Italian workers have turned into chicken; on the other, the native Swiss are being mistaken for gods (they have crowned themselves with flowers). What interaction can possibly connect these two stations? Between the lord and his serfs what is there, except finance? Without money there is no time for leisurely activities. This syntagma brings the viewer back to the beginning of the film. How far has Nino advanced in this society? Not very far. If anything, he has worsened his fate.

According to French archeologist Jean-Paul Demoule, the millennia that preceded the rise of capitalism clearly shows that migrants moved from rural to urban zones.[8] Immigration is not only the move from one country to another. It is also the move from the country to the city. This episode clearly indicates the opposite; Italians have never left their rural setting. They are exactly in the same situation they were in before they emigrated. No, religion cannot help the emigrant peasant. Brusati's attack on Italy here is unforgiving.

Chapter 13: Assimilating
88:52-98:32

52. Scene. Becoming blond. Int. Public washroom. Day.
51-52=edit with effect. 88:52-90:08

The music from the bucolic landscape of the previous syntagma overlaps a photographic image of a typical Swiss landscape. From the real world we go to the fake one, from reality to the imaginary. A more stereotypical *trompe-l'œil* — Alps, hills, trees, lake — would be difficult to find. And it is with this foreshadowing image that an "unreal" Nino will appear.

An elderly plump woman, cigarette in mouth, walks across the screen, from left to right, breaking the spell of the *trompe-l'œil*. Reality sets in. The picturesque as nice as it might seem is not for real. An image is but an image. It is closing time. Bizet's symphony fades out; reality noises fade in: justified, authentic, synchronized, except for the sound of a siren reminding us that the police is never far away in Switzerland.

A washroom cabinet is locked. The cleaning-lady calls out; a man responds in German. The door opens; a man steps out; it is Nino, but we do not recognize him at first. His footsteps on the marble floor resonate loudly. Nino has dyed his hair blond. He examines himself in a mirror. This instance of vanity provokes doubleness: there is the one, and then the other; the one who is, and the other who seems, who is not. We are asked to follow this other Nino — Nino the Swiss. In other words, Nino who has assimilated, disappeared into the majority. We wonder if this episode was not influenced Eddy Murphy in the writing of his splendid *Saturday Night Live* sketch "White Like Me", about a black man passing over as white.

A close up of Nino fingering a lock of his blond hair brilliantly links the end of one syntagma to the beginning of the next.

There are a few instances of such "double-jointed" (overlapping) shots found throughout film history: a shot that is at once the closing of a syntagma and the opening of the following. Such shots compress time but also thrust the viewer deeper into the magic space, the unreal world of film.

53. Bracket Syntagma. Reflections. Ext. Street. Day.
52-53=zero. 90:09-91:36

What comes next is what Christian Metz labelled as "the bracket syntagma": "different successive evocations... strung together through optical effect" (126). Nino crosses the city, mesmerized by his own image reflected on store windowpanes. Narcissus falls in love with his own reflection. Music, like in a video on MTV, overwhelms the soundtrack: not justified, inauthentic, unsynchronized. This is video music and images working together to sell a product: the assimilated immigrant! "Assimilate", "Become like us" screams this syntagma that unites snippets of incomplete actions that follow one another in chronological order. Bumping into a passerby turns into a dance.

Assimilation alleviates life. Brusati seems to be saying that "blonds have more fun!" Even a young Swiss girl calls out to Nino and hands him a magazine that he does not even belong to him. Brusati's acerbity is clear, lest we forget what horrible things Swiss men are capable of doing to children. *Si se non nouerit:* as long as he doesn't know himself, he will be happy – such would be Ovid's advice to Nino.[8] This syntagma ends with another double-jointed (overlapping) shot: Nino walking at night into a bar.

54. Scene. Woman at bar. Int. Bar. Evening.
53-54=zero. 91:37-93:09

Men and women are watching TV. Nino orders a beer in his broken German. The Italian waiter is not amused: "This guy doesn't know what the hell he wants." Not knowing what one wants comes hand in hand with not knowing who one is. This is not Giovanni Garofoli speaking, but the shade of Giovanni Garofoli, his mirror reflection. A fair-haired woman at the bar throws glances at Nino who pretends to be engrossed in a German-language newspaper. When Nino finally lifts up his eyes, the woman invites him to join her. Nino is about to step out when the Italian national anthem blares out of the television set. Instead of following the woman, Nino chooses to look at a soccer match between Switzerland and Italy. Nationalism is stronger than sex, stronger than love.

This peripeteia is ambiguous. No matter how much Nino wants to run away from Italy, Italy like a spiritual entity refuses to leave his body. Why does the image of exorcism suddenly come to our mind at this instance? Would ethnicity be that spiritual demon that nations which to through out of certain of its undesirable citizens? What follows might be comparable to the manifestation of being possessed. Of course, Nino's possession is expressed with humor. Still, the outbreak is not at all appreciated by the people in the bar.

55. Scene. Soccer Int. TV room. Evening.
54-55=zero. 93:10-96:45

From the television the camera zooms into the crowd in the bar whistling in disfavor against the Italian team. The fair-haired woman, dejected, walks back into the bar looking for Nino. Nino's Swiss armor loosens at the hinges when the Italian team fails to score. It is the first display of Nino's downfall. When a player on the Italian national team finally kicks the ball inside the opponent's net, Nino is unable contain the spirit screaming inside him. Out bursts the yelling: "Goal". Nino bawling "Goal" is repeated four times by Brusati (much like the ending in Antonioni's *Zabriskie Point*), reverberating the message loud and clear. It is interesting to note that the final sequence of the exploding desert mansion very much resembles a device that Eisenstein used several times. The effect is striking because... its reliance on montage represents a great departure from Antonioni's usual style.

One is reminded of the recurring plate-breaking sequence in *The Battleship Potemkin* or of the horse and carriage repeatedly sliding off the bridge in October. Rarely used, the device of repeating a shot becomes a convention, much like italics in type, to suggest, as Seymour Chatman writes, general emotional intensification (168). In *Pane*, the effect is troubling. Nino seems possessed by a power that has taken hold of him. Something inside is stronger than the mask Nino wears.

Almost a decade before the Italian Mundial victory of 1982, Brusati associates Italian pride with the Italian soccer team. Why the filmmaker chooses soccer to capture a fervent "emotional intensification" of cultural awareness is intriguing. This moment of pride is intense and emotional, and out of control. This moment of hysteria cannot be what the Italic is. The forces within must be controlled.

Nino screams: "I'm Italian… You don't like it… Go on, threaten me…" Clearly at the end of the road, barely passed the ninety-minute mark the final object of desire is offered. These objects of desire keep turning the narrative gears; Nino might be ready to assimilate but it is quite possible that the host country is too xenophobic to admit the xenos (the foreigner, the barbarian). But it might also be the case that Nino is not ready to let go of the past, and embrace a new Self.

A new identity permutes into a cultural alloy; neither inferior to its original, nor superior to the depositary. I am tempted to use what ethnographer Clark Wissler refers to as the *Age Area* hypothesis of culture[9] to explain the Italic space which is neither there nor here, but everywhere at the same time, the span between the point of departure and present point (and not arrival point). The Italic carries the cultural traits that tend to diffuse outward from the center, avoiding to become a center itself. Not necessarily older than the origin, but certainly more stalwart. Nino must destroy the old Self.

> 56. Scene. Mirror. Int. Bar corridor. Evening.
> 55-56=zero. 96:46-96:51

Footsteps and television rumbling in the background, unperturbed, Nino rambles out of the television room. He makes his way toward the blond woman sitting at the bar, but is arrested by his own reflection in a door window. He stops, pulls a lock of his hair back, laughs at himself. The blond woman smiles at Nino: Nino in blond. Follows the shock: Nino violently smashes his head through the glass. This suicidal act is a necessary moment in Nino's process to becoming another person. He must get rid of the head on his body. Karl Menninger suggests that various parts of the body could represent the genitals and that many psychotic patients would harm themselves purposely in these isolated parts where, for example, fetishists find pleasure.

> The unconscious symbolic substitution of one organ for another is by no means limited to hysterical persons or fetishists. It is only more obvious in them. But we all do it (233).

The part stands for the whole, what is known as metonymy and synecdoche. Nino displaces his source of pain to his head. What this pain is in truth is difficult to pinpoint with exactitude. Floating, fluctuating, rambling, going adrift, meaning is never clearly cut and dry.

The subject is incapable of attaining his real object of desire. Whenever an object of desire emerges in the horizon, an opponent interferes and pushes the object out of reach (or, more precisely, the object transforms itself into something else). The full-time job as a waiter, his love for Elena, the money promised by the industrialist, the strange homo-erotic love between Gigi and Renzo: trust in other Italians. These are metaphors for a deeper quandary. Si se non nouerit: onanism lasts but a short time. Narcissus must give in to Echo so that a beginning of happiness can be set in motion. Symbolically speaking, auto-eroticism is the death-call of immigration. One doesn't fling one's head into a windowpane without a reason. Self-mutilation is a sign of a disordered mind. If we were to trawl the metaphor a little further, sharp images of castration and, most perturbing, self-castration emerge. Nino runs amuck; the Swiss dodge over to him and expel him from the bar. The significance of this ejection is manifold:

    i. a foreigner, am not permitted in the bar;
    ii. liars are not wanted; Swiss (Nino as a Swiss) attacking the Swiss are banished;
    iii. violence is strictly forbidden;
    iv. destruction of property will not be tolerated;
    v. no sexual gestures are allowed in public spaces;
    vi. lunatics must get out. Nino has broken too many rules and must be punished.

              57. Scene. Rejection. Ext. Road. Night.
                   56-57=zero. 96:52-98:32

Nino falls to the ground; a bicycle bell rings; church bell chimes. The spectator laughs but doesn't find the joke funny. Bergson writes: "A deformity that may become comic is a deformity that a normally built person could successfully imitate" (75).

Can dyeing one's hair blond be considered a symbolic deformity? Or is the desire to cut off his own head be the exorcist ritual that he much needs to embark on the trip to the virtual space that awaits him?

The blond woman from the bar joins Nino outside, sprawled on garbage plastic bags. She extends her hand to him, and utters a few words in a language Nino, face covered with blood, does not understand. He asks, "You're not German?" Smiling, the woman pulls off her wig, radiantly exclaims, "No, Spanish." Nino cringes as he lets himself collapse on the garbage, exhausted. The is the end of the act. Ultimately, all immigrant has to face him/herself.

Chapter 14: The End
98:33-108:43

58. Scene. Papers. Int. Police station. Day.
57-58=edit with effect. 98:33-104:47

The high angle shot of male hands stamping papers. A dolly back establishes that this is a police station. Nino is handed expulsion papers. Unshaven, band-aid on his forehead, Nino offers a military salute to the policeman who orders him out of the country. Nino smiles mischievously. Wearing a tie on a checkered black and white shirt, dishevelled, and glad to be on his way, Nino follows a police officer. Kristeva writers that

> In the end, breaking down repression pushes one to cross the border et to find himself in a foreign land. To break away from one's family, from one's mother tongue, from one's country, in order to land elsewhere, is an audacious act that can only follow sexual frenzy: no more taboos, everything becomes possible. No matter if the trip abroad is accompanied by debauchery or, its opposite, with-drawing into fear, exile always implies the fragmentation of the old body (47).

We have witnessed the unravelling of an Italian unable to continue to be either an Italian or a Swiss. The country Nino has left behind, and the country Nino wants to live in are not havens for the new individual he has become. We have entered the symbolic world totally. Realism has been discarded.

59. Sequence. Mischief. Ext. Train station. Evening.
58-59=zero. 94:48-101:06

Back in the corridor to the train station, Giovanni Garofoli reads his expulsion papers. Nino, being a public nuisance, tears a poster and gently puts it in a garbage bin which he then pushes to the floor. He is an accumulation of misdemeanors. Nino gently slaps the buttocks of an elderly woman crossing his path. Later, he runs to a pillar and urinates. Nino's gone awry. Under the influence of some unknown force, Nino kisses the officer in gratitude.

Manfredi imitates Chaplin in *Modern Times:* humiliation, prejudice, disillusionment, or simply self-knowledge? Whoever he might be at this point it is clear that he no longer is simply an unwanted immigrant. There is no paradise after hell. In the train, he recites a line that sounds more like verse than prose: "Is there a small place for a guy who can't find a home anywhere?"

Pane e cioccolata can be resumed by this simple and direct sentence. And unexpectedly a voice on the intercom calls for him: "Do they want me?" Nino asks his fellow passengers, who in turn ask him, "What is your name?" Elena stands outside the train. Nino calls out to her, and rushes to meet the woman he could have loved.

    60. Sequence. "Neither here nor there." Ext. Train station. Evening. 59-60=zero. 101:07-104:28

Scenic spaces are stretched yet combined: an extended filmic geography. Nino moves from one set to another, the action is nevertheless continuous. The secondary character alights like *deus ex machina*, but she isn't. The film has prepared us to accept Elena as a savior. Elena appears every time Nino is in trouble. They could have been an item, but Elena preferred the immigration officer who offers her the necessary stability she needed for her son Grigory.

"You're half blond and half brunette," she notes. To which Nino replies, "That's me. Neither here nor there." How many times have Italian immigrants pronounced those words: neither here not there. The essence of the Italic is just that: a deterritorialized identity based on the hope of cultural survival. Elena hands Nino an envelope, his residency permit.

Elena: "The problem isn't Italy or Switzerland. Choose any country... But choose to live. Don't give up."

Nino jumps back on the train, his head on a window. Elena extends the envelop in her hands. It is too late. Yet this envelop will always be there for Nino to pick up if he ever wishes to come back. An important detail for those spectators who need a real solution in lieu of the magic ending that awaits them. No matter how unreal a film is, the story must in the end deliver a real solution to all questions asked through the work. In this case, that answer is the envelop.

    61. Bracket syntagma. Going back. Int. Train cabin. Evening/daytime. 60-61=zero. 104:29-108:43

Successive scenettes illustrate the passage of time and the crossing over the Swiss border. The loud whistle as well as the strident noise of wheels on tracts are justified, authentic, but not synchronized. From night to day, time passes on. Nino wakes up, his hand on his forehead. An insert of card players in silhouette, then a zoom in on Nino asleep. Italian music fades in. Nino's eyes open plaintively: is he dreaming? A man, with rotten teeth, plays an accordion and belts out "Simmo e Napule paisà" (G. Fiorelli and N. Valente). Nino shakes his head in the negative. And then the unexpected occurs. The spectator is asked to accept the fact that Nino has pulled on the emergency brains of the train that is dashing into the gallery, receding into a black hole. A light outside the gallery goes on and off. The film's theme melody is being played on an accordion and is placed in the background. Nino slouches out of the darkness in shirtsleeves, brown suitcase in his right hand, jacket in the left. He stops and stares into the camera. Dishevelled, band-aid on his hairline, he turns his head to his right, before returning to us, the spectator, fixing us, his witnesses, his accusers, his friends, as the soundtrack breaks into violins.

He has arrived in No-Land. Credits appear on this final image frozen and slowly made to go out of focus until Giovanni Garofoli is reduced to red dot lastly disintegrating into the black screen.

Nino has touched the limits of being and civility. There is no turning back, no retiring, no more mirrors to reflect an illusion of self. Black hair might go blond, but eventually even dye washes away. With unshaven face, shirt soiled by sweat, Nino might have spent the night in a park. Questions remain unanswered. Does it matter at this point? In a review Giovanni Grazzini unfairly criticizes Nino Manfredi for not being able to accurately juggle "between the comic and the pathetic."[11]

The "secret flavors" Manfredi delivers, on the contrary, have matured quite well with time. Giving up one's dignity leads to mental illness. In the police station when he was given his expulsion papers, the light on the ceiling and over Nino's head shines like a fallen halo.

Giovanni Garofoli is neither an angel, nor a good father, but the incarnation of failure travelling between two worlds; this transient space provides equilibrium for those who shuffle between departure and arrival, wavering between incubus and euphoria. This is No-Land, the virtual territory: alternation can be a substitute for stability if the immigrant is not detained in solitary confinement and finds appeasement in a newfound family, which, as *Bread and Chocolate* demonstrates, is never a given.

Conclusion

The film can be divided in ten functions, each described in a succinct phrase faithful to Syd Field's paradigm.

> 1. Giovanni Garofoli is presented to the spectator, discovers a dead girl in a park. (0:00-6:55)
> 2. Nino is found innocent of the killing, urinates in public (Inciting Incident). (6:56-11:08)
> 3. Nino works as a waiter, meets Elena, and a rich Italian industrialist. (11:09-29:18)

4. Nino is fired for urinating in public. (29:13-33:56)
5. Nino is hired by the industrialist, who takes Nino's money, discovers family ties with Elena and her son. (33:57-59:16)
6. Nino finds the industrialist has committed suicide, gone is all of Nino's money, Elena leaves. (59:17-66:17)
7. Nino returns to the barracks, which he leaves to work on a chicken farm. (67:18-88:51)
8. Nino leaves the farm and dyes his hair blond, but is unmasked during a soccer game. (88:52-98:32)
9. The police escort Nino out of the country, Elena has a working permit for Nino. (98:33-104:28)
10. Nino gets off the train, goes to No-Land. (104:29-108:43)

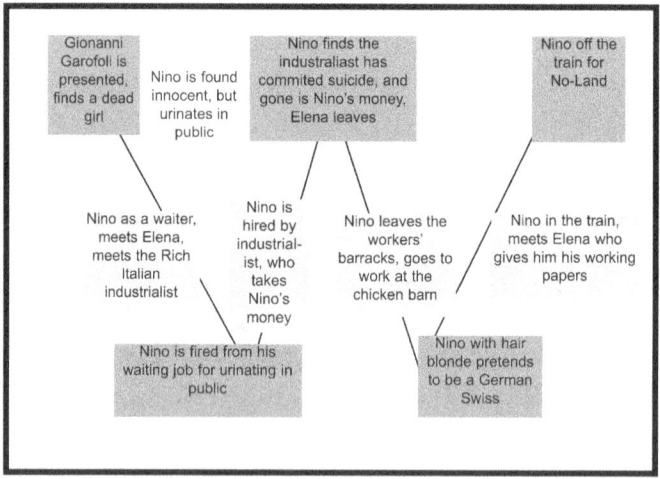

Figure 8

According to the top shaded boxes of our diagram we can disclose the film's premise. (figure 8). *Pane e cioccolata* describes the journey taken by Giovanni (Nino) Garofoli that leads him from his work as a waiter in Switzerland to his being expelled as an illegal immigration for urinating in a public space. Nino then finds a job as a personal butler for an industrialist who unfortunately commits suicide. Nino finally decides on the train back Italy that it is better to live in a virtual territory, we call No-Land, than to submit to what Sergio Valli calls the "canta che ti passa" syndrome.[12] Nino refuses to sing "Torna a Surriento" by Ernesto De Curtis or rush back to the past. Nino wants something else, even if the future is unsure.

The obstacles (the second level in our diagram, light shaded) he must cross over are symbolic endeavors that bring him from reality to unreality, from solid territorial ground to abstract virtuality, from personal struggle to cultural re-construction, from individualism to collectivism. By following semantically the functions one sees how each action leads to the other in a quasi-mathematical equation.

From the start, Nino did not stand a chance of integrating: his eating manners, his finding the dead girl's body logically lead him to the police station. Out of fear, or simply because he had held the urge, Nino ends up releasing himself in a public place which bring about the ultimate misfortunes awaiting Nino. Meeting Elena, the Italian industrialist, the workers in the barracks, the chicken-people are symbolic tribulations (proxies of families) that Nino must overcome. The three objects of desire (the lower line in our diagram in dark and the midpoint) are

1. He gets fired;
2. The industrialist commits suicide (taking along Nino's money);
3. Nino's true identity is revealed at the pub during the soccer tournament. And so from family to family, from one dark event to another, Nino gradually loses patience (his mind?), getting off a rolling train, stubbornly returning to the place he was kicked from.

If these main hurdles do not amount to the creation of an identity, the surmounting of these obstacles, however, do enable Nino to find himself, so to speak, independently, without ever having to return to the point of departure. Never is it a question of going back to Italy; Nino confesses this much to Elena. He has expressed similar feelings to his Italian wife during his imaginary dialogue in his bedroom.

These hindrances are not cul-de-sac; in each dead-end a key is giving to open the door to the next home. The family in Italy is waiting to receive from Nino, from the "father: that he is the formal invitation to emigrate to Switzerland which is, in spite of all its flaws and shortcomings, a better place to live in than Italy. The suicide and the money stolen by the industrialist reduce Nino's chances of becoming a legal worker. Nino finds himself in a marginalized position, and is unable to exist in any recognizable "Little Italy" — a *Ritalie*. (Are the barracks and the chicken coop not metaphors of Little Italy?)

Nino stands at the crossroads: the strada that leads him further into the forest of assimilation (the path taken, say, by Elena), or the second *strada* which takes him into the world of the imaginary: a No-Land, a virtual space where the non-assimilated immigrants gather. It is here that the ethnic is born.

> To treat ethnicity only within a cultural context presents the risk of ignoring those "direct or indirect relationships with the distribution of power, wealth, status, and occupations" that ethnicity cannot refrain from entertaining, in the words of an outspoken and controversial of "new ethnicity". [13]

The agencies that empower cultural communities to fight for their individual collective rights as well as their members individual rights are needed. *Bread and Chocolate* awakens the spectators to the plight emigrants and immigrants face on a daily basis. As a finished product this film clearly encourages a subtle kind of militancy that had not been present in Italy in any direct form up till then. Dino Brusati and Nino Manfredi open wide the doors to a cultural entity that goes out and above any Italian national identity.

Notes

1. Pier Paolo Pasolini, *Empirismo eretico* (1972), Milano: Aldo Garzanti, 2010, 285: "E dunque per quest'ultimo è illecito dimenticare anche per comodo e per un solo momento la sua successività sintattica, la 'la grande lassa temporale' in cui solo esso ritrova il suo senso: e bisognerà piuttosto fare di tale successività una 'categoria' che permanga come elemento concreto e operante anche nel ragionare della doppia articolazione..." Pasolini insisted that "film is an unending sequence shot" ["Il cinema è un piano-sequence infinito"] (249).
2. Piero Scaruffi, "The History of Cinema: Franco Brusati", translated from the Italian by Judith Harris, www.scaruffi.com/director/brusati.html.
3. Vincent Canby, "Four Movies, Two for Children and Two From Abroad, Open: Screen: *Bread and Chocolate*", *The New York Times,* 14 July 1978.
4. Kenneth Mackinnon, *Greek Tragedy into Film,* London: Croom Helm, 1986.
5. Jean A. Gili, *Le cinéma italien 2,* 185. "Je suis accusé [...] de faire des films qui ne sont jamais réalistes: au fond même *Pane e cioccolata* n'est pas un film réaliste, malgré son point de départ et son sujet."
6. Maddalena Tirabassi, "Le emigrate italiane in prospettiva comparata", in *Altreitalie 9,* gennaio-giugno 1993, Torino: Edizione della Fondazione Giovanni Agnelli, 141, with a quote from Michela De Giorgio, *Le italiane dall'Unità ad oggi,* Bari, Laterza, 1992.
7. David Cooper, *The Death of the Family,* 16: "In this sense the psycho-analytic situation can ideally, become a sort of anti-family — a family that one can enter by choice and leave by choice when one has done what one has to do in it."
8. Vide "Trois millions d'années d'immigration", in *Émigrer immigrer.* 26-27.
9. Vide Ovid. *Metamorphosis.* Book III.
10. Vide Merritt Ruhlen, *The Origin of Language: Tracing the Evolution of the Mother Tongue,* 1994.
11. Giovanni Grazzini, *Gli anni Settanta in cento film,* Bari: Laterza, 1977, 230.
12. Sergio Valli, http://www.radioland.it/recensioni-films, *"Pane e cioccolata".*
13. Anna Maria Martellone, "A Plea against the Deconstruction of Ethnicity and in Favor of Political History", in *Altreitalie 6,* November 1991, Torino, Edizioni della Fondazione Giovanni Agnelli, 109.

2

A PAIN IN THE ASS (L'EMMERDEUR)

Synopsis

A Pain in the Ass (L'Emmerdeur) was direct by Édouard Molinaro in 1973.

Based on a script was by Francis Verber, himself a filmmaker, the film features Lino Ventura (Ralf Milan), Jacques Brel (François Pignon), Caroline Cellier (Louise Pignon), Jean-Pierre Darras (Dr. Edgar Fuchs), Nino Castelnuovo (Bellhop), Angela Cardile (Pregnant woman), and Xavier Depraz (Louis Randoni).

After a failed attempt by a hitman at killing Louis Randoni (Xavier Depras), who is about to squeal to the police giving it details on mobster activity in France, a professional hit-man, Ralph Milan (Lino Ventura), from Italy is hired.

Milan rents a room at the Hôtel du Palais in Montpellier with the mission of killing Randoni. In the adjacent room, François Pignon tries to kill himself but fails. Heart-broken because his wife (Caroline Cellier) has left him for the famous psychiatrist, Dr. Fuchs (Jean-Pierre Darras). In order to avoid further complications and get his job done, Milan offers to help Pignon win his wife back. In the end Pignon chooses a friendship with Milan over the love for his wife.

Around and about the film

Édouard Molinaro, born on May 13, 1928, in Bordeaux, France, was a contemporary of the Nouvelle Vague, but not one of the group. Having directed more than thirty-five films, he attained world fame for his comedies. In retrospect, during a 2010 interview, Molinaro admitted that he was pigeon-holed for being a commercial burlesque filmmaker: "When you make a successful comedy that is all they expect from you. These films did not start with me; they were not the sort of things I wanted to do. I regret not having been more audacious in my choices. I often made films I consider 'films for provisional payments', because I had spouses and children to feed."[1]

Molinaro worked with comic Louis de Funès, *Oscar* (1967) and *Hibernatus* (1969), and with Ugo Tognazzi in the two super-hits, *La Cage aux folles* (1978) and *La Cage aux folles 2* (1980). Such comedies brought him international recognition which unfortunately overshadowed his more personal films, such as *L'Ironie du sort* (1974), with cult figure, Pierre Clémenti. Molinaro is harsh and unfair about his true artistic merit, and overly self-critical; some of his comedies are superb works which under the sheen of crass commercialism posit troubling insights on the individual and his/her place in society. His film *L'Emmerdeur* surpasses the remakes directed by Billy Wilder *(Buddy, Buddy)* and by Francis Veber (*L'Emmerdeur*), the original scriptwriter (proving that one might be the writer of a script but not necessarily its best interpreter). The distance that separates intent and execution disappears in the hands of an artist of great talent and vision. If one glances at a short list of films that were released in 1973, it is easy to understand why a comedy like *A Pain in the Ass* did not stand a chance to win the favors of critics.

Play it Again, Sam, by Herbert Ross.
Film d'amore e d'anarchia, by Lina Wertmüller.
Ludwig, by Luchino Visconti.
Le charme discret de la bourgeoisie, by Luis Buñuel.
Cries and Whispers, by Ingmar Bergman.
La grande bouffe, by Marco Ferreri.
Lucky Luciano, by Francesco Rosi.
Amarcord, by Federico Fellini.
La Société du spectacle, by Guy Debord.
American Graffiti, by George Lucas.
La nuit américaine, by François Truffaut.
La planète sauvage, by René Laloux.
The Exorcist, by William Friedkin.
La maman et la putain, by Jean Eustache.
Mean Streets, by Martin Scorsese.
The Sting, by George Roy Hill.
Serpico, by Sidney Lumet.
L'Invitation, by Claude Goretta.
Don't Look Now, by Nicolas Roeg.

This breath-taking list, which includes the epitome of filmmakers, makes little room for the intelligent parodies developed by Molinaro. Nevertheless, *A Pain in the Ass* stands out today as one of the fine films of that year. The one other comedy in the list, *Play it again, Sam,* introduced us to the film world of Woody Allen. Martin Scorsese initiated us to his nervous visit of *Italian-Americana.* Federico Fellini plunged deeper into the hidden recesses of his memory, as did George Lucas. Jean Eustache produced what many critics consider the swan song of la Nouvelle Vague. Nicolas Roeg, Sidney Lumet, William Friedkin, René Laroux, Guy Debord, Luis Buñuel, Claude Goretta, Marco Ferrari, Lina Wertmüller, Ingmar Bergman, Francesco Rosi, Luchino Visconti exposed with singularity the moral corruption of the post-war bourgeoisie.

The individual hero has been replaced by the collective voice, what Furio Scarpelli calls the "chorus-film".[2] Édouard Molinaro's *A Pain in the Ass* is the film adaptation by Francis Veber of a play he wrote called *Le Contrat* (1971). Of the five films, this film is the one that provides the least elements of the Italic experience. And yet, precisely because of this absence of overt Italian references, the wager seemed attractive. This scarcity, on the contrary, can welcome cultural parameters.

Francis Veber, born on 28 July 1937, in Neuilly-sur-Seine, France, can be considered one of the best comedy writers in the world today. Born of a Jewish father and an Armenian mother, he has been quoted as saying that "two genocides and two bloody walls of lamentations are enough to make me a comedy writer". His works deal primarily with the meeting of opposites which Veber arrives at by using the comedy-duo formula.

Retelling the narrative of a killer entangled with one who wants to be killed entails a reading far from being innocent. Impossible as it is to capture the numerous congruent narratives in the film we will address how the confrontation of the August and white clown, the agile versus the klutz, leads to the metaphorical. In other words, this film is more about cohabitation of cultures in France than about the mob or infidelity. This sort of B-film humor was so well received worldwide that the American Billy Wilder decided to do remake entitled *Buddy Buddy* (1981), which starred Jack Lemmon (Victor Clooney), Walter Matthau (Trabucco), Paula Prentiss (Celia) and Klaus Kinski (Dr. Zucherbrot).

Wilder's last film — launched with a more judicious and satisfactory title than the title used for the subtitled version of the Molinaro film, *A Pain in the Ass* — was as much a box-office flop as was the French remake, *L'Emmerdeur* (2008), by Francis Veber. Veber has become a film director in his own right, in particular after directing his own successful and excellent comedy, *Le dîner de cons* (1998).

The synopses of these three films sound dramatically different. In *Buddy Buddy*, hitman Trabucco (Walter Matthau) is hired to eliminate Gambola. He negotiates the price of his job, $10,000, and gets it. Victor Clooney (magisterially performed by Jack Lemmon), on the verge of committing suicide, is François Pignon.

Dr. Zuckerbrot (Klaus Kinski), a curiosity for the viewer, is the fake that Clooney accuses him to be. In Molinaro's *A Pain in the Ass*, Pierre Darras, as Dr. Fuchs, albeit an imposter, possesses a candor that appears rather authentic to the spectator. Regardless of the deceptive practices Pignon accuses him of, Darras' Fuchs (better wit in a name is hard to come by) is a real doctor, whereas Kinski's Zucherbrot is a quack through and through. The attire for both incarnations of the doctor shares nothing in common. Darras' Dr. Fuchs works in a controlled environment assisted by male and female nurses, while Kinski's American doctor comes off as the sex guru who is the leader of a sect. In Zucherbrot's clinic, men and women stroll naked for all to see.

Nevertheless, *Buddy Buddy* contains a number of excellent moments, one being Victor's phone call to his wife Celia, filmed in a long sequence shot, which reveals Lemmon at the height of his acting powers. Yet critics were not gentle toward Wilder's directorial performance. Roger Egbert wrote:

> This movie is appalling... *Buddy Buddy* is very bad. It is a comedy without any laughs. (And, yes, I mean literally that it contains no laughs.)... Can you imagine a film that co-stars Walter Matthau and Jack Lemmon and yet contains no charm, ebullience, wit, charisma – even friendliness?... *Buddy Buddy* is incompetent."[3]

Billy Wilder admitted that he should have used Clint Eastwood as the lead instead of comic Walter Matthau, whose physicality sobs awkwardly when compared to the agile Lemmon. Wilder, here, suggests the interesting idea that the use of two comics in a film end up negating one another. Wilder sadly conceded in an interview: "The best thing for me about *Buddy Buddy* was that not very many people saw it. It hurts to strike out on your last picture."[4]

Where *Buddy Buddy* fails is in its insistence on a nonsensical plot, *A Pain in the Ass* by Édouard Molinaro excels. The French director takes the spectator down the road where she can appreciate the friendship between two genuinely antithetical characters. In Wilder's B-film two comics meet, but no one believes in this meeting. Molinaro turns the B-movie into a masterpiece, in which two non-comedians fall into one another arms and light up the screen with on-going laughter.

> The comedy is excellent, with two actors in really good shape. The highlight is to see that Brel and Ventura are so different and share nothing in common. Each, in his own side, is not funny – one is serious and cold, the other is sad and a loser. But their combination is absolutely comical. (The way Brel calls Ventura "Monsieur Milan" is irresistible.)[5]

James Travers also praises the magical chemistry between Ventura and Brel:

> The popular Belgian singer Jacques Brel stars along side Lino Ventura — the great hard man of French cinema — in this unique, totally bizarre black comedy. The film was adapted from a popular stag play by Francis Veber and directed by Édouard Molinaro. The same director-writer team would achieve even greater success in 1978 with the almost legendary hit *La Cage aux folles*. *L'Emmerdeur* is a very different kind of film, eschewing face and "obvious" comic dialogue for underplayed deadpan humor in realistic settings — with a few brilliant visual gags thrown in along the way... The rapport between Ventura and Brel is perfect — their act resembling a surly panther whose sleep is being disturbed by a rather too playful lamb. As the film develops, there's a marvellous sense of growing tension, an expectation that Ventura will lose his cool at any moment and swat Brel dead with the mere flick of a wrist. The characters are well-developed (the script is one of Veber's best) and skilfully portrayed. It's impossible not to feel for either character, although our sympathies ultimately end up on the side of the beleaguered Ventura (the actor is really on top form here, showing the same unbeatable flair for black comedy that he has for straight dramatic roles).[6]

Lino Ventura (Angiolino Giuseppe Pasquale Ventura) was born in Parma, on 14 July 1919, and died on 22 October 1987. Lino and his mother left Italy in 1927, and moved to Paris, joining Lino's father who worked as a salesman. Ventura began as a professional middle-weight wrestler and won, in 1950, the European championship for Greco-Roman wrestling competition. Jacques Becker would give him his first break in 1953, by getting him to act beside Jean Gabin in *Touchez pas au grisbi*. Lino Ventura never gave up his Italian citizenship, which is quite remarkable since he was considered by many as one of the most foremost actors in France. As stony-faced Ralf Milan,

Ventura radiates, conceding only one smile in the entire 84 minutes and 30 seconds (and, then, only when under the influence of some drug).

Jacques Brel (Jacques Romain Georges Brel), born on 8 April 1928, in Schaerbeek, Brussels, Belgium, and died on 9 October 1978 in Bobigny, France, was a singer and composer who, though Flemish, worked primarily in French. Interestingly, he considered himself a Francophone Flemish artist — an interesting anti-nationalist oxymoron, if ever there was one! His singing career began in 1953 and ended on 17 May 1967.

In 1971, he directed his moving film *Franz* with singer Barbara in the lead role, unjustly disliked by film critics. He acted in Édouard Molinaro's film *Mon oncle Benjamin* in 1969 and, in 1972, in the hilarious *L'Aventure c'est l'aventure* by Claude Lelouch, beside Lino Ventura. *A Pain in the Ass* in 1973 would turn out to be his last film work.

Jacques Brel was the first actor to usher in the François Pignon character Francis Veber would eventually develop in subsequent films. Pignon was interpreted by Pierre Richard in *Les Compères* (1983) accompanied by Gérard Depardieu; played again by Pierre Richard in *Les Fugitifs* (1986), also with Gérard Depardieu (Veber directed the American remake, *Three Fugitives* (1989), with Nick Nolte and Martin Short. And then Pignon was memorably performed by Jacques Villeret in *Le Dîner des cons* (1998); this film became the awful American remake, starring Steve Carell — as a point of interest, Carell's paternal grandfather was Italian; his father, born with the surname "Caroselli", shortened it to "Carell", and Paul Rudd, called *Dinner for Schmucks* which was released in 2010.

Later, Pignon was magnificently incarnated by Daniel Auteuil in *Le Placard* (2001), and exemplified by Gad Elmaleh in *La Doublure* (2005). Most recently, Pignon was catastrophically played by Patrick Timsit in Veber's remake of *L'Emmerdeur* (2008).

Who is François Pignon? Every actor who played Pignon brought an original reading of the role, reinventing Francis Pignon, each with his own particular colors and spices, yet remained faithful to that character's principal trait: Pignon's innocence and generosity. Never a mean spirit, Pignon inevitably falls into the well-organized traps set up by his "enemies" who for some miraculous reason in the end turns out a winner to everyone's astonishment.

> Nevertheless, it would be an exaggeration to speak only of a single character, because incarnated by many actors who expressed themselves differently through physically and verbally.[7]

Jacques Brel's personification of Pignon is quite unique when compared to

Pignon's ulterior incarnations. The script, though, not purposely written for Brel — the stage play predates the script — it could very well have been "written" for him. We get this strange feeling that Molinaro's camera not only films Pignon the character, but Brel playing Pignon.

At the age of eighty-two, Molinaro in a 2010 interview admitted that it was with Jacques Brel that he most enjoyed his work:

> ...Jacques Brel. He was in film my warmest experience. I was able to witness him at work, and he was curious about directing. We were talking all the time. He was genuinely faithful, extraordinary honest when dealing with people. He is a person still very present in my heart; there is not a day I do not think of him.[8]

This double presence (the character and the actor playing the character) extends to Brel playing against Ventura, who also is the exemplar of the actor playing a role.

A cascade of perceptions results: simultaneously, the spectator is aware of the actor being aware of their real person playing a fictional role against another real person playing a fictional role. This multi-levelled complicity is what produces laughter.

Pignon develops an intimate relationship with Milan that is detrimental to the film's success. The not-so-subtle expression of friendship turns into a cultural motive; why else would Pignon abandon the woman for whom he was about to commit suicide and follow Ventura all the way to prison? Perhaps unconsciously, perhaps consciously, this male-male infatuation may be seen as a foreshadowing of *Le Placard*, where Daniel Auteuil's Pignon unwillingly pushes Gérard Depardieu's Santini to have a sexual breakdown.

We are permitted to speculate whether or not the fact that Brel's Pignon and Ventura's Milan end up living together in prison has something to do with the creation of homosexual relationship between Depardieu's Santini and Auteuil's Pignon.

In *Le Placard*, Veber confronts homosexuality candidly, unabashedly. In Molinaro's *A Pain in the Ass*, no matter how much love François Pignon is willing to invest in Ralf Milan, male affection does not intentionally overflow into homosexuality. Such might be the outcome, but it is not *a priori*. Depardieu's Santini does fall in love with Auteuil's Pignon.

Brel's Pignon does not fall in love with Milan sexually; Pignon is entirely smitten by Milan, indeed, but it is there, at that point on contention, that the film fades out. What comes after is speculation, and in that speculation the metaphor surges.

Women stand at the margins in *L'Emmerdeur*, even when accountable for the pleasure and pain of men. Randino's wife gets up, goes to the window, throws the concierge the keys for the car that will explode and slips back to sleep beside her husband; two other women (one at the airport, seen from the back; the other who is putting lipstick), behind counters, hand Milan envelopes to assist him in his mission; Louise leaves her husband François Pignon who then fails at killing himself. In the end, like most women in Veber's script, they lose out to men altogether.

In Molinaro's film, Louise is distant, riding on a horse or driving a Jeep, a shadow that nourishes Pignon's obsession. Apparently bad sex pushed Louise to choose Dr. Edgar Fuchs, who gladly offers this information to Pignon in syntagma 61. Dr. Fuchs: the iconic playfully transparent surname, a proper noun that can converted into a verb, doesn't the name say it all? Sadly in both remakes the writers changed the bold surname for the more fanciful German name Dr. Hugo Zuckerbrot (in Wilder's film, which translates into "sugarloaf") and for the tamer Dr. Edgar Wolf (in Veber's film — an eager wolf?). Coming out of a private screening of *Buddy Buddy*, Molinaro admits his dismay:

> While I ran away from the vaudeville by shooting Veber's play as a thriller, Wilder preferred to re-stage the play. Jack Lemmon and Walter Matthau seem to be enjoying themselves, but no one else is (*Intérieur*, 206)

The physical attraction of male contraries, Brel and Ventura, gives rise to a comedy duo that is more similar to Stan Laurel and Oliver Hardy, Abbott and Costello, Dean Martin and Jerry Lewis than to the male relationships exposed in the art-house films of Paul Morrissey, *Flesh* (1968), *Trash* (1970) and *Heat* (1972). Milan, the wise guy, pitted against Brel, the goof, bounce against one another and ignite an interplay of serious and unorthodox confrontations that instantaneously spark off laughter. This "odd couple", these incongruous men, killer and shirt salesman, cannot but make the spectators smile. (Let us add that, off the set, Brel and Ventura were friends.)

Instead of the usual female counterpart, the comic foil in *A Pain in the Ass* is sustained by the Bellhop, played by Nino Castelnuovo, who made a name for himself as the young lover drafted by the army in Jacques Demy's *Les Parapluies de Cherbourg* (1964). At the 80-minute mark (syntagma 95), it is the bellboy, and not Milan, who will baptize Pignon "a pain in the ass" ("un emmerdeur") in front of Louise, Pignon's wife.

Molinaro's film is not about individuals, but about something in between and beyond individuals. It is this complex impetus that Francis Veber (as a filmmaker) and Billy Wilder were unable to access to the fullest. Molinaro subtly prods the world of sameness and otherness. By hiring two "foreign" actors (one Italian, the other Belgian) he fosters a reading of events that Jack Lemmon and Walter Matthau, and Patrick Timsit and Richard Berry, could never tap into, at least not in the way that their directors, Billy Wilder and Francis Veber, had conducted them. This script is not about killing Randoni, but about two cultures meeting, face to face, on equal standing.

Billy Wilder never depicts the culture of his characters; if he "fails" in correlating the contentious forces in the script (and Molinaro's film), it is because he chose to remain faithful to the pre-filmic script instead of reading the script that emerged from the Molinaro film. If anything, Molinaro proves that he is a director to contend with, because he knows that a script is a tool that must be scraped once the director begins to shoot. Wilder did not take his eyes off of the written word; he directed words, and not actors. Molinaro multiplied his comedic duo by two: the persons as actors, and the actors as fiction-simulation. The vanishing points generated are multiform, baroque in the true sense of the term: an irregular formed pearl reflected light in all directions.

Francis Veber's enterprise was, to put it bluntly, irresponsible, incomprehensible; no wonder critics panned the film immediately upon its arrival in theaters. The reviewer at *Le Parisien* is ruthless: "L'un des plus gros ratages au cinéma français de ces dix dernières années."[9] Another critic, Arnaud Mangin, pitilessly attacks the project for being outright "dishonest":

> It's as if its author did not accept the idea that another filmmaker could give life to fetish characters... *L'Emmerdeur 2008* is above all the story of a man, a little on the decline, who is received less and less well by the public and critics, who is striving to tell the same stories... a man who understood the financial potential of a franchise and a story like *L'Emmerdeur*, a man who unwittingly unpacks the full extent of a misplaced ego with the pretension to correct what he did not like in the 1973 film... In the end, he brings nothing at all.[10]

Martin Gignac sums it all in a short sentence: "87 minutes of stupid and useless fantasies where the gag repeats itself tirelessly."[11] Francis Veber himself will finally concede that his remake was an incredible gaffe:

> I was attacked by critics as if I had performed a burial desecration, as if I had wanted to humiliate Lino Ventura and Jacques Brel, the two actors

of the original film, by asking Richard Berry and Patrick Timsit to resume their roles. People stopped judging the film and focused on my filmic approach. I blame myself for it, because it was a mistake on my part [to have wanted to do a remake]..[12]

After *Le Placard*, Veber could have gone all the way, and could have histrionically exacerbated the odd couple by inviting Pignon and Milan to live together as lovers. One can question the motives that would encourage the director to propel the story in that ostentatious conclusion, yet, in refusing to do so, he (and unfortunately he did) thrust himself into the extreme opposite direction, that is, in the bleak corners of the homophobic. The dark beauty of Molinaro's film is that, in the end, homosexuality remains, as small as it might be, a real possibility; the spectator laughs, but he is not sure what he is laughing about (or at). Perhaps more than sexualness (and not sexuality), the original *L'Emmerdeur* is, as we shall see, mostly about embracing difference, and for this precise reason, the original version has aged marvellously well.

Structure of the film

The entire plot, except for the final scene, unfolds in a single day. The eight mega-syntagmas in *A Pain in the Ass*, of various lengths, offer a clear overall view of its main storyline. Though initially set in the Hôtel du Palais, the film depicts movable settings — the car scenes, highways, rest-stop, clinic, countryside — that carry the spectator far from the fixed theatrical stage.

> Chapter 1. Louis Randoni. 0:00-4:31
> Chapter 2. Ralf Milan. 4:32-10:02
> Chapter 3. François Pignon. 10:03-13:36
> Chapter 4. The Hotel. 13:46-28:46
> Chapter 5: The Highway. 28:47-48:23
> Chapter 6: Mistaken Identity. 48:24-62:12
> Chapter 7: Dr. Edgar Fuchs. 62:13-70:46
> Chapter 8: Friendship. 70:47-84:30

By dividing the film according to Syd Field's paradigm, we get four distinct acts:

Act One:
Chapter 1. Louis Randoni (0:00-4:31); Chapter 2. Ralf Milan: 4:32-10:02; Chapter 3. François Pignon. 10:03-13:36; Chapter 4. The Hotel. 13:46-28:46. The main characters and their motives established, the story brings the spectator to the first Turning Point — Pignon's failed suicide, which forces Ralf Milan to take care of Pignon.

Act Two:
Chapter 5: The Highway. 28:47-48:23 and Chapter 6: Mistaken Identity. 48:24-62:12. Suddenly, we embark on a mixture of a road movie and a tale of mistaken identity. What seemed so certain (a. Milan's mission, b. Pignon's unrequited love become suicide) fizzles out and a switch in identity ensues whereby Pignon becomes Milan, and Milan becomes Pignon.

Act Three:
Chapter 7: Dr. Fuchs. 62:13-70:46, with the mid-point being the moment Milan and Pignon's true identities are revealed, not to the spectator who knows who is who, but to Dr. Fuchs who finds out which man is the true competitor, and the serious contender.

Act Four:
the longest mega-syntagma of the film, Chapter 8: Friendship. 70:47-84:30. All narrative threads converge to Milan's mission, but "thanks" to Pignon's intervention and what estimably should have ended in murder ends in friendship. There is a third Turning Point: Pignon finds Milan's rifle. The rifle shots by Pignon unexpectedly topples the story into a semi-chase with the police chasing the two suspects.

By splitting up the film into syntagmas, we notice a formal pattern in the manner the filmmaker structured his adaptation of the play. Édouard Molinaro approaches his material with clockwork methodology. Four major syntagmatic types seem to have been used: Scene (42); Autonomous shot (sequence shot as well as inserts, mostly explanatory) (33); 3. Sequence (20); 4. Alternate syntagma (7).

Though the scene seems to be the prevalent form adopted by Molinaro, he, unlike Brusati, prefers the sequence shot and sequence filmed rapidly, mostly via Raoul Coutard's hand-held camera (even the scene per se seems to be assembled around one single long take). The alternate syntagma, too, is usually composed of one sequence shot interjected with inserts; however, in these six cases the inserts work more like a separate scene than as a foil to the main action. Despite the fact that the script is an adaptation of a play, Molinaro refuses to use the fixed theatrical setting where actors can develop their characters. We could consider this film a "road movie". Compare this film to Wim Wenders' great *Kings of the Road (Im Lauf der Zeit:* "in the course of time", 1976) and the viewer will find syntactical and narrative similarities.

Instead of filming through various angles a fixed action, Molinaro uses the versatile sequence to bring us into the reality of live action. There is a paradox here, because though the scene might seem more "real", this realness is achieved through artificial means; whereas the sequence is more real per se, and more authentic than the fixed and "assembled" scene; time shown on screen corresponds to the time unfolding in real time. Pasolini says:

> Time in the sequence, understood as a schematic and primordial element of cinema — that is, as an infinite subject — is the present. Cinema, therefore, "reproduces the present" (*Emprisimo,* 237).

The actor, forced to walk for some time in front of the camera, is split in two: on the one hand, we have the character as character; and on the other hand, we have the actor playing the character. This double unfolding of reality and fiction in real time positions the spectator in a sort of voyeur's position, eyeing past the storyline and into the heart of the man and woman playing the role. It is second best thing to being in a theater looking at the play on stage with live actors. Brusati used a similar technique with Nino Manfredi. In a sense, Molinaro can be said to be using the techniques of cinéma vérité and cinéma direct and applying them to film fiction, regardless of the fact that everything in this narrative space is invented. He shot the handheld footage with an Arriflex BL.

Having Jacques Brel act was a feat, especially as a jester to a solemn Ventura. Claude Lelouch had already combined Ventura *le Rital* (French term for the Italian) and Brel in the hilarious *L'aventure c'est l'aventure* (1972) with surprising results. Who could imagine the sombre-spirited Brel of his personal musical repertoire performing a white clown? Strangely, Brel remains Brel on screen. In scene 14, Molinaro, acting as the bar owner, is holding a record by Jacques Brel. The audience in the know plunges into a world of intimacy and friendliness; this collective communication is special, and assures the film's popularity with the general public.

The soundtrack as well respects the pattern of realism. Most of the sounds are justified, authentic, synchronic, that is faithful to the sound sources seen on screen (even the radio announcer finds its source on camera: the portable radio and the car radio), if not "reproduced" during the shooting, "rendered" faithfully by the sound editor. Only once does Molinaro tamper with the soundtrack and that is when the shutter breaks in Milan's room (syntagma 32). In the other versions of the film, the rumble of a passing airplane is responsible for the blinds to roll down; in Molinaro's film though we hear the sound of an airplane, no airplane is ever shown on screen. What we have is a babel of curious sounds that prompt the unrolling of the blind shutter. Excluding this singular act of sound make-up, the elements on the track are rendered as truthfully as possible.

In his book, *L'audio-vision,* Michel Chion distinguishes "reproduced" sounds from those "rendered" later in a studio; "real" sounds rarely sound authentic during a live take; they must be enhanced and refurbished so as to give the spectator the appearance of truthfulness (Audio-vision 94). The few instances of "acousmatic"[13] sounds (what is heard without its source being shown) revolve mostly around the musical leitmotiv, always off screen, identified to either Ralf Milan (a detuned piano piece) or François Pignon (a nostalgic accordion-driven instrumental), which Molinaro introduces at first "redundantly" (on images of the character linked to the melody) and later in off.

Chapter 1: Louis Randoni
0:00-4:31

1. Autonomous shot. Ext. Street: No Parking.
0-1=0. 0:00-0:41
2. Alternating syntagma. Int/Ext. House-Garage.
1-2=0. 0:42-2:57
3. Autonomous shot. Int. Felix's Apartment.
2-3=0. 2:58-4:31

The chapter (composed of one mega-sequence) begins with a 41 second sequence shot with a zoom-out of a *No Parking* sign (which echoes the later *Do Not Disturb* signs) and zoom-in on a home, where a man, early in the morning, is having trouble with the ceiling light, and ends with second long sequence shot of Felix, the hired hitman, walking into his apartment, turning on the radio, shaving, and discovering that he did not kill the right man. In between an extended scene which alternates between the neighbor being upset about Randoni's car parked in front of his garage door and Randoni and his wife fast asleep in their apartment. This alternating syntagma ends on Randoni's expression when he realizes that he could have been the one, and not their concierge, blown up with his booby-trapped car.

Chapter 2: Ralf Milan
4:32-10:02

4. Autonomous shot. Ext. Airport: Airplanes.
3-4=0. 4:32-4:51
5. Sequence. Int. Airport: Milan's Arrival.
4-5=0. 4:52-6:26
6. Scene. Int. Office: Secretary hands note with instructions.
5-6=0. 6:27-7:00
7. Scene. Ext. Car: Reading and burning of instructions.
6-7=0. 7:01-7:53
8. Autonomous. Shot. Ext. Street: Felix getting shot.
7-8=0. 7:54-8:31
9. Scene. Ext. Construction site: Milan leaving site: Gaze.
8-9=0. 8:32-9:12
10. Scene. Int. Airport: Airplane.
9-10. 9:13-9:48
11. Sequence. Ext. Milan on Highway.
10-11=0. 9:49-10:02.

The second chapter, dedicated to our solemn, sullen protagonist, Ralf Milan, presents itself in three mega-sequences: the first, Ralf Milan's arrival at the airport; driving a rented BMW to an fixed address; picking up his assignment from a receptionist (putting on lipstick); his killing of Felix; the second, the arrival of Louis Randoni in Montpellier; the third, Milan driving down to Montpellier. The scenes herein are short, the camera handheld, the off-beat piano march supposed to revive suspense is tagged on Milan as a leitmotiv.

What is in a name? Barely ten minutes into the film and the spectators are given two foreign sounding names: Randoni and Milan (though this name will be pronounced later, yet Ventura's ethnicity is apparent). A coincidence, perhaps, yet there is the indication sign "foreigner" that pops up into the spectator's mind. Randoni might be Italian or Corsican; it is clearly Italic. Milan sends us, as we will be told later on, to the northern city in Italy. We are dealing with foreigners; far from the French baguette and cheese stereotypical images of Parisian men with berets.

Chapter 3: François Pignon
10:03-14:05

12. Sequence. Ext. Pignon on Highway.
11-12=0. 10:03-10:34
13. Alternate syntagma. Ext. Highway: Hitchhiker in rain.
12-13=0. 10:35-11:31
14. Scene. Int. Rest-Stop: Parked car Incident.
13-14=0. 11:32-12:24
15. Scene. Int. Pignon and Hitchhiker conversation.
14-15=0. 12:25-13:00
16. Autonomous shot. Ext. Rest-Stop: Milan's departure.
15-16=0. 13:01-13:16
17. Scene. Ext. Hôtel du Palais: Pignon and Tourist.
16-17=montage with effect. 13:17-13:45
18. Autonomous shot. Int. Hotel-Lobby: Journalists.
17-18=0. 13:46-13:51
19. Autonomous shot. Int. Hotel-Lobby: Pignon signs in.
18-19=0. 13:52-14:05

In the form of mega-alternating syntagma, this chapter is made up of two mega-sequences. We cut from the dour face of Milan driving his car to smile-smeared Pignon in his car listening to a joyous accordion melody; the entire package reminding us of monsieur Hulot and his fancy two-seater in *Les Vacances de monsieur Hulot* (1953), by Jacques Tati, and, if I may, Hrundi V. Bakshi in his sports car in *The Party* (1968) by Blake Edwards, and to press the point somewhat, Mr. Bean (Rowman Atkinson) in his Mini in *Mr. Bean's Holiday* (2007) – filled with references to Tati's film — by Steve Bendelack. Except for a couple of inserts, the major part of these scenes is dedicated to Pignon. Defective windshield wipers squeak like voices from another world. Pignon offers a lift to a tourist hitchhiking in the rain. Pignon is French, the tourist an American. Upon arriving at destination, the American tourist thanks Pignon who walks into the hotel lobby, presents himself as "monsieur Pignon" (sounding strangely like "monsieur Hulot").

Chapter 4: The Hotel
14:06-28:46

20. Autonomous shot. Int. Pignon's Room-Bellhop-phone call. 19-20:0. 14:06-15:24
21. Autonomous shot. Ext. Hotel Street: Milan's Arrival. 20-21=0. 15:25-15:51
22. Scene. Int. Hotel-Lobby: Milan signs in. 21-22=0. 15:52-16:36
23. Scene. Int. Milan's Room: Bellhop. 22-23=montage with effect. 16:37-16:59
24. Autonomous shot. Int. Hotel Corridor: Neighbors. 23-24=0. 17:00-17:07
25. Alternate syntagma. Int. Pignon/Milan's Rooms. 24-25=0. 17:08-18:08
26. Alternate syntagma. Int. Milan/Police on street. 25-26=0. 18:09-18:57
27. Scene. Int. Milan's Room: Map-Roof. 26-27=0. 18:58-19:49
28. Scene. Int. Pignon's Room: Mirrors. 27-28=0. 19:50-20:24
29. Autonomous shot. Int. Milan's Room: Rifle Suitcase. 28-29=0. 20:25-20:40
30. Scene. Int. Pignon's Washroom: Preparing for suicide. 29-30=0. 20:41-21:12
31. Autonomous shot. Int. Milan's Shutter breaks. 30-31=0. 21:13-21:57
32. Autonomous shot. Int. Shutter. 31-32-31=0
33. Autonomous shot. Int. Hotel-Lobby: Manager. 33-31-33=0
34. Scene. Int. Pignon's Suicide. 33-34=0. 21:58-23:07
35. Sequence. Int. Rooms: Milan/Bellhop/Pignon in bathtub. 34-35=0. 23:08-26:16
36. Autonomous shot. Int. Pignon's Room: Bellhop/Milan. 28:17-28:46

Presented again as a continuous mega-alternating syntagma, this chapter introduces the three main characters of the film: Pignon, Milan, the bellhop.

The Hotel manager — who seems to be in the know of the plan; in the Veber version this is clearly the case, as if expecting Milan. Milan room's room is adjacent to Pignon's room. Simultaneously both Milan and Pignon hang a *Do Not Disturb* sign on their doorknobs. Each man with his musical leitmotiv music, each busy with his task, grisly similar in a way: Milan about to kill Randoni at two o'clock; Pignon to kill himself. Milan studies the courthouse from his window, while Pignon looks at himself in the mirrors. In the washroom, as he is about to hang himself, Pignon turns over mirror flaps over. He cannot bare to watch himself die. Pignon as self and as the other: mirrors prevent Pignon from taking that final step which he will fail to accomplish. The Turning Point is Pignon's failed suicide (scene 34). Because of Pignon's blunder, Milan's plans will be fall apart.

Most of the shots are handheld, the editing is rapid; scenes advance without visual or aural punctuation. Like with *Pane e cioccolata*, there is not a single fade out or dissolve.

Chapter 5: The Highway
28:47-48:23

37. Alternate Syntagma. Int. Milan's Room/Police on street. 36-37=0. 28:47-29:45
38. Scene. Int. Pignon's Room/Milan: Phone. 37-38=0. 29:46-30:51
39. Autonomous shot. Insert of Dr. Fuchs on phone. 38-39-38=0
40. Sequence. Int. Rooms: Milan/Bellhop/Pignon on toilet bowl. 39-40=0. 30:52-32:56
41. Scene. Int. Pignon's Toilet: Bellhop wiping the floor. 40-41=0. 32:57-33:31
42. Scene. Int. Milan's Room: Suitcase/Bellhop/Pignon Note. 41-42=0. 33:32-35:55
43. Sequence. Int. Hotel Corridor: Milan and Pignon. 42-43=0. 35:56-36:05
44. Sequence. Int. Hotel Elevator: Milan and Pignon, Introductions. 43-44=0. 36:06-36:42
45. Sequence. Int/Ext. Hotel Street: Wrong car skit. 44-45=0. 36:43-39:31

46. Sequence. Ext. Highway: Shirt business, fidelity and radio. 45-46=0. 39:32-41:49
47. Scene. Ext. Highway: Pignon and Milan: photographs, accident. 46-47=0. 41:50-42:29
48. Sequence. Ext. Car: pregnant woman, police escort, kicking Pignon out. 47-48=0. 42:30-44:06
49. Autonomous shot. Ext. Pignon alone hitchhiking. 48-49=0. 44:07-44:15
50. Scene. Ext. Pignon in truck. 49-50=0. 44:16-44:40
51. Scene. Ext. Milan outside hospital. 50-51=0. 44:41-45:10
52. Sequence. Ext. Horse Park: Pignon and Louise on a horse. 51-52=0. 45:11-47:43
53. Sequence. Ext. Milan on highway, police block. 52-53=0. 47:44-48:23
54. Autonomous shot a, b, c. Insert of car clock, police patrol 54-53-54

This chapter contains various mega-sequences. We counted nine of them: syntagmas 37; 38-41; 42-44; 45; 46-48; 49-50; 51; 52; 53. After Pignon's botched suicide attempt, Milan offers to drive Pignon to his wife. In the elevator sequence shot 44, formal presentations are made. Up till this point only the audience knows the real identity of both these men, strangers to one another. "François Pignon." "Milan, comme la ville" ("Milan, like the city"). A Frenchman faces an Italian; this oddest of couples share a handshake. Pignon, which means a gable, a gear wheel, a cog, to be well-established, expresses his gratitude:

"Vous êtes très gentil avec moi... J'ai la chance d'être tombé sur vous."
["It's kind of you to help me. I'm lucky I bumped into you."]

This chapter offers some of the finest gags in the entire film. Sequence 45 — starting from outside the hotel up to Milan's car, again shot with a handheld camera, Pignon and Milan try to open the trunk of what turns out to be a stranger's car — initiates what could be considered a double-act (comedy duo). Sequence 46: The radio jingle is tagged on to Randoni, the same way the harpsichord march is linked to Milan, and the accordion melody to Pignon: each person is allotted his bit of identity music. The film's entire plot is conditioned by time: the booby-trap blew up early in the morning; at two,

Randoni will appear in court. Time is of the essence. The Italian element makes itself felt as well in this chapter. First, in the elevator (Milan's name), and then on the highway (scene 47) when Milan, grabbing the collar of the excited Italian father-to-be, whispers words in Italian. Police on motor-bicycles passing by oblige in accompanying everyone in Milan's car, bouncing to the screams of the mother-to-be.

Pignon refuses to be quiet: "Fate chose you to help bring one more little life into the world." The sentence, directed to Milan, in reference to the child to be born, can very well be aimed at Pignon and Milan. Are they not waiting to be born? Minutes later, Milan and Pignon have their first couple's quarrel, Milan throwing Pignon out of his vehicle. In the extended sequence 52, made up of various interlinking scenes: Pignon himself has become a hitchhiker, finds a ride in a truck, is friendly with the driver, and when he finally meets up with his wife Louise, he understands that Louise has no desire whatsoever to get back with her husband, and this in spite of Pignon's continuous emotional blackmail (all underscored by the accordion melody).

The urgency is comical. The chapter ends a prolonged sequence with Milan driving back to the hotel. Molinaro seems to have a predilection for ending his sequences with a short scene: here, Milan's speeding car screeches to a halt; sequence 52 ends with the scene between Louise and Pignon; sequence 45 leads, after the car gag, to Pignon and Milan quarrelling. Not true episodes, these brief moments move from one location to another and form, nonetheless, a single temporal unit without obvious punctuation.

Chapter 6: Mistaken Identity
48:24-62:12

55. Scene. Int. Hotel Staircase with Bellhop.
54-55=montage with effect. 48:24-49:03
56. Autonomous shot. Int. Milan in hotel Corridor to room
54. 55-56=0. 49:04-49:12
57. Sequence. Int. Milan's Room/Pignon/Windowsill/Lovers' Room. 56-57=0. 49:13-52:55
58. Sequence. Int. Hotel Stairway: Police, Bellhop, Dr. Fuchs.
57-58=0. 52:56-53:07
59. Autonomous shot. Int. Hotel Corridor: Milan and Pignon.
58-59=0. 53:08-53:43

60. Autonomous shot. Int. Hotel Stairway: Police, Bellhop, Dr. Fuchs. 59-60=0. 53:44-53:55
61. Autonomous shot. Int. Elevator: Bellop and Dr. Fuchs. 60-61=0. 53:56-54:09
62. Scene. Int. Milan's Room: Pignon/Dr. Fuchs. 61-62=0. 54:10-56:16
63. Autonomous shot. Int. Hotel Corridor: Pignon and Dr. Fuchs. 62-63=0. 56:12-56:40
64. Scene. Int. Milan's Room: Pignon and Milan with tranquilizer. 63-64=0. 56:41.-58:16
65. Autonomous shot. Int. Elevator: Pignon and Milan. 64-65=0. 58:17-58:28
66. Scene. Int. Hotel Stairway. 65-66=0. 58:29-58:39
67. Sequence. Ext/Int. Car: Pignon driving Milan to Dr. Fuchs. 66-67=0. 58:40-59:36
68. Scene. Ext. Car: Red light. Police stops Pignon. 67-68=0. 59:37-60:68
69. Sequence. Ext. A groggy Milan on a street. 68-69=0. 60:19-60:47
70. Sequence. Ext. Car: Pignon and Milan back in the car. 69-70=0. 60:48-61:41
71. Autonomous shot. Ext. Car stalled on highway: Pignon and Milan walk. 70-71=0. 61:47-62:12

Five mega-sequences make up this chapter: syntagmas 55-56; 57; 58-63; 64-66; 67-71. Milan returns to his hotel room in a hurry. Time has been wasted. But Pignon will not stop pestering Milan, and eventually slips off the windowsill, his legs hanging in the void.

In wanting to help him, Milan himself falls off the balcony, when the shutter drops on his hands. Milan breaks into the window of the room below where a couple is making love (an elderly gentleman and a younger woman): the only direct allusion to sex in the entire movie. Dr. Fuchs appears and, mistaking Milan for Pignon, injects a tranquilizer into Milan's arm. "Suicide is self-directed aggression…" From Dr. Fuchs the real Pignon learns that his wife Louise "was bored to death" in her marriage to Pignon.

Sprawled on the bed, Milan, groggy, sedated, smiles for the first and only time in the entire film. He orders that he be brought to Dr. Fuchs for an antidote. It is 1h30, and he has only one half an hour to regain his consciousness. In the car Pignon unrolls a monologue on friendship: "I like talking to you…

We could be real friends." These words set in motion a new emotion in Pignon, and a new stimulus in the narrative.

Chapter 7: Dr. Fuchs
62:13-70:46

 72. Scene. Int. Dr. Fuchs's Office: female patient/ Milan aggressive. 71-72=0. 62:13-63:33
 73. Scene. Ext. Clinic: Bouncers get thrown out. 72-73=0. 63:34-63:45
 74. Scene. Ext. Louise in a jeep/Pignon/ Dr. Fuchs: Identity revealed. 73-74=0. 63:45-64:59
 75. Sequence. Int. Clinic: Milan in a straight jacket/all. 74-75=0. 65:00-66:59
 76. Scene. Int. Dr. Fuchs's Office: Milan/all/pills. 75-76=0. 67:00-68:35
 77. Scene. Ext. Road: Milan and American tourist. 76-77=0. 68:36-69:44
 78. Sequence. Ext. Race Car/Tourist vanishes. 77-78=0. 69:45-70:46

This chapter is basically made of two mega-sequences: syntagmas 72-76; and 77-78. A bored Dr. Fuchs glimpses at his watch as female patient, lying on a couch, describes a dream: "They have no sex organs. Just big red hands covered with hair."

Milan breaks into the office and orders the doctor to "straighten him out". Louise and Pignon meet at the clinic, and the real identities of Milan and Pignon are revealed. Not amused, Milan has been tied up in a chair and in a straight jacket. Milan commands he be given amphetamines. When a frustrated Dr. Fuchs strikes Louise, Pignon jumps to her rescue. During the skirmish Pignon inquires about Milan's whereabouts.

A staggering Milan is driving on the highway. Because so much of its plot revolves around cars and highways, the "road movie" code re-asserts itself. In truth, this supra-code gathers numerous codes: the narrative code, the symbolic code, the visual code, the montage code, the semantic code, and compositional code. This travelling to and fro exemplifies the journey to self-discovery. Nothing is fixed, even the clear-cut scene begs to belong to a larger unit, the non-stop sequence where symbols coalesce allegorically into a sort of fable.

Though Milan might not undergo a major change by the end of the trip, François Pignon certainly does. The splitting off is external more than internal, the objects of desire change but not the subjects who keep coming back to the point of departure. This chapter ends with a magical moment, one that resembles the magic disappearance of the mini-pot ball in *Raging Bull*.

A number of gags follow. Unable to find a ride, Milan positions himself in the middle of the road and forces the upcoming car to a complete stop. He slides money under the windshield wiper and orders the driver to get to the Hôtel du Palais in five minutes. The irony is that this driver is a rally driver, and does get Milan to his room on time.

If this were not enough of a comic episode, the next scenette includes the American tourist who decides to imitate Milan. He too stations himself in the middle of the highway but regrettably the upcoming car does not stop. The driver rushes out of his car, looking for the victim's body but it is nowhere to be found. Comes the twist to the gag.

Up in the treetops, there is the tourist's backpack tangling on a branch. And where's the tourist? He is nowhere to be found. His situation, precarious from the start, was always that of the outsider. He resembles the messenger who never reaches his destination. Though only a tourist, he embodies the perfect metaphor of the ethnic who is neither here, nor there, always elsewhere.

Chapter 8: Friendship
70:47-84:30

79. Sequence. Int. Police Station: police and Randoni. 78-79=0. 70:47-71:13
80. Autonomous shot. Ext. Hotel Street: Milan in race car arrives. 79-80=0. 71:14-71:33
81. Autonomous shot. Int. Hotel Corridor: Milan. 80-81=0. 71:34-71:38
82. Scene. Int. Milan's Room: Milan prepares his rifle. 81-82=0. 71:39-72:10
83. Autonomous shot. Ext. Street: Pignon arrives. 82-83=0. 72:11-72:21
84. Alternate syntagma. Int. Hotel Rooms: Pignon/Milan. 83-84=montage with effect. 72:22-73:24
85. Autonomous shot. Ext. Street: Police inspector. 84-85=0. 73:25-73:36

86. Scene. Int. Pignon's Room: Milan/Pignon/Bellhop/Inspector. 85-86=0. 73:37-75:00
87. Scene. Int. Hotel Corridor: Milan and Inspector speak. 86-87=0. 75:01-75:35
88. Scene. Int. Rooms: Pignon with shirts enters Milan's room. 87-88=0. 75:36-75:53
89. Autonomous shot. Int. Corridor: Milan hits Inspector. 88-89=0. 75:54-76:11
90. Scene. Int. Milan's Room: Pignon with rifle, police shoot Milan/Louise. 89-90=0. 76:12-79:00
91. Autonomous shot a, b. Inserts: Int. Corridor. Louise at the door.
92. Autonomous shot. Inserts: Ext. Street: Randoni arrives.
93. Autonomous shot. Int. Hotel Corridor. Police breaks out of cupboard. 92-93=0. 79:01-79:03
94. Alternate syntagma. Int. Milan's Room/Police firing gun shots. 93-94=0. 79:04-79:50
95. Scene. Int. Hotel-Lobby: Bellhop/Louise/Police. 94-95=0. 79:51-80:00
96. Scene. Ext. Roof: Milan and Pignon run away. 95-96=0. 80:01-80:12
97. Scene. Ext. Street: Dr. Fuchs in car. 96-97=0. 80:13-80:29
98. Scene. Ext. Roof: Milan and Pignon escaping, Milan drops his gun. 97-98=0. 80:30-80:44
99. Scene. Ext. Street: Dr. Fuchs picks up Milan's gun/police. 98-99=0. 80:45-80:57
100. Scene. Ext. Roof: Milan and Pignon. 99-100=0. 80:58-81:40
101. Sequence. Int/Ext. House: Stairways: Milan and Pignon on road. 100-101=0. 81:41-81:83:13
102. Scene. Ext. Prison. 101-102=montage with effect. 83:14-84:30

This final chapter consists of five mega-sequences: syntagmas 79-84; 85-89; 90-95; 96-101; 102. The denouement is when all the narrative threads roll out to the end. This mega-syntagma has the form of one long sequence. A clock in front of the courthouse reads five to two. Randoni, in shirt sleeves, smokes a cigarette, is led out.

Accompanied by his theme melody, Milan rushes into his room. Time is running out. He has just five minutes left. Pignon, in his room, converses with Milan from behind the door. "I think it's going to work out with my wife... What's your neck size?" Pignon wants to offer Milan a shirt. Milan stumps into Pignon's room, in Milan's hand the curtain chain with which he would like to strangle Pignon, who innocently queries Milan about his neck size — a fine subtle gag. Milan is willing to facilitate Pignon's suicide: funny.

A police inspector knocks at the door, ordering to see identification papers, and seconds later, is dragged through the corridor by Milan, who drops deadweight body into a cupboard. When Milan returns to his room, he notices Pignon with the shotgun in his hands. Milan relates his situation to Pignon:

> "I work for people who don't fool around. If I fail, they'll find me and kill me."

A clumsy Pignon accidentally pulls on the trigger which kindles a rampage of gun shots from the police down below. Milan is wounded at the shoulder. "Monsieur Milan" becomes the leitmotiv on Pignon's lips, as both fugitives run over rooftops, and down to the street.

In the lobby, the bellhop complains to Louise about her husband being "a royal pain in the ass". This is how Pignon is baptized by the community. Follows his last monologue:

> Mr. Milan, I'll stand by you... A friend in need is a friend indeed. Who cares if you have a rifle in your suitcase. I'm really glad I met you. I've been lonely for three months. We'll steal a car, Mr. Milan. You can have my room. I'll sleep on the couch. We'll run the roadblocks. We'll make it, you'll see. I'll take care of you. We'll get organized.

The accordion melody fades out. Sirens blare in the distance, policemen yell in megaphones. An abrupt cut, the only serious jump cut in the entire film, shows prisoners walking in a circle, with Milan ahead of Pignon behind him who whispers: "I asked them to put us in the same cell. It's all arranged. Mr. Milan..." An unexpected freeze frame on Milan's stunted expression, the accordion melody begins. And then back to the strolling prisoners in a low angle shot; the end credits superimposed in fiery red.

Components of the film

Let us now break down this road movie into its main components.

> 1. After Felix's failed attempted to kill Randoni, Ralf Milan arrives in Montpellier to finish the job. 0:00-7:53.
> 2. The Inciting Incident: Milan kills Felix. 7:54 8:31.
> 3. François Pignon is introduced. 10:03-10:34
> 4. Hotel is the Sender: both Milan and Pignon sign in. 13:52-16:36.
> 5. François Pignon's botched suicide. Milan promises to help Pignon. (Plot Point One.) 21:58-28:46.
> 6. Milan agrees to drive Pignon to a hospital to meet Louise, his wife. 36:43-39:31
> 7. Milan kicks Pignon out of the car (Pinch Point One). 44:07-44:15.
> 8. Dr. Fuchs administers Milan, thinking he is Pignon, some tranquilizers (Midpoint plot point). 54:10-56:40
> 9. Pignon drives Milan to Dr. Fuchs who gives him amphetamines. 67:00-68.35.
> 10. Back at the hotel, a police inspector questions Milan and Pignon about the ledge incident. Milan hits the inspector. (Pinch Point Two.) 75:01-76:11.
> 11. Pignon finds Milan's rifle; Pignon refuses to leave with his wife; he shoots, the police retaliate and shoot Milan. (Plot Point Three.) 77:53-79:50.
> 12. Ending: Pignon and Milan in prison. 83:14-84:30.

We could synthesize the plot by taking the first lines (dark shade) of the above diagram (figure 9). Milan arrives in Montpellier to kill Randoni; through a number of fluky events, Milan gets mistaken for Pignon who is administered tranquilizers; Milan is too drugged to kill Randoni; Pignon fires Milan's rifle which brings them to prison (Randoni is never killed). In conclusion, what we have a reversal of fate whereby Milan symbolically becomes Pignon who himself becomes Milan. Both end up in prison.

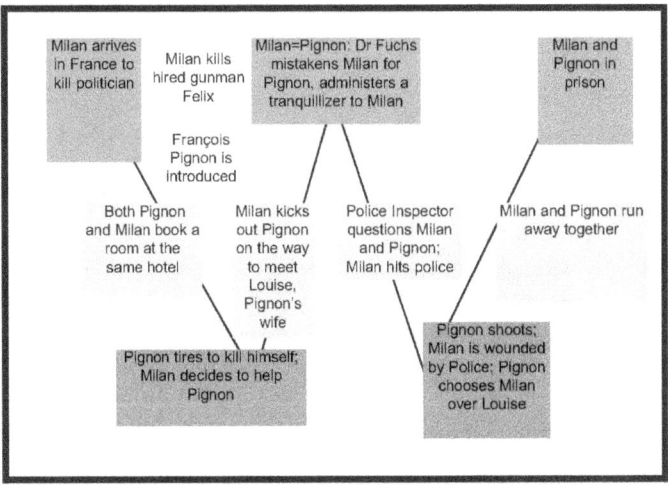

Figure 9

The Pinch Points (light shade) include both Milan and Pignon booking rooms in the same hotel; Milan kicks Pignon out of his car; Milan strikes a Police inspector; Milan and Pignon become fugitives. At this level, conflicts and obstacles separate and climatically bring the two men together.

The plot points (dark shade) include Milan helps Pignon win his wife back; Dr. Fuchs mistakes Milan for Pignon (midpoint); Pignon fires a gunshot, and Milan is wounded by the police. Pignon symbolically shoots Milan who prevented him from killing himself. An Italian killer saves a French shirt salesman who in turn shoots the killer. This is Aristotle's *peripeteia*, a true reversal of intention. No matter who these men are essentially, both end up ostracized by society. The humorous twist of fate makes French society reject an Italian who acts outside of its laws, and a French person who will try to kill himself; yet, that same society will grant a symbolic asylum to a killer and a man who abandons his spouse so that he can live with a foreigner. There is but one condition: they must live outside mainstream society.

Intrusion as transformation

In an article on the dissolve Christian Metz (*Signifiant*, 344) compares this filmic punctuation — used, as we will demonstrate in another chapter, quite masterfully by Nicola Zavaglia in *The Mediterranean Forever* — to Freud's concept of "collective figures": "the uniting of the actual features of two or more people into a single dream-image" (*Interpretation*, 327).

This condensation, this "co-presence", acts more than a simple transitional device; for Metz this juxtaposition is an "progressive extinction" ("extinction progressive"), a sort of "dis-encounter" ("dérencontrer") (*Signifiant*, 344), where two characters cannot meet. A displacement, a movement toward... but where no closure is ever achieved.

What if two characters were to run into each other, embracing one another, both refusing to disappear, neither as self-effacement, nor as separateness, each evolving into a mixture of something old/someone new? Not a before something that dies, not an after about to be born, this moment before and that moment after creating a presence that, to quote Jean-Paul Sartre, becomes a "being-in-pair-with-the-Other" *("être-en-couple-avec-l'autre")* (*Être*, 340). An on-going relationship between subject and object, or if you wish subject-object and object-subject, whereby the other is a world of which one is aware, and willing to cuddle but not to engulf the other, living side by side, making this co-habitation the *locus dramaticus* ("lieu dramatique"), as André Bazin called it.[14] On screen, in the world of fiction, this is where opposites meet, like in the synthesis that constitutes the *fondu enchaîné*, the dissolve, the other place, the virtual territory. Bazin believes that

> Presence, naturally, is defined in terms of time and space. "To be in the presence of someone" is to recognize him as existing contemporaneously with us and to note that he comes within the actual range of our senses... (*What*, 96)

Basically, *A Pain in the Ass* by Édouard Molinaro, more than the remakes (by Billy Wilder and Francis Veber), is about the meeting of opposites. It is not about the individuals that is François Pignon the shirt-salesman and Ralf Milan the hired gunman, going about their respective everyday businesses.

The film describes the "accidental" encounter of two persons becoming one. It is about loving a neighbor who cannot be loved, who does not want to be loved; it is about loving someone more than loving oneself. Francesco Alberoni praises friendship despite the walls of documents and actions that prove the contrary.

> Is there still friendship in the contemporary world?... Moreover, the modern world imposes on us a continuous change. When we change

residence and work we also end up leaving old friends... Friendship is the way to step in front of others... despite this first catastrophic impression... friendship continues to be an essential component of our life (*Amicizia,* 7-8).

Molinaro believes in friendship as well, and demonstrates that the incontro (contact, encounter) between friends, to use a concept advanced by Alberoni, surpasses the love of spouses. Louise, who meant so much to Pignon, for whom Pignon was about to kill himself, slips down the ladder of importance. Friendship is intrusion, agitation, upheaval, turning upside down, inside out. The switching of perspective evokes the issue of focalization. At the beginning of *A Pain in the Ass*, the narrative focalization is, as Gérard Genette calls it, "zero": the camera-narrator knows everything there is to know about every character.[15]

This non-focalization made obvious by how the camera moves from one character to the other, always looking at a character from the outside, at times when dealing with the characters who are distant foils (the owner of the garage, the concierge, Randoni's wife, the American hitchhiker, the Hôtel du Palais manager, Pignon's wife, the secretary putting on lipstick). A hint of something personal is suggested, be it for a fraction of a second, but never more. Some people remain distant. For example, in the first chapter, a man prefers to honk the horn of his car instead of going to ring on his neighbors' door. When the honking does not work the upset man in the garage comes out and orders the concierge of the neighboring building to wake up the owners of the car. We find this "in-direction" in François Truffaut as well, where no single character ever goes straight to the goal: one slogs along obliquely to get to where he/she wants to go, to reach the person he/she wants to speak to. And so gradually the spectator learns the geography of the setting, the people residing in this location, each location depicted in detail: Molinaro presents everyone to us, everything, the upset man who cannot keep his hallway light to go on, who cannot drive out of his garage, the Randoni couple and their apartment.

This focalization will be used later with Milan and his rented car and room, Pignon's car without gas, his hotel room, the hitchhiker, the secretary putting on lipstick, the Bellhop, Dr. Fuchs, Louise. This sharing of idiosyncrasies encourages intimacy. Montpellier is a small town, a civil engineer could draw its physical distribution; everyone knows one another; a boy on a bicycle is able to direct Pignon and Milan to Dr. Fuchs' clinic, located "pass the maternity ward". The maternity ward is where Milan has to drive the expectant Italian woman. Focalization in *A Pain in the Ass* clearly is community driven.

The individual is primarily a piece in a larger puzzle. Molinaro is not interested in one person's evolution; his design is more social in nature. He is speaking about a society, and depicts its reaction to the introduction of a foreigner in this closed environment.

Between society and the foreigner there is the gaze. In syntagma 7 Ventura looks intently out of the frame as if he notices someone or something that attracts his attention. Syntagma 8 shows Felix parking his car and then walking toward the camera, stopping at the door on his right. He rings. The sound of a shot is heard, Felix collapses dead on the street. Was it the stare that fired the shot? Of course, not; syntagma 9 shows Ventura shuffling out of the skeleton of a high-rise, carrying a suitcase. It is only at this moment that we the spectator learn that it was Milan who shot Felix, and from this high-rise. These three shots are linked to one another by their subject and yet are kept apart by their form. Milan does not make the mistakes Felix makes. It takes less than five minutes for Molinaro to describe this character to us. All Milan has to drop his eyes on Randoni and Randoni is a dead man. Molinaro describes these as "*des regards plutôt inquiétants*" ("somewhat disquieting stares") (*Intérieur*, 155). The foreigner is almighty in this closed environment.

At the end of syntagma 9, after shooting Felix, Milan struts to his car and for a moment stares in the direction of the camera, as though he were staring straight at the spectator. Milan has eyes that kill. There is a cut just when we are made aware of Milan's gaze. Syntagma 10, a cut on action, on the gaze, shows Milan in profile, staring out of the frame, as though the spectator had changed position, no longer sitting where he/she was sitting, but had moved to the right, outside of the cinema, in that zone Pascal Bonitzer calls the "blind field" ("*le champ aveugle*").[16]

Displaced, disoriented, the spectator must make an effort to understand that Milan is inspecting the street below where Felix stood a few seconds before. Eerily enough that place, where Felix was standing, is where the spectator is sitting. The gaze of a man with emotionless features, resembling Buster Keaton, is purposely aimed at the spectator like a rifle. This "gaze of death" determines, later, in syntagma 14, the power relationship Milan imposes on the angry truck driver, and in a different setting on the Bellhop. Pignon is the only character who can disarm Milan's "trigger" of death. The police inspector, who at the very end demand that Pignon and Milan produce their identification papers, also breaks the power of this gaze, but Milan luckily uses his physical strength to knock the police down. The law might be powerful, but not powerful enough to control the foreigner. Only the friendship offered by Pignon can achieve this task.

Locations and accessories speak. The radio, clocks on the street, watches, car clocks all remind Milan that time is clicking away. A missed deadline (2 o'clock limit for Randoni) automatically entails Milan's death. The radio acts as a "peridiegetic voice" (*Énonciation*, 55) that keeps the spectator apace on what time it is and what Randoni is about to do. This sound device functions like "imageless alternate syntagma".

The recalls are necessary to the narrative. Without this voice over the spectator would surely have missed a portion of the plot. At the end of syntagma 10, after announcing what crimes Randoni will divulge to the police, the commentator speaks of a jealousy-motivated murder incident.

One wonders why Molinaro would have wanted to include such extra-diegetical information if not to subliminally prepare the spectator to Pignon's jealousy. He is jealous of Dr. Fuchs' sexual prowess. Every character possesses his objects and his setting. The only characters to share a common surrounding are Pignon and Milan. The hotel might be a metonymy of France.

In the last chapter (syntagma 86), Milan tears a shutter string and, frustrated, rushes into Pignon's room with a clear intention of strangling Pignon. The irony of the matter is that it is the same "weapon" with which Pignon wanted to hang himself. The gag is subtle but ever present in the spectator's mind as Pignon measures Milan's neck size for shirts he wishes to offer him as a gift. The doubleness of meaning for that one object sparks laughter. What for one is an object of destruction is changed into an object of affection in the other. Pignon is cured. He can empty his old suitcase and start a new life.

In his suitcase foam Milan carries a mountable rifle. No socks, no shirts, nothing of the sort find there. Milan travels without clothes, with a rifle. This shotgun is Milan's identity, his passport. When it falls into Pignon's hands, all goes astray. Milan's mission but also his identity. If action is what determines a character, then Milan is no longer the character he is when Pignon takes his gun from him. The sexual connotations involved are obvious; what was a tool for murder becomes in Pignon's hand an object for birth. Again, what we have here is a reborn Pignon who surpasses Dr. Fuchs' sexual aptitude. If the radio at the beginning mentioned the tragedy that afflicts a couple, later on this tragedy is transformed, with the appearance of the Italian pregnant woman and her husband, into birthing. The proposition is engaging: foreigners give natality to what wished to die. In *A Pain in the Ass*, foreigners are Italian who open France to new beginnings.

Mirrors reflect the one and the other. From the Latin *speculum*, "mirror" originally meant to speculate, that is to observe the stars with the help of a mirror. It is also linked to the other Latin term *mirare*, to look at. A mirror does not lie; its reflection is sincere, reveals the naked truth, which many ancient traditions equated with awareness and knowledge. Ancient Hindu texts speak of "identity coming from difference; light reflect off of water, but cannot penetrate it". Henceforth two-fold meanings surface from the mirror: knowledge of self versus love of self (vanity), the soul versus the body. The mirror becomes two-sided: on one side, there is fear — to learn about oneself can provoke fear — and, on the flip side, the light which purifies.

> The mirror does not only reflect an image; the soul becomes a perfect mirror that participates with the image and in so doing undergoes a transformation. There exists, therefore, a configuration between the contemplating subject and the mirror that contemplates the subject. [17]

Pignon and Milan are both filmed in front of mirrors, and the mirror like a window where one looks at the other. Like Narcissus and his opposite, these men must learn to look into love of self before they can stare into the depth of otherness. Mirrors cause represent death, in the sense that one who looks into a mirror must "die to oneself".

When Pignon turns the mirror flaps over, it is so that he might not see himself vanishing into someone else (syntagma 34). And yet this gaze turned toward oneself is what is necessary for change to occur. If the mirror were part of an equation, then the units in the equation would be equal (Pignon/mirror = Milan/mirror). Pignon and Milan become one person, hybrids, the outcome of métissage. On side of the mirror, both men have to kill. But they are not capable of killing, because they are interrupted by the flip side of the mirror. Milan ruffles Pignon in his attempt to commit suicide; and Pignon disrupts Milan in his mission to eliminate Randoni. In the ensuing commotion, plans get inverted and magically scrabbled, the same way a monophonic sound source split into stereophony physically erases itself.

Sameness erases itself, opposites attract one another and rise to another entity. When Milan first appears on screen (syntagma 5), a harpsichord led march is heard; from then on every time Milan is seen working on his mission, the melody fades in. That music identifies this character, as do his grey suit, white shirt and black tie. When Pignon is first seen in his toy-filled car, a joyous melody resounds. Riddled with nostalgic connotations, both emotional and social — the past and Pignon are one — it immediately colors the spectator's conception of this character.

Compared to Milan's severe looking grimace, Pignon's face glows with innocence. His black suit, white shirt and patterned tie contrast with Milan's somber attire. Pignon owns his car and has plastic flowers climbing the dashboard and toys on the dash and over the backseat; Milan rents a BMW which has but a radio. When we first see Pignon in his car, the edit momentarily confuses the spectator into believing that Milan is driving in one direction and Pignon in another. Soon it becomes clear that both Milan and Pignon are driving in the same direction: they are heading for Montpellier. If we were to offer a psychoanalytical explanation to the unification of so dissimilar men, we could advance the hypothesis that, like Calvino's halved viscount Medardo, or Bergman's Alma and Elisabeth Vogler in *Persona* (1966), this black (evil) and white (good) dyad belong to an indissoluble entity.

One of the four elements, water is a life-source, an agent for purification and a hearth for rebirth. Water is manifest in a number of instances in *A Pain in the Ass* and in various forms: the water tube from which Pignon hangs himself; the rain drops on the American tourist; the water on Milan's carpet comes from Pignon's room (in which Milan soaks his shoes); the tranquilizer, by extension, is a water-like liquid that is injected by Dr. Fuchs and alters Milan's behavior; the water from the sink tab that washes Pignon, Milan, the Bellhop, Dr. Fuchs' hands.

He who is touched by water is cleansed, purified, purged. The four men will touch water and be changed — Milan the killer does not kill, Pignon the suicide does not commit suicide, Dr. Fuchs the quack ends up a different man (whether he stays with Louise is left unsaid), Bellhop the obedient one is less in a hurry about calling the police.

Only Louise is never seen with the water figure but is shown riding a horse. Of course, at its most basic level, the horse is a pass-time, a sport, but it can also be taken to a higher plane and be viewed as an icon for the unconscious, the carrier of beings to other territories; mythology speaks of the horse as being the child of night and mystery. Unlike other animals, the horse is a vehicle. In semantic terms, Louise is a Sender; she appears at the first Pinch Point of the plot (45 minutes, syntagma 52) and propels the story into a different direction altogether. Pignon continues his journey and attempt to win her back, not as himself, but as another person, under Milan's guise, his *doppelgänger*. And all thanks to Dr. Fuchs who mistakes Milan for Pignon. Who is Milan if not a Pignon under the influence. He is the person he claims to be.

The American tourist is like a messenger come from nothing where, incidentally, he returns, disappearing (syntagma 78). How to make sense of the apparition of this fleeting character who suddenly comes — he appears in four syntagmas (13, 15, 17, 78) — and literally vanishes in thin air. What does he bring to the story? To Pignon? Milan who notices the tourist in the rain does not stop for him. Pignon does however, and thanks to the ensuing conversation of syntagma 15, under the otherworldly squeaks of windshield wipers, we find out that Pignon has a brother who works in Paris for an American company in Boston, that he would like to speak English, that he is a simple French person who knows only France and French goods. In other words, the hitchhiker is a perfect foil to permits this French person to express his limitations. And yet by being there, the tourist reveals information that could not be known otherwise: the cultural identity of François Pignon.

The Bellhop stands at the opposite end of the tourist. He does not disappear; he imposes his presence at the smallest occasion. Milan and Pignon enforce their need of silence by pulling up the *Do Not Disturb* sign to his face. The Bellhop gives the title to the film. The Bellhop names the film, by going against the grain of the narrative. *A Pain in the Ass* is more about Milan than Pignon. So why name the film that points to the secondary character? Molinaro answers:

> The distributor forced the title on us: *L'Emmerdeur*. Veber the first, Venture, Brel and myself, we all hated it and we fought till the end to reject it. In vain (*Intérieur*, 155).

The title has money attached to it; a price has been put on Pignon's but also on Milan's head. Again like in a western Milan the loner disrupts the community he has slipped into. He is as much an *emmerdeur* as Pignon is.

The Italic

If we drop the main characters of the film onto the A. J. Greimas' actant model, with its double axes (the axe of desire and the axe of communication), the results are revealing. Both Milan and Pignon are searching for calmness in their lives. Milan fears for his life, if he does not kill Randoni; Pignon can find peace only if he wins his wife back.

The coincidence that Milan and Pignon should meet in the Hôtel du Palais totally derails both men's plans. The goals do not change immediately, but when they do the story does a somersault. Neither Milan nor Pignon get the object they most desired: Milan is more or less highjacked by Pignon's insistence; Pignon is turned inside out by Milan's assiduities. Pignon accepts Milan for who he is. Film, perhaps more than any other art form, is never about the story being told. Other levels of significance (aesthetic, cinematographic, dramatic, literary, cultural, social, political) converge or open up at the most unexpected moments, like a black hole where suddenly connotations multiply manifold. Ventura has played the tough guy more than once. It was probably the reason why Molinaro hired him.

That this is a comedy about an Italian killer becomes ironic. Milan meddles with the stereotypical image of the Italian mobster. The people who hired this gunman move in the upper scale of the political sphere, not at the margins of organized crime. Randoni professes having important documents that can overturn the "real" criminals in various echelons of the French government. Milan is a hired foreigner, a professional *Gastarbeiter*, no different, say, than Nino in *Bread and Chocolate*. After his mission accomplished, he is expected to leave. He does not. Like Nino. Like Danilo's friend Mario in *Queen of Hearts*. He is a foreigner who will stay in France.

The name Milan also stands in French for kite, the raptor, of the Accipitridae family. Similar to this falcon, the milan bird spends most of its time moving in the air, because it possesses strong wings but weak legs. It feeds off carrion. A kite flies between sky and earth, a bird that lives half in the hereness and half in the thereness Ralf Milan is a falcon-like nomad who makes a living off of dead men. Standing behind the window of his hotel room, he soars with the eyes of a kite and surveys the prey (Randoni) down below. Milan, Randoni, Molinaro, Ventura and, to a certain extent even Felix, which is a name Veber will use again in *Le Placard* (Depardieu's character is called Felix Santini) are Italian names. Whatever their origin, they point indirectly to Italy. With Milan, there is no doubt.

The moment the tall Pignon, with buck teeth, standing on the edge of self-destruction pleadingly touches the stoic shorter Milan on the arm, the spectator expects the gaze of death to be triggered off. Yet we break into laughter. Once the forbidden is ambushed there is no running back. Raymond Queneau advances the theory that "all great works of art are either an *Illiad* or an *Odyssey*".[18] The *Illiads* are vertical narratives taking place in a "huis clos", closed chambers; whereas the *Odysseys* are horizontal narratives, which unfold in various territories, moving along like a "road movie".

When Pignon breaks the barrier of no return, the film narrative slides from the vertical to the horizontal, from an *Illiad* it becomes an *Odyssey*. The hotel, the two connecting rooms, Montpellier, the roads that lead in and out of the center, the playground for this story is no longer confined to one space. The limits of private and social tenacity collapse. The cultural corrodes; the stereotypical narrow-minded French Pignon finds himself in a dead-end. We must keep in mind that Pignon is interpreted by a non-French: a voluntary appropriation of voice. Molinaro could have used a French actor; he didn't. Neither Ventura nor Castelnuovo are French. The main characters of this French film are played by foreigners. The critique of French society could not be more virulent. It begins with the American hitchhiker who activates self-doubt in Pignon admits he is incapable of learning another language.

Throughout the first half of the film Pignon's drone against anything that is not French is relentless: American jobs, blond tobacco cigarettes smoked by Milan, Milan's quality shirt not made in France, Milan being Italian, the guest worker Bellhop kneeling at his feet, wiping water in the toilet, and Pignon having lost his wife to Dr. Fuchs, most probably German-origin (this is consistent in all three versions of the film). If Pignon represents the ordinary French person, what does Milan stand for? Italianness? Italianness as a metonymy for otherness?

A story of such latitude could not be limited to one room. Like *Bread and Chocolate*, *Queen of Hearts*, and *The Mediterranean Forever*, *A Pain in the Ass* is not a chamber film. This is about a journey, a one-way trip, to Nowhereland, to No-Land. Nostalgia, suicide, madness, all false pretences must be surpassed. This is not about individuals; Molinaro's film is about collectivity; not about stereotypes, but archetypes. These characters represent more than themselves. The hotel, the streets and highways, the cars form a virtual territory on which opposites do not collide but co-habit. Here is a synthesis of what is not French. Contrary to the outcome of *Bread and Chocolate*, *A Pain in the Ass* ends on a positive note. Pignon wants Milan to stay. They might spend a number of years in prison, but in that confined space there is hope, there is acceptance. The happy ending is not dissimilar to the ending of *Queen of Hearts*. Once the crime is vacated, the future is auspicious. Consent is total. Opposites stand on equal footing in front of the law. This is real success. As Édouard Molinaro himself admits: "Success sanctifies everything."

Ettore Scola is quoted as saying that "il cinema italiano... parla la lingua che molti tra voi ancora parlano".[19] The idea here being that Italians in France still have a connection to Italian the language. Or is it the idea of being Italian? Hopefully more than the Italian language it is Italian immigration that interests Italians living in France. However, reading Jean-Charles Vegliante's article one senses that justice for Italians living in France, those men and women who live in *Ritalie*, as Antonio Canovi calls it,[20] was not always easy.

Films on Italians in France are rare: *Vie des travailleurs italiens en France* (1926), by Jean Grémillon, *Toni* (1934), by Jean Renoir, *Deux corniauds au régiment* (1971), by Nado Cicero, *Beau-masque* (1972), by Bernard Paul, *Il sospetto* (1975), by Francesco Maselli, *La Cecilia* (1976), de Jean-Louis Comolli, *Le rôle économique des travailleurs étrangers* (1978), by Dominique Juliani, *L'exile est une longue insomnie* (1979), by Sabine Mamou, *La trace* (1983), by Bernard Favre, *La vallée des espoirs* (1987), by Jean-Pierre Marchand et Jean-Pierre Sinapi, et *Mima* (1991), by Philomène Esposito.[21]

An autobiography, *Les Ritals* (1978), by French writer François Cavanna, towers as a major monument for the Ritals in France. Across the border, in Belgium, in 1983, Claude Barzotti releases his hit, "Le Rital", about his attachment to his Italian roots that was very popular.[22] Much like Toto Cotugno's 1983 success, "L'Italiano (Lasciatemi cantare)", Barzotti's song became an anthem for francophone Italians. A cry not for the country, but for individual's right in a foreign system. Comparable to the American "Dago' or Canadian "Wop", Rital is a derogatory term derived from the French argot. Its origins however obscure (perhaps a play on the fact that Italians tend to roll their "r") refers to any person in France and Belgium that is of Italian origin. Clearly an attack to Italian immigrants in francophone territories. (In Canada, Wop is the term of scorn used against Italians.) Fascism had put a legal stop to "its migratory calling".[23] But emigration came back in full force after 1945. As Antonio Bechelloni presumes, the reason for this need for emigration is without doubt due in part to the helplessness Italy found itself after the war, with its economical and social turmoils.[24] Article 35, 3 of the new Italian Constitution is clear:

> La Repubblica... riconosce la libertà di emigrazione, salvo gli obblighi stabiliti dalla legge nell'interesse generale, e tutela il lavoro italiano all'estero.
> [The Republic recognizes the freedom to emigrate, within the limits established by the law in the interest of the many, and protects the Italian workers abroad.][25]

Soon ensues a not-so-subtle battle between France and South America which country will attract the most Italians. Thanks to the workers union on the one hand, and the Catholic associations on the other, France would inherit the unspecialized workers on the Left of the political spectrum, whereas Argentina and Brazil would invite the workers on the Right. Though the Left Wing element is not unique to France — there was Sacco and Vanzetti in the U.S.A. — something about emigrants in France is special. Studies on the Italian communities in France and Belgium are only now being undertaken. Books such as *Les Italiens en France depuis 1945*, edited by Marie-Claude Blanc-Chaléard are fulfilling an unfortunate void.

If I did not analyze *Toni* by Jean Renoir, it is because the emigration the film depicted is the earlier one at the beginning of the Twentieth Century. Renoir's *Toni* (Visconti worked on the film) would influence Italian neo-realism. The camera offers depth of field that made André Bazin happy, and the drama that unfolds in this southeastern part of France proves once again that Renoir is a humanist of the greatest kind. Renoir jumps over stereotypes and scrutinizes the workings of the universal soul. Here, an Italian immigrant takes it upon himself to accept the blame for a murder he did not commit. When the vigilante finally guns him down, the spectator's emotions are propelled full force. Empathy is total.

The other film of interest is *La Cecilia,* by Jean-Louis Comolli, about a group of anarchists (ten men and one woman) who, under the "leadership' of Giovanni Rossi, established a commune, in 1890, in Palmeiras, Paranà, Brazil. The anarchist "Cecilia Colony", with its membership of 100 men and women, failed after five years of existence, due to difficulties arising from the practice of "free love' (come about primarily to the lack of women in the commune). Analyzing the truly fascinating *La Cecilia* would have led us to far away from the premises of our study. (Other films, though fascinating, are still unavailable to the general public.)

Both *Toni* and *La Cecilia* delve into the world of love, sex and community, and though many critics are quick to talk about tragedy on one hand and destruction brought about on the other, it is death of the family that is ultimately responsible for the consequent catastrophe. For the better or the worse, social relationships act as a glue that facilitates communal graciousness and survival. David Cooper spoke of the "de-structuring of the family'.[26] More than "blood relationships", it is the invented family (the re-invention of a nuclear unit) that is to be encouraged in order to maintain social stability.

Albeit not outright about being Italian, *A Pain in the Ass* does involve an Italian man and his association with a host country. This film acts as a perfect bridge between the very Italian *Bread and Chocolate* and the very British *Queen of Hearts*. Emigrating outside Italy but remaining on the European continent makes a difference; Italy, not far away, remains a possible outlet if things abroad do not go according to plan. For the Americas, Italy is not always a recourse. Little Italy can act as a haven. The topic of Little Italy is hinted at in *Queen of Hearts* and studied in depth in *The Mediterranean Forever.* The Imaginary place that Little Italy becomes for every emigrant/immigrant plays an important role in the building of a para-individual, collective identity. The Italic reality (and all modern ethnic reality) is more about this building of this Virtual territory than about the actual country left behind.

Notes

1. In "Édouard Molinaro: Sans regret ou presque", interview with Éric Clément, *La Presse*, 23 August 2010.
2. Furio Scarpelli, quoted in Francis Vanoye, *Scénarios modèles, modèles de scénarios*, 2nd ed., Paris: Armand Colin, 2008, 52.
3. Roger Ebert, *Chicago Sun-Times*, 1 January 1981.
4. In Charlotte Chandler, *Nobody's Perfect: Billy Wilder, A Personal Biography*, New York, Simon & Schuster, 2002, 299-304.
5. Michele Realini, "Monsieur Milan' broadcasted at Radio svizzera italiana, 2 October, 2005.
6. James Travers, *The Toronto Star*, 2005, reprinted in *Films de France*, filmsdefrance.com, 2010.
7. Amélie Chauvet, commeaucinema.com, December 2008.
8. Édouard Molinaro, Interview, op. cit.
9. *Le Parisien*, 15 December 2008.
10. Arnaud Mangin, FilmsActu.com, 9 December 2008.
11. Martin Gignac, "L'Emmerdeur porte bien son nom", *Le frelon vert*, 14 January 2011.
12. Isabelle Hontebeyrie, interview with Francis Veber, "J'ai eu trop de succès, j'ai été puni", 7 jours, 19 April 2009.
13. The concept was found by Jérôme Peignot but elaborated by Pierre Schaeffer, quoted in Michel Chion, *L'audio-vision*, 63.
14. André Bazin, "Théâtre et cinéma' in *Qu'est-ce que le cinéma*, Paris: Éditions du Cerf, 158. The term *locus dramaticus*, a marvellous find, is by Bazin's translator, Hugh Gray, *What Is Cinema*, Volume 1, Berkeley: University of California, 104-105.
15. Francesco Alberoni, *L'amicizia*, Milano: Garzanti, 1984, 7-8.
16. Pascal Bonitzer, *Le Champ aveugle*, Paris: Cahiers du cinéma, 1999.
17. Jean Chevalier et Alain Gheerbrant, *Dictionnaire des Symboles*, Paris: Robert Lafont/Jupiter, 1982, 638. This section of the 'mirror' owes much to this work.
18. Raymond Queneau, *Bâton, chiffres et lettres*, Paris: Gallimard, 1965, 117. Quoted by Francis Vanoye in *Scénarios modèles, modèles de scénarios*, 28.
19. Quoted in Jean-Charles Vegliante, "Cinema e presenza italiana in Francia", in *Altreitalie 6*, November 1991, 140.
20. Antonio Canovi, "La communauté italienne d'Argenteuil. Identité et mémoires en question", in *Les Italiens en France depuis 1945*, Rennes: Presses Universitaires de Rennes, 2003, 237.
21. This list is taken from Vegliante fine article in *Altreitalie 6*, 140-147.
22. Here are a few verses to Claude Barzotti's song: "C'est vrai je suis un étranger/On me l'a assez répété/J'ai les cheveux couleur corbeau/Je viens du fond de l'Italie/Et j'ai l'accent de mon pays/Italien jusque dans la peau // Je suis rital et je le reste/Et dans le verbe et dans le geste/Vos saisons sont devenues miennes/Ma musique est Italienne/Je suis rital dans mes colères/Dans mes douceurs et mes prières/J'ai la mémoire de mon espèce... //Mon nom à moi c'est Barzotti/Et j'ai l'accent de mon pays/Italien jusque dans la peau.'

23. Antonio Bechelloni introduces this idea of the "vocation migratoire' in his article "Le choix de la destination française vu du côté italien", in *Les Italien en France depuis 1945*, edited by Marie-Claude Blanc-Chaléard, Rennes: Presses Universitaires de Rennes, 2003, 30.
24. Antonio Bechelloni, "Le choix de la destination française vu côté italien", 30: "Les bruits vont bon train sur les destinations possibles d'une nouvelle émigration. Certes, le désarroi d'un pays à moitié détruit, avec d'immenses problèmes économiques et sociaux sur le tapis, y est pour beaucoup.'
25. Quoted in Antonio Bechelloni, op. cit., 30. My translation.
26. David Cooper, *The Death of the Family*, 24: "...the possibility of a de-structuring of the family on the basis of a full realization of the destructiveness of that institution. A de-structuring that will be so radical, precisely because of the lucidity that finally points the way to it, that it demands a revolution in the whole society.'

3

QUEEN OF HEARTS

Synopsis

Directed by Jon Amiel, in 1989, and based on a screenplay by Tony Grisoni, *Queen of Hearts* stars Joseph Long (Danilo Lucca), Anita Zagaria (Rosa), Eileen Way (Mamma Sibilla), Vittorio Duse (Nonno), Vittorio Amandola (Barbariccia), Ian Hawkes (Edoardo, Eddie), Tat Whalley (Beetle), Anna Pernicci (Angelica), Jimmy Lambert (Bruno), and Ray Marioni (Mario).

Circa 1960s. Danilo and Rosa escape from Italy, Danilo marries Rosa who had been promised (fixed by an arranged marriage) to Barbariccia, the wealthy butcher's son. The young couple elope and emigrate to Britain, where Danilo, thanks to gambling, becomes the owner of a restaurant, The Lucky Café.

Situated in London's Soho section (Lucca is Danilo's surname), the café becomes the metaphorical center for what happens to an Italian family in Britain. With the mother-in-law watching their every move, the young couple starts a new life in London's Little Italy. Four children (Bruno, Angelica, Teresa, and Edoardo (Eddie), who is the film's narrator) are born. Prosperity and happiness, however, comes to an end when the vengeful Barbariccia arrives in London, many years later, to claim back his woman, Danilo's wife, Rose. With the help of a friend, Beetle, and his grandfather, the youngest child, Eddie, saves the broken Luca family.

The ethnic fable

Following the practices produced by Anne Golio-Lété and Francis Vanoye,[1] we have broken the film *Queen of Hearts* up into chapters which enable us to capture its filmic narrative structure. How was this film put together? These two authors explain that

> [d]escribing the film, narrating the film, is also interpreting the film, since it is, in a certain way, reconstructing (or deconstructing) the film (*Précis*, 41).

According to Anne Goliot-Lété and Francis Vanvoye, filmic analysis follows a double process by which at any single "moment"[2] the analyst must "describe" systematically what the object being studies first is, by using a precise terminology which will act as a guide throughout the analysis, and then to "observe", structure the object, and pull informative details from this complex object.

Breaking up the film into disparate fragments is a fundamental moment in the analysis. Without a pre-established hypothesis, we describe and observe as accurately as possible the syntax used by the filmmaker and to what purpose. Film, we know, is not a language. Christan Metz tried to establish a nomenclature for patterns used repeatedly from one film to another. These "phrases", these syntagmas, though not equivalent to the linguistic concepts of monene and phoneme, do nonetheless function in a repetitive and ritualistic manner. Presenting a scene in one way or another produces meaning that cannot be easily discarded.

The famous parallel syntagma in *The Godfather 1*, whereby Michael Corleone assists his nephew's baptism while he is simultaneously assisting *in absentia* at the killings of his enemies, would not have had the same effect had these two separate syntagmas been presented in a linear fashion, one scene after the other. The church scene (perfectly linear) announces Michael's religiosity, regardless of the sincerity of the gesture. Here is a religious man who goes to church and prays to God, and believes in the sacrament of Holy Baptism. Whether or not, this belief is sincere cannot be demonstrated by this scene alone.

In the second segment (totally nonlinear), we have a bracket syntagma where one very short scene is succeeded by another, each grouped together by the same kind of action: murder at work. Corleone's job has led him to kill his competitors: capitalism gone wild. By pitting one scene against the other, Coppola suddenly lifts the entire macro-sequence to another level of significance. All of a sudden the spectator is being asked to re-evaluate the psychological complexities of what has just unfolded, and this thanks to the syntax of the language adopted. Intercutting the church scenes with the murder scenes, a new symbolic dimension is added to Michael Corleone's personality: we are left with more questions, more doubts, than answers that both the sequences would have initially offered.

There is no way of escaping the weight of narrativity when analysing a work of fiction. Narrative contents get organized and this organization is entrenched in its formulation. Very much like language, the sentence structure has been stable for over hundred years, even when it is purposely toyed with, as in the case of the films by Jean-Luc Godard (*Our Music*, 2004) David Lynch (*Mulholland Drive*, 2001), Quentin Tarantino (*Pulp Fiction*, 1994), or Christopher Smith (*Triangle*, 2009). Somehow the storyline wants to impose itself in form.

D.W. Griffith's filmic syntax has colored much of storytelling worldwide. Soviet expression (Poudovkin, Eisenstein), dadaism and surrealism (Clair, Picabia, Buñuel, Dali), German expressionism (Weine, Lang) or what Gilles Deleuze calls in *L'Image-temps*,[2] la modernité cinématographique (cinematographic modernity), which begins with Italian neo-realism with the introduction of "pure optical and aural situations", has been unable to dislodge the Hollywoodian precepts of film narrative. Stylistic elements from other formal sources might filter inside the narrative mode, but, outside these brief allusions, narration remained stubbornly linear when it comes to works of fiction. Most of the experience of viewing a film relies heavily on the story being told and less on the invisible storyteller. The analyst has no choice but to deconstruct the story into "moments' in order to sketch out the filmmaker's idiosyncratic stylistic tics. Self-expression blurts out often as a filmic Freudian slip more than as an essence total and direct.

Remove the weight of the storyline and we have storytelling become the story that is in fact being told. We will have the occasion to elucidate this axis more deeply in the chapter dedicated to *The Mediterranean Forever* by Nicola Zavaglia who fashions his narrative "plot" most exclusively on this "formal" stratum. In fact, of the five films Zavaglia's film is the one that most exhaustively relies on this "formal' (what other term to use) platform for the "story" (if such narrativity should be labelled) to exist.

The story told is an *a posteriori* product, the story told is the form unfolding (the story is logically induced, an effect more than a cause). Contrary to the other four films which had a story *a priori* that had to be fit into a style or a genre for it to be told, the story being an effect deduced from a pre-ordained cause, Zavaglia's story is the telling of the story. What is extraordinary about such a proposition is that Zavaglia's film is a so-called documentary, whereas the other four are so-called works of fiction, which, students and spectators have been made to believe, are works of total creation. Documentaries are utterly works of fiction as well.

We must now delve in the accepted split between the one slab of expressivity (the filmmaker) and the second (ascribed to the scriptwriter, the inventor of the story being told). In *Bread and Chocolate,* such a schism, though present and very real, remained minimal because the filmmaker and the actor were also the composers of the film (the third writer being at the service to the other two). What we are looking at emerges from the same source of inspiration. There isn't so much of a spread between the story written and the story filmed. What we see is without doubt what lay at the inception of the project.

Brusati and Manfredi never lose sight of the initial source, whatever inspired them nourished the *mise en œuvre* (within the confines established by the producer). The artists were free, yet not totally free. We have 1. the individuals in *Bread and Chocolate;* 2. who are identifiable by their nationality (the artists Italians from Italy do not hide this fact); 3. they are conscious of their ethnicity, more or less proud to be Italian, in spite of the criticisms directed against them; 4. they are hired to make this film by producers. The core group we have in *Bread and Chocolate* is what of we call "dependent artists". Had they produced the film themselves they would have been "free artists", but they were not completely without attachments.[3]

Brusati and Manfredi were bound by a contract, working under the work and financial conditions established by the producer. We could say that Brusati and Manfredi were pretty much free to do what they wanted, regardless of their being sealed waxed by an exterior financier. When the source and final product do not radiate in a one-to-one relationship, when elements collide in a division of labor, we need not be a Marxist economist to understand what bobs up is a separation of intent. The critics from *Les Cahiers du cinéma* and critics like Andrew Sarris, Pauline Kael, and Peter Wollen advanced methods to juggle with who is the real "author", the authentic voice of a film. This quest for "truth: becomes more urgent when it comes to ethnic films, because for some reason, during this transitory moment in the history of global emigration, much is at stake. Marcia Landy's comment on the Italian film industry under Fascism could be extended to the rest of the world. "Filmmaking was central to the regime's objectives of shaping the culture according to the objectives of Fascism" (*Italian,* 49).

Frank Capra dedicated for a time much his energy to the making of war propaganda films for the U.S. military during World War II. Germany (the Nazi), England (the government postal service), Canada (National Film Board), to name a few, also used the film to influence, engage, indoctrinate, cajole, intimidate, coerce, brainwash the citizens of their respective countries. Those images and sounds flashing at 24 images per second on the glowing screens of the world are never as innocent of intent as they proclaim. Steven J. Belluscio claims that the "passing" scenario (as Gunnar Myrdal defines it: "passing means that a Negro *(sic)* becomes a white man, that is, moves from the lower to the higher caste")[4] must be lifted from the very confined Afro-American setting and widened to include all ethnic communities. Is this not what a controversial film such as *Green Book* (2018) by Peter Farrelly achieves?

If so, then we should also be able to include those in ethnic communities who refuse to "pass" for what they are not. Indeed, we cannot fix the criteria that make up identity, for identity is not a fixed entity. Always fluctuating, identity of an individual is no less complicated as is the identity of a community. Nevertheless, it is not wrong to think that there are many individuals who do not wish to sell out to the culture that very kindly opened its doors to the foreigner. If the free artist is one who controls his work entirely, the dependent artist is one who is almost free. But he/she is not totally free. His contract to whatever "power" that enabled him/her to produce his/her work is binding in whatsoever form or content.

Queen of Hearts for the very first time raises this significant issue. Who is the storyteller? Between point A and point Z, there are a number of delicate stations which require what Samuel Taylor Coleridge called a "willing suspension of disbelief".[5] There is no irony (no dissimulation) on the part of one creator that is juxtaposed on the story being told by a second creator. That would have been insulting to the Italian-British community. Such a stylistic tactic would only demonize an account that presents itself as autobiographical, surely, and honestly as sheer entertainment. Nor do we believe that there is any stereotyping (fixed depiction or preconception) involved. This would have tipped the work into outright discrimination, which would not have been wished by the producers who backed the film. At most, the creators of *Queen of Hearts* might have sought archetypes to represent transposed and modernized *commedia dell'arte* characters, if these can at all be compared to doll-like supernumerary figures. Nothing about production is *déjà vu,* nor is the spectator for a single instant expected to view this film as a realistic film. Every aspect of this work operates as though part of a fable.

This fabula, the mythological tale, an allegorical reminiscence, might not be telling the whole truth, but it cannot be an exercise in deception. Not to speak the whole truth is not the same as telling a lie. Though the protagonists of fables tend to be animals (one thinks of Aesop and de La Fontaine), in this modern *fabulatio* which does resort to cartoon divos and divas (Bugs Bunny, Sylvester the Cat, Betty Boop), the cast was asked to play the role with a dose of humor. And yet... It is something *in bilico,* balancing between drama and comedy, between the past and the future, between Italy and England. *Queen of Hearts* is a serious comedy, or if you wish a comical drama. The form balances as well between realism and exaggeration.

In the *New York Times Review*, Caryn James describes the film as being a "melodrama", "a perfect caricature", with a "deliciously funny and disarming perspective", "exaggerated storytelling".[6]

TV Guide calls *Queen of Heart* a "mystical fable of love and revenge".[7] Gene Seymour, in his video review speaks of a "goof grin" of the "fanciful and the mundane" a "soap opera" with "enchantment" — terms that can be easily applicable any fable-like movie.[8] No mention of stereotypes is made whatsoever.

For Hal Hinson, of the *Washington Post*, this "revenge story... [is]... so operatic that you expect the characters to burst ecstatically into song" and a narrative "born on a current of headless romanticism".[9] Two days later, in the same newspaper — one wonders if the editors of the *Washington Post* felt they had to overload the praise after Hinson's outright negative review — Joe Brown, one of the staff writers, begins his review with "A fairy tale about everyday people", with a "dizzy climax" unfolding with "giddy momentum" and its "comically surrealist visions", the "mundane made marvellous".[10]

Finally, Roger Ebert steps in on 20 October 1989 and sticks the gold star of quality on the work, by comparing *Queen of Hearts* to *Moonstruck* (1987) by Norman Jewison, produced two years earlier, which had won six Oscars. Ebert explains how *Queen of Heart* delivers "magical romanticism", as told by a "kid with a hyperactive imagination". He, too, uses the adjective "goofy", but is quick to add nouns such as "fantasy", "humor", and "a fairly substantial story: a story about what it means to belong to a family".[11]

Nowhere is there a mention of stereotype or irony. These stakes are too high to dip one's pen in the ink of ridicule. Film is a big money-making industry. Men and women who wish to make films must gamble, like Danilo, their spouses and children away. Tony Grisoni can only hint at abuse of power, and, to quote Joe Brown, Jon Amiel is left to cover this all under his "engaging and inventive' filmic language.

On deconstructing the film

Film critic and programmer, Kent Jones of the Film Society of Lincoln Centre in his analysis of *L'Argent* (1983), by Robert Bresson, gives an intelligent advice to anyone who wishes to study a film in depth:

> Close analysis is often scorned by regular cinema goers, for the simple

reason it prompts its own way of looking at a film, miles from the experience of just sitting and watching a movie. More often than not, analysis leans on metaphor and interpretation, the pursuit of interlocking patterns, a mechanical process at work behind the film that has next to nothing to do with the way that an artist proceeds when he or she is producing something interesting.[12]

Jon Amiel used the scene (52 times), the sequence (16), the alternate syntagma (7), the sequence shot (6), the episodic sequence (4), the descriptive syntagma (1), and the parallel syntagma (1), to create *Queen of Hearts*. Characters are made to face one another and converse, and for the rest of the time they are moving from one place to another or else are being displaced through time and place in order to lift realism to the symbolic level. Realism is clearly not a primary concern for the filmmaker who is more interested in the art of narrating than in the "realness" behind the narrative told.

Twelve chapters resume the film's narrative plot which is not quite equivalent to the original synopsis given at the beginning of this chapter.

1. Chapter One. Running away. 0:00-8:00 minutes.
2. Chapter Two. Setting Up in Britain. 8:01-16:38.
3. Chapter Three. The Wedding. 16:39-22:03.
4. Chapter Four. The Shadow. 22:04-29:56.
5. Chapter Five. The Nightmare. 29:57-32:59.
6. Chapter Six. Nonno Arrives in London. 31:00- 47:58.
7. Chapter Seven. The family is growing. 47:58-52:15.
8. Chapter Eight. The past that will not sleep. 52:14-57:15.
9. Chapter Nine. Bella terra. 57:16-62:54.
10. Chapter Ten. Nonno Dies. 62:55-:80:56.
11. Chapter Eleven. Rosa and Barbariccia. 80:57-93:45.
12. Chapter Twelve. Happy Ending. 93:46-1:10.00.

Without going into details here, the structure with its plot points emerges nevertheless quite discernibly. 1. Someone runs away from Italy, 2. settles in Britain, 3. marries, receives *una busta*, 4. someone called the Shadow appears, 5. it is a nightmare, 6. Nonno arrives in London, 7. the person's family grows, 8. but his past that will not sleep, 9. on this bella terra, 10. Nonno dies, 11. this person's wife Rosa meets the Shadow (Barbariccia), 12. then there is a happy ending for our protagonist when his wife comes back to him.

Even without mentioning the content of each scene and sequence the plot seems easy to describe. A couple runs away, and sets itself up in London,

England. One of their four children marries. At the Turning Point (according to Syd Field's paradigm) is the appearance of the Shadow (the jilted lover).

The happy family begins to breakdown (the nightmare being an metonymy of this collapse) that will be momentarily remedied by the unexpected arrival of the grandfather. A grandchild is born, the grandfather encourages the son to settle down in England ("This is pure land") and not to look back at the past (the earth is the metaphor of the present and new life). Once this message has been passed on to son and grandchildren, the adjuvant "grandfather" dies.

This symbolic (and very real) helper has temporarily stepped aside (the grandfather will come back as a vision near the end of the film), the second Turning Point presents itself with the appearance of the jilted lover who is coming back to reclaim the love stolen from him. A number of gambling episodes lead to the third major Turning Point of the film: the once-promised lovers must meet again. Meet they do in order to settle the accounts...

The (gambling/lovers') debt must be paid back. The final episodes are metaphors of the combat between two men vying for the same woman. Chosen love stands against pre-arranged marriage, whereby the chosen man is made to win. The conflicts resolved, the film concludes with its promised ending. Everyone lives happy ever after.

There are various plots at work in this film, crisscrossing, moving up and down, going from the foreground to background of the narrative screen, each "actant" (Greimas) moving according to the role he has been ascribed to.

> 1. Danilo and Rosa run away, move to England, start a business, and lose everything to owned; Danilo even gambles his wife away, and must win her back by winning a battle against the old lover.

> 2. It is the story about a boy growing up Italian in a foreign land (England) and possibly turning into a writer or an artist. Who is he speaking to? Who is his monologue addressed to? Why does he need to tell someone his story?

> 3. This story is at once an autobiography and ethnographic study of Italian immigrants.

> 4. There is the revenge plot: two subjects after the same one object of desire. Barbariccia does everything in his power to win back the woman he loved dearly. More than just a promised bride, Rosa represents the universe to Barbariccia.

The suffering Barbariccia experiences — if we are to believe all that is said in the major monologue during the gambling scene uniting Barbariccia, Danilo, Bruno, and Eddie fast asleep behind his father — is very real. Yes, we are right in supposing that Rosa is the reason why Barbariccia has become a bitter, angry man.

> Barbariccia: "The ace, the three, the King of Swords... what are you thinking about, Dany. I want to know what you are thinking at this moment... you won't feel it right now, Danilo. You just feel a kind of empty, like, a dream. You can't understand it, but slowly slowly it comes into your blood and then you realize that you've lost everything, that you've got nothing, that you're nothing, and then you start to be angry... okay one more... Double or quits..."
> Danilo: "I've got nothing."
> Barbariccia: "You're not clean out. You've still got a chance. You can still..." At this point Barbariccia grabs Danilo's hand with his wedding band: "You've got this. Put it on the line. Double or quits" (Scene 61).

These four narrative axes constitute the core of *Queen of Hearts*. The other characters act as adjuvants and opponents to the quest whose object is found at the end of the film. Here is a film with simple magic plotlines that reviewers have labelled it, and rightly so, a cinematic fable. More than the delving into modern adaptation of commedia dell'arte, *Queen of Hearts* is the first film fable in our study that offers a social commentary about an Italian culture outside of Italy.

From the first image up to the happy ending, we assist at the making of an Italian family that finds contentment in a foreign land, that is, outside their place of origin. This process to joy is painful. Yet the suffering is acceptable thanks to humor and irony. Is this transformation the result of what Elie Faure called *les effets du métissage*?[13] The gradual mixture of cultures, what the editors at the magazine *Vice Versa*, defined in the early 1980s as "transculturalism",[14] enables the ethnic artist, as post-emigrant, to dislodge assimilation and criticize it (with simple irony).

This emerging voice,[15] as Pasquale Verdicchio calls it, is in reality the coupling of agency and irony. This will to create and criticize both the non-assimilated Self and the assimilated Other is unique to the post-emigrant artist. Contrary to Franco Brusati's perspective (which remains, no matter how political, profoundly rooted in Italian History and the Italian territory), Tony Grisoni brilliantly swerves away the pillars of Italian national filmmaking. *Queen of Hearts* is not an Italian film; it does not belong to the History of Italian cinema defended say by Peter Bondanella, Millicent Marcus, and Marcia Landy,[16] none of whom ever define what it is that they call "Italian cinema". These scholars take their "Italian" corpus for granted. What is "Italian' about the films made by the Italian nation? That is the snag in most books about "Italian" cinema. Never are we given a precise definition of the thing they call Italian film.

The closest definition Marcus ever comes up with is by quoting Angela Dalle Vacche: "The body on screen serves as the reflection of a fictional, national self... terms of identification, an image of how they need to see themselves in order to have access to a national identity and imagine their roles in the historical process."[17] We find something similar with Marcel Jean who gives himself the challenging task of defining what is meant by "le cinéma québécois". Scholars and critics are hard pressed to define what their "national' corpus entails.[18]

National cinema? The cinema of the nation? Break away from the nation and you break national cinema, at least this is what Francesco Rosi's hypothesis seems to imply (Marcus suggests that "[f]or Rosi, the waning... of national cinema is attributable to the loss of a unified self-image... a social disintegration").[19] The fact of the matter is that no one has yet created a satisfactory definition of the term "nation". In his book *Nations and Nationalism since 1780*, E. J. Hobsbawn explicitly demonstrates how the original term *(naciuns=pagans)* was used to designate the foreigner.

The word then evolved to exclude anyone who lived on a territory, owned by the Nation-State, that did not speak the language nor believed in the same god of the citizens of that society.[20] This shift in meaning (going from inclusion to exclusion), facilitated by the "hardened" of territorial borders, colored the ethnic dimension. There was a time when the nation included peoples from different backgrounds and who spoke different languages, but by the end of World War II this conception of citizenry shifted tremendously. From being heterogeneous and complex entities, nations strived for a more homogeneous sort of territory.

Our contention is that crossover — not the nostalgic proxy for a nation, but the indisputable acceptance of otherness in one's territory — establishes for the first time in a post-nation-state reality a confident new identity. Though there already existed dispositions for recognizing indirectly "nations" that shared many different territories (the Jewish people, for example), post-1945 biases have yet to expand our understanding of culture, people and geography. Splintered groups today find themselves vying on their own for their survival in different parts of the world.

This cultural evidence abroad for the Italian reality is the Italic, though, the Italic should be the equivalent of Anglophonia, Francophonia, and Lusophonia. We reserve the term Italian to all the peoples living in Italy, regardless of their origin, religion, and language who work for the Italian nation. The Italian-hyphenated-host-country and the Italic includes anyone who wishes to contribute to a higher, more abstract order of cultural distinctiveness for things Italian, but not national.[21] Each individual minority group will deal with its particular issues and to learn to cope with its new collective but not nationalist ideal.

With *Queen of Hearts* we can specify that what we have here, in this film about Italian culture in Britain, is the wager (is it a coincidence that the film is about gambling?) that a displaced, deterritorialized Italic culture exists and is doing well in the United Kingdom. It is a gamble whose stake are far from being secured. Some individuals will win their bet, and foster "a politics of cultural pluralism"[22] (to quote Michael Novac). Others will lose everything, and jump onto the train of the "passing", those vehicles for the "Uncle Toms" *(sic)* who chose to disappear under the banners of another community.

The filmmaker and the scriptwriter

Acclaimed for his television work on Dennis Potter's *Singing Detective,* Jon Amiel (b. May 20,1948) tackled his first feature film, *Queen of Hearts,* scripted by Tony Grisoni (October 28, 1952). Amiel went on to have a respectful film career, directing films such as *Sommersby* (1993), *Copycat* (1995), *The Man Who Knew Too Little* (1997), *Entrapment* (1999) and, more recently, *Angel Makers* (2010).

Inevitably when it comes to the ethnic we are forced to deal with the "authentic", suggests Michael Novak in his book *The Rise of the Unmeltable Ethnics.*[23] The term "authenticity" automatically implies its antonym "inauthentic", "counterfeit", as though one were indissociable from the other, the double face of a single coin. When it comes to ethnic artistic expression, people find it very difficult to sever the means of production from the product offered.

More often than not, in popular commercial works, content is all an audience notices: we praise the storyline, or an actor's performance in such and such a scene. At times, the *auteur theory* takes precedence over content: a certain film develops a specific aspect or quality in a particular filmmaker's work. Seldom do we twaddle on the cultural merits of a film directed entirely by an ethnic group of artists. Seldom, because true ethnic works of art, in the proper sense of the word, are a rarity.

The majority films produced are works produced by artists born and living in nations. *Bread and Chocolate* is without question an Italian film written and directed by an Italian Franco Brusati. *Teorema* (1968) is an Italian film directed by an Italian Pier Paolo Pasolini, though the protagonist is interpreted by British star Terence Stamp. *Un prophète* (2010) by French Jacques Audiard is a French film, in spite of its poignantly multicultural spices (North African, Corsican, Italian, French flavors).

As culturally vibrant as these elements might be, not one of these works can be considered an ethnic film; all spring from a defined geographical location, each one expressing itself in one main cultural language, unfolding a single history, with people with faiths dedicated to pretty much one religion. These are national films, produced by a nation for its people.

These are Italian or French films produced to mirror the image of a specific society. What they review about their own society may or may not be applicable to other societies; people conclude: It is an Italian problem, it is a French problem, it is not our problem. For example, *Fish Tank* (2009) by Andrea Arnold depicts a British social problem which has very little to do with the U.S.A, Italy, or Canada. There might be similarities but ultimately what Arnold does is lift a mirror for her society to look into.

The best of ethnic works dig deeper into the soil and come out from the other side. The ethnic film does not limit itself to the nation from which it rises; in fact, in many cases the ethnic film when produced independently speak against the nation in which it was made. John Cassavetes could be considered an ethnic filmmaker; until very recently his films were not even available to the public. He need not have talked about his Greek-ness, but every film he did direct had that something more that pushed his work to the margins of society. Similar commentary could be extended to Woody Allen (in some cases) and Spike Lee (in most cases).

When I say "ethnic" in this book, I am speaking mainly of the descendants of the immigrants of southern and eastern Europe: Poles, Italians, Greeks, and Slavs. These include, of course, Armenians, Lebanese, Slovenes, Ruthenians, Croats, Serbs, Czechs (Bohemians and Moravians), Slovaks, Lithuanians, Estonians, Russians, Spanish, and Portuguese... What is an ethnic group?

It is a group with historical memory, real or imaginary. One belongs to an ethnic group in part involuntarily, in part by choice. Given a grandparent or two, one chooses to shape one's consciousness by one history rather than another. Ethnic memory is not a set of events remembered, but rather a set of instincts, feelings, intimacies, expectations, patterns of emotion and behavior; a sense of reality; a set of stories for individuals — and for the people as a whole — to live out."[24]

Ethnic identity has widened to enclose more groups. The criteria to account for ethnicity get more complicated than we might have imagined. The debates kindled by ethnicity of the 1970s, at the time when Michael Novak was first sounding his theories of otherness, have been pushed open to actively embrace the twenty-first century spectrum of peoples, cultures, histories and religions. Ethnicity requires that we put ourselves in a different mindset in order to extract new meanings usually from old contents. No longer in search of a particular stylistic tic on the part of the director, we find ourselves unravelling obscure social and cultural concerns.

Queen of Hearts dabbles with "Hansen's law" which Marcus Lee Hansen advanced in a 1938 essay, "The Problem of the Third Generation Immigrant": "the son wishes to forget the grandson wishes to remember."[25] Though *Queen of Hearts* does delve in the ethnic experience, superficially, ironically, intelligently, on various levels — indeed, "a grandson who wishes to remember" — it is not an ethnic film. It is, after all, a British film.

Where does one start when dealing with a story about a culture that is not one's own? Jon Amiel is not, we imagine, of Italian descent. Why make a film on a culture one knows little or nothing about? Through research and analysis, much study, a filmmaker can eventually manage to pull out some of the authentic experience, however, the filmmaker, unlike an actor, need not be a follower of Lee Strasberg and the Actors' Studio. The paycheck provides the necessary stimulation-to-order to direct a film.

There have been, of course, many Italian filmmakers who made films on Italians. Yet national culture is not ethnic culture. It would be interesting to compare how non-Italian filmmakers fair compared to Italian filmmakers when approaching the thematic of ethnic Italianness. We can ask ourselves how do works by non-Italians differ from those by Italians. What intrigues us most is to know, if this had been possible, how would an Italian ethnic filmmaker have directed *Queen of Hearts?* Imagine how dissimilar the Italian version, the British version, and the ethnic version of a single script of *Queen of Hearts* would be? (Quality put aside, and quality is the ultimate judge.)

In the 1980s the Canadian councils for the Arts had to deal with this delicate thematic; behind this "appropriation of voice" issue lay complex financial parameters that determine the well-being of artists. Every art piece should also make its artist live. Some critics claim that commercial practices (what else could they be?) of this sort "denaturalize" grassroots artistic expression. Granting one to make a film about an ethnic group that is not one's own automatically raises political questions. "Why choose/allow one 'foreign' artist to create a work about 'our' people? Why not hire someone from the same ethnic background as us?"

This is especially in the case of *Queen of Hearts*. Why choose Amiel who had never directed a feature-film before? Producer John Hardy could very well have approached a filmmaker from Italy or, if he were more daring, an Italian ethnic filmmaker from the Italian community in Britain.

Moving outside of national culture alters the nature of the game. A film might still be a film, but suddenly another level of significance opens up before the attentive viewer that question the whos and the whys of the multiplicity of artistic gestures.

This reasoning seditiously brings us to the notion authorship: who is, in reality, the author of *Queen of Hearts?* Is it the director, Jon Amiel, as advanced by the auteurist movement in the 1950s by the critics-filmmakers of the *Les Cahiers du cinéma?* Is it the scriptwriter, Tony Grisoni? Is it the producer, John Hardy? Though it is not the purpose of our study to visit the history of the politics of authorship, as Andrew Bennett does in his thorough examination of the "author", we must, nonetheless, ask ourselves this very important question: who is the author of this film?

Thanks to Roland Barthes' 1967 stimulating essay, "La mort de l'auteur" ("The Death of the Author"), Michel Foucault's exploration of the author as a function in his provoking 1969 article, "Qu'est-ce qu'un auteur?" ("What Is an Author"), and the works by countless feminist scholars, the author has come to the fore. He might be an individual, or a collaboration. The author can also be what Pierre Bourdieu calls a "cultural capital".[26]

Each position is valid and can be a proposition that takes us to various destinations. Roland Barthes' line of reasoning in his essay is clear; the author is of no importance. There was something there before the author started to write his story; the author is a person who copied words out of a dictionary readymade ("dictionnaire tout composé"), a life dictionary from which he pulled, like from a magician's hat, images and ideas. The author is but a mediator of a "before" and an "after" of the story, a sort of shaman, whose talent is recognized according to his "performance".

It is the reader who is responsible to piece all of these elements together and make sense of these fragments that come from no single source. Barthes will push these concepts to the maximum in *S/Z*.[27] What is needed here is a running through of the text in order to pull out one by one the threads that ultimately produce pleasure in us. Accordingly, we can say that Jon Amiel is a mediator between the producer and Tony Grisoni. As Grisoni is the mediator of between Britain and the Italian community he was born into.

Michel Foucault produces an altogether different point of view about the author and his/her functions in society. Basically, the author-function possesses four characteristics: 1. Juridical and institutional; 2. Temporally and geographically confined; 3. Complexity of roles; 4. Plurality of egos. In the case of film, we are mostly confronted by the last function; one can never tell who is speaking what and, in the end, as Foucault himself says: what does it matter who is speaking?[28]

In *Queen of Hearts* the author is a plurality of voices. The film is the mediation between Amiel's technical virtuosity (but not only) and Grisoni's lyrical resourcefulness. It is, to use an object in the film itself, a "bella macchina", a collector's piece that interlocks different components of the narration (story telling outside of film), the plot per se, the filmic story ("le texte est un tissu de citations", as Barthes would have it), and the manner in which the film is (re)telling the story.

In some cases, who speaks matters. For speaking is a right that is not always granted. The right to speak for an ethnic is a rather recent invention. When given this right, often it is not always acknowledged. In scene 50, a barely noticeable incident attracts our attention. Joyous about the plot of land, Nonno greets a neighbor who refuses to acknowledge him. A simple greeting that is rebutted. Metaphorically, one might be given the freedom of speech but speech is valid if and only if there is someone out who is willing to listen. Without a listener speech is just as good (or futile) as silence (or talking to oneself).

If the ethnic voice is not filtered through the tunnels of the legitimate powers of the canon, it is silenced, ignored, deleted. With film, these powers, terribly political, are neither given, nor unchangeable. Imagine this film being directed by a totally independent Grisoni, producing it with his own money, unfretted by any financial, political, business, national, and cultural considerations? Because it is impossible to imagine such a script is proof that the position the ethnic artist finds himself (and a thousandfold herself) remains inclement to say the least.

We want to visit more what in *Queen of Hearts* is particularly Italic than to unravel the semantic structure in Jon Amiel's artistic signature. It is Tony Grisoni's creative imagination that sparked our need to study this film, not Amiel's style (though we will unresistingly map those directorial signs).

We will move up and down the elevator of meaning (style and narrative) concentrating on the codes that most interest us which, at this time, are those that lead more directly to the Italian cultural synergy.

Chapiter 1: Running Away
0:00-8:00 minutes

1. Sequence. Ext. Italian town. Day. 0-1=fade in.
0:00-1:31: Producers' credits.

This chapter is divided into two mega-sequences: syntagmas 1-6 and 7-9. Luscious strings filled with operatic Italianness over a stone wall, the camera pans from left to right, stopping on a hamlet in Italy. Title film credits begin, the stone wall acting like a stage curtail. In *Les vacances de monsieur Hulot* (1953), Jacques Tati used window curtains and sails swishing over the screen to call forth the start of a scene. The music rises to an ironic crescendo on the film title, *Queen of Hearts*. Not "verbo-centric", as Michel Chion terms it (*Audio*, 71), this chapter unrolls like a silent movie. Justified and synchronized sounds are authentic, yet they do not call out to the spectator. The main element on the soundtrack is the melody score uniting what in reality are disparate fragments spliced together in a logical and chronological order.

2. Sequence shot. Ext./Int. Bar-Café. Day.
1-2=zero. 1:32-1:51

A slow back dolly on the Italian town in the sweltering heat. Italian voices (justified, synchronized, authentic) in off over the image of the father of the protagonist, with a kepi, asleep on a chair, in the entrance of an empty café. The music rises (unjustified, asynchronic, non-authentic) and fades out as the camera dollies back to a large polished espresso coffee machine. This espresso maker coolly placed off-center will play a prominent role in the film. Without this silent Mac Guffin (to use a concept devised by Alfred Hitchcock) nonchalantly tossed in the foreground, there would be no Turning Point.

3. Scene. Ext./Int. House. Day.
2-3=zero. 1:52-2:18

A man in shirt sleeve (Danilo Lucca) leans against the window frame sadly yearning for a neighbor, a woman (Rosa) dressed in white, combing her long hair. The music, non-justified, non-synchronized, non-authentic, is "empathetic" as well as "music from the pit", to use terms introduced by Michel Chion (*Audio*, 71). It simulates operatic melodrama which suggests that a tragedy will soon folding before the spectator's eyes. The source of the music is not revealed on screen. The director put music here to attract our attention. The love gaze of pining lovers is interrupted by the Italian mother in a black dress (is she in mourning?), who abruptly shuts the windows on Danilo.

4. Scene. Int. Bar-Café. Day. 3-4=zero. 2:19-2:48
Danilo in shirtsleeves walks into the bar café from behind the curtain, fear in his eyes, tiptoes so as to not awaken his sleeping father. Steam from the espresso machine blurts out unexpectedly, stirring awake the father who taps his finger on the box laid on his lap, indubitably a personal treasure. The significance of this box will be apparent later. From the box the camera tilts to a cane cutting across the screen. The father, moral lawmaker, shakes a powerful "no" with his head. Out pours the son's plea: "Papa." The son walks away. Danilo has no mother; and Rosa has no father. Few images to express the forbidden (paternal, social, cultural); the complimentary elements of the story: Danilo and Rosa. Yet neither Rosa's mother (a widow?), nor Danilo's father (a widower?) acknowledge this star-crossed love.

5. Scene. Int. Room. Day. 4-5=zero. 2:49-3:50
The orchestral music "from the pit" persists. Two men in black suits smile: one is the future husband (Barbariccia); the other the best-man, the witness, the chaperon. The dowry is bestowed to the future mother-in-law, who invites her reluctant daughter into the living room.

A crucifix reminds the spectator that this is a Catholic family. A Catholic woman is about to marry. A displaced diegetic insert of the neighbor (Danilo) cutting a clothesline. The festive moment ends curtly; there are no crucifixes in Danilo's house.

The bride-to-be frowns, says in Italian: "Mi sento male" ("I feel awful"). Out she runs to her room. No English subtitles are added.

No need to explain: Rose does not want to marry Barbariccia. The mother picks up the dowry (a golden colored embroidered quilt). Barbariccia sneers.

6. Scene. Ext./Int. Rosa's Room. Day.
5-6=zero. 3:51-4:32
The mother climbs to her daughter's room. Rosa is crying on her bed, clutching a pillow. The jilted husband-to-be knocks on the door. The door latch-locked. Inside, in low angle Rosa looks up, smiling off screen, the shadow of a ladder above her head, like an aura. This is the man Rosa truly loves.

When finally Barbariccia and mother break down the door, the room is empty. Rosa is nowhere to be seen. From the window Barbariccia and Rosa's mother look down, as a tomato drops to the ground.

7. Sequence. Ext. Village roads. Day.
6-7=zero. 4:33-5:47

Danilo, still unnamed (the spectator still has not heard the protagonist's name), and Rosa race through the labyrinthine roads of San Geminiano. This is the Keystone cops *à l'italienne*... A mixture of the noir by Fritz Lang (*Metropolis*, 1927) and the pink of Charles Chaplin (*Modern Times*, 1936). Danilo in a black suit and Rosa in her white dress are very much like a married couple! No dialogue added. Just a melodramatic music. Jilted, Barbariccia asks his best-man for a knife.

8. Sequence. Int. Tower staircase. Day.
7-8=zero. 5:48-6:13

Horns blare out the despair of this couple running away. This myriad of staircases reminds us of Hitchcock's majestic film, *Vertigo* (1958).

9. Alternate syntagma. Ext. Tower. Day.
8-9=zero. 6:14-8:00

The horns subside. Violins take over the melody; voices rise from the street. All is synchronized, justified, authentic. In this alternate syntagma scenes we move from the top of the tower where the lovers stand to the villagers down below. Heart-crossing Rosa's mother spits on Danilo's father, at her side.

The couple jumps. On-lookers scream. The music screams. Then silence, as the couple safely drop onto the straw pile behind a truck passing by. Soft music fades in. Eddie, the couple's youngest child, begins a monologue in a British accent. His words bind the following disparate narrative segments together. Out of control, Barbariccia slides the knife blade in his fist, blood drips to the ground.

Chapter 2: Setting Up in Britain
8:01-16:38

10. Scene. Ext. Boat. Evening.
9-10=montage with effect. 8:01-8:18

This chapter is made up of four mega-sequences: syntagmas 10-15, 16, 17-21, 22. Eddie's monologue links two syntagmas, a new chapter announces a new life. Against the setting sun, Rosa and her lover kiss. In the background Rosa's mother.

Brusati in *Bread and Chocolate* used this ingenious trick in what we called a "double-jointed" (overlapping) syntagma, which brings one syntagma to its conclusion and opens the following one. Without a fade-in, without a fade-out, without a dissolve, the couple is on its way to England. This absence of visual punctuation quickens the pace of the action.

> 11. Sequence shot. Int. Home. Day.
> 11-12=montage with effect. 8:19-8:48

We assist at the birth of the Lucca family. This entire mega-sequence in form of an episodic sequence details scenettes of this Italian emigrant family setting up a business in London in the early 1960s.

On the soundtrack: accompanying joyful music, reminiscent of Nino Rota's circus compositions for Fellini, is slightly higher in volume than the natural sounds whose sources can be viewed on screen. This interplay between synchronism and asynchronism brings us back to the silent-movie era; the voice-over acting as an inter-title. No subtitles appear.

Amiel reassures his spectator that he need not count on words to understand the film. From a close up of the photograph of Blessed Pope John XXIII (1958-63) and statuettes of the Holy Mary and saints on a wardrobe with a mirror the camera dollies back out of a tent in a room with a leaking roof where are sitting Nonna Sabila knitting, a crucifix on her breast, Dad in a black tuxedo (has yet to be given a name) and Rosa waiting to give birth. Dad goes to work, holding an open umbrella inside the house. This is not going to be a serious drama; a fairy-tale quality charges the atmosphere. This is not the lifestyle Barbariccia would have given Rosa, now holding her tummy with her first child.

> 12. Episodic sequence. Int. Home. Day.
> 11-12=montage with effect. 8:49-9:20

A sequence of episodes: scenes of the birth of the four children: Bruno, Angelica, Teresa, and (Danilo, in the foreground in his undershirt, Rosa in the background, curtain pulled, is giving birth to) Eddie, whose fate is put in the hands of religious superstition. ("The angels decided to make me stay.") Such a sentence prepares the viewer to the fable-like unfolding of future events.

> 13. Sequence shot. Int. Room. Evening.
> 12-13=montage with effect. 9:21-9:29

Against a black backdrop, a child's hand tightens an adult's index finger. Michelangelo's *Birth of Adam* comes to mind. Father and son, God and Adam. The beginning of life.

14. Scene. Int. House. Night.
13-14=montage with effect. 9:30-9:36

Here is what Laurent Jullier and Michel Marie call a "circus shot": the camera faces a character spinning around. Danilo holds Eddie, turning a full 360 degree. Not a sequence shot, there are cuts to and fro between Father and son, between God and Adam.

15. Scene. Int. House. Night.
14-15=montage with effect. 9:40-10:06

Danilo and Rosa waltzing, laughing, Eddie looking up. It is not truly music the couple can dance to. A few edits reveal the children, grown-up, eating on the floor. Bruno, *Monday's Child*, is already critical of his father who is unable to pay the bills. Eddie does not recall "any of that stuff". These three last syntagmas could be read as being part of the episodic sequence 12. If in this syntagma we are offered more than glimpses of the birth of a family, the first two syntagmas intimate the growing harmony between father Danilo and son Eddie, and the Bruno-Danilo dissension.

16. Scene. Int. Restaurant. Evening.
15-16=montage with effect. 10:07-11:32

We do not consider this scene as forming a new chapter, because what follows postulates a continuity of action. A sign hangs from the ceiling of a restaurant, "Merry Christmas", dangling over Danilo and a second waiter standing, looking bored. Interestingly, Grisoni has chosen to give his character the same job as Brusati gave Nino. Italian emigrants work as waiters in the new land. A body-less hand calls Danilo who speedily walks up to the table. This is the first realistic "verbo-centric scene" (to quote Chion) of the film: screen dialogue and synchronic sounds score the action. It must be the end of the night, the restaurant is empty, except for these drunken clients laughing.

Behind their table, a large decorated Christmas tree. This eleven-minute scene must be counted as a Turning Point of sorts, an Inciting Incident. In order to stimulate our curiosity, the scriptwriter must devise a diegetic switch in order to keep the spectator's interest alert.

In *Bread and Chocolate*, it was the scene where a couple catches Nino urinating in public and, in *A Pain in the Ass,* it is Milan shooting Felix. Here a couple asks Danilo to smile, and if he does he will win a five-pound bill. Danilo does not know what to make of this wager.

Then the head of the dead pig on the table in front of the couple speaks to Danilo: "Money is like the sun. Only if you trust the coin will you become a man of property. Only then will you be happy. Trust the coins. Beware the King of Swords."

The narrative switches register. The spectator is given a hint to what will unfold: three words the encompass all of the plot: "Coins. Property. King of Swords"; money, to have and not to have any; ownership, the café; another man who will become an obstacle, Barbariccia.

17. Sequence. Ext. Streets. Night.
16-17=zero. 11:33-12:17

Danilo walks down a street at night, with a music-box melody in the background. The sounds of footsteps are justified, synchronized, authentic, except for a man's voice (the pig's voice) calling out to him: "Danilo, Danilo, trust the coins. I will show you a game, any game you want."

The music rises, Danilo ("Dad" finally receives a name) searches for the source of the voice. It is an unidentified man standing in the dark. The film turns mysteriously thriller-like, the foggy back-alley lit with blue light, the footsteps become louder and inauthentic. Danilo rings the door of a place appropriately named *Cassa d'Oro* (the Golden Coffer). The title conveys an Italian clientele. The ghetto suggests that Italian immigration was alive and well in London of the 1950 and 1960s. Danilo is not alone; he is one among many.

18. Sequence. Ext./Int. Cassa d'Oro. Night.
17-18=zero. 12:18-12:59

Danilo's finger presses on a doorbell; an eye in the door-eye. The camera alternates between Danilo's subjective point of view and that of other men looking at Danilo. The music, a mixture of suspense and playfulness; realistic justified sounds audible in the background.

19. Episodic sequence. Int. Room. Night.
18-19=zero. 13:00-14:28

Danilo sits at a table where players play. Dead moments are skipped.

20. Scene. Ext. Road. Day.
19-20=zero. 14:29-15:03

Snow on the ground, music in the air, the magic melody fades into real sounds. Eddie continues his monologue in voice over. Danilo holds suitcases, his family stands behind him, Eddie to his side. They stare at their new property. "A man with property." Gambling ("coins") has enabled Danilo to become the owner of property, an old hardware store which he transforms into a house and a café shop ("Dad has plans"). As will become evident,

Eddie is Danilo's confidant, and the spectator's narrative filter: the narrator is Eddie. Focalization is subjective: what he sees is what the spectator sees.

21. Scene. Int. The Lucky Café. Day.
20-21=montage with effect. 15:04-15:51

Time has passed. Most of the sounds are justified, synchronized, authentic. The hardware store has become a café. Standing in front of a coffee machine, a friend Mario scribbles in his palm the amount that Danilo will have to pay for the espresso machine, on credit.

"This takes a thousand years to pay back," says Danilo, discouraged. He asks his son what he thinks; Eddie acquiesces enthusiastically. Danilo and Mario spit in the palms of their hands and seal the deal with a handshake. Accordion music ("Torna a Surriento" by Ernesto De Curtis) rises to the fore. This well-known melody was heard in *Bread and Chocolate*. This wink at Italy is stereotypical, more or less real, in the minds of the creators, in the minds of the spectators, yet the music works, kindles nostalgia.

22. Scene. Int. Café. Day.
21-22=montage with effect. 15:52-16:39

Between scene 21 and scene 22, five more years have passed by. A close-up of the eagle on the *bella macchina*, the grandmother is sweeping the floor.

Eddie's monologue wraps the introduction to the "lucky" family: Rosa and Teresa shine the coffee machine; behind them, Angelica; Pepe, a man who spends his time eating "yesterday's sandwiches"; Nonna "who hasn't smiled since the day Queen Victoria died."

Outside, a sign with the name of the coffee shop: *The Lucky Café (Danilo Lucca e figli)*; Eddie, Danilo and Bruno, dressed in the best suits, stare into the camera of a photographer.

"Now we've got our own business. I'm ten now, and I'm a partner. Bruno says I live in a dream. Some people think I'm stupid. I know how things really are. I know the truth. My name is Eddie Lucca and my dad says I'm special."

An accordion interpretation of "Torna a Surriento" comes to an end, bringing this second chapter to a close. There is an element of the unreal in this simple scene. This film does not rely on realism.

Chapter 3: The Wedding, *La Busta*
16:39-22:03

23\. Descriptive Syntagma. Int. The Lucky Café. Day.
22-23=montage with effect. 16:39-19:25

Two mega-sequences make up this chapter: syntagmas 23-24, and 25. Jon Amiel refuses to pause on these episodes unrolling with feverish rapidity. Scene after scene, information is thrown at the spectator and, thanks to the Eddie's monologue which binds disparate fragments together, the narrative unity feels seamless. Mike Southon's inspired mobile camera captures these individual segments with such smoothness that the whole appears to the view as unbroken entity.

This scene wants to be realistic, visually, aurally: it is the wedding of the daughter Angelica. Eddie warns the spectator of trouble soon to come in the shape of a brown envelope. An envelope *(la busta)* at weddings usually contains money a guest brings to the newly-weds. Mario's brown envelope, however, is no one such gift. Ironically, Rosa comments on her son Bruno's bad behavior (he is seen as the most rebellious against the Lucca family): "Our children are moving into other worlds." To which Mario replies, quite innocuously, as he hands her his envelope: "Me too, Rosa." Old customs are dying out, and new attitudes, we will soon discover, are taking over. This envelope is the half-hour Turning Point. The plot changes direction.

24\. Scene. Int./Ext. Street. Day.
23-24=zero. 19:26-20:44

The photographer in his heavy Italian accent (stereotypes quickly act like strong identifiers) begs the wedding guests to step outside so that he can take the last and only photograph of the marriage — all his other images having been destroyed by children who have stolen his bag. There is a sort of visual enjambement between the last scene and this one… an ingenious method to further practice the invisible edit. All get ready for the final family picture, but nothing seems to work as it is supposed to. A red car frightens the screaming photographer who accidentally pulls the camera off of its tripod, producing the memorial slanted wedding picture that is a presage of the ills to come.

25\. Scene. Int. Café. Day.
24-25=montage with effect. 20:45-22:03

Another shift in time. The same location, it is a few days later. The first Turning Point of the film happens here. The scene begins with the wedding photograph in a frame on the wall of the café. The contents of the brown envelope are disclosed. Danilo, Eddie (arms on his father's shoulder), Mario with hat and Pepe (cigarette over his ear), are playing cards. Over Mario's should a picture of Blessed Pope John XXIII. Mario's new landlord (Barbariccia) has paid him to get out of his home.

Mario has decided to return to the old country: "One million pounds. I'm going to be a big shot. I'm going back to the old country, and I'm going to open a little business." Danilo's son Bruno refuses to make coffee for his dad. Alone, Eddie, the faithful son, is too glad to make an espresso for his dear beloved father. Mario, more than just a friend, is the Sender whose presents (the *bella macchina* and the *busta*) are keys that open doors to a new horizon.

Chapter 4: The Shadow
22:04-29:56

26. Sequence. Ext. Road. Day.
25-26=montage with effect. 22:04-22:40

The chapter, though shaped like an episodic mega-sequence, is linear, less fragmentary; slight temporal blocks have been edited out. Instead of presenting each scene in depth, this mega-sequence reveals the double-levelled plot. On one level, Eddie acquaints us to this Little Italy, and, more particularly, to Beetle, his dear friend; on the second level, another story, which we had left behind, now comes to the surface: the Shadow Barbariccia, the mysterious landlord who has given Mario a million pounds. Reduced to a looming Shadow, Barbariccia appears everywhere. A Zorro hat on his head and in shorts, Eddie runs out of the café.

27. Scene. Int. Gennaro's Betting Office. Day.
26-27=zero. 22:41-23:38

The scene is realistic, both on the sound and visual tracks. Sounds are justified, authentic, synchronic. The action is confined to one large room, which will be the setting where the outcome of this story unfolds. Eddie walks into the betting den, owed by Beetle's father. The barber asks Eddie for his advice on a bet. Eddie is a begetter of luck.

The Lucca surname (also the name of a Tuscan city) translates humorously into Lucky. Perhaps this play of vowels ("a" and "I") foreshadows the ironic twist of bad luck that awaits Danilo. The missed double-suicide, the pig, now Eddie's supra-natural powers (what else to call it?): reality is invested with otherworldly wizardry.

"That kid's blessed," the barber mutters as he collects his booty. Eddie's childish wager (on Singalong) has brought the barber real money.

28. Sequence. Ext. Hardware store/street. Day.
27-28=zero. 23:38-25:08

From the Lucky Café, the spectator visits the creation of Little Italy ("Ritalie", "Wopland") as viewed by Eddie and Beetle. Mario's abandoned hardware is under construction, curtains hang in front of the building. Eddie compares the building to an "empty skull". This seemingly banal comment in fact contains unexpected connotations. Little Italy prevails if inhabited, or else — dare we think say it? — it is reduced to head without thought. Being Italian outside of Italy is a willed thought; one must want it to be, otherwise it simply disappears.

29. Alternate syntagma. Ext. Street. Evening.
28-29=montage with effect. 25:09-25:50

Music again accompanies the image. This new syntagma begins with an establishing shot of what the Shadow sees. Someone is looking at the Lucky Café, and it is not the boys. Mario in an overcoat embraces Rosa. The Nonna in the background sews, as Danilo watches on. Mario speaks first in Italian, then switches to English: *"Ciao, bella macchina."* Danilo, hand on his friend's shoulder, complains about not being able to pay him back. "Just look after it." Outside, the Shadow waits. Scared, the boys run into the frame, Eddie screaming "Dad." Two more inserts show the shadow of a man in the dark.

30. Alternate Syntagma. Int. The Lucky Café. Evening.
29-30=zero. 25:51-27:08

This syntagma alternates between shots from the café and shots of the film shown on the television (*The Vikings* (1958), by Richard Fleischer, director of the masterpiece, *The Boston Strangler*, 1968, about Albert De Salvo, the presumed Boston serial killer.)

The family sitting in front of a television set: *Bread and Chocolate* has a similar scene, with Nino, Elena and her son. Families spend a lot of time in front of television sets hypnotized by moving image: cartoons, a movie. "This is where the bird takes out his eyes," the grandmother mutters. Danilo and Pepe, unable to play a game of cards, turn to watch. Einar and Eric are two Viking half-brothers; the former, a great warrior, the other, an ex-slave, both are unaware of the true identity of the other. Tony Curtis holds a bird that attacks Kirk Douglas and pulls out his eyes.

Sadly, the television breaks down, Beetle proposes to fix it. Danilo screams, "Don't let him near it." Nonna intercedes dismissing Danilo who threatens her to put her in an old people's home, "like English grannies". Eddie identifies the sound of a car.

31. Scene. Ext. Street. Evening. 30-31=zero.
27:08:-29:56

A couple kiss, Bruno gets out of his girlfriend's car. His sister Teresa weeps in a second car. Upset, Bruno pulls his sister out, ready to fight with the man inside. Teresa runs into the Café accusing Bruno of acting like a "big Italian brother".

Neighbors applaud at the scrimmage on the street below. Rosa scolds her son. Nonna applauds Bruno's fury: "Just like Tony Curtis." Danilo accuses Bruno of acting like a movie star. Bruno accuses his father of being a drunkard and a gambler. When Rosa suggests that Bruno find a wife, Bruno retorts: "You need a husband... He is a weak man, Mamma."

Rosa replies: "He is strong enough for me."

From the TV set, Kirk Douglas says: "If I can have your love, I'll have your hate."

Bruno has but hatred for his father.

Chapter 5: The Nightmare
29:57-32:59

32. Scene. Int. Bedroom. Night.
31-32=zero. 29:57-30:47

This chapter presents itself in two separate mega-sequences: syntagmas 32 and 33. Eddie has nightmare to which we are privy to. An eagle (the bird from The Vikings) attacks Bruno dresses as a gladiator. The bird sound is loud, inauthentic (yet synchronized and justified).

Amiel acknowledges Alfred Hitchcock's *The Birds* (1963). As the glittering sword strikes down in the dark, Eddie awakens, screaming. Eddie sits up in the bed he shares with Bruno, realizes that his brother is not the gladiator at all but is sound asleep. From the thunderous music we glide into a soft background music barely audible.

33. Alternate Syntagma. Ext./Int. Bedroom. Night.
32-33=zero. 30:48-30:59

A low angel shot of Rosa pulling the curtains, from the point of view of someone below. Who is looking? Three quick inserts reveal the answer: it is Barbariccia. This revelation, a Turning Point, brings this mega-syntagma to a close. Empathetic music rolls on a close-up of Barbariccia. The past has caught up with Danilo.

Chapter 6: Nonno Arrives in London
31:00- 47:58

34. Scene. Int. Bedroom. Day.
33-34=zero. 31:00-31:50

Chapter six contains six mega-sequences: syntagmas 34-38; 39; 40-44; 45; 46; 47-49. Syntagma 45 could very well be part of mega-sequence 6 but it offers a moment of intimacy with Danilo that is unique in the entire film. Danilo and Rosa are kissing in bed. It is a lazy morning. Eddie walks into the bedroom, asking for socks. Danilo jokingly tells him to put newspapers instead, claiming that is what he used to do in Italy. This bringing up Italy foreshadows the arrival of Nonno.

35. Scene. Int. The Lucky Café. Day.
34-35=zero. 31:51-32:50

Teresa, all dressed, walks into the café, kisses her Nonna, eating breakfast, on the cheek, walks right by Bruno, behind the counter, refusing to talk to him.

A postwoman plods forward, head down, male clients whistle at her. She greets Bruno warmly ("Buon giorno, Bruno"), hands him a letter, which Nonna pulls from his hand.

"He [Danilo] don't have no secrets from me."

Eddie eats a soup, watches, silent. The focalization is his. In the background, the accordion interpretation of "Torna a Surriento", an inversion of nostalgia: it is not Danilo who is going back to Surriento (Italy), but Italy that is ironically coming to London.

36. Scene. Int. Bedroom. Day.
35-36=zero. 32:51-33:14

One is tempted to see this scene and scene 34 as belonging to one syntagma, with an insert in between. But it is not the case. For what scene 35 does is extend the duration the lovers spend in bed. It prepares us for Nonna's one liner: "You want more kids or something?" Danilo and Rosa, still in bed, are kissing and laughing.

Nonna breaks into the bedroom, disgusted. There is no privacy (even less for sex) for husband and wife. Interestingly, there is little sex in the films we are studying. No so much a taboo as a ritual taken for granted. Nonna continues (to Rosa): "His filthy father is coming here... today." A military march links Danilo's smiling face and the next scene.

37. Scene. Int. The Lucky Café. Day.
36-37=zero. 33:15-34:28

The camera zooms in on a photograph of Danilo's father dressed in an Alpini military outfit, a gun in his hand. Eddie and Beetle stand in command in front of this picture; a military march (more humorous than serious) smothers the realistic sounds. Nonna is going to church to pray for their "black souls, especially yours" (staring into Danilo's eyes).

Danilo sends her a flying kiss, as he boasts his father's triumphs: "He could run through the mountains like a goat." Bruno refuses to accompany Danilo to meet his father at the station. Beetle and Eddie, Zorro hat on his head, newspaper in lieu of socks, follow Danilo.

38. Sequence. Ext. Street. Day.
37-38=zero. 34:29-34:45

A sequence shot. Natural sounds. Danilo, Eddie, and Beetle strut down the road. Their backs to us, Danilo holds the boys' hands.

Eddie: "Dad, have you ever worn a condom? ... I can't imagine you in a condom."

Progeny continues... minus the sex.

39. Scene. Int. Confessional. Day.
38-39=zero. 34:46-35:26

Nonna in a confessional box. The camera is on the priest listening not to the woman's sin, but to her complaining about Nonno's "filthy sins". The soundtrack, realistic, enhances the comical nature of the scene. Nonna's harping brings a smile to the spectator's lips, endears the priest to the spectator.

40. Scene. Ext. Station. Day.
34:26-36:30

Danilo's father is not the evil man Nonna makes him to be. A social man surrounded by young women conversing with him. The grandfather (wearing hearing aids) kisses the boys aggressively on the cheek. He baptizes Beetle (ie., Beatle) with his new name. (Eddie: "This is how Beetle got his name.")

41. Sequence. Ext. Taxi stand. Day.
40-41=zero. 36:31-37:19

People cross the frame as we move from one shot to another. A technique Amiel has repeated before: using human bodies as an editing device. Nonno greets the taxi driver who returns the salutation with "Shalom, Papa." Openness to otherness is implanted. Emigrants must help one another. The Jewish taxi driver brings the group to the Italian quarter via the short scenic route. The soundtrack is realistic: Nonno sings. London is a multicultural city; the spectator wonders where are the English among all of these ethnics.

42. Sequence shot. Ext. Road. Day.
41-42=zero. 37:20-37:41

The four get out of the taxi and walk the rest of the way home, their backs to us. Road noise makes up the soundtrack. Lack of money has been an issue for Danilo who does not have enough to pay for the complete ride home.

43. Scene. In. The Lucky Café. Day.
42-43=zero. 37:42-39:17

In the café, Nonno embraces Rosa, his daughter-in-law, congratulating her on her beauty. He hands out gifts (salami and cheese Italian tourists would normally carry in their suitcases). Nonno compares the coffee machine to "a big heart" *("un grosso cuore")*, it is the heart of Danilo's survival. Rosa's mother keeps her distant, refusing to address Nonno in Italian. But Danilo's father will have none of this cold-shoulder behavior, braves the moment: "How you do, old Chap? Please to met *(sic)* you..." Everyone breaks out in laughter, which infuriates Nonna. Eddie, the narrator, watches from a distance. What we are seeing is what Eddie is seeing.

44. Scene. Int. The Lucky Café. Day.
43-44=montage with effect. 39:19-40:25

Rosa is wiping cups as Danilo walks in, restless, surprised to see Pepe and Bruno missing. The café-bar is empty. Husband and wife speak in English. Are they speaking in English for real? Or is their speaking Italian being "translated" into English for the British spectator? A technique that we noticed in *Bread and Chocolate*. Rosa complains about Danilo's relationship with their son Bruno. Cigarette in hand, he staggers out, refusing to quarrel with his wife. Sounds are simple: justified, synchronized, authentic. This missed confrontation becomes the vehicle for the up-coming Pinch Point.

45. Sequence. Ext. The Lucky Café. Day.
44-45=zero. 40:26-40:57

The orchestra shot around Danilo, standing outside his café, ends with a close up. Here is a private moment with Danilo smoking, lasting less than a minute. Focalization has moved from Eddie's point of view to a general one. Or is all of this action being imagined by Eddie? Eddie signals a crucial moment: this is the end of the old life, the end of a dream, the end of innocence. Awareness will soon set it. This complicated camera shot is like a flash from heaven. Narrative significance needs not be lengthy. Seconds suffice to predict disaster or revelation.

46. Scene. Int. Nonno's bedroom. Day.
45-46=zero. 40:58-42:49

Eddie and Beetle step into Nonno's room. Nonno is lying on the bed. "This box," Nonno explains, "is the family treasure. This corrects what goes wrong... It brings you great dignity and magic." Music underscores the mysteriousness of the low-angle shot on Nonno. The box will become a center piece later on. A "family treasure" that will change the course of things to come. The spectator does not know that in the box is a gun. What Nonno is passing on to Eddie is how violence can sometimes save your dignity. A troubling secret to pass on to a grandson.

47. Scene. Ext. Road. Day.
46-47=zero. 42:50-43:27

The Italian ghetto is a small part of town. Around the corner Danilo notices the sign "Barbariccia" on the building that once belonged to Mario. Under the music of violins swirling in the background, Eddie speaks to the spectator: "It was as though Dad had always known it." Disaster is a revelation. Barbariccia, the mirror shadow, the jilted lover, Danilo's negative double, has come back to haunt Danilo. Barbariccia will take over the ghetto, mirroring how Danilo had stolen Rosa from him. With sheer brutality.

48. Alternating syntagma. Int. Barbariccia's store. Day.
47-48=zero. 43:28-45:51

Focalization is Eddie's, even if the action takes the spectator inside the shop. Barbariccia boasts the quality of his cutting machines (a metaphor for himself). They "cut everything in two seconds... I need someone for this place. A cigar...? You are a lucky man," says Barbariccia. Few words are spoken, each one to the point. Danilo Lucca, lucky? The irony is fierce. Is Barbariccia's job offer serious? A rhetorical question that spells irony. Barbariccia has been to

America. "Danny boy, there is nothing better than losing to make you sharp. Don't look so nervous. It was a long time ago... another world..." Barbariccia invites Danilo to a game of cards, an invitation which Danilo turns down. Barbariccia is aware of Danilo's weakness for gambling.

The alternating syntagma brings Barbariccia and Eddie together; this braid of distinct actions foreshadows the plot that will unfold. We're at the forty-five-minute point, when the Sender and the object of desire clash. Two subjects in want of the same object of desire. Barbariccia is an antagonist subject demanding his object of desire (Rosa). Danilo is the protagonist who must vie to keep Rosa he stole from Barbariccia, who scolds Pepe, in suit and tie, now Barbariccia's employee. "Looks like Mafia business," says Eddie. "Na, my father says the Mafia is just fairy tales," replies Beetle. Mafia business — fairy tales? Barbariccia fits the picture of the Mafioso prototype. Beetle will soon personally discover that the Mafia is no fairy tale.

49. Scene. Int. The Lucky Café. Evening.
48-49=montage with effect. 45:52-47:57

As the Lucca family celebrates Nonno's arrival, Bruno drops a bomb. He has found a new job in the entertainment business. He is working for Barbariccia, his debt collector. All hell breaks loose. Danilo and Bruno argue, Nonno insinuates that Teresa is pregnant. Teresa leaves abruptly, weeping. Nonna accuses Nonno of being "Satan" in Italian. Nonno smirks: "Only speak English?" All players who have been introduced now must follow the layout of roles. What better way to end tragedy than with a smile.

Chapter 7: The family is growing
47:58-52:15

50. Episodic sequence. Int. The Lucky Café. Day.
49-50=montage with effect. 47:58-52:14

This episodic sequence acts both as a mega-sequence and a chapter. It is not length but intention that qualifies a filmic segment. This sequence captures various moments of the day. These clips respect a chronological order. These fragments, episodes of emotionally charged action, conceal the non-linear structure of this film. "Flashes" of memorable moments are brought together by Eddie's monologue. His point of view dominates, he is the storyteller. What is trivial is neglected. The narrative might be misconstrued, unarticulated, dissimulated by his narration. We must accept what is said and shown as truth. "People are acting strange," says Eddie when he notices the postwoman obviously in love.

In this sequence Eddie divulges a number of consequential events that mark his burgeoning maturity: work (café), love (postwoman), gambling (Nonno), religion (Nonna, baptism, limbo), tradition (the plot of land), birth and social moral laws (Teresa giving birth as an unmarried woman). Instead of plunging deep into each individual instant, Eddie (ultimately, Grisoni and Amiel) choses the allegorical construction, as a sort of *scholium* (an explanatory note on a boy growing to be a young man). Eddie has taken over Bruno's job behind the counter, handling the espresso machine. Nonno listens to the horse race on radio. He is a gambler, like his son, and as unlucky. Is addiction genetic, or an acquired taste? Is Eddie doomed to be an unlucky gambler like his father and grandfather?

The accordion rendition of "Torna a Surriento" alludes not only to Italy, but to Barbariccia as well. Ironically, Italy presents itself both as a safeguard (Nonno) and an ominous entity (the butcher's son come back to claim his stolen girlfriend). The espresso machine's steam is a leitmotif bridging these moments dedicated to earth, religion, and birthing.

The soundtrack is mostly responsible for giving linearity to fragmented story. What is brought to us are key moments in the life of the Lucca family. Danilo and Nonno, shovel in hand, count the length of a plot of land. Danilo is "getting back to his roots". Interestingly, a little incident of racism is hinted at: Nonno greets a neighbor who refuses to acknowledge him.

Months have gone by. Teresa and Rosa flip through the pages of a magazine on babies. In the confessional, Nonna curses Danilo's father. The espresso machine spits steam as Teresa screams in pain giving birth. The child's baptism follows. Nonna compares Danilo's father to the devil. Beetle is told that his soul will rest in limbo for not being baptized. Everyone changes except Nonna's dislike of her son-in-law. A dissolve should follow; there is no such punctuation.

Chapter 8: The Past that will not sleep
52:14-57:15

51. Scene. Int. Nonno's Bedroom. Day.
50-51=zero. 52:14-55:31

Chapter eight presents three main moments in the story, announcing the median point, each of these syntagmas act as narrative mega-sequences. The first scene demonstrates Grisoni's comic genius. In his room, Nonno is listening to the horse races on the radio. The radio has been rigged by Beetle and Eddie, who control the horse-race broadcast in the adjacent room.

Beetle mimics the race commentator's voice, yells out the name of the winning horse. But it is not the horse Nonno has bet on. Nonno is aware of the kid's contraption. He pretends to be upset. Curses in Italian in North Italian accent. He places his hand on his heart, begins to cough, collapses on the bed, stone dead! Eddie and Beetle are shocked. When the boys come into the room, Nonno jumps out of bed and frightens the surprised boys away. The gag could have ended here; it doesn't. Follows the twist. Nonno returns to his room, calling the boys "bastards". He coughs, then spits blood into a handkerchief. The audience is taken by surprise, as were Eddie and Beetle. A masterful Grisoni touch — he pulls the audience into the story, by pushing us in that spot left empty of the escaping boys.

52. Scene. Int. Lucky Café. Day.
51-52=zero. 55:32-56:10

Pepe has come back with a note to reclaim la bella macchina. The edits are natural, sounds natural as well. We are getting close to the midpoint of the film where what is negative becomes positive, and what is positive negative.

53. Scene. Int. Bedroom. Night.
52-53=montage with effect. 56:11-57:15

The two brothers share their room with Nonno. On his bed, Nonno holds his magic box on his chest, whispering to himself in the dark. On the soundtrack, noises coming from outside: a barking dog, the ticking of a clock, music in the distance, voices from the war echoing. A non-diegetic insert of Nonno, as a younger man in a military outfit on a mountain.

Eddie, light caressing his face, stares at his grandfather, as though he were inside his grandfather's mind. Eddie can see Nonno's past. This dream-insert is both a flashback (analepsis) and a flashforward (prolepsis). From one perspective (Nonno's), the spectator is given a glimpse of Nonno's past; from another perspective (Eddie's), this insert projects the forthcoming death scene, and Eddie's potential "magical" powers. This insert asserts the subtle connection between grandfather and grandson... all of this unbeknownst to Bruno, the other grandson, shut off to the past and future.

Chapter 9: Bella terra
57:16-62:54

54. Scene. Ext. Garden. Day.
53-54=fade in. 57:16-57:45

This chapter is divided into three main components (mega-sequences): syntagmas 54; 55-57; 58. Nonno and Danilo talk about planting vegetables in this *"bella terra"*. Danilo is dismissive; Nonno ecstatic: "This is pure land." What is positive for the father is negative for the son (and positive for the grandson: Hansen's law at work. It is on this plot of land that Eddie will open the treasure box that will save Danilo from Barbariccia's clutch. Nonno's euphoria, however, is curtailed by coughing. Danilo runs in horror. Just twenty-nine seconds are needed to depict Nonno's physical attrition. All shot from a distance, as though what counted lay elsewhere: Eddie, the narrator.

55. Scene. Int. Barbariccia's shop. Day.
55-56=zero. 57:46-58:03

Eddie and Beetle knock on the windowpane of Barbariccia's shop. Pepe turns around smiling, but the boys make insulting faces and pull the finger to him.

56. Scene. Exterior. Street. Day.
55-56=zero. 58:04-59:55

Gennaro is standing outside his betting office, reading a letter. A garbage truck divides in two the space between Beetle and his father, and Eddie standing across the street, alone. Gennaro, upset, screams, pointing his finger to Eddie who cannot hear what is being said. Gennaro is weeping. The camera does a circus shot, turning a full 360 degrees around the quarrelling friends. On the soundtrack, the rumble of the garbage truck.

Beetle, visibly angry, walks up to Eddie: "I thought you were my friend, Eddie. Why has your brother kicked us out? Your brother is a debt collector. My dad owes money, but he hasn't got any… Your brother is a scum… Like the rest of your family." This harsh attack takes Eddie by surprise who strikes back: "At least I got a family. Not like you. Everyone knows about your mom. She did not die, she ran away with a man. She did not love you." Before Beetle can react, Gennaro pulls his son away: "You'll never speak to them again."

This was a comedy that sharply switches register. This is the break we were expecting. The midpoint is Bruno's betrayal of his family. Eddie walks into Lucky Café, with a "Closed" signboard on the door. Bruno, the son who has no attachments to the Lucca past, has become Barbariccia's debt collector, the enemy's collaborator. This theme of Italians betraying other Italians is a trait that is found in the four fiction films. The "I could have been a contender" syndrome. In a way, Bruno recalls Joey LaMotta. The enemy is family.

57. Scene. Int. The Lucky Café. Day.
56-57=zero. 60:00-62:35

Chairs are stacked in the café. Dressed up to the nines, Bruno hands Rosa a bouquet of flowers, slips Eddie a toy Ferrari Testa Rossa. Eddie refuses to thank his brother. Bruno treats Danilo with Havana cigars. Eddie strikes: "He's a scummy debt collector." The Mafia connection is discovered. Danilo slaps Bruno. Music fades in emphatically with the slap. Bruno points to Eddie: "This is your family, and that's your son." Bruno is divorcing himself from the Lucca family totally. Danilo, exasperated, says to Rosa in English: "This Bruno is killing me" – to which Rosa answers in Italian, *"Non è Bruno."* Evil is not the assimilated son, but Barbariccia — the unwanted Italy.

58. Sequence Shot. Int. Church. Night.
57-58=montage with effect. 62:36-62:54

A statue of the Virgin Mary, with Jesus in Her arms. Barbariccia is praying. The melody introduced in the previous shot completely invades the soundtrack.

Chapter 10: Nonno Dies
62:55-:80:56

59. Scene. Int. Bedroom. Night.
58-59=zero. 62:55-64:31

Five mega-sequences make up chapter ten: syntagmas 59; 60-62; 63-65; 66; 67-68. The soundtrack has realistic sounds at their normal volume. Eddie, in pajamas, whispers, "Nonno." Nonno's health is dwindling. There is code-switching: the younger generation speaks in English. The older generation continues to speak in Italian. Nonno's advice is simple: "Talk to your father. He knows what has to be done." Nonno brings the magic black box up to his chest. Michel Chion distinguishes two types of accessories: the functional kind (for example, a gun or an alarm clock), and the symbolic kind (the objects that represents a character as in a metonymy) (*Écrire*, 100).

Nonno's box is at this point a mystery. We have no idea what is in it. Whatever it is, it plays the role of what Hitchcock called a "Mac Guffin", that secret object that takes over the plot (*Écrire*, 136). Whatever it is, it is what will free the Lucca family.

60. Sequence. Int. Bedroom. Night.
59-60=zero. 64:31-65:54

Eddie steps into his father's room. Danilo, a deck of cards in his hands, asks Eddie to put on his suit. Eddie shines his shoes with his hand, humming the theme melody of *The Good, the Bad and the Ugly*. Like a posse, the father-son team make their way to Barbariccia's gambling den, Golden Goblet. An inspired name: a mixture of money and alcohol, Danilo's weaknesses. The camera angles are inventive, balancing on the uplifting music, contradicting the seriousness of what follows.

61. Scene. Int. Golden Goblet. Night.
60-61=zero. 65:55-73:39

Barbariccia welcomes Danilo to a fresh game of cards. Danilo is with Eddie; Barbariccia with Bruno. The prize: Gennaro's place.

"Remember what the Pig said: go for the coins," whispers Eddie, who has not forgotten the fairy tale story of the pig and coins.

A nondiegetic insert of Rosa sitting by Nonno in bed. Nonno is ill. Enters Rosa's mother who offers her assistance: "Get some sleep." This tangent brings a smile to the viewer's lips.

The "shoot-out" between Danilo and Barbariccia ends ironically with the King of Swords. The Pig's prediction has come true. Danilo's luck has run out. Eddie has fallen asleep on a chair behind Danilo. Bruno in his black suit sits behind Barbariccia. Barbariccia demands Danilo gamble his wedding band. Danilo accepts, despite Bruno's disapprobation. Is this too much disgrace for the assimilated Bruno?

The ring drops on the table it resonates inauthentically loud. A displaced diegetic insert of Rosa in bed waiting nervously. Eddie wakes up asking his father if he has won. The spectator knows otherwise. A lie is being said. Eddie, who is the narrator, should know the truth. Here is the second object of desire, not so much the desire that one wishes, as much as the object that keeps Danilo sinking deeper into depression. This is the second Pinch Point.

62. Sequence Shot. Ext. The Lucky Café. Night.
61-62=montage with effect. 73:40-74:04

Danilo to Eddie: "Not one word to your mother." Danilo the loser has stepped into his worst nightmare. He has lost everything, including his wife, the reason why he left Italy in the first place.

Barbariccia's words spoken during the game express exactly the emotion eating away at Danilo: "Slowly you realize that you've lost everything. That you've got nothing, that you are nothing, and then you start to be angry." But

Danilo is too weak to be angry. Nonno would have gotten angry. Danilo, no. Anger skips a generation, so to speak (Hansen's law.) Eddie will be the one who gets angry.

63. Alternate syntagma. Int. Bedroom. Night.
62-63=zero. 74:05-76:36

Nonno, the saviour box on his chest, lies in bed. A transformed Nonna is sitting by the bedside. Eddie joins her. Nonna says in English: "He's only dying." Eddie retorts with a child's innocent question: "Does it hurt?" Nonna answers: "Sometimes. Not this time."

The grandchildren take the place of their grandparents, they see, however, no use in the language, or in certain traditions. "Age wisdom" is, nevertheless, transmitted, even if through a foreign tongue.

Cultural wisdom passes on from one group to another, regardless of the idiom used. As Merritt Ruhlen reminds us in his indispensable work, *The Origin of Language* (1994):

> ...there is no intrinsic connection between language and ethnicity... different languages and different ethnic groups do not represent different stages of our evolution... there is no direct connection between a person's gene and the language he speaks... language families and biologically distinct human population are, jointly, the consequence of certain (or more often prehistorical) events (149-152).

If Nonno is dying physically, then Danilo is withering away metaphorically. Because of his addictions, his family is breaking down. Help can come only from the transmission of culture. Eddie is the only one who can save the family. But first Danilo must "die" for transformation to be complete.

Cut to: Int. Bar. Night. 74:36-76:17

We pondered at length about naming this syntagma. We could not consider this an insert, displaced diegetic insert. The narrative importance of this scene (and the following) refuses us to see them as simple "narrative asides".

This is why we think that they belong to a larger syntagma, the alternate syntagma, which is the form which best contains these two memorable but separate moments of the film. Two deaths occur simultaneously, in a single house, but in separate rooms.

Here the camera cranes down on Danilo sitting alone in the dark of his Lucky Café. He is weeping, his wedding band missing, which Rosa shockingly notices. On the soundtrack, the sound of rain. Upstairs, Nonno is dying.

Cut to: Int. Bedroom. Night. 76:18-76:25
Nonna and Eddie sit by Nonno in bed, closer to death than life. Eddie asks: "What is happening now?" Nonna replies: "He can hear the angels' wings..." Death of a family can be physical and symbolic. One can't be avoided, the other can. Life must be chosen.

Cut to: Int. Café. Night. 76:26-76:36
In a sequence shot Rosa walks away from Danilo, in extreme close up.

64. Scene. Ext. Mountain. Day.
63-64=montage with effect. 76:37-77:04
A dream sequence (more than a flashback, since what is depicted is unreal): Nonno in an Alpino uniform and pistol in hand on a snow-covered mountain. On the soundtrack, people are cheering. What sort of performance is this that merits an applause? A dark figure in cape and hood stands before Nonno. it is the angel of darkness. Nonno aims his gun at the silhouette, but cannot shoot. String music accompany Nonno stumbling along, about to collapse under the weight of the mist.

65. Sequence. Int. Bedroom. Day.
64-65=zero. 77:05-78:30
Children voices and a church bell ringing awake Eddie. Danilo caresses his father's face, drops his head on the pillow, weeps. Nonno is dead. Danilo picks up the box. Eddie asks, if they can open it. Danilo answers, "No... come with me... we've got something to do." The scene ends with operatic music.

66. Scene. Ext. Garden. Day.
65-66=zero. 78:31-79:34
On the plot of land, Eddie stands at a distance. Danilo in a winter coat buries the magic box in the garden. The music reigns, competing with the sound of the shovel. The voice of the priest introduces the next scene. Here lies tradition. The burial of a treasure.

67. Scene. Int. Church. Day.
66-67=zero. 79:35-80:20
An establishing pan stops on the family. Bruno stays away, in the background. Mourning music. A priest prays. A nondiegetic insert of Nonno trying to shoot at the angel of death in the mist. The gun drops from his hand. On the soundtrack, wind is blowing, music. Eddie's delivers his monologue:

"Sometime I wonder what is life in limbo. It is like you're running and running, but you don't go anywhere. You shout but no sound comes out. It's like you're not there at all. It's like you're a ghost." The word "ghost" is spoken on the image of the angel of darkness standing at the doorstep of the café, waiting for Danilo.

68. Scene. Ext. Street. Day.
67-68=zero. 80:21-80:56

The Lucca family (Danilo, Eddie, Angelica, her husband, Teresa with her baby in her arms, and Nonna) return home. A faceless dark figure (a mirage) waits in front of Lucky Café. Danilo joins the angel of darkness (a metaphor for Nonno's death, but also for Danilo's symbolic death) who turns out to be a man with a bowler hat who serves Danilo a court order. Eddie wears Nonno's earing aid. More than the foreigner, it is one's own family that implodes. Betrayal of this nature comes not from the outside but from within. We will have a chance to explore betrayal more in depth in the chapter dedicated to *Raging Bull*.

Chapter 11: Rosa and Barbariccia
80:57-93:45

69. Sequence shot. Int. Room. Day.
68-69=zero. 80:57-81:07

Seven mega-sequences constitute chapter eleven: syntagmas 69; 70; 71; 73-74; 75-76; 77; 78-79. Rosa opens a suitcase. She is hurting, yet decided. Dressed in black, she pulls out the golden blanket offered to her by Barbariccia, as a wedding present. A low angle bestows on Rosa with a majestic quality. Rosa must meet Barbariccia.

70. Scene. Int. The Lucky Café. Day.
69-70=zero. 81:08-82:08

The family is sitting around the table. Teresa realizes the horror of what Danilo's gambling has produced. Nonna interjects: "He gambled with all of us. Do you want to support a gambler?" Teresa abruptly defends her father: "He supports you." Nonna mutters: "I wish I were dead." Rosa steps into the café, with Barbariccia's wrapped gift in her arms. The children try to stop Rosa from leaving. Nonna proudly adds: "She is going where she should have gone in the first place." Eddie rushes out, in vain. Danilo's "it's too late" proves only too well the uselessness of this man unable to protect his family. As we saw in both *Bread and Chocolate* and *A Pain in the Ass*, the family as a concept (old as well as new) must come to an end before it can reinvent itself.

Without this re-invention, this awakening consciousness, there can be no community. Metaphorically, the first-generation immigrant is too weak to carry on the tradition; as though, the burden of Italy prevents them for acting appropriately in the continuation of culture. As a norm, we advance that the Italic begins with the second generation, the generation born abroad, who are free of the nation's ballast.

71. Scene. Int. Barbariccia's Office. Day.
70-71=zero. 82:09-85:12

This is the moment Barbariccia has been waiting for (and the moment most feared by Danilo). Rosa, the object of his desire, greets the man she was supposed to marry. Standing in the shadows, brown envelope on her breast, Rosa faces Barbariccia. She rejects any manifestation of intimacy, expresses herself in English. Again, we wonder if this idiom is the idiom for the film, and not the language actually spoken by these emigrants. On her hand in clear view, her wedding band: "Mr. Barbariccia, this gift... It was wrong for my mother to accept it. I wish to return it to you."

The suitcase she holds is not her own, but her mother's. Nonna had safely kept Barbariccia's gift throughout the years. (Nonna's non-acceptance of Danilo as a son-in-law could not have been expressed more fiercely.) But now that Nonna has changed attitude, assisting Nonno Lucca at his bedside, Rosa can make the final break with the past. Rosa returns the dowry, the nuptial gift offered by a young Barbariccia.

> Barbariccia: "For twenty-one years I thought of no one and nothing else but you. Everyday I fight to keep you out of my head."
> Rosa: "Look at me. I'm not a schoolgirl. I'm forty years olds. I've got four children. I'm a grandmother."
> Barbariccia: "I am a man who has lost his honor."

A lifetime of passion (Barbariccia) versus quotidian brutality (Rosa on her knees). Bruno is weeping, finally switches sides, chooses his family over Barbariccia's authority. Betrayal forgiven. Rosa whispers to Barbariccia (but also to her son): "I feel sorry for you." It is Rosa who permits her family to reinvent itself. It is a question of days before Bruno makes his way back into the fold, into the reinvented family. Nonno, as a specter, brings about this reinvention, this transformation of the family; but it is Eddie who, by speaking with Nonno's voice, will reinvent the family. Danilo can't do it by himself.

Like Nino in *Bread and Chocolate*, Danilo is unable to do reinvent himself, let alone his family. He needs outside help. If Pignon could reinvent himself and his "family", it is only thanks to Milan. If the family wishes to reinvent itself, it needs to refresh itself with tradition, but a refashioned tradition. Not an inherited culture but a reinvented one, an acquired one.

72. Scene. Int. Dark place. Night.
71-72=zero. 85:13-85:58

Emotionally charged violins flow over the sounds of Eddie sniffling. The camera dollies over the empty matrimonial bed, and stops on Danilo unbuttoning his shirt collar.

73. Sequence. Ext. Street. Night.
72-73=montage with effect. 85:59-86:23

A number of shots of Danilo walking through the streets of London. The sound of his footsteps like a solo over the violins of despair. Not only is he revisiting Little Italy, he is going through an autocriticism right now. The new rises from what disappears.

74. Scene. Ext. Bridge. Night.
73-74=zero. 86:24-87:34

With the crescendo of emphatic violins Danilo sinks into the night, his white shirt the only place where light is reflected. Danilo climbs a bridge and throws himself into the Thames.

The repetitious music becomes hypnotic, the London Bridge is seen from Danilo's point of view. Wishing to compare this scene to Frank Capra's *It's a Wonderful World* with the memorable James Stewart's failed suicide would not be an exaggeration. Both films depict a man pushed to the limit.

75. Scene. Int. Dark place. Night.
74-75=zero. 87:34-89:59

Eddie is awakened by the ringing in Nonno's hearing aid. In the background sirens and strange city noises. As he gets up the spectator realizes that Eddie was sleeping in the cabin on the Lucca plot of land. Eddie unearths the magic box Danilo had buried.

Eddie's white shirt, like Danilo's white shirt in the previous scene, is the only source of light. Inside the box, wrapped in a jersey cloth, there is a handgun. The handgun we had seen Nonno handle against the angel of darkness. Eddie pretends to shoot at the stars, the camera cutting and moving further away in each subsequent shot. Rosa, Danilo and Eddie form the narrative triangle and constitute the basic foundation of the plot. Eddie has found his object of desire, delivered to him from Italy by his Nonno. In *The Mediterranean Forever*, it is the fig tree. This metonymy of cultural transmission becomes in the next scene the instrument of counter-revenge.

76. Scene. Ext./Int. Golden Goblet. Night.
75-76=montage with effect. 89:00-91-09

A man's eye in the door-eye. With a subjective camera we are Eddie pointing the gun. The doorman with eye cup tries to calm Eddie speaking a mixture of English and Italian. "Be careful, don't shoot." Eddie fires directly at Barbariccia. When Bruno steps into the room, Eddie accidentally fires the gun at him too. Eddie topples onto the floor. Fratricide? Symbolic, or real? Eddie has shot the man who has brought trouble to the family, the man who has pushed his brother into a position of betrayal.

77. Scene. Ext. Fast Food joint. Night.
76-77=montage with effect. 91:10-92:40

The camera tilts up from the Thames to the fast-food joint belonging to Mario. Yes, the spectator is surprised to see Mario there. Mario says in English, unaware of what Danilo is up to (or is he making light a sober situation?): "It's a crazy time to go swimming, Danny. The water's filthy. You could've got really sick. You're lucky it's low tide."

Mario spikes the coffee with grappa which he hands Danilo, a towel over his shoulders. Mario talks about his failed return to Turino: "I was even dreaming in English." What linguists call code-switching: using more than one idiom at the same time. Mario and Danilo are speaking to each other in Italian, with a British accent. Or are they speaking in Italian which is being translated into English for filmic reasons?

Language, accented speech, are ambiguous commodities of storytelling. Idioms, accents must be taken with a grain of salt. The film would have been quite different, had Amiel shot it in Italian (or dialect) and used English subtitles. With the growth of ethnic acceptance, subtitles will resolve this unfortunate moment in filmmaking with an accent.

78. Sequence. Ext. Street. Night.
77-78=zero. 92:41-93:31

Under a full moon, Bruno is walking back home with Eddie in his arms. Bruno was not shot at all. Eddie had imagined it all. Whether true or untrue, Eddie is taking Bruno back into the family. It is ironic that it is Bruno who is carrying the savior of the family. Much like St. Christopher. The music is heartwarming. Could this be the sort of "anempathetic music" Michel Chion is talking out? The music that so naturally accompanies the image we forget it is there? Eddie asks: "Bruno, are you dead?" Bruno smiles, says no, and mutters something that is totally muffled. Eddie tightens his embrace around his Bruno. Eddie has rescued Bruno. The same way Mario has "rescued" Danilo.

79. Sequence shot. Int. Bedroom. Night.
78-79=montage with effect. 93:32-93:45

Bruno, Eddie, Danilo, and Mario are in this scene. Bruno tucks his younger brother into bed, where Danilo is sleeping as well. Mario and Bruno look onto the sleeping pair with affection. Nonno's death, debts accumulated by Danilo, Bruno's betrayal recanted: this chapter ends at the lowest point in the narrative. Ninety-three minutes and false objects of desire exhausted, we are now ready for a major shift in the plot.

Chapter 12: Happy Ending
93:46-1:10.00

80. Scene. Int. The Lucky Café. Day.
79-80=zero. 93:46-94:34

The last chapter contains five mega-sequences: syntagmas 80-81; 82; 83-84; 85-86; 87. Eddie is preparing instant coffee. Neither *la bella macchina*, nor Rosa are there. Bruno is on the phone with his mother Rosa to whom Danilo does not speak. Beetle walks in, asks: "What is for breakfast?" The storm has subsided. Forgiveness has calmed the fury. The call for a renewed family reunion.

81. Scene. Int. The Lucky Café. Day.
80-81=zero. 94:35-95:22

Eddie and Beetle are breaking bread (a symbolic gesture of friendship), dropping the pieces in their caffelatte bowls. Beetle inspects the hearing aid: "That'll do. I'll put things right again." Friendship (Mario, Beetle) saves the family. As Eddie was Zorro when holding his Nonno's handgun, so Beetle, the motherless Italian boy next door, acquires the role of Zorro.

82. Episodic Sequence. Ext./Int. Street/rooms. Night.
81-82=zero. 95:23-96:28

Short scenettes present the spectator Eddie and Beetle rigging up wires outside Gennaro's ex-legal gambling office. Bruno is in the coup as well; in short, the idea is to control the information incoming from the horse-race commentator. Except for the music, lively, cheerful, the soundtrack is justified, synchronized, authentic. More than just the one individual — Danilo — it is the community at large that gains from this friendly *deus ex machina* intervention.

Caryn James in Washington Post wrote that "the film becomes more focussed and resonant when Danilo's father arrives."[29] With Nonno's spiritual assistance, Eddies carries the entire last portion of *Queen of Hearts*. Two generations converge and save the lost generation in between (Danilo's).

83. Parallel Syntagma. Ext./Int. Street/room. Day.
82-83=zero. 96:29-1.03.09

The continuous going-to-and-fro, cutting from Eddie to Beetle in the monitoring room, constitutes a single syntagma that pits two settings against one another, with the temporal unit presented as one. A low angle shot of Danilo, Bruno and Eddie, in black suits, walking toward Gennaro's ex-betting grounds recall the western posse.

This is the second time an obvious reference to Sergio Leone is made: already Eddie had hummed the theme song of *The Good, the Bad, and the Ugly*; here we have an ironic reference to the western duel. While the ethnic film awaits to be born as a genre, it must camouflage itself in other generic vestments.

In his room, on the second floor, Beetle fidgets with his radio gadget. Eddie nods affirmatively. Nonno, one more time, has come to save the hour: first the gun, now *in absentia*, via the hearing aid. The anempathetic music, repetitive like a bolero, rolls us into a sort of trance. Expectancy, suspense, tension. Bruno puts in the first bet, one thousand pounds, a skeptical Danilo to his side. The faces behind the grid are Italic. We are in the Italian quarter, Gennaro, the barber, Bruno, all applaud Danilo who gets his first win, a lot of money. At last, the alternate syntagma develops into a single scene, no longer the need to go to Beetle now caught red-handed. An insert of Barbariccia, the new owner of Gennaro's gambling den, getting out of his car. The "octopus" has its hands in every business in the ghetto.

Down comes the *deus ex machina:* Nonno (through the hearing aid). Here Nonno is a voice from a distant galaxy speaking through his grandson Eddie in a trance who shouts in Italian, "Play numbers 6 and 3... It is Nonno who speaks," explains Eddie.

In comedy the *deus ex machina* does not disturb. The unexpected hearing aid (scarcely noticeable on Nonno) adds spice to the general atmosphere of relief. Danilo bets the numbers Eddie yells out who is getting this inside information from his dead grandfather. The announcer details the evolution of the horse race, the customers scream in unison, "Six and three, six and three."

When Danilo wins convincingly, there is wild jubilation. Lifted on men's shoulders Danilo becomes the hero he never was. Mario and Rosa enter; there is forgiveness in Rosa's eyes. Barbariccia, sore, stares at his rival in disgust. In the end, after sending everyone away, Barbariccia finds himself alone with Danilo and Rosa.

84. Scene. Int. Gambling Parlor.
83-84=zero. 1.03.10-1.06.34

Danilo, in one corner; Rosa, in the other, near the exit; in between Barbariccia mutters: "It's like purgatory, you and me, you win, I win, you win, for eternity." Danilo swaps all his gains for his wedding band he lost at gambling. Barbariccia turns to Rosa — "You were promised to me"— as he pulls his necklace on which he had attached the ring; he hands it to Rosa, and turns his back to the reunited couple below a signpost that reads "Pay Out".

Rosa and Danilo commiserate with Barbariccia, hands on his back, Rosa first, then Danilo, Barbariccia is weeping, melodic music fades in. Rosa and Danilo walk out, leaving Barbariccia alone, his back to the camera, too broken to face the audience, the jilted lover, the gangster lost in London's Little Italy, the butcher's son who has nothing, the man who is left with empty power, but with no love or friendship. Neither Amiel nor Grisoni smirk at this hurt, they respect the pain of the bad guy. Danilo wins his wife back from the broken-hearted King of Swords.

85. Scene. Ext. Mountain. Day.
84-85=montage with effect. 1.06.35-1.06.44

The angel of darkness in the mist near the Alps. A flashback, Nonno in military uniform, no longer alive, appears in this metaphorical enclave. What is the significance of this return to the past, a past of a cherished deceased (grand)father?

In the next scene Amiel-Grisoni bring us further back to Nonno's childhood. The orchestral music, unjustified, non synchronized, inauthentic, creates a non-realness rich for the spectator's imaginary. The writer and director are purposely forcing the spectator to "dream". This cut away from reality, from the realness of fiction, brings us deep into another world of metaphor. Fiction with fiction quickly turns into metaphor.

> 86. Alternate syntagma. Ext. Country Home. Day.
> 85-86=dissolve. 1:06:45-1:07:38

A dissolve on Nonno in military uniform running: an Italian town in sepia and Nonno throwing away his Alpine hat. A young woman (Nonno's mother) waits for him. Just as Nonno is about to embrace her, a young boy appears and completes the final embrace. The change is physical, metaphorical. Nonno clearly becomes Eddie. Eddie runs to his mother, as Nonno runs to his mother, as Danilo runs to his stepmother. A coming back not to home, but a renewed home, an invented home. A No-Land.

> 87. Scene. Int. The Lucky Café. Day.
> 86-87=dissolve. 1:07:39-1:10:00

A second dissolve carries the narrative from the past to the present, from metaphor to the reality. Eddie is sitting between Bruno and Beetle, staring at his parents smiling. Grisoni has brought in all of the after-death/post-life possible locations into this film: heaven, limbo, purgatory and hell. For Eddie (Nonno gives Eddie agency), heaven is "like coming home".

The danger vanished, they find happiness in the newly re-created family home. Is it not this meaning that Scene 85 is whispering to us? Mother and son reunion is like being in heaven, it is, to paraphrase Eddie, the best time in one's life. Pepe serves wine behind the counter where the *bella macchina* has returned. Nonna is finally smiling with a tray of cakes. The artist photographer makes his way around the table of guests, camera on his tripod. Everyone is laughing, speaking loudly. The picture taken, the camera dollies back, behind curtains pulled shut, the instrumental melody concluding the emotions "empathetically".

As the camera pulls all the way back into the street, Eddie begins his concluding monologue. These awkward photographs are metaphors of the past gone by. A memory that is never clear, stable, true. Eddie's souvenirs are his alone.

> "My name is Eddie Lucca. And that's my story. It's up to you if you want to believe it or not. But that's the truth. Well, that's the way I remember it anyway. Sometimes I turn a corner and think I got to see the place again..."

[At this point, Eddie's young voice is juxtaposed and then replaced with Eddie as an older man as the images dissolve into one another as we move away.] "...The café, the betting shop where Beetle lived, Mario's store... I can even smell the dark coffee... the warm bread rolls. But somehow I can never seem to find the right street, those familiar grey bricks streets. But I know they're there. And I know that some day I will find them again."

The music rises to an emotional climax as the camera moves over the brick wall with which the film began... Credits follow and the orchestral film melody dissolves into the more folkloric accordion interpretation of "Turno a Surriento". End. (1.12.30)

Commentary

The main problem with film analysis is the linearity limitations of the book form. One can appreciate the breathtaking didactical work that Jean-Luc Godard has undertook since the early 1970s. Many of his post-1968 films are precisely a struggle to capture the understanding of how film works.

In *Queen of Hearts*, the character Barbariccia unexpectedly speaks about how loss, failure, about being "empty like a dream". He does not say like in a dream, but like a dream. A dream is not a container for emptiness, but it is itself something that is empty, that is, without any content inside it. Like a dream pain is such that there is nothing left over in one's life. Film analysis is very much about making sense of this dreamlike empty-ness, for there is so much to analysis that one feels a sort of empty-ness after watching a film. Empty here being no different from being full. It is its opposite corresponding entity; the semantic negative of full-ness; emptiness is the opposite of fulness. It is not that there is nothing in empty-ness. (Grisoni does use, interestingly enough, the word "empty" and not "emptiness"; it takes a number of attentive readings before we make out the words pronounced. One expects an error to slip in; actors do not always speak properly, do not always pronounce their lines eloquently, do not always enunciate the words distinctly...

In that scene, however, Vittorio Amandola — who is absolutely brilliant in his role as villain, who is not always a bad guy, and especially in the gambling scene (with the four main male characters of the film present: Barbariccia, Danilo, Bruno, Eddie), accent and all — distinctly pronounces the word "empty".

To be able to break up this empty-ness (for everything reads as natural, when nothing is natural in a film), to be able to dissect the complete panorama of a film, one needs to place the denotative exploration of the film in one column, the narrative analysis in a second column, in a third column the commentary of, say, how music is used throughout the film, a fourth column to make the "quote-unquote" references in all films, the fifth column about such and such a detail in the actor, and so forth. This mammoth task is, strictly speaking, impossible to accomplish. We must necessarily trample along cautiously, putting out among the thousands of details the things that seem to matter most. Film is so entirely full, that it feels paradoxically empty. Too full in fact, that one mind cannot encompass the entirety of the filmic experience. We inescapably blank out.

There are many references to suicide in this film: killing oneself presents itself for Danilo as the only possible way out of the madness, the emotions that are too full and too empty as the same time. Perhaps, suicide in *Queen of Hearts* is the equivalent figure of the "madness" encountered in *Pane e cioccolata*. Reality is so stifling that it has to be punctured in some way.

Queen of Hearts is about putting a damper on the blanking out under the crushing heaviness of the symbolic. The surcharge of intensity in Grisoni's world requires it to be "controlled" by an outside force, in this case, by the "foreigner" Jon Amiel. Amiel is not Italian, and it is because he is not Italian that he is unable to give a measured first reading of Grison's story. To transpose his own experience onto fiction is already a need to put a distance between reality and self. (The writer could have chosen to produce a documentary on the Italians of London; he didn't.)

What seems to be at work is a sort of kenosis, an emptying, a voluntary abdication of one's powers. Few artists dare to venture in the precarious fields where on questions the very foundation of capitalist entertainment. Ethnic works are indeed rare; true independently produced films are scarcer. The financial resources are extremely difficult for ordinary, "national" works; one can only guess how near to impossible it is to find money for artists living at the margins of the national mainstream.

There must inescapably be for the time being much compromise. And this compromise manifests itself in various forms: one can hire "non-ethnic" directors and actors; one must work in fixed genres to be able to attract the audience at the box office. All of this is part of the compromise, and this compromise reflects itself in the work and its relationship with the audience.

A filmmaker as ferociously independent as Spike Lee had to come to some sort of compromise for his later films. If he wanted to direct money-making films, he needed to rev up the system he had used to make *She Gotto*

Have It (1986). It does not suffice to limit analysis to the filmmakers. Scholars should be wary to compartmentalize the expression of ethnic artistry strictly from one person's point of view. Means of production must be included in the discussion. Who puts in money decides. There are compromises to make, and these include the audience.

Amiel brings lightness to the overwhelming formal intensities inherent to Grisoni's Italic imagination. If Barbariccia is empty-ness, Danilo represents full-ness. This duality of purpose might be considered a common denominator in many Italic films. We find such binary manipulations in the five films studied in this work: Manfreddi deflates the suffocating world of the characters in *Bread and Chocolate;* Jacques Brel pokes a hole right into the gravity of *A Pain in the Ass;* Joe Pesci subverts the asceticism prevalent in *Raging Bull*; Joseph Long delinquently escapes from the darkness hanging over *Queen of Hearts;* the director Zavaglia outplays the severity of the immigrant world through his formal playfulness. Compromise unavoidably entails a loss of entitlement. *Queen of Hearts* is throughly an expression of this quest and/or loss of deserving entitlement.

The title

The story begins, the music rises to an ironic crescendo on the film title, *Queen of Hearts*. We sense something being "too much", something that was added on a "thing" proclaiming itself to be Italianness. There is "Italianness" in the "acousmatic" music, that is, the prerecorded musical score whose source on screen. A layer of self-awareness gets attached to this music. This Italianness screams out its name over what is (seems to be) already Italian. It is as if Amiel needs to make sure that the spectator knows we are in Italy.

The dual-layered details, at once essence and the robe covering the essence, contain the ironic. Object can manifest themselves brashly in stereophonic mode. An ironic figure implies the opposite or a difference of what is expressed.[30]

Let us consider the title: what (who?) can the title *Queen of Hearts* refer to? The Queen: this mention of royalty (the monarchy) intrigues us. There has been only one queen in Italy, Margherita di Savoia (1851-1926), who was the grandmother of the last Italian king, the May King (Re di Maggio), King Umberto II, who ruled for thirty-five days, between 9 May up to 13 June 1946. The 2 June 1946 referendum put a term to the rule of the House of Savoy, and transformed Italy into a Republic. Is the "Queen" in the title of this film an explicit reference to Margherita of Savoy? If this were the case, we would be in the heart of an historical drama. But, of course, this is not the case as the spectator soon finds out.

Perhaps this queen of hearts is not the Italian Queen at all but the British Queen? Are we going to looking at the story about British monarchy? However, the ambiguity is quickly resolved. There is no talk about monarchy nor the Queen *per se,* but perhaps metaphorically to the territory this queen represents: Britain. No, this film is not about the monarchy (neither the British nor the Italian monarchy). *Queen of Hearts* is about Italians living in Britain. It is more precisely a love story between an Italian man and an Italian woman — or should we speak of two Italian men who love the same Italian woman? — who have emigrated to Britain.

Finally, the Queen of hearts might be Rosa, the woman who is coveted by two Italian men; she is in part the reason for the character's emigration. The queen of hearts is also an image in a deck of cards. We have the symbol of the heart (love), yes, but also the card in a deck of playing cards. This is then an allusion to card playing and gambling.

One pan, a curtain, an Italian hamlet, an ambiguous title, the entire story given to us in a less than one minute. Roland Barthes would have said that this is a cluster of the major codes of textual signifiers: the hermeneutic code (W5, the rule of five: who? where? what? when? why?), the semantic code (territory, ethnicity, love, rivalry), the symbolic code (the heart of emotions), the proairetic code (falling in love, gambling), and the reference codes (Italian vs British culture).

Though the images introduce an hamlet on an Italian hill (San Gimignano), are we not being explicitly told that this is a British film (directed by British Jon Amiel) about Italians (from British writer Tony Grisoni's imagination)? The combination of the image of the Italian hamlet on the hill underscored by the lavish music composed by Michael Convertino takes the spectator to a special territory. What this initial sequence conveys is immediately recognizable as British, even if the action unfolds elsewhere.

This film with images of Italy is made for the British public, whereby the British spectator is asked to become a tourist for an hour or so. Surely, it is not the other way round. This is not the film for an Italian spectator looking into the British world. It is more about the British spectator giving the chance to peep at the Italian world.

This narrative strategy is a significant tool that frees Amiel of any "wrongdoing" (of any accusation of tampering with a foreign culture). The filmmaker's position is encoded: Amiel does not pretend to be someone he is not. As a guest director, he is no different than the average British spectator watching a film on Italians. We are guests invited to visit Tony Grisoni's (invented, fictionalized) family. We are looking at Italians not from within, which was the case with *Bread and Chocolate,* but from the point of the Other (the British). Yet this story is told (even if the narrator is the Italian boy born in London) from the Other's perspective, from the point of view of an Italian born in Britain. (Imagine Brusati's *Bread and Chocolate* directed by a Swiss director?)

Queen of Hearts does not show us how the British view Italians in their country, but how Italians view themselves in a foreign country. There are no pure-blood Brits (if such a thing is possible?) in *Queen of Hearts.* The boy's narrative is unquestionably British (Edoardo is more British than Italian, because he was born in Britain).

These considerations are detrimental to the production as well as viewing experience. Elie Faure is clear on this point:

> L'ethnicité et le milieu historique et géographique insistent à tel point sur la détermination des formes que ces formes même infligent leurs caractères essentiels aux modes d'expression le plus éloignés d'elles (108).
> [Ethnicity and the historical and geographical environment insist to such an extent on the determination of forms that these forms themselves inflict their essential characteristics on the modes of expression most distant from them.]

In what year does this story take place? Some images suggest the end of 1950s, others the 1960s: we see a photograph of Pope John XXIII, yet there is mention of the Beatles (Beatlemania starts after 1963).

The question, however, will never receive a clear-cut answer, because the creators themselves do not give a clear-cut answer. The spectator is purposely forced to doubt the temporal fixture of this ethnic narrative. This story can happen anytime, anywhere. This film is about emigration. It is dedicated to emigrants who, unlike Nino in *Bread and Chocolate,* find happiness abroad.

Structure of the film

By dropping the Turning Points in our W-paradigm we can pull out other meanings that underline the film's narration (figure 10). If we read the first level of the story (the dark squares), we have Danilo Lucca and Rosa running away from Barbariccia and moving to London; one day at work Danilo hears the Pig proffer words of wisdom about gambling; Barbariccia imposes his power by taking Gennaro's gambling outfit under his wing. Barbariccia uses Danilo and Rosa's son, Bruno, to collect the debt owed; but in the end Barbariccia is defeated; Rosa choses once again Danilo; the family is re-united.

On the second level (light-shaded squares), the Pinch Points, what we have concerns Barbariccia. At the Lucca wedding, Mario hands Rosa the *busta*, which turns out to be the beginning of Lucca's nightmare (Barbariccia is partially responsible for Mario's departure); then follows Danilo accidentally falling onto Barbariccia's shop; Danilo gambles his wife away and loses her to Barbariccia, and his father dies; lastly, Eddie hears his Nonno's voice that give him the numbers that help Danilo win against Barbariccia.

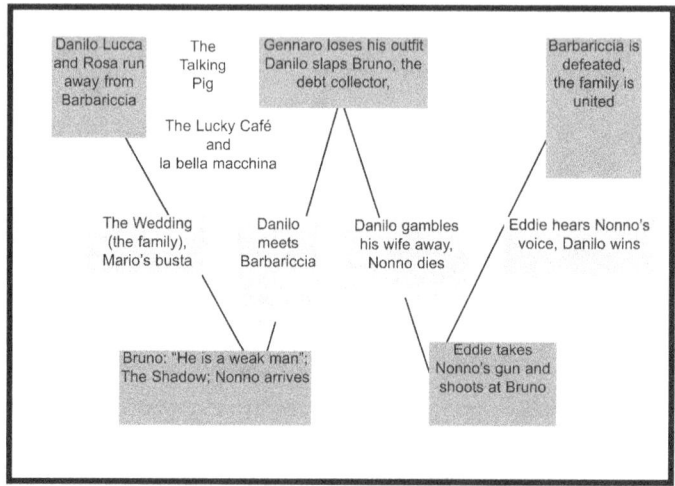

Figure 10

We end with the Turning Points. The creation of Lucky Café and *la bella macchina* offered by Mario is a key moment which sets the stage for the three major narrative transformations: the first switch occurs around the thirty-minute mark which can be divided into three parts: Bruno's attack of his father; Barbariccia the Shadow making his presence felt; the announcing of Nonno's arrival (which will take over the following section). This Turning Point will in turn bring about two major events: Gennaro loses his gambling outlet in the hands of Barbariccia (via Bruno); Danilo slaps Bruno for what he did; Eddies takes Nonno's gun and shoots Barbariccia and then his own brother, Bruno.

La bella macchina

The espresso machine enables the Lucca family to make a living. Danilo purchases it from Mario on credit. When Mario's building is bought by Barbariccia, the credit is transferred to the new owner who has one thing in mind: destroy the Lucca family, in order to win back Rosa. It will be Pepe, a colleague of Danilo's who will remove the machine from the bar-café. Is this not Barbariccia's way of emasculating Danilo, decapitating him, castrating him, de-Italianizing him, deterritorializing him? Without the espresso machine Danilo loses his identity. Why should we not be surprised that suicide appears as a way out of this existence?

The espresso machine combines added connotations in Chapter Seven, a segment of the film dedicated to the extension of the family unit. In a symbolic sense the *bella macchina* becomes equated to a fertility rite, or even the male sexual organ. Plainly, Teresa's screams converge with the steaming of the coffee machine. A sort of facile trick which frankly works. Eddie speaks of "people acting strange", and when he speaks of strangeness what he should have said is that he was become aware of sexual attraction. The Postwoman is distinctly a prolongation of this growing boy's awareness of sexuality. Always around the machine. People caress the machine, they shine the machine, they remove the machine, and all hell breaks loose.

The entire family's well being depends on this apparatus, naturally a reference to Italy. The espresso machine is noticed for the first time at the very beginning of the film, when Danilo is about to run out of the house to snatch Rosa away. An act that is abruptly censored by his father. Sex is censored, but it is too late, the flame is lit.

Barbariccia

Italy, two men, one woman, a mother without a husband, a father without a wife; poverty against newfound wealth; an arranged marriage versus the romantic coupling of lovers; an escape; physical pain is nothing compared to the humiliation and the turmoil this once-husband-to-be experiences; here is a big man who is hurting like a baby.

This story is about Barbariccia ("curly beard") who goes out of his way to fix, what he considers, a social mistake: he purchases anything that surrounds Rosa with the hope of suffocating her out of her environment. Thanks to money, Barbariccia manages to do the impossible. Never totally in the center of our attention, never in the background, Barbariccia with his thick extended goatee is present everywhere: a young man, a jilted lover, a shadow, finally a mobster.

Between the first word he pronounces ("Rosa) to the last words he speaks ("You were promised to me"), Barbariccia follows a trajectory from which will never digress; the goal he has fixed for himself, the object of his desire, Rosa, Danilo's wife, is found at the end of a straight line.

This man weeps at the beginning of the film, weeps at the end of the film; in between it is his tears that drive him to revenge. The narrative and symbolic paths the writers assigned to him are unambiguous, direct, with no deviation, no drifting, no turning about. A criminal from the start (who else would have as best man someone who carries a switchblade?), a criminal to the end, a victim of unrequited love, a prisoner of desire for a woman who prefers a loser, Danilo.

This wise guy, unaware, will make right what is wrong. By fighting to regain his lost love he will push Rosa further away from him, and back to his enemy's arms. At the beginning of this film, paradoxically, the good guy (Danilo) is presented as bad, and the bad guy (Barbariccia) as good. The reversal of truth, the peripeteia, turns things right side up again. This film converts a love story into one of revenge, or should we say this story of revenge transmutes into a love story? In reality, it is both a love story and a story of revenge, and something else as well: the story of emigrants and immigrants. More than just two simple men, these are two archetypes of Italians: 1. The successful businessman; 2. The unsuccessful businessman. Or if you wish 1. The successful criminal; 2. The honest complete failure.

Furthermore, this duality demonstrates how a bad man (Barbariccia) could have been a good man had he be given a chance to love. The Mafia boss wants to enter society, but he is never given the opportunity to do so. Forever tossed to the margins of society (we are told nothing of his interpersonal status) Barbariccia spends most of his time at work and, when he is not working, desperately yearns for Rosa.

When Rosa begs Barbariccia to stop harassing her family, he responds with disconcerting honesty: "For twenty-one years I thought of no one and nothing else but you. Everyday I fight to keep you out of my head... I am a man who has lost his honor." One thing Barbariccia is not, is a liar. He is truthful about who and what he wants. This criminal has lost his honor because denied the love he had been promised. This criminal has been slighted in public. And this idea of *brutta figura* surfaces and never seems to vanish. Having lost his honor, having been refused the right to love, he stands at the margin of society. By purchasing most of the buildings in the Italian ghetto, he hopes to be a guest, but he is never really invited anywhere. He works in

British society alright, but he is not part of the Italian community.

Moving about in a hiatus that lies between the inside and the outside the new world, the criminal is the only person of the ghetto to be permitted to evolve in the new world outside the ghetto. Other characters seem to be dependent of small family businesses. When Gennario loses his gambling den, he becomes an unemployed immigrant. Mario, as well, fails to make a life for himself in Italy ("I was dreaming in English"), and can only feel content with a greasy spoon food stand on the bank of the Thames. Danilo relies on a single espresso machine to the well-being of his family.

Reduced to a looming Shadow, Barbariccia's undefined presence is like the octopus (like the Mafia). Barbariccia is not only a large man but his hands are everywhere. He has purchased half of the ghetto: Gennaro's gambling store, Mario's company, has become the main supplier for gambler's needs. We notice his Shadow three times:

1. In Mario's store: the Shadow will come downstairs and scare the two boys away;
2. In a non-diegetic insert that lasts no more than two seconds;
3. At the end of a sequence, when the boys enter the Café accompanied by Danilo.

Rosa says to Barbariccia, "I feel sorry for you." Rosa is not impressed by this mobster become half a man. This Shadow of a man controls the narration as well. His triple narrative presence (the boys at the Hardware store, Mario's departure and the presence of the Shadow) makes sense only if surveyed from the Shadow's viewpoint. The Mafia is not investigated in *Queen of Hearts*. The Mafia presence is felt as all powerful, but Eddie and Beetle toss that idea as a "fairy tale". The Shadow is a voyeur, and a controller. The Shadow first looks and then is responsible for Mario's departure, Eddie's bruised hand, the breakdown of the Lucky Café, and the takeover of Gennario's den. With the excuse of being love-hurt, a criminal surveys movement in Little Italy and monopolizes every individual. The weakness of the men in the community — the ironic leitmotif "My lucky friend, Danny" is a reminder of this weakness — enables Barbariccia to win. When at the end, he forcefully grabs Danilo who is caught cheating, and forces him to gamble all his illegal wins, Danilo, frightened, alone, knows that as a weak man he has no chance. Only Eddie manages to outplay the Mobster.

Beetle

What is remarkable about Beetle is the space he occupies. This red-headed Italian boy possesses talismanic powers. However, unlike Eddie, his charms are real; adjuvant, he can do almost anything he wants. Thanks to Beetle, the Lucca family (become unlucky) wins (for a time), until Nonno steps in with his voice and saves Eddie. Beetle's father Gennaro manages the bets.

Gennaro calls his son Tarzan, and orders him to use the stairs like all simple mortals. His world of make believe is nevertheless wired to the real world. His knowledge of electricity, a commodity rare in Italy of the 1940s and the 1950s, enables Beetle to change the fate of families in the Britain of the 1960s. Friendship plays a major role in this film. The friendship between Eddie and Beetle, between Danilo and Mario, becomes more than the manifestation of affection between acquaintances; upon friendship lies not only a character's destiny but also the future of the entire Italian community.

Friendship also plays a significant role in *Bread and Chocolate* (Nino and Elena; Nino and the rich industrialist; Nino and Gigi), *A Pain in the Ass* (François and Ralph), *The Mediterranean Forever* (Mario and Angelo), and *Raging Bull* (Jake and Joey). When friendship flourishes, so too does the collectivity. When friendship breaks, the collectivity crashes.

Betrayal

Before Beetle can react, Gennaro pulls his son away: "You'll never speak to them again." Something has cracked. Midpoint is Bruno's betrayal of his family. Eddie walks into Lucky Café, a "Closed" sign on the door. The family unit? Dead and broken. These emigrants left Italy for reasons that is not solely lack of money. Danilo and Rose left because of love. Poverty continues in the new country. Danilo, Nonno, Eddie, Nonna, Rosa, Mario, Bruno, Barbariccia, Pepe: each at some point betrays a friend, a partner, his/her family.

In some form or other we encounter double crossing, back-stabbing, transgression of a contract between members of a family, friends, companies, countries. Someone trespasses the bounds erected by a common pact. In the film shown on the television, *The Vikings* (1958), by Richard Fleischer, neither Einar nor Eric know the true identity of the other. Brother against brother, fratricide, be it in fiction (*The Vikings*, Kirk Douglas versus Tony Curtis) or reality (*Queen of Hearts*, Eddie against Bruno), or mega-reality (Italian against Italian), petrifies. Social and cultural pilferage terrorizes the individual. In the nightmare section of the film, Eddie speaks to the spectator:

> Dreams always mean the exact opposite of what they say. So, if you dream you're going to be poor, it means you're going to be rich. And if you dream someone is going to kill you, it means they will really love you a lot. That's right, isn't it?

To whom is Eddie addressing this question? Who is listening to this frightened boy? The speechless spectator. The spectator who smiles at this old wives' tale. Of course, dreams tell the truth. Alfred Adler explains his view of the dream:

> ...we dream only if we are not sure of the solution of our problems, only if reality is pressing in on us even in our sleep and offering us difficulties. This is the task of the dream: to meet the difficulties with which we are confronted and to provide a solution (99).

Eddie senses the family problems. He might be unable to formulate a clear interpretation of the troubles tearing his family apart, but his unconscious is trying to cope with these "difficulties".

In *The Interpretation of Dreams*, Freud exposes his view of the enigma of the "dream within a dream" (374). Eddie's dream is not merely a "dream within a dream" in the true sense; it could be viewed as a mirage, if we consider *Queen of Hearts* a dream itself. Just as the film *The Vikings* is a dreamlike event in *Queen of Hearts*. A triple "mirror construction" (Metz, *Film*, 228) which demonstrates Eddie's indecision — "That's right, isn't it?" — his fluctuating between truth (Eddie's fear) and untruth (Bruno killing Eddie) is a *mise en abyme* equivalent, according to Freud, "to wishing the thing described as a dream [that] had never happened" (374). The fratricide of *The Vikings* never happened (it was only a movie), just as fratricide does not happen in his own dream (Eddie wakes up before the sword strikes him), nor does facticide occur in *Queen of Hearts* (Eddie does not kill Bruno with the gun). Cain kills Abel because Abel is the one chosen by God. In *Queen of Hearts* which of the two "brothers" has God chosen? Which of the two brothers has society chosen?

The parallelling of fiction and reality (filmic reality), this *mise en abyme*, this "inescutcheon construction" (Metz, *Film*, 228), to use Christian Metz term, permits via this "mirror construction" to reflect the story as a narrative of "two half-brothers". One might be tempted to compare Einar and Eric to

Danilo and Bruno, but that would be misleading. Bruno can never be a brother to Danilo. What we need to do is to return to the first part of this mega-sequence to fully comprehend what "brothers" are being referred to. The structure of this fourth chapter cannot be properly grasped if we do not reduce the range of the narrative to the presence of one and only one person: the Shadow.

Eddie introduces the Shadow to the spectator. He knows something he did not know back then. He is recounting a story that happened in the past. But being in the past, Eddie must lose himself in past events by adopting the present tense. Eddie is an intelligent narrator; what message he discloses actualizes itself as a post-narration.

Eddie (Tony Grisoni?) is divulging a lesson he learnt later. By unearthing what materialized in the past, he becomes aware of the origin of the hurt. Eddie does not "know" the identity of the Shadow. That is, he must pretend that he does not know.

Eddie is aware that Barbariccia and his father Danilo are "half-brothers" who killed one another when they should have loved one another. From this lesson, he learns that he might want to kill Bruno but can't. He fantasizes about such a killing, but does not act upon this wish. He must forgive, not kill. We are assisting once again, as we did in *Bread and Chocolate* (and in *Raging Bull* and *A Pain in the Ass*), to the betrayal of "brothers" (both as a metaphor and a metonymy), not necessarily physical facticide, but unequivocally to the betrayal that destroys culture and encourages assimilation (cultural fratricide).

Barbariccia's skilful maneuvering enables him to quicken, at least for a while, Danilo's independence. By forcing Danilo to forfeit his home and Café, Barbariccia has in fact denaturalized him of his identity. Michael Novak explains the process in *The Rise of the Unmeltable Ethnics:*

> . . .[t]he threat today is homogenization, a coercive sameness, a dreary standardization. The melting-pot ideology... may have been a rationale for deculturalizing immigrants, depriving them of their cultural values, and strength, and thus reducing their political and economic power. If one deprives people of their affective bonds to family, culture, and value, then one can reconstruct them afresh. While they are confused and without identity, one can manipulate them more freely, telling them what they ought to be. One takes their souls and gives them bread and circuses. For a while – until the awake – they are grateful (229).

Near the end of the film, Eddie half asleep in his brother's arms, asks, "Bruno, are you dead?" Dead in which sense? we are encouraged to asked. Bruno who became a pawn for Barbariccia is a prodigal son. When Eddie fires his gun Bruno performs a psychological switch. After having witness his father gambling off his mother to Barbariccia, Bruno must make amends and demand for atonement, which Danilo accepts.

The traitor offers an apology, and the victim must without question accept it without any sort of retribution. Eddie's gun shots pointed at Barbariccia and accidentally toward Bruno provokes retribution. When at the end Beetle enters the café, without bearing a grudge, as though nothing of the betrayal on the part of the Lucca family had happened, he provides the tools to overturn the state of things as managed by Barbariccia, without asking a single question. No penalty in view, all is forgiveness. Forgiveness is one of the denominators of the Italic.

Cassa d'Oro

Italian cards consists of forty cards and four suits following two styles: the Neapolitan, Piacentine, Triestine divided into *coppe* (cups), *ori* or *denari* (golds or coins), *spade* (swords), and *bastoni* (clubs); and the *Piemontesi, Milanesi,* and *Toscane* style which uses suits that what we in North American are used to playing with; that is, the French style, with *cuori* (hearts), *quadri* (diamonds), *fiori* (flowers, clubs), and *picche* (spades).

What is not apparent here is that Eddie speaks of "coins", and the deck used in the scene corresponds to the Neapolitan style, whereas the title of the film refers to the second (French) style of card (with hearts, diamonds, clubs, and spades).

A little semantic friction heightens the seriousness of the gambling fever. No matter what cards are used the wager is serious. No wonder the sound of cards thrown on the table are magnified and distorted with reverb and echoes. This is serious business indeed: Danilo is a gambler. The gains and loses are tremendous in consequences. How can Danilo explain such things to his son without being a little fanciful? Danilo drinks, smokes, gambles, but he does not have a lover. He is seriously in love with his wife Rosa. In the end he gambles all his gains in order to win back his wife, the only reason for living, the key to family-hood.

The family

In the evening, the family sits in front of a television set and enjoys a movie. *Bread and Chocolate* has a similar scene, which includes Nino, Elena, and her son. Like in *Bread and Chocolate*, the family as a social unit for individual salvation resonates throughout. Not to be part of a family jars, as is the case for Beetle. (Think of Milan the loner in *A Pain in the Ass.*)

Beetle never eats meals with his father. Barbariccia is without a family. Pepe is a adopted "relative" by the Lucca family. Nonna and Nonno live with their offspring.

One can emigrate as a single person, but one must create or adopt a new family unit to be able to accommodate oneself to the new context. Poignantly, Rosa comes from a single parent home; as do Danilo and Beetle. The only concrete family in this film is Danilo's family, which he manages to keep together against all odds.

The narrative trick of children opening the photographers' film bag is an excuse to move the party guests outside. The wedding game with electricity is to introduce Beetle to the spectator. Eddie (via Bruno) betrays this close friend. Bruno grows apart from Danilo, and there is nothing he can do.

This generational gap translates also another malaise but, poignantly, as later scenes will indicate, Bruno never really gives up his cultural roots; he simply needs to modify them, adapt them to the new British reality (via Barbariccia's organized crime outfit). There is never rejection of Italian culture, nor is assimilation a possibility. Bruno turns into debt collector but still labors in the ghetto. The criminals deal principally with Italians, often members of the extended family. This is where trouble begins.

How can one perform his criminal duty and respect his family? The Lucca family falls apart because Danilo is powerless to piece it back together. When Bruno interjects: "Daddy, you're just going to sit there," it is because the son rebels against his weakling of a father. Danilo needs his military father (Nonno) by his side to fight the enemy within and without. Elsewhere Bruno tells his mother: "You need a husband… He is a weak man, Mamma." What kind of husband does Bruno have in mind: Barbariccia? Most probably, a criminal. Until he comes to understand that even crime is not the solution for social advancement and personal well-being. Only the family can guarantee this sort of stability.

God, Eve, Sex, Satan

Leaving Italy: the connotation is challenging. Does this mean that life would not have been possible in Italy? Grisoni echoes Brusati's argument. The orchestral music is soft on this silent sequence shot. In voice over, Eddie's revealing monologue: "It's funny how you can't remember it: being born. It must be strange, sitting in the dark, nothing to do. Then suddenly you can hear and see and feel things right."

Stretch the image of birth and we have the full extent of the attack against the past. Italy is not God. Nor is sex. Sex is more or less on everyone's mind (Scene 34-35-36-37-38), but sex is not an end. In fact, the entire chapter six could have been called "Sex". What could Danilo's father be guilty of to deserve the epithet: "filthy". Nonna calls him "filthy" but it obviously does not refer to Nonno's wealth (filthy lucre, filthy rich). No, it is more probably the other kind of filth: "obscene language or thoughts, anything that corrupts and defiles" (Webster's Dictionary).

Is Danilo's father sexual to the hilt? In one scene Nonna calls Nonno "Satan" in Italian. Barbariccia's obsession for Rosa, undoubtedly sexual, is never translated as a sexual attraction. Are Italians prudes? Reserved? When dealing with homosexuality (*Bread and Chocolate*, *A Pain in the Ass*, *Raging Bull*), it is as if same-sex love were not a sexual issue. Immigration and change of language do not alter the issue. No matter where Italians live, their morals are similar. Language does not modify the Italian's behavior. Though a major theme, sex is always treated with humor and irony, meant to attract the spectator to the family and its problems.

The Italian ghetto

We get a modest view of the streets of London's Little Italy. A barber "shop" (which we never get to see, except for the barber who is a regular at Gennario's), a betting den, a road leading to Mario's building, the small piazza in front of the Lucca home. Eddie crosses the street and screams "Good Morning" to the barber, and rings Beetle from a contraption connected to the ground below. Everyone knows one another. And yet in the end we wonder if this quarter actually existed at all; the older Eddie admits not recalling where the neighborhood is... If Little Italy did exist, it is not the one that was, nor is it the one which might still exist today. Eddie's Little Italy might be a fantasy.

Italian Men and Women

When Nonno loses at the races, he curses Gennaro from his window. What image is being projected to the British spectator about Italian men? Italian-British men are gamblers, weak men. Barbariccia is a mobster. Bruno is a violent brother who will stop at nothing to protect his sister ("big Italian brother act again"). Danilo gambles not only his own life but also his wife away. Mario lives in make believe world, unable to live in Northern Italy or in Britain. Nostalgia is an emotion that is more or less real.

This reaching back to Italy which is personified at various occasions in the film with the melody of "Torna a Surriento" by Ernesto and G. B. De Curtis.

> "Vir 'o mare quant'è bello, / Ispira tantu sentimento, / Comme tu a chi tiene a' mente, / Ca scetato 'o faie sunnà. / guarda gua' chistu ciardino; / Siente, sie' sti sciure arance: / Nu profumo accussi fino / Dinto 'o core se ne va ./ E tu dice: "I' parto, addio!" / ... // T'alluntane da stu core / Da la terra de l'ammore / Tiene 'o core 'e nun turnà? / Ma nun me lassà, / Nun darme stu turmiento! / Torna a Surriento, / Famme campà!"[31]

This song is the cry from those who stay behind apostrophized to those who leave. It solidifies the need for a return to the place of birth. The receiver of the song might be a woman, but this woman represents more than just the loved one, and warrants the viability of the Italian center. Without this cry to the departed, emigrants become homeless nomads. The song appeared in Pane e cioccolata as well, and it served the same nostalgic purpose: the call for temporary relief from the endless journey by forcing one to look back.

This land of love can be carried elsewhere away. The garden, the lot of land, can be cultivated beyond the confines of their native land. With love, friendship, and consciousness emigrants can reproduce the love left behind.

Barbariccia (who is identified at various time to the melody) represents the past, Italy. His love for Rosa, is it not a fantasy of the past, of the Italy of his youth? No wonder Rosa prefers Danilo the uncertain, because he represents the now. And Eddie, the future. Rosa wants a love she can cultivate like new earth. Richard Gambino suggests that

The Italian-American woman is the center of the life of the entire ethnic group. The privileges transmitted to her give her a status which evokes the special position of women in the legend of chivalry... The equivocal status of the woman as the core of the family, and hence of life, and in service to *l'ordine della famiglia*... Under other conditions of adversity these same men respond by steeling themselves. When necessary to the preservation of *l'ordine della famiglia*, they can press back tears and emotions and present a stony determination to the World that can even out do the stoic aspect of their men... (160-63).

Men act according to the demands made by these female ministers of immigrant culture. Mario, who seems to be without a female presence in his life, wanders from place to place like a nomad. Gennaro, Beetle's father, is a widower. His wife either died or ran away with another man; he too is a man without a center. In the end, even Nonno finds a partner in the reluctant Nonna.

Richard Gambino's comment on Italian-American women is in general applicable to Italian emigrant women living outside of Italy. In *Queen of Hearts*, Italian-British women are more solid. The end of a fixed marriage does not frazzle Rosa. From a fatherless family (there is no mention of Rosa having a father), she is a beautiful woman who, though promised to a rich butcher's son from the village, choses the neighbor's poor son. A free-thinking woman.

A strong woman, she reprimands her son Bruno when he becomes violent against her sister's boyfriend. Why is Rosa not authorized to marry the man next door? Had this woman stayed in Italy, she might have had to marry the butcher's son who promised her financial stability. Rosa takes the path less travelled on, whether her protective mother would faithfully follow or not.

Nonna, a rigid and severe woman, is protective of her daughter. A difficult elderly woman who criticizes her son-in-law for being a weak man; and Nonno for being wicked. Nonna's surrendering to a higher pursuit demonstrates once again how in essence it is the woman who carries the culture forward. She cannot decline Nonno's need for help. The Lucca family is made up of women: Nonna, Rosa, Angelica, Teresa; they will carry the tradition a step further. Men, as we have been shown, tend to find refuge in friendship or non-reality.

Eddie's narrative "I" is never lyrical, seldom poetic, yet often trips in the traps of imagination. His descriptions of his grandfather in the Alps are not nostalgic. They are strange, frightening, haunted by ghosts, but never sentimental. Eddie does not feel a longing to go back to the "old country". Italy is not his home. His very last monologue contains a hint of nostalgia, but it is for the Italian ghetto in London. "Sometimes I wonder what it's like in heaven. It must be like the best time in your life. And it just goes on and on forever. It must be like coming home."

Eddie's home is his mother's home. The mother stands at the opposite end of the metaphorical spectrum. A mother gives birth, death takes life away. The mother is a sign of re-naissance, re-birth. Nonno on the Alps is an awakening for Eddie. Eddie cannot return to Italy.

Eddie's past resembles a fairy tale. We can't assume that the unearthing of the gun and the shooting in Barbariccia's bar actually took place. Which parent would leave his/her child out so late at night? Which criminal would be frightened of a child with a gun? Which doorman of an organized crime open the doors to a boy with a gun?

Viewed from Eddie's point of view, the fairy tale has a lesson to transmit. Grisoni wants to show how the new generation can save the older generation from vanishing into memory. It is the Eddie's and the Beetle's of this fictionalized universe who will continue the tradition brought over from Italy. This is the lesson in hope.

Like Grigory in *Bread and Chocolate*, Eddie represents a will-to-be that does not easily disappear, notwithstanding their existence be limited to works of fiction. The stubbornness of the ethnic persists, against all odds, even when everything around the child of emigrants vanishes.

The possibility of a cultural continuation suffices to conclude that assimilation is not guaranteed for the host nation. Through the magic of the imagination, we can jump off a running train and, bruised, make our back to the place that rejected us (Nino). We can shoot ourselves because of friendship and live off of the affection one has for another's culture (Pignon). We can dig out of gardens treasure boxes with instruments that will help us get rid of whatever obstacle that stands before our goals (Eddie). If we will it, the likelihood of the resurgence, in fiction or in reality, of a community that today seems silenced is assured.

Language

In this film the standard Italian is spiced with a regional accent from the North. If it were not for the English spoken by the characters, we would swear that we were in a town in Northen Italy. But we're not in Italy, we are in Little Italy. Merritt Ruhlen reminds us that

...there is no intrinsic connection between language and ethnicity... different languages and different ethnic groups do not represent different stages of our evolution... there is no direct connection between a person's gene and the language he speaks... language families and biologically distinct human population are, jointly, the consequence of certain (or more often prehistorical) events (149-52).

The family comes full circle. Language is not an issue with these people. They move from one idiom to another easily, without a translation, to the obvious exclusion of unilingual English-speaking spectators. There is non-stop code-switching and code-mixing. One generation speaks in English, the other generation speaks in Italian; one person speaks alternatively English and Italian; another mixes a number of languages. The logos adopts to the circumstances, to different settings. Italians in Italy are Italians regardless of the nation's linguistic impositions.

The monologue

The narrator is voiced by a character named Edoardo, aka Eddie. A first-generation born Italian-British boy who revisits his childhood in the Italian ghetto which today no longer exists. Why is the ghetto no longer there? Maybe the ghetto has been absorbed by mainstream Britain. Maybe the ghetto was destroyed and paved over with high-rise buildings and superstructures. We don't know. The answer remains ambiguous, uncertain.

Eddie speaks, to use a concept by Michel Chion, in voice over using the I-voice *(voix-je)*.[32] This is the "juxtadiegetic" voice, as Christian Metz calls it: "a character is diegetic, but his voice, as a voice, is not really diegetic, for we are never shown the narrator in the act of speaking... That voice... enables the diegetic character to remove himself and yet still be there" (Metz, *Énonciation*, 142).

The youngest of the Lucca family, Eddie, speaks as a child, but it is not a boy's consciousness that transpires his idiom. He expresses himself with the awareness of a mature man. The voice itself therefore is a lie. It might be speaking the truth, yet the lexis is not entirely truthful.

What we hear is the retelling of a story that might never have happened, or if it did occur, it did not unfold exactly as the story is told to us. The monologue mixes fact and invention. The mode is ironic: "So that's how Mom and Dad married. It was incredibly romantic."

According to Eddie, Danilo his father is responsible for the fairy tale quality of the plot. But there is a discrepancy between the time continuum of the story and the story as it appears on screen. The ellipses and the formal manipulation of the material presented enhances the fictional quality of the narrative. Jon Amiel was not the only one responsible for the distanciation in the material at hand.

Between the raw life-event and the life-story that made it to the screen, there is more than a description; one is faced with a double "de-monstration" ("monstration" in French) advanced by André Gaudreault.[33] Irony appears in the describing of the recounted story. The I-Voice splits into many utterances: Eddie the child, Eddie the adult, Eddie the storyteller, Eddie the censor, Eddie the fabulator, Eddie the mask of Jon Amiel, Eddie the mask of Tony Grisoni. At all times, these persons make their presences felt, and so modulate the realistic and the filmic modes. This is not neo-realism. For the third time in our study, realism is tossed aside in order to amplify the magic in the narration. Artistic creation is perceptibly another parameter of the Italic. Italic is artistic invention.

The pig

The woman and the man at the table, intentionally outlandish, wish Danilo the waiter to "honor" (the client's actual term) them with a smile and, in doing so, will be recompensed with a five-pound note. Danilo is a man who never smiles. The clients' faces taken in extreme close-up, their features distorted by a wide-angle lens, contrast with Danilo's face not yet the clown-like mask he will acquire later in the film. In this scene Danilo has not grown a moustache yet, which will appear only after he becomes the owner of the café. One distinguishes a hint of Leopoldo Trieste in *Lo sceicco bianco* (1952) by Federico Fellini, and perhaps a little of early Chaplin as the Tramp.

Before an annoyed Danilo answers, he is distracted by a pig's stuffed head on the table, shining there, in between the man and woman, like the statue of a taxidermic animal, that persuasively turns its eyes to him. Eddie the narrator calls this scene "the vision". The Pig is given the gift of speech: "Money is like the sun. Only if you trust the coin will you become a man of property. Only then will you be happy. Trust the coins. But beware the King of Swords."

Danilo fathoms the message given to him from this telluric god and breaks out in a smile which instantly wins him the freshly printed five-pound note. What is the significance of this highly stylized scene, if not to bring the spectator to other events: the title credits and the suicide-attempt scene.

The queen of hearts of the title and the suicide plunge of the escaping lovers are both expressions of the wager. Eddie embellishes the rather harsh reality of a childhood spent living under the weak rule of a gambler-father who foolishly believes pig our heavenly gods. With this subtle mention of the King of Swords as well as coins we are right in the gist of the problematic of this plot. Queen of Hearts has transparently to do with gambling, and taking chances against all odds. The outcome of the Pig's divination pushes Danilo to suicide. This pact with demons is a wager that brings the Lucca family to its collapse.

At another more metaphorical level, fiction (fairy tales) can be viewed as a dangerous apparatus for it turns pain to joy and joy to pain. Fiction is a gambler's wand that does not guarantee exemplary results. The Italic is a gamble, a wager against all odds.

Suicide

Eddie tells an incredulous Beetle (repeated to the spectator) that Mario is receiving a million pounds for selling his warehouse. During this conversation, Barbariccia's shadow ambles down the stairs, frightening the boys away. As they flee, Eddie trips to the ground and injures his hand on broken glass. The blood that drops from Eddie's hand eerily is reminiscent of Barbariccia's blood dripping to the ground on the day that Danilo and Rosa jumped into the void. Had the straw-filled truck not been there, there would have died. The symbolic equivalence, enabled by a visual simile, permits the spectator to deduce that this Shadow is none other than Barbariccia, the landlord who handed Mario the large sum of money.

Few words are exchanged between the boys about Beetle's mother. Unaware, Beetle reveals how his mother's blood squirted out of her veins. Eddie asks him about her dying from the bite of a tsetse fly. Beetle refuses to elaborate. This is the second time suicide is mentioned in the film (in less than twenty-five minutes): the first being Danilo and Rosa's suicide pact (the desire to jump off the tower), and the second is Beetle's mother cutting her veins. *Deliberata morte ferocior* ("Made more ferocious by this desire to die").[34] Self-destruction is a complex issue receiving as many definitions as there are cultures. Ethics immediately come into play and blur the meaning of this self-induced death. Émile Durkheim gives his definition of "suicide":

> We consider *suicide* any case involving death that is the outcome of a direct, or an indirect, action, no matter if positive or negative, produced

by a victim on himself, and who was fully aware of the outcome of such an action (5).

The term "suicide" comes from the Latin *suicidium,* that is from *sui caedere,* "to kill oneself". Suicide, like insanity, mentioned in an earlier chapter dealing with Nino's mental state in *Bread and Chocolate,* seems to play an important role in immigration. According to Hawton and van Heeringen, over one million people a year commit suicide.[35] Eustace Chesser believes that there seems to be a link between ethnicity and suicide rates.[36] In England, World Health Organization reported 1.1 female and 2.9 male suicides per 100,000 people for 1952-54. Chesser believes that passivity in integration is no better than total radicalism against assimilation.

> Whether integration with society is a good or bad thing depends, of course, on the type of society. It may not be desirable for everyone to accept passively the social order in which they are born. But when that order breaks down the strain will prove too great for some individuals (104).

Do Danilo and Rosa fit this description, they who preferred to throw themselves from the heights of a tower than to continue living in a society that refused to recognize their salubrious love? Does Beetle's mother belong to one of these statistics of those who prefer to kill themselves than to accept their fate? Not being able to adapt is a strong motive to kill oneself. In *Man Against Himself* Karl Menninger describes the three components in the suicidal act — the wish to kill, the wish to be killed, the wish to die.

Keeping in mind these drives facilitate our understand of the baffling attitudes behind alcoholism, problem gambling and outright self-induced murder (*auto-lysis* (from the Greek *[auto-]* and *[lúsis]* destruction). Danilo wishes to die: he wants to kill his girlfriend (tower), he wants to kill himself (London Bridge), he wants to kill his family (betting his wife away to Barbariccia). Viewed under this light, Bruno's growing belligerence against his father Danilo might be justifiable; his enmity leads him to behave in the most antagonistic way. Bruno will have none of his father's desultoriness (jumping from wine-drinking and card-playing to daydreaming). What we are witnessing is the splitting up of individualism and culture. Behind his destructive behavior, Danilo manifests his difficulty to integrate into the British society. It is this refusal that Bruno attacks. More poignantly, Danilo's wish to commit suicide (via his addictions) is what his son Bruno rejects. Culture cannot survive without a loved one, nor can it survive with a suicidal father.

The end

This mixture of past and present opens the way to possible happiness. This *mescolanza* (mixing) can be achieved through friendship and familial ties. The ghetto, the setting for such family affairs, James Stuart Olson explains, "had two dimensions, cultural and residential... the ghettos were neither pathological expressions of fear nor walled, escape-proof communities. Ethnic groups lived there in part because of the emotional security they offered. Havens rather than prisons..." (346-47).

At least, this is what the Amiel-Grisoni tandem seems to be suggesting. Franco Brusati's message is somewhat different; in his point of view the ghetto is a dangerous zone; solitude leads to illness (mental and physical); suicide and madness are symptoms of emotional instability. Cultural survival necessitates cooperation, technological (Beetle) as well as emotional plurality (Rosa and Danilo consoling Barbariccia). As for language, it needs a setting without which culture must attach itself to another idiom. Edward Sapir conjectured "that language and culture are not intrinsically associated. Totally unrelated languages share in one culture, closely related language -- even a single language -- belong to distinct cultural spheres" (213).

Past traditions can blossom if one enters a trance; that is, if one blanks out, is pulled outside himself or, dissimilarly, becomes totally immersed in meditation (prayer and confession). Survival depends on parameters associated with exaggeration (irony) and inventiveness (fiction).

Interestingly, Grisoni and Amiel prefer to overplay religion as a primordial parameter of ethnicity. In *Pane e cioccolata*, religion is scarcely mentioned; Zavaglia and Scorsese include religion in their theses. Molinaro does not. Some filmmakers state through their works that the further we go from the "age area" (the center of a culture) the more vital a role religion plays (even if it is nothing more than a moral crutch).

The main issue raised in *Queen of Hearts* is the need for Italy (metaphorically speaking) to rejuvenate what has detached itself from Italian culture transplanted abroad. Nonno represents this positive agent of emotional and social revitalization. New blood must be reintroduced for the old blood to replenish itself. Metonymically, the handgun and his hearing aid provide a medium for cultural revival and provides the help so badly needed in this languorous family. Addiction (gambling, alcohol, private ambition) eventually dictates a person's social attitude and behavior; Nonno's influence changes all of that, without being himself the manipulator in any direct way. He is quick to remind his grandson Eddie that Danilo knew what had to be done. Nonno is a source for new direction when all seems to move to a dead-end.

The dream sequences (Nonno's military past and Eddie's rampage in Barbariccia's gambling joint) might be a fanciful method for introducing the angel of death, but these dreams allow the Amiel-Grisoni tandem to re-introduce the Figure of change (what is death but a change of status): the messenger (Eddie about Nonno and the plot of land: "he needs to get back to his roots") who recalls Nonno's youthful plunge into his mother's (Italian) arms.

Italian culture abroad risks becoming stale if inactive. Barbariccia cannot be considered a symbol of reinvigoration, because he comes not from Italy; he is from Italy, yes, but then he moved to America, and from America he went over to Britain. Barbariccia is doubly an emigrant: once from Italy, then from America. Barbariccia, we are told, owns a bar in New York. He might have learnt his trade in Italy, but he honed his criminal vocation abroad. The manner in which he is able to take complete control of the Italian ghetto is not the outcome of some special inborn characteristic. He knows too well (the courts including: the agent in a bowler hat) what has to be done to reclaim what he loses. Barbariccia cares nothing for barter systems. He gets what he wants by paying for it (Mario's hardware store). He can hire people who will get him what he wants (Bruno, Pepe). Nonno does not possess that sort of power. One wonders if he was ever able to use that handgun. Strangely, Eddie seems more at ease with a gun than Nonno. Even when facing the angel of darkness, Nonno is too tired to fire.

The weak link in the chain is Danilo, he who is the "bad guy" (he stole another man's woman) ends up being a "good guy". Without Nonno's presence, however, Eddie, his brother and sisters would not have made their way into the light. Nonna Sabilla emphasizes this fact; are we to blame her for refusing to give her daughter to Nonno's son? She can't admire a gambler who loses everything. Nonna criticizes Nonno and Danilo for being a family of "black souls" (understand "lost souls"). If Danilo finally wins all he has lost (his family), it is thanks to Nonno who interjects, via his otherworldly presence (using Eddie's body as a vehicle). To claim back his wife, the mother of his children, Danilo needs his father's assistance. "Going to heaven", to paraphrase Eddie, means accepting to give up everything one owns, including the one million pounds loot. To keep his culture, he has to lose everything he owns. Going back to Italy (as Mario did) is not the solution. The alternative is to bring a piece of Italy (his father) into the new world; his father revitalizes whatever culture that has been exhausted. This is the lesson Eddie passes on to Italians-outside-Italy ("Italiani fuori patria", as Gianfranco Lotti calls them). He, the grandson, wishes to remember what the son wishes to forget.

Notes

1. Anne Goliot-Léte and Francis Vanoye, *Précise d'analyse filmique* (1992), 2nd ed., Paris: Armand Colin, 2009., 105.
2. Goliot-Léte, op. cit., 10: "Il s'agit de 'moments", plutôt que d'étapes".
3. This classification of sixteen expressions of the ethnic writer was devised and published in *L'Impossible*, 2, February 1993, edited by André Beaudet, under the title, "L'autel de l'assimilation". A translation of this essay was published in *In Italics: In Defense of Ethnicity*, Toronto: Guernica Editions, 1996. This essay also has appeared in various versions of *In Italics* (or as a separate article) and in various languages across the world
4. Quoted in Steven J. Belluscio, *To Be Suddenly White: Literary and Racial Passing*, Columbia and London: University of Missouri Press, 2006, 1.
5. Samuel Taylor Coleridge, *Biographia Literaria*, Chapter XIV, 285. See also T.S. Eliot, "Dante", in *Selected Prose of T.S. Eliot*, edited by Frank Kermode, 1975, 223. "What is necessary to appreciate the poetry of the Purgatorio is not belief, but suspension of belief... I mean a state of mind in which one sees certain beliefs... as possible, so that we suspend our judgment altogether."
6. Caryn James, *New York Times Review*, 20 September 1989.
7. TV Guide, Review, http://movies.tvguide.com/queen-of-hearts/review/110767, 1989.
8. Gene Seymour, EW.com *(Entertainment Weekly)*, 16 March 1990.
9. Hal Hinson, *Washington Post*, 11 October 1989.
10. Joe Brown, *Washington Post*, 13 October 1989.
11. Roger Ebert, *Chicago Sun-Times*, 20 October 1989.
12. Ken Jones, *L'Argent*, London: British Film Institute, 1999, 36.
13. Elie Faure, *Fonction du cinéma*, Paris: Éditions Gonthier, 1964. (Éditions d'Histoire et d'Art, 1953). "L'homme et le groupe, très longuement formés par des complexes ethniques, empruntent au milieu le langage dans lequel ils exprimeront les idées et les images qui germent d'une confrontation millénaire entre les impulsions poétique et leur ordre intellectuel. Il y a action et réaction incessantes entre l'espèce et l'habitat."
14. Beginning in 1983, Fulvio Caccia, Lamberto Tassinari, Bruno Ramirez and Antonio D'Alfonso published a magazine that would greatly alter the landscape of cultural criticism. Much has been published about *Vice Versa* and its policy of transculturalism, the most recent of these publications is *La transculture et "Vive Versa"*, edited by Fulvio Caccia (Montreal, Éditions Triptyque), 2010.
15. I owe much to Pasquale Verdicchio's essays dedicated to the perspective of cultural criticism from the post-emigrant. See *Devils in Paradise: Writings on Post-Emigrant Cultures* (Toronto, Guernica Editions, 1997) and *Bound by Distance: Rethinking Nationalism through the Italian Diaspora* (Cranbury, Fairleigh Dickinson University Press, 1997). *Bound by Distance*, 122.
16. See Peter Bondenella, *Italian Cinema: From Neorealism to the Present* (1983), Edition, New York, Continuum, 2001; Millicent Marcus, *Italian Film in the Light of Neorealism*, Princeton University Press, 1986; Millicent Marcus, *After Fellini: National Cinema in the Postmodern Age*, Baltimore: John Hopkins University Press, 2002; Marcia Landy, Italian Film, Cambridge: Cambridge University Press, 2000.

17. Angela Dalle Vacche, *The Body in the Mirror: Shapes of History in Italian Cinema*, Princeton: Princeton University Pres, 1992, quoted in Millicent Marcus's *After Fellini*, 286.
18. Marcel Jean, *Le Cinéma québécois*, Montréal: Boréal, 2005. "[Le présent ouvrage] est consacré uniquement au cinéma francophone, mais cette séparation linguistique ne répond pas à des motifs politiques. Elle est plutôt induite par la problématique qui sous-tend le cinéma anglo-québécois et qui, pour l'essentiel, rejoint celle de l'ensemble du cinéma canadian" (13). Such a programme, we will see, excludes the plurilinguistic works of a filmmaker like Nicola Zavaglia.
19. Millicent Marcus, *After Fellini*, 285.
20. E. J. Hobsbawn, *Nations and Nationalism Since 1780* (1990), Cambridge (U.K.): Cambridge University Press, 1997.
21. Italian-American scholar, Anthony J. Tamburri published a book *To Hyphenate or Not to Hyphenate: The Italian/American Writer: An Other American,* Montreal: Guernica, 1991, in which he proposed the use of the slash instead on the hyphen when speaking of ethnics. Instead of Italian-American he suggests Italian/American, the slash here being a symbol of unification, unifying as it is the two terms instead of semantically dividing them, as the hyphen ultimately does in its own manner by putting one of the criteria at a disadvantage. Tamburri believes that the hyphen more than unites, diminishes one or both of the terms around the symbol. Only the slash creates an active confrontation that keeps the meaning of the term vibrant, both individually and conjointly.
22. Michael Novak, *The Rise of the Unmeltable Ethnics* (1971), New York: The MacMillan Company, 1972, 8.
23. Michael Novak, op. cit., 150 and 186.
24. Michael Novak, op. cit., 46-48.
25. Quoted in Horace M. Kallen, *Culture and Democracy in the United States* (1924), New Brunswick (U.S.A.): Transaction Publishers, 1998.
26. Quoted in Andrew Bennett, *The Author,* London: Routeledge, 2005, 49.
27. Roland Barthes, "La mort de l'auteur", published in *Manteia,* 1968, reprinted in *Le bruissement de la langue,* Paris: Éditions du Seuil, 1984.
28. Michel Foucault, "What Is an Author?", published in the *Bulletin de la Société de Philosophie,* LXIV, 3, 1969. Published in *English in Screen,* 20, 1, Spring 1979, translated by Donald F. Bouchard.
29. Caryn James, *The Washington Post,* 20 September1989.
30. M.H. Abrams, *A Glossary of Literary Terms* (1957), New York: Holt, Rinehart and Winston, Inc., 1971.
31. "Torna a Surriento", a Neapolitan song, composed by Ernesto De Curtis to lyrics by his brother, Giambattista. It was copyrighted in 1905.
32. Michel Chion, *La Voix au cinéma,* Paris, Éditions de l'Étoile, 1982, quoted in Anne Golio-Lété and Francis Vanoye, *Précis d'analyse filmique,* 38.
33. Quoted in Anne Goliot-Lété and Francis Vanoye, *Précise d'analyse filmique,* 36.
34. Horace, "Ode XXXVII", line 29.
35. Hawton K, van Heeringen K, "Suicide", *Lancet* 373 (9672), 1372–81.
36. Eustace Chesser, *Why Suicide?,* 89: "Suicide is less common among Roman Catholics, Moslems and Jews than Protestants."

4

THE MEDITERRANEAN FOREVER

The personal Ddocumentary

Mediterraneo sempre (also known as *Méditerranée pour toujours* and *The Mediterranean Forever,* by Nicola Zavaglia, released in 2000, documents an Italian ghetto in Montreal, Canada. Absent in *Bread and Chocolate* and *A Pain in the Ass,* and hinted at in *Queen of Hearts,* Little Italy (or La Petite Italie, as it is known in Montreal) is vibrant and as distant as anything that might have been conjured in the term "Ritalie" (Wopland). Zavaglia makes no apology for the existence of this cultural territory. Displayed as a vital center of personal and collective exchange, the Little Italy depicted in his film is so deeply inscribed in a new immigrant tradition that, at times, it can pass as a visual political manifesto. The title itself forcefully asserts its position. *Sempre, toujours, forever:* whatever noun this adverb qualifies, almost like an adjective, will never die, disappear, disintegrate. The Mediterranean is viewed as a sea but also as a metaphor, a metonymy for the peoples who live around that sea, and, more specifically, the peoples of the Italian peninsula.

> We believe that the cinema's capacity for getting around, for observing and selecting from life itself, can be exploited in a new and vital art form.[1]

These words were written by John Grierson in 1936. It was Grierson who, in fact, coined the term "documentary" in a review published in the *New York Sun* in February 1926. The French had used the term earlier when speaking of travel films, but it was John Grierson who used the term to qualify *Moana* (1926) by Robert Flaherty, which he considered to be the first documentary ever to be made.

What is a documentary? "The creative treatment of actuality" (Grierson, 13) is Grierson's answer. The word "documentaire", an adjective introduced in 1877 to describe commercial activity, such as in "crédit documentaire", gradually made its entry into film vocabulary in 1906, as "scène documentaire". By 1915, the term evolved and gained the status of a noun: the "documentaire" was used to describe the short- and medium-length non-fiction films which usually had little success with the general public.

Grierson had noticed how "the use of natural material" and "the camera shot on the spot" (145) distinguished documentaries from works of fiction. The thought that a filmmaker could work outside the centralized Hollywood system made documentaries enviable, because the directors had to work far from the places where the "ready-made dramatic shape" (147) was imposed on natural (raw) material. Documentaries were stories pulled out of reality with the help of the "spontaneous gesture" (145). To observe, expose, uncover, demonstrate, refute, such were the documentary filmmaker's job descriptions.

Grierson immediately realized the didactic and propagandist possibilities of non-fiction films and how they would serve the Allies during War World II. In May 1938, invited by the Canadian government, Grierson produced a report on the Canadian film work, and in October 1938, his recommendations were approved in parliament. By March 1939, the government passed a bill which established the National Film Board and, on 2 May 1939, the National Film Board becomes a legal entity. "In his conception the National Film Board was using films as they had never been used before, in a planned and scientific way to provide what might be described as a supplementary system of national education" (26). Grierson elaborated his vision:

> The main thing is to see this National Film Board as a service to the Canadian public, as an attempt to create a better understanding of Canada's present... A country is only as vital as its processes of self-education are vital (28).

According to film critic Marcel Jean, before 1914, only eighty films were made in Canada and these were registered by Edison at the Library of Congress (Jean, *Cinéma*, 15).

Because of Canada's official cultures (plus the overdue recognition of the Amerindian cultures), government subsidies had to be divided (and continue to be divided), more or less equitably, among the Francophones and Anglophones of the country. French-speaking Canadian filmmaking developed through the decades independently of the English-speaking Canadian reality, so much so that one could safely consider, regardless of one's political denomination, Quebec as a separate cultural entity. Interestingly, Grierson never addressed this extremely sensitive issue in his report. An oversight? Tactful intellectualism? Not really. Grierson's position on the issue, in reality, was quite clear: "It is not necessary that films be made in French..." (Jean, *Cinéma*, 33) Quebec did not appreciate the comment.

Between 1952 and 1956, 1109 films were produced in Canada, of which only 69 were in French (Jean, *Cinéma*, 35). We cannot name all of the filmmakers belonging to the French-Canadian tradition; this would lead us far beyond the scope of our study. Nevertheless, let us mention a few names of persons who might have shaped Nicolas Zavaglia's mind: Albert Tessier, a priest who is a monument in the field for his regionalist and community-oriented documentaries; Maurice Proulx, another priest who responsible for the first sound feature-length documentary in Canada, *En pays neuf* (1934-1937); Louis-Roger Lafleur, who specialized in making films on Amerindians in the 1930s; Paul Provencher, also a specialist in filming Amerindians; and Herménégilde Lavoie, who worked primarily on French-Canadian culture. It would be only in 1963 that the Canadian government started to take French-Canadian film culture seriously.

Many of the filmmakers who played an important role in the 1960s, 1970s and the 1980s were closely associated to poet Gaston Miron and his publishing house, L'Hexagone. Louis Portugais and Gilles Carle (a major French-Canadian fiction filmmaker) were actual co-owners of the literary press, which was established in 1953. Considered the first non-religious French-language press in the country, l'Hexagone would be at the forefront of the *Révolution tranquille* that was to transform Quebec the province into Quebec a nation. Pierre Perrault, who was one of the first filmmakers to explore cinéma vérité, was also published by Miron.

The fiction and non-fiction films produced in Quebec during the 1960s by the French Canadians were remarkable in their social and cultural sensitivity. Under the influence of Roberto Rossellini and Vittorio De Sica's neo-realism and France's *cinéma vérité*, French-Canadians came up with their singular version of realist filmmaking: the *cinéma direct*. Gilles Marsolais explained the neologism:

> Comme son nom l'indique, il désigne donc ce nouveau type de cinéma (documentaire, à l'origine) qui, au moyen d'un matériel de prises de vues et de son synchrone (alors de format 16mm), autonome, silencieux, léger, totalement mobile et aisément maniable, tente de cerner "sur le terrain" la parole et le geste de l'homme en action, placé dans un contexte naturel, ainsi que l'événement au moment même où il se produit. Il s'agit d'un

cinéma qui tente de coller le plus possible aux situations observées, allant même jusqu'à y participer, et de restituer honnêtement à l'écran "la réalité" des gens et des phénomènes ainsi approchés (12).

The invention of portable cameras (Aaton), light-weight tape recorders (Nagra), and ultra-sensitive film (400 ASA and higher) facilitated work for the small crew by giving film directors greater mobility and the possibility to make live sound recordings in the tiniest corners of a city or village. Jean Rouch's sketch, *Gare du Nord*, in Paris vu par... (1963), shot mostly in one sequence shot, moving from a small apartment and down the road and over a bridge, became a landmark. Filmmakers were now free to move beyond the confines of studio walls and explored subjects outside of stylized fiction and the morbidity of television talking heads.

The first film in the cinéma direct mode was *Les Raquetteurs* (1958), by Michel Brault and Gilles Groulx. Marcel Carrière recorded the first synchronic ambient sounds in film. One scene, the mayor giving his speech, was shot and taped in perfect synchronism. Michel Brault and Pierre Perrault pushed this quest for realism further in the masterpiece, *Pour la suite du monde* (1963). From 1963 onward, French-speaking filmmakers in Quebec produced some of the finest films in the country. Their unique brand of political awareness helped them create their own film industry, distinct from the highly Americanized films of English Canada.

Nicola Zavaglia, born in 1954, in Mammolla, Calabra, emigrated to Canada with his parents in the 1960s, gravitates outside these two disconnected cultural centers. Though he produced some of his films with the assistance of the Montreal office of the French-language National Film Board, Zavaglia cannot be considered either a French-language or a English-language filmmaker. As much an outsider as is possible — a totally independent filmmaker is an impossibility in Canada — Zavaglia stubbornly directs his films that contain traces of neo-realism, cinéma vérité, and cinéma direct. In Rome, Zavaglia studied with Marco Bellocchio and Cesare Zavattini.

Zavaglia's first film, *A Poet in the Family*, was released in 1979. A moving portrait of handicapped poet Vincenzo Albanese, the film also presents honest impressions of the Italian-Montreal community. Zavaglia directed documentaries for the provincial television station, Télé-Québec, in the 1980s, which brought him some notoriety. However, his longer films such as *L'espoir violent* (1989), *L'Eclipse du sacré* (1998), and *Barbed Wire and Mandolins* (2002) would crown Zavaglia an imperative documentary filmmaker.

In 2000, he wrote and directed *The Mediterranean Forever*, a multilingual film on the Italians of Montreal, produced by the National Film Board of

Canada. Zavaglia is one of the first Italian-Quebecois filmmakers to explore the various aspects of cultural and social identity. Unlike Carlo Liconti (*Concrete Angels,* 1987) or Paul Tana (*La Sarrasine,* 1992, and *La déroute,* 1998), Zavaglia never uses fiction to map the intricacies of otherness, nor does he use re-creation in his documentaries, as Paul Tana did in *Caffè Italia-Montréal* (1985).

Zavaglia uses "natural material" which he then orchestrates into intricate and interlocking compartments. Free of any sort of prescribed plot, Zavaglia assembles disparate photographs and shots and masterfully reorganizes these fragments in syntagmas which constantly move inside and out of an original narrative. Remove a single element from his social commentaries and the whole suffers. Zavaglia has a predilection for the bracket syntagma, that is a "system of allusions... series... occurrences..." (Metz, *Film,* 126) which act much like words in between bracket or parentheses; he also use the alternate syntagma — the switching between two or more linear actions — and the descriptive syntagma — which gathers in a single segment various details of one large unit (for example, a landscape divided into distinct shots). Zavaglia prefers shooting his interviews in long takes, which he then cuts by interjecting images, drawings, sounds, scenes shot at another time and space.

He rarely shoots scenes in their entirety; there are jump cuts and ellipses, and often uses a voice over (usually his own voice) to bring the separate pieces together. Zavaglia shoots his scenes with a single camera and works with an extremely small crew. He normally is the editor of his films, which enables him to slowly, carefully mixing disparate shots to create an ordinary scene. His scenes resemble sequences, more like a cubist painting than the uniform theatrical scene with two or characters chatting around a table. A Zavaglia scene is never totally complete; a piece or two of the puzzle somehow seems missing; the spectator is never permitted to take anything of what is being depicted for granted.

The spectator is refused the privileged right of acting as the calm "entertained" visitor or witness. Zavaglia never encourages the voyeur to jump out of the spectator. Before our eyes an obstacle is placed to disrupt the joy of total spectator abandonment. The person who watches a film by Zavaglia must figure out what is happening on screen, and always be on the look-out and critical.

In the 1991 edition of *Le Cinéma québécois,*[2] Marcel Jean pointed out, and rightly so, that even when presenting interviews Zavaglia refuses to limit himself to the "talking head" formula. This quest for a different kind of formal identity has put Zavaglia at the margins of Quebec and English-Canadian film criticism, as can be attested by Marcel Jean's 2005 revised edition of *Le*

Cinéma québécois, in which Zavaglia no longer figures. Jean retains the name of Sylvie Groulx, who, in the previous edition, had been mentioned alongside Zavaglia, but for some unknown reason Zavaglia's name has been cancelled.

This trifle for some is indicative of the ostracization taking place in this country, on both side of the linguistic barrier. This devaluation of a filmmaker reveals the narrow-mindedness of the bureaucrats governing the artistic policies of this country's national cinemas. Whenever an artist does not sink in the folds of the accepted vocabulary, s/he is erased from the official registry. And this attitude can be found across the artistic spectrum.

Nicola Zavaglia is not a man known for his political outspokenness, even less for being an anti-assimiliationist. He considers himself a Canadian filmmaker in the true sense of the terms (French-English-Canadian-Italian). Nonetheless, the fact that he is of Italian origin creates somewhat a problem, for those who would like to fit him in a clear-cut category. There is no legal provision for filmmakers like Zavaglia. Where does an Italian-Canadian filmmaker fit in a bilingual and bicultural Canada?

Zavaglia's films are plurilingual. Men and women speak in dialect, standard Italian, French, joual, and English. He belongs to artistic movement. He is a solitary artist who makes personal films.

People who appear in his film speak with Nicola Zavaglia. His films have a special quality to them; most of the time the spectator feels s/he is eavesdropping on a conversation among friends at a dinner party. His is a filmmaking of complicities, unique and authentic; his images sound the secrets of a non-mainstream Canada.

Creativity at work

The Mediterranean Forever captures Angelo Finaldi in the act of creation. This creativity-in-the-works, so to speak, reveals itself before us in ways that are reminiscent of The Rolling Stones in Jean-Luc Godard's *One plus One* (1968), and of the Rita Mitsouko in *Soigne ta droite* (1987). In his film, Zavaglia has chosen to explore musician Angelo Finaldi, a famous rock and roll composer and performer from Quebec, as he is writing the theme song for *The Mediterranean Forever.* If this were not enough, Zavaglia places Angelo Finaldi with his father, mother, and daughter. And it is in this very private family setting that Zavaglia records the birth of the theme song, as well as something wonderfully intimate: the becoming of an Italic.

Zavaglia accomplishes inwardness by observing Finaldi's song maturity in bits and pieces, but never giving it to the spectator in its entirety. The filmmaker then uses this birthing as the premise for the film's unavowed theme: the transmission of culture and tradition from one generation to the next. This instance of creative powers brings together three generations (grandfather, father, daughter) in a single room. While the son Angelo Finaldi fidgets with his song in the background, his father Carmine Finaldi explains tradition to the granddaughter, Coco. Magic erupts before our eyes. Such sophistication is exclusive to Zavaglia's documents, which should not be compared extempore to the other documentary on Montreal's Little Italy by Paul Tana, *Caffè Italia-Montréal*.

Scholar Maria Gabriella Adamo does a superb job in outlining certain undercurrents found in both filmmakers' relationship to the question of Italian immigration in Montreal, but one should be cautious about mixing appearances with depth analysis.[3] Furthermore, to correlate this film to Marco Micone's récit *Le figuier enchanté* can only lead us astray.[4] The only point in common with these three Montreal artists (Zavaglia, Tana, Micone) is their use of the fig tree, and nothing else. For the three, the fig tree represents rebirth, a coming out of a winter slumber. However, what happens in the springtime with these three fig trees is completely different.

Paul Tana and Bruno Ramirez summarize their political-cultural position quite adequately in their forward to the published film script:

> For the Italians in Quebec, the cultivation of this tree is a way of taming a country that is not quite theirs yet, of appropriating it — to a certain extent — by giving it things that are familiar to them, that belong to their culture and their past. In doing so, they transform this country and transform themselves...(*Sarrasine*, 7).

Marco Micone uses pretty much the same wording to express his concept of the *culture immigrée* (immigrant culture):

> No culture can fully absorb another or avoid being transformed in contact with it. Immigrant culture is a culture of transition that, if it cannot survive as such, can, in a harmonious exchange, enrich Quebec culture and thus perpetuate it (100).

Maria Gabriella Adamo concludes her brilliant essay stating:

> But this Otherness, which is at the same time a sense of belonging, becomes symbiotic, in the context of an integration process where interculturality begins with everyday living ("Méditerranée", 192).

Manifestly, the message in these three fragments is similar: death, integration, interculturality, rebirth as another. Micone writes: "L'immigré est tiraillé entre l'impossibilité de rester tel qu'il était et la difficulté de devenir autre" (*Figuier*, 87).

Let us not delve into the Francophilia and the proto-nationalist discourse blatant in Tana-Ramirez and Micone's propositions. These intellectuals prove what Michael Novak wrote back in the early 1970s: "The more educated people are, the more they cherish *enlightened* values — it is almost a tautology" (223-24) [my Italics, used ironically].

A similar kind of situation recently developed with Italian-American writer Helen Barolini who, after years of promoting Italian-American culture, spins around and disparagingly refutes the existence of anything multicultural, and arrogantly proclaims the "end of Italian-American literature". As if a single statement could erase a culture firmly established in the country; as if the simple fact of one individual's wealth and success automatically entails the renunciation of the cultural existence of another individual's unwillingness to disappear into mainstream culture.[5]

No single artist creates a cultural entity, no single artist can destroy a culture. Cultural membership surpasses individual allegiance and dissension, be the person wealthy or poor, famous or unknown, educated or not. Be it as it may, Seymour M. Lipset controversailly suggests that "the lower strata are the least tolerant",[6] perhaps because the lower strata of a cultural community can be manipulated more easily, or perhaps because the desire to succeed within that group seems more pressing. *The Mediterranean Forever* also depicts the lower strata of the Italian immigrant community in Montreal, the men and women who work (or have worked) long, hard hours to make ends meet. The artists interviewed (Angelo Finaldi, Mary di Michele, Raffaele) fit more comfortably in the echelon of laborers than in the high spheres of decision-making elites. We must be wary of terms that sound synonymous, but are awry.

If, for some, the fig tree symbolizes rebirth; for others, it represents a foreign fruit tree that survived a transplant. A tree can die, and once dead no fruit will blossom on its branch. Reincarnation or assimilation? As Oscar Handlin claims, "the ties, once severed, could never be replaced."[7] What we are witnessing through the use of a figure of speech is an attempt to dislocate the target of the discussion. The fig tree episode in Zavaglia's film is not comparable to Tana-Ramirez and Micone's fig tree, because unlike the others Zavaglia's tree is not a metaphor. By placing too much emphasis on the burial of the tree, we forget who is digging the ground.

Zavaglia's fig tree is an excuse for him to follow the persons digging the tree. Zavaglia attaches more importance on the persons than on the ritual; more on the individuals than on the plant which is bound to die. For Zavaglia, the metaphor divests itself of its symbolism. Moving from a metonymy (the folkloric crown of thorns for Italian immigrants) to a synecdoche (the assimilation of Italian immigrants to their eventual disappearance), Zavaglia then shows why the burying of the tree, somehow, goes beyond Italian-Canadian mythology and encompasses every citizen in the country. There is an African American involved in the burial scene. Why call it a burial scene at all? Putting to sleep a tree is a new ethnographical practice of a society unaccustomed to fig trees.

This is not the nostalgic pursuit of the past, nor is it the sounding of an alarm for persons being assimilated into another culture. No, this is about gardening management devoid of memoric connotation whatsoever. Zavaglia demonstrates how Italians alter the country they live in. They don't need recall. They are not disappearing. They are well planted in this ground. They are the fig tree that has altered the country's landscape.

Such a trend in Quebec is indeed rare. English Canada — where the discourse on transculturalism, interculturalism, multiculturalism, and pluriculturalism is quasi-absent among intellectuals of Italian origin — is not free of blame. English Canada's nationalism resembles Francophone nationalism in Quebec. What the citizen in Canada hears on a daily basis is the overt appeal in favor of the melting pot ideology, be it British or French.

Tana and Micone are known to be outspoken Quebec nationalists; they are not advocates of a multicultural society, which is the official Quebec government position. This ideological position might explain part of their success. Their Italianness is a transitional phenomenon, they might claim. Many of the younger generation emulate this "die-and-become-mainstream" approach with the hope of being accepted by the mainstream. Interestingly, the fact that both Tana-Ramirez and Micone have ceased to produce artistic works is indicative of how insidious assimilation really is; moving out of their culture of origin and into the culture of assimilation has ironically silenced them. Artists born in a cultural community who allow themselves to be absorbed into another culture become paradoxically, to use the title of one of Marco Micone's play, *a gens du silence*, a "voiceless people".

What is the past is considered, as Novak would say, immoral, and what is the future, moral progress (199). Wherein wriggle the ambiguities. For instance, the last scene in Paul Tana's film, *La Sarrasine* (1992), depicts Ninetta urinating in the snow. The gesture is clearly meant to be a metaphor. But as a simile something is unclear.

Is the spectator asked to consider the urinating the prolongation of the past? This discharging of a part of self seems to contain nothing valuable to offer the present and even less the future. Should we interpret the passing of water as act of aggression on the land that put to death the one person Ninetta loved? The equivocalness of this scatological gesture is disturbing. The spectators, as voyeurs, sense no pleasure at gazing at this woman urinating, unless as a fetish. We are being asked to enjoy what is not enjoyable? Otherwise, why include the scene? If this pleasure is refused to the spectator, then there is something incomplete about the imagery. Perhaps, the denotation of the act is quite straightforward: Ninetta feels so at ease that she is ready to embrace the new reality as her own.

The published script of *La Sarrasine*, where words normally explain what an image leaves ambiguous, purposely silences the significance of this incongruent gesture on the part of an otherwise respectable Italian woman. The term incongruent here is used in its artistic definition and not in its moral or religious connotation. Ambiguousness in cases like this might be dishonest.

Zavaglia's *The Mediterranean Forever* is free of such ambiguities. The constant recall of creativity acts as defiance against those who would only too happily embrace submissiveness and passiveness. There is nothing offensive in Zavaglia's documentation. No one is tagged as a failure. No one is accused of passing away, of disappearing into the mass of sameness. There is no individualism in Zavaglia's film; men and women form families and friendships, each tying up to a larger community which has the potentiality of resisting disappearance. Celestina, the Finaldi, Antonio, Mario, Mary di Michele, Michele, Giovanni, Raffaele... these are active individuals part of a community and, as such, keep the body politic (should we call it the body ethnic?) awake. One is free to participate in the community or not. The choice is theirs. With Tana-Ramirez and Micone, there is no choice. Ninetta is a prisoner of the world she is forced to live in.

Nicola Zavaglia's voice

Throughout the film, Nicola Zavaglia the director becomes the narrator, the commentator, the private person, the interviewer, the historian, the companion. The physicality of his voice is immediately, regularly felt. In the thickness of its enunciation one senses a foreign presence, unlike Eddie's voice in *Queen of Hearts* whose voice, both as a child and as a man, sounds typically British: words are pronounced as someone on national radio or TV would pronounce them. In the case of Zavaglia, its foreignness strikes the listener as authentic, an authenticity that can annoy, especially to any person intolerant of strangers. The accented voice (with its pointers of *there-ness*) is an aggression, for it affirms its being not from here. No French Canadian (in or outside Quebec), no English Canadian speaks like Nicola Zavaglia. His is a voice that simply and brazenly states its entity. A peridiegetic voice,[8] confessing its otherness, pronouncing its idea of something not from here. When its source is eventually shown on screen, it is without a doubt from elsewhere (Italy).

Being from elsewhere and working here, Zavaglia embraces omnipresence. His voice adds layers of beingness on what seems arbitrary. When Zavaglia turns into a commentator, he can be ironic, humorous, harsh. When conducting the interviews, however, the voice refrains from appearing as a face on screen. He respects whoever or whatever is shown on screen. He prefers to remain *in absentia*, a voice and its presence sensed, but adjacent. The interviewee converses with the director, who remains off screen. The eyes are rarely directed to the spectator. The person speaking is looking to the side of the camera lens which records with aloofness history unfolding.

When Zavaglia the historian unravels lists of figures, dates, and encounters, he does so efficiently. In some scenes, he allows himself to speak with an I-voice,[9] revealing private information which seems too personal for the context. In these instances the narrator, the commentator, the interviewer and the historian remove a mask, and emotion is divulged, acknowledged, respected. *The Mediterranean Forever* is not, however, about Nicola Zavaglia. If the narrating voice gains an identity (the film director, Nicola Zavaglia) at the very end of the film, it does so like a second thought.

Post-Italy: The interior domain

La demeure intérieure, the house within, the interior domain, the Mediterranean Sea as a space within: Nicola Zavaglia designates his goal with the film image. The world that one abandons remains within like a heart, a mind. The experience of departing never erases the past, nor is the past forgotten in the present. If anything, both the past and present are essential tools to the creation of the future in its becoming, a growth, an appendix within the body's interior body. Cut this new limb and the wound bleeds. The spectator is required to keep this double world in mind while watching this documentary on Italian immigration in Canada. Carole Gagliardi in her review of the film, published in *Le Journal de Montréal,* resumes these ideas:

> *Mediterraneo sempre,* Mediterranean forever. The sea as far as the eye can see, sumptuous images of Italy, immigrants in search of America and, above all, the dream of a better life. Immigration is a painful gesture and nostalgia for the country of origin persists for a long time, sometimes always... The immigrant maintains a sentimental relationship with this country which is no longer quite his...Nicola Zavaglia knew how to recount with tenderness the love of these immigrants for their country of origin, the pain caused by an absent father, the attraction of America... the importance of the Italian presence at the beginning of the colonization...[10]

Gagliardi speaks of nostalgia, tenderness, sentimentality, presence. A new dimension is added to the worlds introduced by *Bread and Chocolate, A Pain in the Ass,* and *Queen of Hearts*: the post-emigrant experience. Brusati opens the door to departure; the Grisoni-Amiel duo examine the establishment of a community, though it seems to have vanished since; Molinaro lifts the issue to a more subtly political level; Zavaglia surveys the first generation and the second generation (Coco is born in Canada).

The first generation consists of people who left Italy and emigrated; however, the definition should be widened, since Angelo Finaldi, Mary di Michele, and Zavaglia himself, though born in Italy, arrive in Canada at a young age; the second generation consists of children of foreign-born parents but they themselves were born on foreign soil. The country left behind, and a new identity found abroad, in Montreal, these Italians achieve synthesis by traditions prolonged, extended, remodelled in order to accommodate themselves in a new territory.

The father acts as link between the trauma of abandonment and the birthing. This is the birth of a compound identity, more plural than hybrid, more mosaic than layered, every thread leading in various (singular) and composite (multiple) directions.

Louise Blanchard's iterates similar concepts in her review published a few weeks later, again, in *Le Journal de Montréal:*

> Italy has remained entrenched in the heads and hearts of the members of the Italian community, a complex landscape, that of a soul troubled both by the history of uprooting and the difficult reality of integration into Quebec life. The film... also seeks to help understand this community to those who have been around it for a long time and who often know nothing about it...[11]

Two new terms are brought forward in Blanchard's piece: "communauté" (community) and "intégration" (integration). Immigrants have moved beyond individual existence; a larger entity, the social-political realm, awaits them. Glimpses of an Italian community exist in *Bread and Chocolate*, though, in that particular case, the community was reduced to a workers' quarter or a chicken coop. One could question whether Brusati is being ironic, sarcastic, or simply viscous by transposing real places, such as Little Italies, into metaphoric boxes where freaks, loners, deviants, eccentrics, lunatics are lumped together. There can be no community if the individuals are neither organized, nor living some kind of familial stability. Workers in Switzerland and Germany are guests who might be unexpectedly ordered to leave.

In *Queen of Hearts*, a community seems to be hinted at, but it is in its infancy (not yet entirely formed), or perhaps it is dead (Eddie admits not being able to know where his house used to in London). A spectacle of disappearance or birth? Italians in Britain continue to exist no doubt, but not necessarily in the same one location. There is a chance that Italian immigrants have moved away from the ghetto, common at the beginning of emigration, and relocated in some less obvious urban center.

This moving away from the ghetto occurred in Montreal and in Toronto. Yet this dwindling away does not lessen the impact of a "cultural community" ("communuaté culturelle"), as ethnic communities are baptized in Quebec. With the move from emigration to immigration emerge new questions: "Will emigrants return to where they came from?" (as claimed in *Bread and Chocolate*); "Will this physical immigrant center peter out through its own volition?" (as hinted in *Queen of Hearts*); "Will these outsiders finally melt down into the single pot?" (as assimilationists, such as Louise Blanchard, demand — "integration" being nothing less than camouflaged assimilation)? Suddenly, the political is erected in front of emigrants. It is this new quiddity that is subtly, cunningly, studied by Zavaglia. Nathan Glazer calls this experience the "familistic allegiance":

> ...in mass society there is the need in the individual for some kind of identity — smaller than the state, larger than the family, something akin to a "familistic allegiance" (*Ethnic*, 250).

It would not be amiss to point out that it is precisely the failure to create a family that brings about the downfall of Giovanni Rossi's anarchist commune depicted in Jean-Louis Comolli's film, *La Cecilia*.

In Montreal's intellectual newspaper, *Le Devoir*, an article appeared without signature which raises two more important issues: America as viewed by a citizen of the province of Quebec of Italian origin, and America that incarcerates Italians for their political stances (fascism during World War II).

> The is the story of our compatriots of Italian origin in Montreal... Doors open on the emigrants' past, the misery they fled, the Eldorado they did not find in the mythical "America", but also the dark hours of the last war... Quebecers of Italian origin were then hostages to a witch hunt, some sent to camps as prisoners of war, suspected of being followers of Mussolini..[12]

Italian Canadians no more, Italians become full-fledged citizens of the country, whether they liked it or not. This concept of being a full-fledged citizen will be raised in Comolli's *La Cecilia*. As the military tells Rossi, "You might be Italians in Italy, but here you are Brazilians." Italians no longer represent simply a workforce of emigrants, but have become, by the mid-twentieth century, a thorn in Canada's political body. Bandits (*Bread and Chocolate* and *A Pain in the Ass*), waiters (*Bread and Chocolate* and *Queen of Heart*s), men and women with strange-sounding names exemplify a counterforce in the battle of Quebec society in the trough of self-determination. From one year to another, these foreigners determine the future of a country. With *Caffè Italia-Montréal*, Paul Tana promoted the idea that Italians choose to fight on the side of the *indépendantistes* (separatists).

The Mediterranean Forever comes out thirty years after the October crisis, twenty years after the failed referendum, six years after a Quebec Prime Minister blamed "money people and the ethnic vote" (that is, the Jewish and mostly Italian people) for the defeat of the second referendum. The truth of the matter is that neither the Jewish nor Italian people combined would not have put a dent in these referendums even if they had all voted against this call for separatism.

Failure to bring about Quebec's separation is and will remain a brother-against-brother affair; in this, the French Canadians of Quebec, though they refuse to consider themselves an ethnic group, follow the collective patterns as those of other ethnic groups in this country. The tug of war within any one cultural community is systematically similar; one brother pushes for success (assimilation in the large group); the other pulls for the protection of group rights.[13] The call to nationhood, though granted, as least verbally by the Prime Minister of Canada, conceals untenable positions if ever they were to become a country. Countries normally grant equal rights to all its citizens; countries are not represented by a particular parameter of identification (be it linguistic, religious, ethnic) belonging to a single minority or majority collective within its boundaries. As E. J. Hobsbawn notes about the birth of certain xenophobic attitudes that basically led to World War I:

> Merely by dint of becoming a "people", the citizens of a country became a sort of community, though an imagined one, and its members therefore found themselves seeking for, and consequently finding, things in common, places, practices, personages, memories, signs and symbols... For the period from 1880 to 1914 was that of the greatest mass migrations yet known, within and between states, of imperialism and of growing international rivalries ending in world war. These elements underlined the differences between "us" and "them". There is no more effective way of bonding together the disparate sections of restless peoples than by uniting them against outsiders (90-91)

Far from my intention, by this quote, to suggest that the province's justifiable demands will lead to war, any kind of war. What I do wish to stress is that the French Canadians (and this can be debated) who were making claims for an independent country did nothing to involve and attract the Italian community to their cause. Italians might have been cousins (through their linguistic and religious links), but they were, for historical reasons, associated with the enemy camp (the Anglophones). These challenges and deliberations are the backdrop of Zavaglia's film.

The makers of *Caffè Italia-Montréal* pled for the separatist cause; Zavaglia argues, not for the opposite side — the Canadian cause — but for the Italic cause, for what we call a "virtual territory". This cause is advanced in his film regardless of what Zavaglia might himself think or express in interviews on the meaning of his films. Often what an artist believes he is doing does not correspond to what the work produced actually does. Intent and product do not have a one-to-one relationship. The leitmotiv of the Mediterranean Sea is not a call for a return to the Old country. This film prompts the spectator to approach the question of ethnicity differently. Glazer defines ethnicity:

> "Ethnic groups", groups sharing a common history and experience and defined by descent, real or mythical..." The term "ethnic" refers — and this usage by now is quite common among sociologists and other social scientists — to a social group that consciously shares some aspects of a common culture and is defined primarily by descent. It is part of a family of terms of similar or related meaning, such as "minority group", "race",

and "nation"; and it is not often easy to make sharp distinctions between these terms (74, 234).

Werner Sollors plunges deep in the etymology of the term:

> To say it in the simplest and clearest terms, an ethnic, etymologically speaking is a goy. The Greek word *ethnikos*, from which the English "ethnic" and "ethnicity" are derived, means "gentile", "heathen". Going back to the noun ethnos, the word was used to refer not just to people in general but more specifically to the "others"... In the Christianized context the word "ethnic" (sometimes spelled "hethnic" recurred, from the fourteenth to the nineteenth century, in the sense of "heathen" (25).

The French Canadians in Quebec saw Italians as heathens, as not belonging to the in-group. It is with the films of Paul Tana and Nicola Zavaglia that the French gradually refocused their lenses. Zavaglia's enterprise was to readjust the historical reading of the Italian/French-language Quebecois relationship. This is, in my opinion, the motor that propels *The Mediterranean Forever*. It is not the paying of respects to anti-Quebec sentiments that might at times be shared by Italians and English Canadians.

I would be loath to consider Zavaglia's film a Canadian film. If Canada is an officially bilingual country, with two official cultures (the French and the English), than it is not a far-fetch deduction to assert that this film is an Italian-Canadian film, and therefore an ethnic film, and not a Canadian film which can be produced legally on by a member of either one of the official peoples of this country. Because *The Mediterranean Forever* cannot be an Italian film (though Italian is spoken), because it is neither a French-Canadian film (though French is spoken), nor an English-language Canadian film (though English is spoken), one is obliged to ask the simple question, no one dares to ask: Where does such a film, in the strictest legal sense of the word, fit? It does not fit. It exists only in a virtual territory. The Italic is the accumulation of all works that are and are not Italian, but which ratiocinate, reflect, question, challenge things Italic. The virtuality of such a No-Land is exceptional, because not territorial, not religious, not linguistic.

> It has even been argued that popular spoken Italian as an idiom capable of expressing the full range of what a twentieth-century language needs outside the domestic and face-to-face sphere of communication, is only being constructed today as a function of the needs of national television programming.[14]

Without going as far as what is being claimed above by Antonio Sorella, we can conjecture that the Italic is a "post-Italy" phenomenon, in the same way historian Shlomo Sand speaks of his position being "post-Zionism" (11). The Italic does not replace Italy. The same way as the Francophonie does not replace France, Haiti, or Quebec; or as the Anglophone cultural does not replace the United Kingdom, English Canada, Australia, or the United States of America.

What is desired is receptivity, admittance, inclusion, not ostracization, dispossession, proscription. Italian peoples are extremely divided, and according to *Ethnologue*,[15] hardly amount to 61 million people who speak the standard language (including dialects). Legally speaking, the individuals of Italian origin born abroad are Italian only if they possess an Italian passport, regardless of the language they speak. Where do these persons, culturally speaking, fit in the larger scheme of things cultural if they do not have the legal right to call themselves Italian? Such individuals delude themselves when they call themselves Italian.

When this solitary delusion takes on ponderous proportions that can be recorded, always according to *Ethnologue*, in as many as thirty-four countries; when the loner's predicament exceeds the individual's scope and becomes a collective condition, then a name in required to adjust our definitions. The Italian-outside-Italy is a global marvel. Scholars and critics have been slow in regarding this outburst as a universal occurrence.

Many content themselves with the glorification or the condemnation of this sort of cultural ferment, and usually consider such a local disruption as a passing subculture. Contrary to Helen Barolini, we do not believe this Italic outpour is a fad. This decentralization of culture is a growing phenomenon, most clearly expressed in the Italian community up till now, but soon this manner of expressing one's culture, away from the center of nations, will become prevalent amongst other cultures, as is noticeable with the Indian and Arabic communities established abroad.

With the possibility of non-assimilation, future cultures will be redefined, remodelled, expanded by "interior domains". Very much like Massimo d'Azeglio who wrote, "L'Italia è fatta. Restano da fare gli Italiani,"[16] one will say, "Adesso che l'Italico è fatto. Restano da fare gli Italici" ["Now that the Italic has been established, we need to create Italics'].

The formal dissection of The Mediterranean Forever

Contrary to the narrative fiction films, we noticed that the basis of Nicola Zavaglia's film is not the scene (8) but the sequence shot (32), the bracket syntagma (13), the episodic sequence (6), the descriptive syntagma (5), the parallel syntagma (4) and the alternate syntagma (2). The director resorts to various points of view in order to get his narrative across.

Though one finds a narrative voice — Nicola Zavaglia narrates the text — the outcome is never one that rises from individualism. What the spectator hears is the collectivity singing. This collective is the Italic, neither from Italy, nor from Quebec, it is a nameless country that belongs to no single territory. It constitutes a cultural awareness that unities people above and beyond borders. The persons interviewed in this film live in Montreal. Surprisingly, for the shortest of the films analyzed in this studied, *The Mediterranean Forever* contains the most chapters. This formal idiosyncrasy indicates the baroque nature of Zavaglia's fragmented narrative.

1. Chapter 1. Prologue. 0:00-2:27
2. Chapter 2: Il était une fois l'Amérique. 2:28-3:59
3. Chapter 3. The Finaldi Family. 4:00-5:35
4. Chapter 4. Celestina. 5:36-10:47
5. Chapter 5. Mario. 10:48-14:21
6. Chapter 6. 1400. 14:22-18:23
7. Chapter 7. 1900. 18:24-19:40
8. Chapter 8. Antonio. 19:41-27:04
9. Chapter 9. Mary di Michele. 27:05-33:22.
10. Chapter 10. America Invented. 33:23-38:44
11. Chapter 11. 1524. 38:45-45:00
12. Chapter 12. Giovanni. 45:01-47:11
13. Chapter 13. Raffaele. 47:12-49:38
14. Chapter 14. Carmine et Coco. 49:39-50:50
15. Chapter 15. 1642: Francesco Giuseppe Bressani. 50:51-60:46
16. Chapter 16. 1665. 60:47-62:21
17. Chapter 17. 1756: Carlo Francesco Burlamacchi. 62:22-72:30

Various vanishing points coincidence with the multitude of voices heard. If nostalgia is present, its references are multiple, the scope plural. The Italy reflected is elastic, pliant, tough, but not brittle; as wide as the spatial expanse depicted, time is supple and lasting. The narrative moves to and fro simultaneously on many levels. Culture is muscular, resolved, will not vanish.

Chapter 1: Prologue
The Mediterranean… as an interior home,
retreat, an interior domain
0:00-2:27

1. Bracket syntagma. 0:00-2:16

Shots of Southern Italy dissolve into photographs of immigrants. There are justified, synchronic and authentic sounds (voices, waves, ships) associated to the sea. On the soundtrack, a melody played on pan's flute which gives way to a cello and voix instrumental, a theme which at various occasions will be repeated throughout. Film credits appear and end in a fade.

A particular sound (inauthentic, enhanced by echo) resounds. Are these coins tumbling into a machine? Or chains of an anchor being lifted? A boat leaves the shoreline. The spectator is expected to believe that this ferry is equivalent to the boat taken by Italian emigrants. For this film to work, the artistic gesture requires a "willing suspension of disbelief". T.S. Eliot wrote about a similar feeling:

> When I speak of understanding, I do not mean merely knowledge of books or words, any more than I mean belief: I mean a state of mind in which one sees certain beliefs… as possible, so that we suspend our judgment altogether (*Prose,* 222).

As Eliot suggests the spectator of this film must put aside his/her prejudices and truths, and trust the filmmaker on this ride through time. A trip into the past can resemble a touristic voyage. The emigrant who travels becomes an immigrant. This change of status is now made to go backwards the other way round. We are asked to view the immigrant as an emigrant. *The Mediterranean Forever* proposes a study of real events (it is, after all, a documentary), with real people, in real settings. We arrive at the one minute and thirty-nine second mark, a French subtitle appears, *Méditerranée pour toujours*. The spectator has been dealt all the cards necessary to appreciate the film. The Mediterranean Sea is a metonymy for Italy. Here is a peninsula, with its special geographical structure made to receive and dispatch boatloads of people.

2\. Autonomous shot. Ext. Mountain. Day.
1-2-1=fade. 2:17-2:27

A new mega-sequence begins. For Zavaglia the mega-sequence often corresponds to the chapter unit. A sequence shot of an accordion player. A pause is filmed before he begins to play. This melody fades in and out a number of times throughout the film. Often it is accompanied by a male voice. Nicola Zavaglia instigates a visual routine that will also be repeated in this film. He introduces a chapter with a "teaser". For example, this shot of the musician does not belong to the Prologue; it should normally have been placed in the second chapter. Instead of a clear cut between one section of the film and another, Zavaglia engages in this play of overlapping shots ("double-jointed" scenes) which end of section and begin another.

The accordion player stares directly at the camera. This musician could have stepped out of a Pier Paolo Pasolini film. His face emerges from another world, the landscape of history. The man nods. As though he were acquiescing the director's signal to start playing. Why would Zavaglia have kept this short moment of indecision, when he could have eliminated, and started the scene seconds later. This awkward gesture so clearly non-cinematic, why does Zavaglia underline this gesture of approbation that strikingly makes the director's presence so pervasive?

Behind this voluntary mark, one senses the wish to express, on the part of the director, the generosity of cooperation. Of course, the director is there to direct the action, it is his film, his vision. But the accordion player's nod, annoying to the perfectionist wishing complete control, is comparable to the signature at the bottom of a contract. Zavaglia and the musician come to an agreement. This acceptance of participation colors the film with truthfulness. The musician and the director appear more honest; they have agreed to follow a set of rules. This is not the Hitchcockian wink to the attentive spectator, this looking at the camera. This smile signals authenticity, what André Bazin called a "parallelepipied of reality" (271). A depth of field of what is in the shot as well as what surrounds the shot, the other spaces that never are spoken about, but which modulate the raw film stock.

The spectrum of documentary stretches out, different from fiction, in a more geometric way. The lens encompasses the objective lives of the director, the characters on screen, and the audience looking at the spectacle. One cannot but bring up Pasolini's concept of the "multiplication of presences" ("moltiplicazione di presenti"): "come se un'azione anziché svolgersi una volta sola davanti ai nostri occhi, si svolgesse più volte" (238). What we are assisting at is a sort of filmic code-switching, whereby the Ur-code turns, as Pasolini would label it, into a "code of reality observed" (293). A "code of reality photographed" (296).

This succession of overlapping realities unfolds rapidly. In a sense what Marcel Jean wrote in his one-line review was that Zavaglia's film-making does not reduce itself to a real person being shot by another person sitting behind a camera. What we are made to watch is a person agreeing to being filmed by a person called Zavaglia. Talking heads do not suffice; the creative act must somehow be filmed in action. "L'uomo cioè si esprime soprattutto con la sua azione... perché è con essa che modifica la realtà e incide nello spirito" (240). Zavaglia's wager to be authentic is essential for the re-presentation on screen. Reality is never a given; it must first release its permission, so to speak, before it reveals itself to the camera.

Chapter 2: Once upon a time there was America
2:28:3:59

3. Bracket syntagma. Various exterior shots.
2-3=fade. 2:28-3:59

The accordion music spreads over the title of the section and the subsequent images. Coco Finaldi's voice rises in the background, singing. Nicola Zavaglia begins his narration in voice over. An insert of the sequence shot 2. Instead of keeping the shot intact, Zavaglia has sliced it in two. A mega-sequence dissolves into the main chapter unit. There are shots of Southern Italy which end with an overlapping scene of the Finaldi home: a shot of a coffee tray, and the Mother in the kitchen making pizza. "Once upon a time, America": the program is bluntly laid out. The tone is fairy-tale-like. A salute to Sergio Leone's *One upon a time in America* (1984). Nicola Zavaglia's I-voice is detached, withholds an emotional articulacy. Audibly this is the voice is juxta-diegetic,[16] played over the images of Southern Italy. Zavaglia speaks:

> I did not grow up dreaming about America. I thought I was there already... My father was gone to America... My friend's fathers were gone to America.

From the general to the particular, from the metaphor to the personal. For every generalization an individual detail is mentioned. For every effusion of the personal, there is a jumping back to the community, as if both were intricately linked. "With time immigration becomes a heritage. From father to son, from mother to daughter, it is a story that they tell one another. At times it is a love story." These crucial lines are the foundation on which the film rests. The title credits that follow divide the syntagma in two. The last shot of this overlapping syntagma could very well belong to the next: a sequence shot of a table with coffee pot and cups. Zavaglia surprises us with these "double-jointed" scenes. Concluding segments begin new syntagmas.

Chapter 3: The Finaldi Family
4:00-5:35

4. Alternate syntagma. Int. Dining Room. Day.
3-4=Fade. 4:00-4:57

We are presented to the Finaldi family: Carmine, Carmine's wife, Angelo the musician (on electric bass), Coco, Angelo's daughter, who is a singer. Angelo speaks about composing a theme song for Celestina, a character in the film. Carmine is writing the lyrics. Carmine's wife, who does not speak, is in the kitchen, rolling out balls of dough for pizza. There is an insert of Celestina fanning herself; the soundtrack is justified, authentic, and synchronic. Nothing linear is to be expected.

Angelo Finaldi is a renowned rock star in Quebec. He has performed with some of the finest musicians in the world. This visit into the privacy of his parents' home triggers curiosity in the knowledgeable spectator. The spectator is invited to view the creation of a theme song, the preparation of a meal, and the making of a film. Every person is action. No idle moment. A person is what he does. Behind this action is the transmission of cultural heritage.

Culture is passing from one hand to another: from the grandfather to the son to the granddaughter. Angelo explains the story, over an insert of Celestina, an aging woman, staring into the camera. Follows a musical interlude. Angelo and his daughter are playing her theme song. Back to the Carmine staring lovingly at his grandchild.

5. Alternate syntagma. Int. Corridor. Day.
4-5=Dissolve. 4:58-5:35

The synchronic music becomes asynchronic as it fades under photographs of young Celestina, and then under a sequence shot of Celestina in the corridor walking toward the camera. This is an overlapping syntagma, part of No. 4 and No. 6, which introduces Chapter 4. Zavaglia uses the dissolve to cancel time. The song begins. Here is the equivalent of the Inciting Incident: Celestina's is a typical Italian-Montreal house, with kitsch lamps and massive fake Victorian furniture. Celestina stands in the corridor, leaning on a cane. This syntagma functions as any other scene, only it appears here in the form of a poetic Inciting Incident. Instead of slicing images together, Zavaglia dissolves one into the other, ridding them of their realism.

Image 1 is juxtaposed onto image 2, and together these create a third image which is half of image 1 and half of image 2 and something that is not tangible but only visible. Our perception of objects is altered; the simple description of a thing gets interwoven into a figurative language. No longer just images A+B=C, they become $A_1+B_1+C_1$, $A_2+B_2+C_2$, and so on. Zavaglia demonstrates how the opposite of weight is not lightness but intensity. Matter dematerializes itself and changes into vision, or if you wish, history in the making, cultural memory becoming heritage.

Chapter 4: Celestina
5:36-10:47

6. Autonomous shot. Int. Celestina. Day.
5-6=Fade. 5:36-8:11

Nicola Zavaglia inquires about Celestina's meeting her husband. Using sequence shot he lets his interviewee speak. Rarely does he leave a long take untouched for very long; he adds inserts to diversify his visual canvas. This is how the chapter acquires the form of an alternate mega-syntagma. Celestina answers, "It started when we were children." Zavaglia inter-cuts the main sequence shot with other images linked thematically thanks to the soundtrack. This technique is used in a number of occasions. First hints of a cello in the background which is then mixed with the theme song dedicated to Celestina. The music is combined with the synchronic voice of Celestina (lapsing in and out of its visual source) and the non-synchronic voice of Nicola Zavaglia.

All sounds are authentic and diegetically justified. Zavaglia builds his narrative cautiously, one block at a time, like a cabinetmaker, one piece interlocking into the other. Not so much a film of transitions, as much as one of interconnectedness of disparate entities. There are French subtitles while Celestina speaks in her regional Italian language tainted with dialect and French words (code-mixing). The director is reduced to an off-camera voice. We will never see Zavaglia in this film. His voice spills into the microphone used to captured Celestina's voice. It must be a hot day, because Celestina fans herself with an exotic dark silk-laced fan. Not a *femme de salon*, but a motherly elder lady. If Celestina were to be classified, she would fall under the heading of mother, or what Janice Welsch calls, the "Archetype":

> The mother is surely the most familiar archetype, the dominant image of adult woman in our society. She nurtures, protects, cares for, encourages. She is home, family, marriage-oriented and generally defines herself and others in terms of the roles each fulfils within the family. In her own case this means the centrality of her functions as childbearer (which she interprets as destiny) and as a familial stabilizing force. She enjoys having others dependent on her. Her willingness to sacrifice for them is influenced by the desire to direct their destinies. She can be emasculating, as well as nurturing, a bitch and a nag as well as an empathic and encouraging protectress of the household.[17]

Holding pictures for the camera, Celestina is flanked by another woman, possibly her daughter. Celestina: "For six years, he lived alone, and then he wrote me to come and join him... My husband was a faithful man." Men were here to work, and not to be promiscuous. Follows single image of the Mediterranean Sea, in the evening, against the light. Documentary relies on the close-up as a way to break up what Eisenstein called "monologuism" of film.[18] With a close-up, scenes would be one long monologue. Physiognomy is an interior landscape, as Jacques Aumont explains:

> Physiognomy is, among other things, moral. It immediately gives the truth about its bearer, since, for this heir of the last "phsyionomists" or physio-gnomonists, the possibility of all the modifications of the soul is inscribed from the beginning in a face (83).

Zavaglia welcomes the close-up. These bustling records of time past stand in parallel to the stillness of the present image of Celestina herself, who broadens her status of motherhood into the sphere of the collective. Celestina is showered with dignity. This is more than the story of one Italian woman; an entire minority group has been summoned here. C.G. Jung explains how this transfer from the individual to the collective occurs:

> A collective problem, if not recognized as such, always appears as a personal problem, and in individual cases may give the impression that something is out of order in the realm of the personal psyche. The personal sphere is indeed disturbed, but such disturbances need not be

primary; they may well be secondary, the consequence of an insupportable change in the social atmosphere. The cause of disturbance is, therefore, not to be sought in the personal surroundings, but rather in the collective situation (*Memories*, 233-34)

Zavaglia does not retreat in personal histories; he invites the spectator to view these men and women as a social phenomenon, or to re-phrase the Jungian concept of archetypes, these are the "organs of the prerational psyche...," "riverbeds which dry up when the water deserts them" (*Reflections*, 38).

This silent woman working away in the kitchen and in the basement, preparing food for the family, for the community, must not be mistaken for the stereotype of the abused and defenseless woman. What Celestina actualizes is Jung's "archetype".

> The archetype as an image of instinct is a spiritual goal toward which the whole nature of man strives; it is the sea to which all rivers wend their way, the prize which the hero wrests from the fight with the dragon (*Reflections*, 42).

The Mediterranean Forever persuades us to re-experience the spiritual transmission of culture. The Mother accompanies the Wanderer across the Mediterranean Sea, around the Aeolian Island, where the parts of the film were shot, and where Ulysses is said to have travelled, and then comes all the way to America.

7. Scene. Int. Finaldi home. Day.
6-7= 0. 8:12-8:59

Coco appears on screen first, and then Angelo on electric bass. Both are humming the Celestina theme. Sound becomes synchronic, authentic, diegetically justified. What Michel Chion labels "point de synchronization" (synchronization point) (*Audio-vision*, 52). Carmine writes the lyrics on the table. The three are sitting at the same table.

8. Episodic Sequence. Int. Celestina. Day.
7-8=0. 9:00-10:25

Celestina holds a picture. There are cuts, breaking the temporal unity, a single shot of the back of a house seen from an alley. Perhaps this is Celestina's house. As Celestina speaks of the past, pictures of Italian immigrants at the beginning of the twentieth century dissolve in and out of the visual track. The Finaldi melody is orchestral music, as Michel Chion would call it

(*Audio-vision*, 71). These shots intervene with the sequence shot of the next syntagma.

Celestina in the sequence shot has been divided up with the photographic inserts. I initially had divided these episodes into separate fragments in order to understand the complex montage involved, but finally chose to group them in to one main block of actions: Celestina and her recounting episodes of her life. Celestina's voice and Zavaglia's voice-over spreads across time, space, and proposition. Celestina's voice (often turning into a voice over) explains how Italians grew chicory and preserved vegetables for the winter season. She speaks of prejudice and hardships endured by Italians.

9. Descriptive syntagma. Ext. The Mediterranean Sea. Evening.
8-9=0. 10:26-10:47

Celestina's voice extends over images of the Mediterranean. The seascape is dark against ominous skies. The accordion music; a man sing a lament, *Il Tango delle capinere*. This syntagma-mega-sequence is a signpost for the past. The Mediterranean Sea promises, however, a sense of temporal freedom. Nothing is provided in clear narrative blocks; the osmose is at once linear and vertical, simultaneously about the present and the non-temporal. Reality becomes symbolic.

Chapter 5: Mario
10:48-14:21

10. Autonomous shot. Int. Kitchen. Day.
9-10=0. 10:48-11:21

Mario, at the kitchen counter, pours wine he has made with grapes from his garden. Mario speaks in a heavy accented broken *joual*. The accordion music from the previous syntagma fades out and is replaced by justified, authentic, and synchronic sounds (except for Zavaglia's off camera voice). A title insert: Mario. Every chapter begins with an in-action scene, a teaser of sorts. The accordion player, the Finaldi, Celestina, Mario, Antonio, Michele... appear before the section credit fades in. A Zavaglia trademark. This entire mega-sequence could be considered an episodic sequence: one theme at a time, unfold in one space, during a fixed time slot (afternoon). The episodes continue through the accumulation of autonomous shots.

11. Episodic sequence.
10-11=0. 11:22-13:36.

Follow three inserts of Mario in the garden and his wife tending to tomatoes and basil. Next is a sequence shot of Mario's wife also in the kitchen, standing in front of the fridge. Zavaglia reacts to her comments on the large quantity of foods she and her husband produce with what comes from their garden. Sounds are justified, authentic, synchronic (except for Zavaglia's off camera voice).

In another sequence shot Mario toasts Nicola Zavaglia, which is interrupted by an insert of Mario preparing a pot of espresso. An overhead travelling shot brings us back alley where Mario and his friend Angelo take their walk below clothes on lines dancing in the gentle wind. A Montreal day, Italian daily actions.

The natural sounds are mixed with Finaldi's bass melody, low in the background: in part justified, authentic, synchronic, in part not at all. The director purposely wants the spectator to feel this strangeness, this aural displacement. Mario and Nicola Zavaglia's voices off-camera, they talk about the lack of jobs in post-War Italy. Gradually we start to detect a slight Northen Italian accent in Mario's speech. The spectator accustomed to Italian and French immediately discerns the double nature of Mario's identity. A man who speaks so well in Italian and who can hardly express himself in French: harsh reality comes into focus as Mario admits sadly: "I was forced to emigrate."

Back to the alley, Mario and Angelo are juxtaposed with an interplay between justified and not justified sounds, authentic and non authentic volumes. Zavaglia moves beyond realism. In spite of the turmoils of unemployment, there is a joie de vivre in his worker. As Mario, his wife, and his friend Angelo sit to savor their coffee and homemade cookies. They are conscious of the camera. Mario echoes the word "Canada", but it is Angelo who ventures a more poignant reply: "When pushed by hunger." A mild embarrassment ensues, the voices and sounds fading out under flute music.

The mosaic-like episodic structure works differently here if compared to the formal structure alternating section with Celestina. In the latter, we had a comparison unfolding; the spectator was led through the labyrinthine funnel of time; Celestina the young naive girl in love to Celestina the elderly citizen pronouncing harsh words against the country she lives in. Zavaglia stresses the hardships endured by the first-generational immigrants of the beginning of the last century, and more especially during their imprisonment in Petawawa during World War II.

This semantic jump into statement could only be attained through an indirect poetic discourse. Baroqueness occurs where point of view is deviated, diverted, sidestepped. With Mario, Zavaglia exposes his direct tribute. Fragmented yet linear realistic images are glued to one another, suggesting passage of time. Fleeting inserts revealing a quality of life spent in this country as compared to the hardships experienced in post-war Italy. Celestina represents the first wave of Italians, who came before World War I; Mario, the second wave of immigrants who came to Montreal after World War II. Two moments in the Italian diaspora of the twentieth century disclosed in two formal ways: the poetically, sinuous baroque style versus the disjointed linearity. In the middle lies the War.

Another clear day, the climate warm. Angelo in a t-shirt throws a bocce ball, the players react, Mario comments on the score. Zavaglia enjoys filming the distinctive faces of men at play: at once harsh and innocent, tough and gentle, pained but never bitter. *Amici:* Friends. Voices of the bocce players carry over to this new syntagm and gradually fade away. At eye-level, from a distant, later, Mario and Angelo stroll toward the camera. The soundtrack offers realistic (justified, authentic, synchronic) sounds, what Chion calls *éléments de décor sonore* (the audible elements of the setting) (*Audio-vision*, 48-49). The sounds set the mood for what follows. Zavaglia's voice intervenes just as other voices dissipate, underling what the spectator clearly understands by now. Zavaglia steps down from his directorial position and becomes personal: "Like my parents, Angelo and Mario belong to the second wave of Italian immigrants come to Canada."

If the director is permitted to confide personal information, it is to a certain measure due to the friendship between Mario and Angelo. As though the reassurance of intimacy granted the director the right to be "friendly" with his audience. This entire chapter is dedicated to friendship. Zavaglia constructs his narrative following a semantic plan: from the family, to the female presence, and the male companionship.

12. Bracket syntagma. Photographs.
11-12=dissolve. 13:37-14:21

A new mega-sequence is introduced: photographs dissolving into one another, accompanied by non-justified, inauthentic, and non-synchronic sounds heard behind the director's voice: "This wave of immigrant belongs to the great waves of last century. These images of Sicilians, Neapolitans, Venetians, alighting on the promise land with their boxes now belong to the iconography of everyday America. However, Italians discovered America way before the twentieth century." Paradoxically, the personal permits the collective and the collective opens up to historical analysis.

Chapter 6: 1400
14:22:18:23

13. Parallel syntagma. Ext. Venice. Day.
12-13=dissolve. 14:22-15:47

Orchestral music, modern-time Venice, drawings from the Renaissance. Follows a long description of the history of thought and navigation. Each idea illustrated by floating images between real footage of Venice and drawings. The director addresses his spectators as a teacher: "In fact, immigration to Canada belongs to an historical moment that began in the fifteenth century. In the Rinascimento. The Renaissance."

Main figures of the Italian past are introduced: Christopher Columbus, Amerigo Vespucci, Leonardo da Vinci, Michelangelo, Machiavelli. The symbolic equation is not as evident as it first appears. Zavaglia equates modern immigration to the travels of sixteenth century explorers; Italian culture has been in Canada longer than historians care to acknowledge. A fact not officially recognized by this country's institutions.

14. Parallel syntagma. Int. Finaldi home. Day.
13-14=montage with effect. 15:48-16:20

A new mega-sequence begins. Present-day Montreal. The reason we consider this segment of the film a parallel syntagma and not a scene is because, on the one side, we have the composer and, on the other hand, we have the taciturn mother composing a meal for the family. Never a hint of female belittlement here (the stereotypical woman in the kitchen). If this were the unconscious disclosure sexism, Coco would not have been featured so predominantly in this film.

Richard Gambino explains the difference of Southern Italian families and (North) American families:

> The status of American families flows from the political and/or economic success of their members, almost always their male members. In the Mezzogiorno power usually flowed from family. The political or economic success of a person most often was dependent on the power and his or her family. And the family was at least as dependent upon the talents and efforts of its women as upon those of its men (169).

The sounds are diegetically justified. Music is introduced after the mention of the major Renaissance artists. The semantic link could not be stronger. Creativity is what those images of tomatoes, roads, and art is all about. Creativity, a parameter in the culture, included invention, hard work, and food (food appears in many segments of *The Mediterranean Forever*). Creativity is what is transmitted from one generation to another. The Finaldi mother might be *in absentia*, she is nevertheless as present in the creative process as the composers.

15. Autonomous shot.
14-15=montage with effect. 16:21-16:24.

Carmine's voice overlaps onto this syntagma. This "overlapping shot" (a "double-jointed" shot) ends metaphorically the Finaldi segment and physically opens the next. "'A Merica", Carmine repeats the word for her granddaughter to pronounce correctly. Coco is being taught the difference between America (reality) and A Merica (dream paradise of Italian immigrants).

The next syntagma, acting as a mega-sequence as well, is a displaced diegetic insert of Mrs. Finaldi slicing green peppers. On the soundtrack, Carmine explains that in Neapolitan words have to be "eaten". A hint of the ludicrous here on the part of the director. A subliminal linking of food and language? Angelo the son will later joke about how "In Naples words are fatty, oily..." On the nondiegetic insert of the Mediterranean glowing under the sunlight Zavaglia repeats the word "America" twice. This "overlapping" insert pulls us out of the real and into the symbolic: the Mediterranean as a "domaine interieur", an obsession, the opposite of navigation, the journey, the crossing.

16. Bracket syntagma. Images and photographs.
15-16=dissolve. 16:25-16:55

One is tempted to consider these syntagmas descriptive, but they are not. There is no temporal link between one segment and the next. Lack of chronological succession turns this segment into a interlocking syntagma. "America. America. Never had a word promised so much hope." Footage of boats dissolve into drawings and posters of famous passenger cross-Atlantic ships: the tourist versus the emigrant. "America. America. A siren's song attracting millions of workers whose homeland turned out to be a mother-sea."

Zavaglia's favorite device in this film is the dissolve. Georges Méliès invented the technique and used it to replace one character by another. A conjunction, more than a punctuation, combines two segments, two events, two images, brings about a certain idea of correspondence: a hyphen (linking), a slash (separation), an equal sign (addition), but also a multiplication sign (a metaphor). One entity pitted against another. The present versus the past. A pass-time versus survival. Zavaglia confronts deception with the joy awaiting emigrants. Sounds of waves give rise to the slow melody of the cello-voice duet.

17. Bracket syntagma. photographs.
16-17=dissolve. 16:56-18:23

The orchestral music bridges two syntagmas. Canada. Travelling shots, zooms... from Giovanni Caboto on a horse at Atwater Square to pictures of Italian immigrants. Instead of talking about Canada, Zavaglia takes us back to Italy. This spatial and metaphorical jump is wanted:

> In 1880, Italy was beginning to take its first steps as a republic. Italy was young and poor. This new country was far from being a country opened to all. 500,000 people died every year from malaria, cholera, bad nutrition. Everywhere across the peninsula fields of tiny white crosses sprang forth. Half of the dead were children.

Pictures of transatlantic ships dissolve in to photographs of families and children in small tombs; the moon crossed by dark clouds; the tolling of a church bell; sunset dissolving into a boat; the cello-female voice duet. The man with the accordion takes over with *Il Tango delle capinere*. If Italy has been identified to this female-cello duet, Canada is identified to the male accordion player. The narrator-director continues:

> To be able to vote, one had to pay an extravagant tax. In spite of all the promises this young Italy made, thousands of people were excluded. For these poor men and woman, America became the motherland Italy had never been.... The exodus took on biblical proportions.

Zavaglia resorts to the bracket syntagma to introduce us to the New World. The formal journey is a prerequisite to understanding the motifs (social, political, communal, personal) blossoming before our eyes. At seventeen minutes, a sunset over the ocean slowly becomes a sunset over a boat which turns into a postcard of a boat. The Zavaglian dissolve does more than simply link, it becomes itself the creator of a virtual image that exists only as a filmic photogram. By the time we get to the half point mark, we become fairly well acquainted to these "virtual photograms" that momentarily imprint themselves onto our minds. To properly capture *Mediterraneo sempre* we would have to print these virtual images side by side... This film is a formal account of the Journey, the crossing which, as Matilde Battistini would say it, "expresses the impulse to search, discover, and seek change. It is depicted as a crossing over the sea or over unfamiliar lands, or as a descent into the Underworld. The journey represents discovery and initiation, and it is presented as an imaginary trip into the realm of the beyond or into uncharted regions."[19] Here is a fine example of how the denotative and connotative strands are intrinsically woven together.

Social misfortune has led to inner knowledge for some immigrants. La demeure intérieure is an achievement, not *a priori* given. Zavaglia overturns cliché: self-knowledge is a social and political journey, ethnicity is an interior journey, impossible to dissipate or assimilate.

Chapter 7: 1900
18:24-19:40

18. Bracket syntagma.
17-18=fade. 18:24-19:04

This chapter foreshadows the Canadian experience. The mega-sequence corresponds to a chapter. America. In the previous segment, Zavaglia channelled his way through the journey as, at once, a personal and social maze. Here, he invites the spectator beyond the social and political realms, and opens the windows to cultural landscapes. Another sunset on an expanse of water; a boat and its wake; the hollow sound of a wind instrument; a boat in the harbor. Without attracting too much attention, Zavaglia moves gingerly onto to the next item on his agenda: the roads to gold.

> Immigrants needed to believe in the myth of the New World, but, as soon as they got off the boats, they learned three truths. First: the roads in America were not paved with gold. Second: the roads of America were not paved at all. Third: they were there to pave the roads of America.

Sarcasm wanted, accepted. Pictures of immigrants turned laborers for Canadian and American companies. A new-age piece plays in the background as "spatial-temporal turntable" (to use an expression advanced by Chion (*Audiovision*, 72-73). Music introduces movement, displacement; Antonio speaks: "This photograph is important for me."

19. Episodic syntagma. Ext. Balcony. Day.
18-19=0. 19:05-19:40

A teaser scene. We are getting used to Zavaglia's teasers. After the sea lull of waves, the dissolve into a virtual reality. Neither past, nor future, Antonio talks of his father, introducing us to a "racist" concept of the *voleur de job* (the "job snatcher", the immigrant comes to Montreal to steal jobs from the French). A photograph of the Father. And a major theme borrows its way to the foreground unexpectedly. The Father. The real immigrant. The *voleur de job*.

Chapter 8: Antonio
19:41:27:04

20. Autonomous shot. Int. Kitchen. Day.
19-20=0. 19:41-23:15

Guitar music fades out, orchestral music fades in; diegetic justified sounds; a window left open. A sequence shot presents Antonio preparing supper in his kitchen. Zavaglia is off screen, on the right, asking Antonio questions. The long take is interrupted by four inserts. Two displaced diegetic inserts of a family picture: Antonio as a young boy. Antonio talks about his father's harshness, the absent father, the Italian who has never seen the Mediterranean Sea. "It is poverty that makes fathers harsh": Antonio's viewpoint is non-dramatically political (Marxist?). Economical strife changes people's behavior. Two nondiegetic shots of the Mediterranean coastline.

An insert of a sunset on the sea, orchestral music, a cut on the word *mort* ("death"). This direct link between the sea and the concept of death appears for the first time. Inadvertently the Mediterranean Sea represents not only the journey, the crossing from the Old to New World, but death of the older generation. Poverty wedges generations apart. At the age of seventy-five Antonio's father sees the Mediterranean Sea for the first time (he passes away shortly after). The elderly father stretching out to his son. Antonio, saddened, admits candidly, never to wish this to happen between himself and his own son.

21. Autonomous shot. Int. Kitchen. Night.
20-21=0. 23:16-25:01

Antonio speaks: "Once an immigrant always an immigrant. The only way out is by possessing economic power." A sequence shot, the camera has been moved to Antonio's right, it is evening. The justified sounds coming from the window. The director stands slightly to the right of the camera, off screen. Antonio, in front of the stove where steam comes out of the kettle, is cooking pasta for his guests (the film crew?). Antonio talks energetically about the immigrant worker.

To be on welfare is considered a public shame. Antonio echoes ethnic preoccupations brought up in Pane e ciccolatta and *Queen of Hearts*: Nino finds himself having to work in a chicken coop; a jobless Danilo is pushed to suicide. To be unemployed is to the crawl before the social ladder, to be at the margins of society, unable to take decisions, incapable of changing society; work means belonging to society, no matter how abstract one's integration to that society might be. Work can be criminal activity (*A Pain in the Ass* and *Raging Bull*), yet it is work. Mediterraneo sempre is perhaps one of the few films made in this country that does not deal Italians and the criminal component. (This is another major difference with *Caffè Italia-Montréal*.)

Zavaglia depicts Italians as honest, law-abiding citizens, be they from the past or present, men and women who by their hard work enable their children to live on an equal basis with the rest of society. A number of inserts (pictures with Italian immigrants) unroll nondiegetically along side Antonio gesticulating to Zavaglia off camera. Pasolini writes on the non-verbal as being a language itself ("Il non verbale dunque, altro non è che un'altra verbalità : quella del Linguaggio della Realtà") (*Empirismo*, 264). Imagine the screen divided in two and the spectator will get an idea of how this syntagma might have been presented.

22. Autonomous shot: Sequence title insert. di Michele's poem. 21-22=fade. 25:02-25:12

> *There is only one heaven,*
> *the heaven of the home.*
> Mary di Michele, *The Stranger in You*

White titles on black, a woman's voice reads the poem in its French translation. Why place a poem at this point? This is a Turning Point in the film. The film changes direction with this second allusion to the Father figure. A teaser that prepares the spectator to Mary di Michele who will speak, as Antonio did before her, about the Father. It was the death of children as well as the impossibility for children to have a future in Italy that encouraged Italians to emigrate. Zavaglia dedicates this entire middle portion of his film to the children of immigrants. First, Carmine, Angelo and Coco; now, English-speaking Italian-Canadian poet, Mary di Michele, and her relationship with her immigrant father.

Zavaglia introduces the first English-speaking person of the film. Mary di Michele is a Toronto poet who moved to Montreal. Mary di Michele writers of "heaven", "home", "paradise", "garden", "children", "adults". In the fragment di Michele places "heaven" and "paradise" on one side, and "home" and "garden" on the other side. For Zavaglia, the home is essential. Characters so far have been filmed in their homes, in their gardens. These di Michele segments contrast with the previous episodes of immigrants shot outside their home. Workers on the construction site look older than a worker drinking wine or sipping an espresso. The wives stand by them, and they by their wives. There might be a division of labor (as in the case of the Finaldi), but both occupations are valid to the same extent, equivalent in importance. Di Michele's poem is the heart of *Mediterraneo sempre*. Is it possible that Zavaglia purposely chose to create his film on the dissolve precisely because nothing is ever fixed in the world of the broken families of immigrants?

> 23. Bracket syntagma. Ext. Balcony. Day.
> 22-23=fade. 25:13-26:31

Images of Italy accompany the director's commentary. Fade in on the Maella mountain in the Abruzzi region (where Mary di Michele comes from) on which appears and disappears the image of Zavaglia's father. Behind the commentary, synthesizer music. The Mediterranean Sea dissolves in and out, as the director mentions his father, hinting at his presence, his absence, his immigrant experience. Paradoxically, the aloofness creates a highly emotionally charged moment. Just two inserts of Zavaglia's father who passes away during the making of this film, the father dissolving like an icon into the landscape. Zavaglia interjects:

> When I think back to my youth, departure is what I remember. There are village scenes of suffering unfolding before the eyes of all. Every evening there was a departure, as punctual as the bells of the church.

A low-angle shot of a church bell tower: this can be a nondiegetic insert (a metaphor); a subjective insert (an image of fear? pain?); the explanatory insert (a detail of the landscape depicted: beside the seashore, there is a church); a displaced diegetic insert (a church mentioned in the commentary). What could be the use of this visual conjunction? To make real a poetic simile? This metaphor serves another purpose.

Pasolini reminds us that the Ur-Code is lived reality ("la Realtà vissuta")

(*Empirismo*, 295). The reality depicted in this segment is Italy and in Southern Italy, where there are plenty of church bell towers. In this bracket syntagma already riddled with cuts and dissolves, Zavaglia needs to underscore his reality as the child immigrant. This is perhaps the essence of documentary: the poetic stemming out of reality, not the imaginary world.

The church bell tolls twice. "Everyone wept. Like laughing, weeping is contagious. I did not cry when my father left. I was too young. When one day in summer he came back it was as if to a son a father was born." A beautifully inspired reversal of fact: normally it is a father who helps in giving birth to a child, but here, thanks to the subtle wordplay, Zavaglia turns a painful reality inside out. The documentary filmmaker changes the document into a poem. A troubling evanescence qualifies fatherhood. Similar to the non-ending dissolves that make objects and persons appear and disappear, what dematerialized re-emerges hauntingly so.

We should freeze frame the dissolve in motion to fully appreciate the intensities at work here. Zavaglia's father is captured on film ever so briefly, a few seconds at most, before he eerily vaporizes into the facade of buildings. The echo of heels striking on the slabs of the balcony. This patriarch, left arm defiantly akimbo, the ghost of a father, an absent father, two images of the Father Figure etched in our minds long after the viewing of this film: visual seconds can last a lifetime.

Zavaglia concludes this half of the film with the following sentences: "The story of immigration is the story of disconnection, the story of distances, wider than distance and the geographic wanderings." To capture fleeting presences. Music fades out.

24. Autonomous shot. Int. Room. Day.
23-24=dissolve. 26:32:-27:04

A dissolve, from the Mediterranean Sea to an image of Mary di Michele as a child. Mary di Michele speaks, the nonjustified music of a music box. Reality has taken proportion of unreality. The Paradoxal Father: a larger-than-life presence that is absent. A book cover on which Zavaglia dissolves twice: once to reveal a picture of her father and her as a child; then to reassure the spectator that this is a writer of some importance who won awards. In a open-collar blouse under a woolen sweater, green as the color of Mary di Michele's eyes: the spectator is hypnotized by this tiny woman who appears so big on screen. The camera is barely lower than eye-level. Behind the poet, Japanese folding panels in white and black: "I was extremely attached to my father... and so it was very painful being separated from him." Here Mary di Michele's lips are pursed; one detects tears in her eyes. Her entire composure tightens up. There is a lot of hurt bundled up in this fragile woman shrugging her shoulders, nodding her head under the weight of pain recalled. The camera stares at the paper burning. Pasolini uses this image of burning paper to speak of film: "Fare del cinema è scrivere su della carta che brucia" ["Making cinema is writing on burning paper"] (*Empirismo*, 245).

Chapter 9: Mary di Michele
27:05-33:22

25. Autonomous shot. Insert.
24-25=dissolve. 27:05-31:42

An insert of the Mediterranean Sea, another chapter begins. A sequence shot of Mary di Michele, in a third-quarter profile, talking to Zavaglia, standing off screen to her left. A syntagma is never linear with Zavaglia. Titles come later, after a chapter has begun. On a displaced diegetic insert of the Mediterranean Sea, di Michele reveals that as a child she come to America where her father was. Di Michele concedes frankly: "I did not recognize him... I started to cry... I thought my mother had taken up with another man... this cannot be my father." The interview is interspersed with a number of displaced diegetic inserts of the Mediterranean Sea under a cloudy sky and the diegetically justified rumble of wave and looming storm. In voice over, di Michele imparts: "For my mother, the primary identification is family... but my father has something else that he's trying to find again... Home... An unqualified home. But there isn't one."

While editing the film, the story to be told comes together. Disparate fragments coalesce. We do not know in which order the film scenes were shot, but what is certain is that these scenes were amalgamated later on the editing board. First, Antonio and his father; second, the death of children in Italy; third, Zavaglia's absent father; fourth, di Michele's homeless father. Alfred Adler offers perhaps the most social view of the role of the father:

> He must prove himself a good fellow man to his wife, to his children and to society. He must meet in a good way the three problems of life — occupation, friendship and love — and he must cooperate on an equal footing with his wife in the care and protection of the family. He should not forget that the woman's part in the creation of family life can never be surpassed. It is not his part to dethrone the mother, but to work with her (134-35).

The absent father creates displacement. Di Michele recognizes that "this displacement is the source of my creative work... The gift my father gave me was the gift of displacement, and the gift of being a stranger even to myself." The source of suffering is transformed into the flame of creativity. "The stranger is in you." Only through creativity can the troubled immigrant (or child of immigrant) redeem himself/herself.

In *Bread and Chocolate,* Nino is unable to redeem himself. His sense of displacement is what remains at the end of the film: he is neither here nor there. Whenever he tries to find a home, his chances for finding stability are shattered.

The only place he can find a sense of meaning is in suicide (smashing his head in a mirror is not something a normal man would do, under any circumstance) and madness (he has lost all sense of reality by the time he is on the last train to Italy). Whether one is on the train or off the train, there is a non-yielding territory.

In *Queen of Hearts,* displacement for both men (Danilo and Barbariccia) cannot be avoided. Criminality is the only way out for Barbariccia, at least this is what the film suggests. Danilo, though a dependent of criminality, stands outside the immediate circles of criminality. He has a chance to redeem himself.

Displacement is aggravated by his continuous losses against the one person who has found stability, his competitor. It is no wonder that suicide and madness (personified by addiction) are the only way out for Danilo. If in the end he does temporarily free himself of his addictions, it is not out of his own volition, but thanks to his father and his youngest son.

In *The Mediterranean Forever*, Zavaglia introduces creativity as a possible way out of a nightmarish maze. Zavaglia has already explored other forms of displacement — political exile, anomaly, deficiency — in other films: *Poet in the Family* (1978), *L'Espoir violent* (1989), *Barbed Wire and Mandolins* (1997); he begins, however, a new thread in this search for the understanding of displacement. Creativity, as one solution to deterritoralization. Is the absence of territory not another name for displacement? The artist as a stranger in oneself?

Another insert, sea and mountain, di Michele's parents moving to and fro from Italy, three times. Another metaphor, Zavaglia interrupts the flow: "The idea of the Saragazzo sea: you leave, but you never reach the destination." No destination home, to quote Bob Dylan, because there is no territory to land on; displacement becomes a permanent essence and no longer a temporary condition. Inserts of the sea and a mountain conclude this mega-sequence dedicated to fatherless and displacement. As the camera travels, as orchestral music fades in and accompanies Mary di Michele reading a poem. Inserts do not form a block, nondiegetical, displaced diegetical inserts add metaphorical depth to the prevalent concept of displacement. Music fades out with the image.

26. Scene. Int. Finaldi Home. Day.
25-26=dissolve. 31:43-33:08

Carmine teaches Coco how to sing his Neapolitan lyrics, Angelo in the background plays the melody on his bass. "Io camina camina/e non sach' dov' vaga/sto sempre briacha/e non beva mai vino..." [I walk, I walk/but I don't know where I'm going/I am always drunk/but I never drink wine."] These words confirm and prolong the image of displacement. Not only does the older generation feel without a home, so does the younger generation. This is a major parameter to the Italian abroad experience. We would go as far and affirm that without the displacement trope the Italic would not be.

27. Autonomous shot. Ext. Venice. Evening.
26-27=0. 33:09-33:22

An insert of Venice on which the refrain "Cuore, cuore..." is repeated by Coco accompanied by her father's bass playing. Mixed here are the justified, but non authentic and nonsynchronized hum of water... the volume of sound is exaggerated. What do we have here if not an equation of an "interior home" (Italy) plus a "cuore" (heart)? This coupling will be revisited later when Carmine will speak directly to Zavaglia on the question of nostalgia, perhaps the only time we actually raise this issue of nostalgia, not as a looking back, however, but as correspondence.

Chapter 10: America Invented
33:23-35:44

28. Bracket syntagma. Images and Pictures.
28-29= fade. 33:23-35:45

Orchestral music (performed on a synthesizer) opens with the title. Not the discovery of America, but the invention of America *(A Merica)*. Invention, also an act of creation, like one invents a boat, an electric bass, a country. The teaser concludes the previous chapter and begins the next — an overlapping syntagma. On this accumulation of footage and images, one dissolving into another, Zavaglia comments off screen. "The name America appears for the first time in 1507 in honor of the Florentine Amerigo Vespucci."

It is he who notes the fact that the place Christopher Columbus "discovered" was another continent. Winter, the statue of Giovanni Caboto in Montreal, facing the Atwater subway station: where many Italians had settled upon their arrival in Quebec. From Venice without snow to the Montreal of snow, a confrontation: hot versus cold, the Old versus the New. Zavaglia never emits a disparaging statement; he refrains, surprisingly so, from chastising. He shows, teaches, informs, never admonishes.

29. Episodic sequence. Ext. Winter street. Day.
28-29=0. 35:46-37:00

We are giving snippets of activities, episodes on a winter day, friends Mario and Angelo.

A. Mario and Angelo walk on snow-covered path.
B. Mario and Angelo: forty-year-old friendship. Accordion player signing "O Sole mio".
C. Dante's statue.
D. Mario and Angelo in back alley.

Accordion music, "O sole mio", Mario and Zavaglia talk about snow, North America, friendship. Zavaglia concludes by mentioning another guest, Salvatore, who, in Italian cafés, "perpetuates an oral tradition that dates by to Homer." Is Zavaglia using film as a form of diary? Scenes are like journal entries.

30. Scene. Int. Caffè Italia. Day.
29-30=montage with effect. 37:01-38:44

Sounds are justified, authentic and synchronized. In the background, the accordion music fades out. Salvatore tells a story in Italian about how during the war German soldiers were surprised urinating, helpless. Violence could have broken out, but soldiers on both sides shook hands and went their separate ways. Zavaglia prolongs friendship to social civility. Cooperation aligned with understanding is better than bloodshed (explored in the next few syntagms). The chapter ends with the insert of Dante's bust.

Chapter 11: 1524
38:45–45:00

31. Bracket syntagma. Giovanni da Verrazzano. Int. Church. Day. 30-31=fade. 38:45–42:57

Images of Italy dissolve into drawings of maps and the militia. Orchestral music and church choir relay on the music track, while Zavaglia offers information on how the Pope Alexander VI, nephew of the King of Spain, divided the New World in two: Brazil going to the Portuguese and all the rest to Spain. François I hired Giovanni da Verrazzano to conquer what he could from the other two powers. Verrazzano explored the Atlantic coastline giving French and Toscan names to places he and his crew visited, ending his voyage in what he called Nova Francia. On a map the name *Mont Real*, which Zavaglia pronounces on the shot of Venice at sunset, equating Montreal to Venice.

What should we make of this ironic statement? Zavaglia, the editor, purposely places his words "Mont Real" on this image of Venice. Like in a rime in poetry, there is, as Alexander Pope wrote, a correspondence between sound and sight. As in poetry, the connotations are multifarious: serious, eloquent, pompous, sarcastic, nostalgic, dualistic. An intertext appears, a quote signed by a Jesuit priest, Father Briard, 1666:

> Je crois que ç'a esté ce Jean Verrazan que a esté le Parrain de cette dénomination de la Nouvelle France. [I believe it was Giovanni da Verrazzano who should be considered the Godfather of New France."]

Italians have been in Quebec from the very beginning. Montreal is born in 1524.

32. Descriptive Syntagma. Little Italy.
31-32=fade. 42:58–43:24

Mandolin music in the background, a man sings Angelo Finaldi's famous song of the 1960s which could be considered Quebec's national anthem. Establishing shots of Little Italy, leading to Caffè Italia.

33. Autonomous shot. Int. Caffè Italia.
32-33=0. 43:25–43:35

Angelo Finaldi is sitting in the café beside Salvatore, and other Italians.

34. Episodic syntagma. Int. Room. Day.
33-34=0. 43:36-44:49

Three autonomous syntagmas (sequence shots) strong together which give us a more personal glimpse of Angelo Finaldi the man. Angelo, in close-up, speaks to Zavaglia, sitting, off camera, to left of Angelo. He clarifies the birth of his song (co-written with François Guy and Richard Tate), "Nous sommes Québécois." Began as an English song entitled "America", the lyrics get translated into French; quickly the song is adopted by the *indépendandiste* movement. "Is it not strange that it should be a Neapolitan who wrote the national anthem?"

Angelo corrects him: "Quebec, not national."

Angelo Finaldi, now in profile, answers the question. We have moved to another location, at a different time. Zavaglia wishes to debunk the foundations of cultural hegemony: Caboto, Colombo, da Verrazzano, Angelo Finaldi. These are Italians at the heart of Quebec's history.

35. Scene. Int. The Finaldi home. Day.
34-35=0. 44:20-44:49

Carmine looks attentive — listening compassionately, to his off-spring (he taps his fingers on the table to the beat of the music) — as Angelo and Coco perform their new Montreal-Neapolitan composition. In voice over, Angelo Finaldi expands on the creation of the song written in 1969, ten years after he had immigrated with his parents. Carmine in voice over talks about his pride in being Neapolitan.

36. Autonomous shot. Int. The Finaldi home 2. Day.
35-36=0. 44:50-45:00

A sequence shot of Carmine, to the right of the screen, explains in perfect French, how he studied French at night. "I am always a Neapolitan; never have I lost the sense of nostalgia. Never... J'ai la nostalgie de l'Italie." "I am homesick..."

Nostalgia: le mal du pays: "Algos": a hurting; and "nostos", the need to go back: I am hurting to get back home. Carmine is emotional, candidly so, as if he were surprised to feel that emotional weight. Such an admission contradicts in many ways what has been the motor of the chapter. Zavaglia contradicts himself, purposely: there is no hardened truth when it comes to identity, to the "interior home". One can be firmly grounded in one place, and yet be firmly rooted elsewhere. This duality of emplacement is a parameter of the Italic. To be at once here and there, both within and without, in No-Land.

Chapter 12: Giovanni
45:01-47:11

37. Scene. Ext. Garden. Day.
36-37=fade. 45:01-45:35

Guitar music introduces the next two mega-sequences: one on Giovanni, the other on Michael and his wife. Giovanni boasts about having the very "first olive" in Canada. Michele smiles. looking off-screan to Giovanni. The gaze, Seymor Chatman elucidates that "[t]he person looking becomes a surrogate narrator, a telling-subject, no longer merely one of the told-objects" (92).

Zavaglia "disappears" for a fraction of a second, allowing another person to recount the tale. The story told is not the story announced, that is, Giovanni's story and his olive tree; friendship is reiterated. Much has been written about the "gaze", but little has been written on hearing, as if the act of listening were less important. The master of film sound, Michel Chion speaks about three kinds of listening:

1. casual listening (identification of sounds);
2. semantic listening (the "how-ness" of sounds);
3. and reduced listening (phenomenological description of sounds (*Audio-vision*, 25-30).

Michele is not only looking, he is listening to his friend speaking (about the olive), listening to how his friend speaks (they are not from the same region of Italy), listening to what is being said, to what is not being said, listening to the pride of being the first Canadian to have an olive in this Northern winter climate. The accents of these Italians are varied. This is a journey through a linguistic landscape, like in Roberto Rossellini's *Paisà*. Every character a dialect: from Northern Italy (Maria, Salvatore) to central Italy (Celestina, Michele and his wife, Antonio, di Michele if they were to speak in dialect), to Naples (the Finaldi), and southern Italy (Giovanni, Zavaglia).

38. Descriptive syntagma. Ext. Garden. Day.
38-39=0. 45:36-45:50

Images of an over-grown green garden, vegetables galore, a church bell echoes. From the church tower of the Madonna della Difesa to the blossoming garden. We move onto Michele and his wife. Where has Giovanni gone to? This chapter should have been called "Michele". It isn't. Giovanni does not warrant such an honor, since he disappears after a few seconds on screen. A wrong sign post? A mistaken identity? A cinematic salute to Michelangelo Antonioni's *L'avventura*, to Anna's disappearance? Possibly. Giovanni vanishes and is replaced by the looker, the listener, Michele, his friend. This multiflorous backdrop is there for one purpose: the revelation of love. The budding greenery is the fruit of happiness and love, of belonging to a place, to the past, to the present. Light of love.

39. Parallel syntagma. Ext. Garden. Day.
38-39=0. 45:51-47:11

Michele and his wife sit in the shade under overgrown plants and vegetables, drinking coffee. She asks her husband if they should put tomatoes in jars. Michele laughs, "And who will do this?" The wife laughs, "Michele." A loving moment. This is not Cary Grant and Ingrid Bergman in Alfred Hitchcock's *Notorious* (1946). Here is a simple couple, a man in a baseball cap and a handsome woman, with white hair, in a dark purple dress, enjoying an afternoon coffee. After lunch. A couple married for fifty years. How rarely do we relate love to this generation of men and women? Parents too were once young and beautifully in love. Remember Celestina. Love that kindles the desire to emigrate, to leave everything behind and to follow our beloved one. Zavaglia asks questions, Mrs. LaVilla answers honestly, always with a smile. Michele pulls weeds in the garden. Orchestral music fades in, brings the segment to an end.

Chapter 13: Raffaele
47:12-49:38

40. Autonomous shot. Int. Room. Day.
39-40=fade. 47:12-47:46

A sequence shot of Raffaele, standing in front of his painting of the Coliseum. He recites a poem about art being a gift from God. He turns his head to Zavaglia (off screen), smiles: "It is longer, but I don't remember the rest." Music fades in. The spectator smiles with Raffaele... To make filmic portraits is what pushed Zavaglia to documentary. A faithful disciple of John Grierson. The director must be attentive, paying close attention to the smallest nuances on faces. With the lightweight Aaton camera, Zavaglia moves about easily, capturing these fleeting flashes of "object correlative", as defined by T.S. Eliot in his essay on "Hamlet":

> A set of objects, a situation, a chain of events which shall be the formula of that particular emotion; such that when the external facts, which must terminate in sensory experience, are given, the emotion is evoked.[20]

41. Episodic sequence. Int. Rooms. Day.
40-41=0. 47:47-49:38

Raffaele is painting in his studio, conversing, at times in voice over, other times on camera, interlocked with images of his paintings dissolving one into another. The accordion player sings "Maria Mari" (by V. Russo and E. Di Capua). "Ah! Maria, Mari! Quanta suonno che predo pe te..." ["How many sleepless nights because of you..."] Maria here being an extension of Italy...

Raffaele says that "painting is a way of staying connected to Italy. Ideally, in thoughts, in emotions, in dreams." The imagination nourishes nostalgia. Raffaele masters the Italian standard language, astonishingly so, for a man of his generation. "A novel of a thousand pages would be too small to tell my story." As Zavaglia says, "L'histoire de l'immigration c'est l'histoire d'une fracture." The story of disconnection can only be mended through works of the imagination. With the Neapolitan air of "Maria Mari" we fade to the Neapolitan world of the Finaldi.

Chapter 14: Carmine et Coco
49:39-50:50

42. Scene. Int. Finaldi home. Day.
41-42=fade. 49:39-50:10

"Maria Mari" fades out, and we are back with the Finaldi. Coco repeats the Neapolitan lyrics for her grandfather who corrects her. Angelo in the background plays on his bass: transmission of knowledge, culture, dialect, music. Carmine mentions figs; images of the fig tree will soon carry the film to its conclusion.

43. Scene. Int. Finaldi. Day.
42-43=montage with effect. 50:11-50:40

Son and daughter perform a song in Neapolitan, Carmine interrupting to correct the pronunciation of "tuost" ["hard"].

44. Descriptive Syntagma. Rome Street.
43-44=0. 50:41-50:50

The Streets and monuments of Rome. Justified, authentic, synchronic sounds. With the Finaldi composition fading, Zavaglia bridges Montreal and Rome. A subtle use of the visual riming scheme.

Chapter 15
1642: Francesco Giuseppe Bressani
50:51-60:46

45. Autonomous shot. The Mediterranean.
44-45=fade. 50:58-51:04

Cello music fades in. The Mediterranean Sea. This is a teaser: the Zavaglia signature. The new mega-sequence is dedicated to Father Francesco Giuseppe Bressani from Rome.

46. Bracket syntagma. Drawings.
45-46=dissolve. 51:05-54:02

Bressani's contribution to the understanding of the Amerindians in invaluable. Various sounds (water, wind, music, voices, noise of tools) have been added to enhance the prints on Amerindians dissolving one into the other. An Italian priest spent a lot of time with Indians. The spectator smiles when Bressani asks himself why the Iroquois did not fatten him before eating him. The joke endears the not-so-liked Church to the spectator.

47. Descriptive syntagma. Int. Church. Day.
46-47=montage with effect. 54:03-55:06

Choral music on moving shots of the Madonna della difesa church — evidently influenced by Alain Renais *L'Année dernière à Marienbad* (1961). This new mega-sequence is dedicated the art of Toscan painter, Guido Nincheri (come to Canada in 1914). In this church a painting showing Benito Mussolini on a horse leads to Nincheri's arrest, locked up in the war camp of Petawawa during World War II. Italians in Canada and their internment during the war have kindled many pages of controversy.

48. Autonomous shot. Int. Church. Day.
47-48=0. 54:07-55:33

Guido Nincheri's son lights votive candles in the church. In a strong French-Canadian accent, he refers to his father as "Popa".

49. Autonomous shot. Int. Church. Day.
48-49=0. 55:34-57:26

Mr. Nincheri conveys his feelings about the time his father spent at the internment camp. After Italy's declaration of war against the United Kingdom on June 10, 1940, over 700 Italian Canadians were interned. : "It was an awful time for the family... after his name he had to add to sign P.O.W., Prisoner of War." The highly emotional man becomes taciturn, teary eyed. This dark moment in the history of Italians in Canada has divided the community in two: some accuse Italians of being Fascists; others attack the government for using their laws to get rid of financially powerful members of the Italian community.[21]

Nicola Zavaglia himself did a forty-eight minute much discussed film entitled *Barbed Wire and Mandolins* (1997) on the issue. In their book *Enemies Within: Italian and Other Internees in Canada and Abroad*,[22] Italian-Canadian scholars Francesca Iacovetta, Robert Ventresca, Angelo Principe castigated Zavaglia for depicting the internees as victims of anti-Italian sentiments. The debate continues and goes beyond the limits of our study.

Guido Nincheri was a believer and produced some refined stained-glass works which are presented in this mega-sequence devoted to faith, another parameter that might have to be included in the Italian in Quebec identity. Might: because Catholic icons and relics have been presented in the films we studied. Addressing organized religion and its ramifications in the Italic film would require a thesis on its own.

50. Autonomous shot. Ext. Little Italy. Day.
49-50=0. 57:27-58:02

A long travelling sequence shot of men playing on the bocce court. The church of the Madonna della difesa is the backdrop to the park. Zavaglia's commentary: "Whoever looked like an Italian was arrested." Seventeen-thousand Italians were arrested, but later freed, though forced to present themselves to the police every month, for the duration of the war. Coco's sings, her voice modified by echo. The Canadian government has yet to excuse itself for its behavior against its citizen of Italian origin.

51. Autonomous shot. Int. Living Room. Day.
50-51=0. 58:03-60:46

Celestina, upset, vents her anger about her husband being arrested during the war. Like other Italians, he had his fingerprints recorded by the Royal Mounted Police. Celestina declares Italians were discriminated. She lists a dozen names of important members of the Italian community who were shipped to Petawawa. Nondiegetical inserts accompanied by their justified and authentic sounds (one in daylight, the other at sunset) bring relief and diversion to the charged atmosphere. Just as the Mediterranean Sea reverts back to Italian, these back alleys ("ruelles") designate Montreal. Coco's hums the theme song.

Chapter 16: 1665
60:47-62:21

52. Bracket syntagma. Ext. Turin: Italy.
51-52=fade. 60.47-62:21

The military played an important role in emigration. Pietmontese and Savoyard solders preferred to stay in New France once the wars against Amerindians ended. Zavaglia: "To fully appreciate the Italian presence in Canada, one must fly to Turin, where on the Palazzo Carignano" an Iroquois symbol appears on the facade of the building. Drawings dissolve one into the other underscored by orchestral music.

The Palazzo Carignano was commissioned by Emmanuel Philibert, son of Thomas Francis, Prince of Carignano and his French wife Marie de Bourbon. Its construction began in 1679. The architect Guarino Guarini designed the cadet house of the House of Savoy, decorating its facade with images of the campaign of the Carignano family with Carignan-Salières Regiment against the Iroquois in 1667.

Chapter 17: 1756: Carlo Francesco Burlamacchi
62:22-72:30

53. Bracket syntagma. Drawings.
52-53=fade. 62:22-64:14

Wars fought by Carlo Francesco Burlamacchi, from Lucca, changed the course of Canada history, especially during the battle on the infamous Plaines d'Abraham, where Quebec's fate was decided. Burlamacchi replaced

General Montcalm. Drawings of the battle dissolve into pictures of Italians in Montreal. France lost to England. The Italian solder fought on the French side. So why is there still this animosity against Italians in Quebec? Synthesized orchestra music makes way for Coco's voice, in a distant echo. Voices of the past resound in time present.

54. Scene. Ext./Int. Caffè Italia. Day.
53-54=dissolve. 64:15-64:39

Back in Caffè Italia. A live sound recording. Antonio, Angelo, Coco, Salvatore, and friends celebrate the end of the film shoot. But also the Italian presence in this country. Zavaglia adds: "Immigrant Italians have had their impact on Canada as Canada has impacted on them." The reciprocity of experience is the basis of an honest relationship, something that was unavailable in *Pane e cioccolata* and *Queen of Hearts* where the immigrant was more or less tossed aside. War memories put to rest, Zavaglia concludes with an optimistic view of ethnic cooperation.

55. Autonomous shot. Int. Finaldi home. Day.
54-55=0. 64:40-65:35

Carmine speaks to Zavaglia off screen. This sequence shot is the same as the earlier one of Carmine (Syntagma 61). Carmine speaks about going to night classes in order to learn French. A displaced insert, a close up of Angelo playing his bass. Coco sings. The spectator notices the narrative threads being pulled together. The film is coming to an end.

56. Autonomous shot. 55-56=0. 65:35-65:43

A sequence shot of the Mediterranean Sea under a cloudy sky. The sound is justified, authentic, synchronic. This metaphoric parallelism rhymes with the surrounding syntagmas.

57. Parallel syntagma. Int. Finaldi home. Day.
56-57=0. 65:44-65:58

Zavaglia asks Angelo: "What is the first impression of Quebec?"
    Angelo laughs: "A back alley. *(Une ruelle.)*."
    Inserts of back alleys, the backbone of east end Montreal. "And the toaster and sliced white bread." Laughter calls forth the bocce court. Angelo explains: "This is Little Italy where people speak Italian." Montreal's Little Italy is a cultural haven. Its role resembles that of a filmic insert: displaced, explicative, subjective, nondiegetic.

58. Autonomous shot. Ext. Neapolitan Piazza. Day.
57-58=0. 66:59-67:07

A piazza in Naples. A stack of sequence shots, Angelo's voice bridges them together.

59. Autonomous shot. Ext. Naples: Street. Day.
58=59=0. 67:08-67:13.

A sequence shot of Neapolitan boys in low angle. Zavaglia asks them: "Have you ever thought about emigrating?" The reaction is immediate, in the negative: "Never... Naples is forever... Naples is too beautiful." Besides being the home of the Finaldi, Naples is being presented as a fortress that resists emigration. But how truthful are the boys? Italy's financial situation is no better today than it was in the late 1900s. Emigration is part of the Italian psyche.

60. Autonomous shot. Int. Music performance. Day.
59-50=0. 67:14-67:37

Angelo, Coco and a third musician perform live. Coco is singing in Neapolitan about Naples. The Neapolitan parameter links these various autonomous shots together. Is Naples in Canada different from Naples in Italy? Like all fine poetry, the rime is ambiguous, yet its meaning directed.

61. Autonomous shot. Int. Finaldi Home. Day.
60-61=0. 67:38-69:29

Angelo praises his daughter's wish to sing in Neapolitan: "Words are fat, oily. They have a rhythm... stories are better when told in Neapolitan... There is always a humor... in everything... even in death."

A zoom out reveals Carmine sitting to the side of his son. Both laugh, when Angelo imagines a dead man awakening to say "ciao" to the people mesmerized by his funeral procession.

Never a categorical solution to the filmmaker's point of view. As soon as you think he offers an answer, he rushes in the opposite direction. Bringing up polyglot Italy at this point is acknowledging the complexity of Italian cultural history. Italy has never been, will never be, unidimensional.

Bridging oneself to Italy is not connecting to one specific element of Italy. Dante might appear as a bust in a park, a symbol, a statue against the northern snows, but threads can be pulled in various directions. The films of François Truffaut, Alain Renais, Éric Rohmer, Jean-Luc Besson, Jean-Jacques Beineix, Nicole Garcia speak the same dialect, the same language. Italian films do not speak a single Italic dialect. The films of Federico Fellini, Pier Paolo Pasolini, Michelangelo Antonioni, Bernando Bertolucci, Mauro Bolognini, Lina Wertmüller, Gianni Moretti, Roberto Benini use a multiplicity of idioms to express complex regional distinctions.

Being Italian today means more than just being from Italy and speaking standard Italian. Zavaglia successfully presents the plurality of languages spoken in Montreal. Being Canadian or Quebecois means more than just speaking English or French. Identity is plurilingual, pluricultural.

A displaced diegetical insert of a street punctuates what Angelo Finaldi says off screen. A second nondiegetical insert of the bust of an unnamed god flashes on screen just as Angelo mentions the word "death".

> 62. Episodic syntagma. Ext. Garden. Day.
> 61-62=0. 69:30-71:01

Angelo's laughter fades on these episodes of men pushing a fig tree into the cold autumn soil. Except for the director-narrator's voice, sounds are realistic, justified, authentic. The cello-voice duet fades in, as the church bell from Madonna della difesa fade out. The fig tree sleeps.

> It takes an Italian genius to be able to cultivate a fig tree in snow. When it gets cold, the tree is put in a deep grave where it is protected from ice and wind. As soon as the warmer season arrives, it is exhumed... awakened. These rituals of death and resurrection symbolizes the Italian experience in Canada. If we can explain immigration by such words as hardships, suffering, mourning, we can also see it as an achievement, a breath of creativity, liberty and renaissance.

The images bespeak what the commentary does not. If the Mediterranean Sea acts as a metaphor of what is and will not die, the fig tree cannot be rebirth. Rebirth would imply death; and there is no death. The same reasoning can be applied to "re-naissance" (a second coming).

The fig tree is not dead, and so there is no rebirth. The tree is protected from the bitter Montreal winter. By suggesting death and renaissance, Zavaglia undermines, in our opinion, the vastness of his project where death did not figure at all. Maybe what he is formulating is the possibility of resurrecting a culture that has been disfranchised. But if this were the case, his message of hope shines as a beacon for future generations.

The key sentence is "It takes an Italian genius to be able to cultivate a fig tree in snow." What Zavaglia celebrates, applauds, salutes is the worker. The Italian immigrant whose genius flows in his/her fingers. It is there, in his hands, as painter, as musician, as garden, as preserver of food, in the handshake of friendship, that the garden grows. The fig tree sleeps in the garden, it is not dead in a grave, for there is no grave in a garden of life.

63. Bracket syntagma. Mediterranean Sea.
62-63=0. 71:02-72:30

And so it is on images of the unruly Mediterranean Sea that the end credits roll, accompanied by the voice of Coco singing "Cuore...cuore..." Take heart, be hopeful. The film concludes on an emotional note of optimism. On a single word: "heart". The heart is the "interior domain". The heart is the hearth where culture continues. The virtual territory of the Italic.

Nicola Zavaglia's aim is not to produce a political film. His didactical approach helps the Quebec spectator to see the Italian of Quebec differently. This is a film made for the French Canadians of Quebec, but it is also made for Italians in Italy. By inviting us into the homes of the Italian Montrealer, Zavaglia instructs us how language, place, faith do not define our citizenship. The borders of countries are removed. There is something otherworldly about these modern nomads who dig their fingers into the North American soil. Not chained to the past, all work for the well-being of their children. By combining the image of the Mediterranean Sea to the "cuore", Nicola Zavaglia traces a path to the future of ethnic consciousness.

Structure of the film

Breaking the documentary into the paradigm is risky business. Nevertheless the exercise yields interesting results. The short length of the film shifts the entire narrative frame forward. On the first level (the dark rectangles) the gist of the film's metaphorical landscape is laid bare: from Southern Italy, we meet the Finaldi family and Celestina (the character for whom Angelo Finaldi composes the theme song, she enters as an Inciting Incident). The Father figure comes next: Antonio, Mary di Michele, Zavaglia eulogize their fathers, Zavaglia's father appearing and disappearing at the climax. The film ends with the garden, the echo abroad of the Mediterranean Sea, the virtual territory. *La demeure intérieure.*

If we inspect the Turning Points, we notice how it is the Father who, as the bearer of tradition and culture, enables synthesis, closure. In *Queen of Hearts* the Father (Nonno) represents cultural continuity. The plot of earth makes hope a possibility; the garden is where Danilo buries his father's gun. Eddie returns to the garden to unearth the treasure Nonno had left him to free his family of the shackles of the past (Barbariccia). As the first Turning Point, Carmine is seen passing on valuable material to Coco, his granddaughter. At the midpoint, the Father (Antonio's, Mary's, and Nicola Zavaglia's father) rises as a point of enlightenment. The third and final Turning Point is Caffè Italia presented as a virtual island for intellectual and emotional discussion.

The space where friendship flourishes. The garden. *The Mediterranean Forever* is a call for self-awareness, made possible with the transmission of cultural knowledge (via the Father). The garden the place knowledge actualized as tradition.

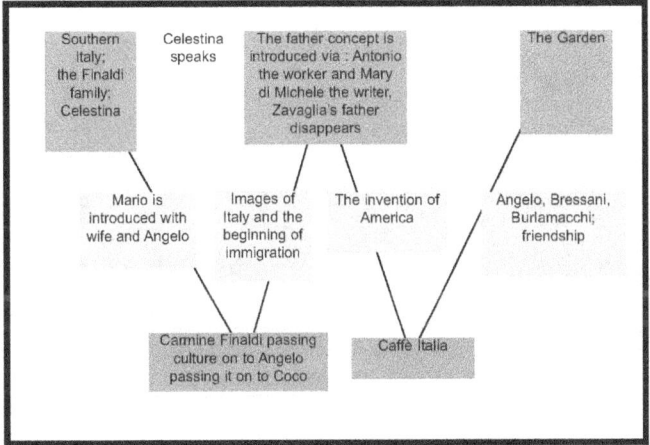

Figure 11

Most interesting is Zavaglia's use of the Pinch Points. Like in the works of fiction, there appears at four moments (light shaded in the diagram): Mario, Mario's wife, and their friend Angelo are introduced to the spectator (friendship); the next Pinch Point consists of Italy and hardship (immigration); the third Pinch Point announces the "Invention" of America: Zavaglia insists on America being not discovered, but invented (A Merica). (Italy owes so much to Amerindians: Italian cuisine was transformed by their fruits, vegetables, and spices.) The last Pinch Point praises camaraderie and love of spouse for being what binds the entire structure.

Without love and friendship, there is no virtual territory called the Italic. *Bread and Chocolate* unreservedly demonstrates that without love and friendship, Nino fails. *A Pain in the Ass* tips the concept of friendship to its most burlesque outcome: friends end in prison. If culture is to survive away from its center, it necessitates the strength of companionship, exactly what is lacking in *Raging Bull*. Though there is no governing body in the Italic, it exists on the condition it is animated by friendship, love, and creativity.

Notes

1. John Grierson, *Grierson on Documentary*, edited and compiled by Forsyth Hardy, London: Faber, 1946, 146.
2. Marcel Jean, *Le Cinéma québécois* (1991), Montréal: Boréal, 2005, 15.
3. Maria Gabriella Adamo, "Méditerranée pour toujours (Nicola Zavaglia, 2000): L'espace des origines, l'altérité, la langue migrante", in *Langue-Culture méditerranéenes en contact*, edited by Yannick Preumont and Régine Laugier, Roma: Aracne editrice, 2007, 184.
4. Marco Micone, *Le figuier enchanté*, Montréal: Boréal, 1992.
5. This point of view is elaborated in Margherita Ganerio, "La fine della letteratura italoamericana in Helen Barolini", *Italian Canadiana*, XXIV, 2010.
6. Seymour M. Lipset, "Working-Class Authoritarianism", quoted in Michael Novak, op. cit., 225.
7. Oscar Handlin, *Race and Nationality in American Life*, quoted in Michael Novak, op. cit., 148.
8. Christian Metz, quoted in Anne Goliot-Lété and Francis Vanoye, *Précis de l'analyse filmique*, 2 nd ed., Paris: Armand Colin, 2009 (1992), 38.
9. Michel Chion, quoted in Anne Goliot-Lété, op. cit., 38.
10. Carole Gagliardi, *Le Journal de Montréal*, Saturday, 20 May 2000.
11. Louise Blanchard, *Le Journal de Montréal*, Tuesday, 6 June 2000.
12. *Le Devoir*, 2010.
13. Further discussion on federalism versus ethnicity cannot be fully understood without Nathan Glazer's unavoidable read, *Ethnic Dimension: 1964-1982*.
14. Antonio Sorella, "La televisione e la lingua italiana", *Trimestre: Periodico di Cultura*, 14, 2-3-4- (1982), 291-300, quoted in E. J. Hobsbawn, op. cit., 10.
15. Massimo d'Azeglio, *I miei ricordi*, 1867.
16. Christian Metz, quoted in quoted in Anne Goliot-Lété, op. cit., 38.
17. Janice Welsch, "Actress Archetypes in the 1950s: Doris Day, Marilyn Monroe, Elizabeth Taylor, Audrey Hepburn", in *Women and the Cinema: A Critical Anthology*, edited by Karyn Kay and Gerald Peary, New York: E.P. Dutton, 1977, 100.
18. Eisenstein quoted in Jacques Aumont, *Du visage au cinéma*, Paris, Cahiers du cinéma, 1992, p. 95.19. Matilde Battistini, *Symbols and Allegories in Arts*, Los Angeles: The J. Paul Getty Museum, 2005, 225.
20. T.S. Eliot, "Hamlet", in *Selected Prose of T.S. Eliot*, edited by Frank Kermode, London: Faber, 1975, 48. Seymour Chatman quotes this same passage by Eliot in his work on Antonioni.
21. See Filippo Salvatore, *Fascism and the Italian of Montreal*, Toronto: Guernica Editions, 1998, and Angelo Principe, The Darkest Side of the Fascist Years, Toronto: Guernica Editions, 1999.
22. Francesca Iacovetta, Roberto Perin, and Angelo Principe, eds. *Enemies Within: Italian and Other Internees in Canada and Abroad*, Toronto: University of Toronto Press, 2000, 393-398.

5

RAGING BULL

Synopsis

Raging Bull, directed by Martin Scorsese in 1980, is taken from a screenplay written by Paul Schrader, Mardik Martin, Martin Scorsese (uncredited), and Robert De Niro (uncredited). The script is based on the autobiography *Raging Bull: My Story,* written by Jake LaMotta, Joseph Carter and Peter Savage. The film stars Robert De Niro, Cathy Moriarty, Joe Pesci, and Frank Vincent.

Raging Bull is the biographical journey of middle-weight boxer, Jake LaMotta. It begins in 1941 and ends in 1964. Twenty years in the life of an Italian-American athlete who stubbornly refuses to collaborate with the Mob. His brother Joey decides to entertain a questionable partnership so that Jake might become the middle-weight champion. Soon the foundation gets shaky on the personal front. Jake leaves his first wife Irma for a fifteen-year-old blond virgin, Vickie, who is friendly with members of the Mob. Jake brutally strikes Joey, believing he has slept with Vickie. This is the end of their relationship; Joey and Jake never talk again. Left to himself, Jake tumbles deep into a world of alcohol, and is thrown in prison for serving alcohol to a fourteen-year-old girl at his Miami bar. Vickie and the children leave Jake. Back in New York Jake earns his livelihood as a stand-up comedian.

The outsider

In *Gangster Priest: The Italian American Cinema of Martin Scorsese,*[1] Robert Casillo spends numerous pages and footnotes explaining how Martin Scorsese is neither an Italian American, nor an American tout court, and yet concludes that Martin Scorsese has made Italian American films:

> Being neither an ethnic outsider nor fully assimilated insider, whether in American society or the film industry, he has never been bound by the claims of his ethnicity but as repeatedly demonstrated his artistic freedom, curiosity, and daring. Many of his films have nothing to do with Italian America. He has directed urban melodramas, satires of contemporary life, thrillers, surrealistic fantasies, costume dramas, historical biographies, musicals, and biblical films. To be sure, these works reflect Scorsese's background as an Italian American Catholic, but he has also brought to them an awareness formed outside Italian America, including a lifelong immersion in American and European cinema. The rich texture of Scorsese's non-Italian American films testifies to this interweaving of cultural strands (65-66).

This quote indicates how a critic can irremediably reduce — following in the footsteps of Jerre Mangione, among others — the definition of Italian-American artworks to "works on Italian American subjects".[2] It is the content that defines the ethnicity of the work, not the filmmaker. This thought draws us to the obvious supposition that if we were to subtract this particular "ethnic" ingredient from the entity, the whole thing would collapse into mainstream sameness.

Individuals are either an ethnic or not an ethnic for the contents they use. Casillo reminds us that the artist stands where the "successful dehyphenated ethnic artist" stands.[3] More explicit an agenda is hard to come by. Aesthetic merit depends on the artist's capacity to transcend his ethnicity. Contrary to Casillo's position, Lee Lourdeaux's hypothesis advances the notion that an artist, consciously or unconsciously, tries to camouflage his cultural references (be he from the land of origin or not) in works that do not overtly pertain to ethnic themes, but to no avail. For Lourdeaux ethnicity is not something one disposes of so easily. Accordingly, ethnicity is not a content; it is a form as well. A scene where characters devour spaghetti does neither make the scene Italian, nor the characters Italian.

We presume Martin Scorsese is an American. That he is an Unitedstatesian is not the issue. The question we should be asking is whether or not Scorsese is a pluricultural artist. Now, that's a valid question. Or is he a die-hard assimilationist, who swears on the melting-pot agenda? Having strong European ties, in itself, means absolutely nothing. Woody Allen has European ties. Does that mean a film by Allen is like a film by Scorsese? Surprisingly, yes. Well, that's the wager.

There is, in reality, that special something in a Woody Allen film that does resemble the special something in a Martin Scorsese film, though their points of reference might be dissimilar. As "ethnic" as *Match Point* (2005) and *Shutter Island* (2010) might be — if such a claim can be made about either of these films, the point to raise is whether these films come across as ethnic films. Beyond their details, is there something about the entirety that we can consider ethnic? And if so, what is it?

On some intangible level these two films, regardless of their content, speak about the cultural background of the filmmakers, if not directly, at least bashfully. In both works there is a pluricultural point of view at work. The directors plunge into the cultural unconsciousness of a country. Granted, the works do not deal with blatant ethnic "contents" (whatever that might mean), but they do touch upon the parameters that constitute the culture that created these films.

Geography does not count when it comes to film. The directors have to make the audience glide, as it were, over the moving territory without being pulled down by gravity. Ethnicity is the opposite of finding one's origins. Ethnicity might include nostalgia, but it is not the blatant wish to return to the homeland. As we have seen in *Queen of Hearts, Bread and Chocolate, A Pain in the Ass,* and *The Mediterranean Forever,* ethnicity is about movement, displacement, the absence or tearing off of roots. The viewer must sense the iffy sensation that it is does not matter where we are, we would end up being exactly like this.

What is at stake is not similitude of experience but dissimilarity of identity, not likeness, but distinction: not an *endo-* (as in "endogenous"), but an *exo-* (as in "exogenous"); not a *syn-* (as in "synonym"), but an *anti-* (as in "antinomy"). Many artists in the U.S.A. fear being identified to ethnicity. If there is a lesson to be learned from *Raging Bull*, it is precisely that to become an ethnic (for one becomes ethnic, one is not an ethnic), it will cost artists everything they have.

The idea raised by Casillo, via Daniel Aaron, according to which Jewish writers have been more successful than Italian American writers in moving between "their ethnic and mainstream identities and inheritances" is an epistemological fallacy. Artistic success is rarely recognizable during one's lifetime. There is no certainty on what will be appreciated tomorrow. If this were not the case than writers such as Rimbaud and Lautréamont would have been rich men during their lifetime. It was not the case then (neither got to distribute their printed books to a reading public), it is not the case today. Whatever fame they have came decades later, after they were buried.

Critics should be wary of speaking of cultural success, momentary and commercial recognition; the universal contribution of any work of art is a gift time alone can bestow. Curiously, pecuniary discourse is nowadays more global than cultural. Furthermore, in the U.S.A., as in many countries today, the ethnic issue entails political considerations that too few artists are willing to raise in public. To speak of "American" or "ethnic flavors" demonstrates just how far we are from fully comprehending the topic.

The limits of contemporary cultural studies, for the most parts, continue to rely heavily on a stereotypical discourse in order to convey what still has no name. To speak of acculturation and assimilation when dealing with third and fourth generation ethnic artist is naive, so too is it debatable to presuppose that the shortcomings of a pluralistic society will force its artists and intellectuals to embrace the melting pot ideology.

The U.S.A., as Scorsese brilliantly demonstrates in *Gangs of New York* (2002), is far from being a monolithic society. The film is not about Italians, but *Gangs* is about ethnicity. Scorsese could not have been more virulent in his political stance than in this particular work. Far from giving a lesson in a melting pot ideology, Scorsese depicts a U.S.A. that savors its parallel differences.

Detachment, aloofness, loneliness, rage, the need for purgation such are the themes that he and fellow filmmaker and script-writer Paul Schrader excel in. Scorsese's ethnicity balances on the Outsider motif, often relying on Schrader's Christ-like figures in order to achieve what is called the seesaw moment. Ethnicity specifically blends the Outsider and Christian themes in such a way that the work of art rises above the seesaw that is tilting toward one side more than the other. The ability to balance metaphor is what lifts Scorsese above the rest of Italian-outside-Italy filmmakers. His contribution exposes the hostility that awaits any artist who tramples on assimilation and multiculturalism. What saves him from failing is his outstanding mastery of form, and it is in form that he controls the ethnic readings of his films.

Chapter 1: Jake and Joey LaMotta
0:00-17:15

1. Autonomous shot. Int. Opening Credits. Night.
0-1= fade in. 0:00-2:54

Black and white images of Jake LaMotta, alone, in the ring, shadow boxing in extreme slow motion, with credits appearing with the adagio of Mascagni's *Cavalleria rusticana*. Casillo observes that "the use of black-and-white implies stylization. The viewer experiences it as essentialism" (229) To make the film in black and white was a political gesture. Scorsese and other filmmakers wanted film-stock companies to change their attitude about the fragility of color films; many films of the past were fading away. Scorsese was not alone in this movement. Woody Allen's *Manhattan* (1979) was produced for the same political motive: determination not to stand out, but to save tradition.

2. Scene. Int. New York City, 1964. Night.
1-2= 0. 2:55-4:06

No fades in, no fade-outs, just edits as powerful as Jake LaMotta's punch. No punctuation to distinguish one time from another. A teaser scene on which a title is juxtaposed: "New York City, 1964". An elderly, overweight Jake LaMotta in a tuxedo in the artist's dressing room recites a poem. A second title appears in superimposition on a close-up of LaMotta: "Jake LaMotta, 1964". Scorsese lays out his narrative cards on the table:

> I recall every fall.
> Every hook, every jab.
> The worst way a guy
> Can get rid of his flab.
> As you know my life wasn't drab...
> "A horse! A horse!
> My kingdom for a horse!..."
> And though I'm no Olivier
> If he fought Sugar Ray
> He would say that the thing
> Ain't the ring, it's the play.
> So give me a stage
> Where this bull here can rage.
> And though I can fight
> I'd much rather recite... That's entertainment!

At the beginning of every film lies its end. LaMotta's last words, "That's entertainment" pretty much sums the meaning of his existence. The film can be seen as an entire flashback, presenting itself as an explanation of what LaMotta has become. LaMotta enjoys a cigar. What is the "entertainment" he is alluding to? The boxing career? His romance with Vickie? Both? Neither? Scorsese himself admits: "to call *[Raging Bull]* a boxing picture is ridiculous. It's sports but it's something to do with living. Jake LaMotta takes on the aspects of everybody" (228). Michel Cieutat pushes this idea a little further:

> *Raging Bull* can only be appreciated as a symbolic expressionist film, which uses the pugilistic setting as a pretext for an iniatic spiritual journey. For, both in terms of its screenplay and its form, *Raging Bull* is a film that presents itself as an invitation to penetrate the soul of a primitive, who unconsciously tends to holiness and whose "true violence is internal" (169)..

Critics seem to agree on the fact that this film is about redemption. Yet, in order to receive grace, Jake LaMotta must descend into hell and what better way to depict the inferno if not by altering one's physical body dimensions. Robert De Niro outplays the actor. Robert De Niro's actual body is thirty kilos fatter. Stylization at every level is at work (which did not sit well with Pauline Kael).

> De Niro wears scar tissue and a big, bent nose that deform his face. It's a miracle that he didn't grow them – he grew everything else. He developed a thick muscled neck and a fighter's body, and for the scenes of the broken, drunken LaMotta he put on so much weight that he seems to have sunk in the fat with hardly a trace of himself left. What De Niro does in this picture isn't acting, exactly. I'm not sure what it is. Though it may at some level be awesome, it definitely isn't pleasurable... He has so little expressive spark that what I found myself thinking about wasn't LaMotta or the movie but the metamorphosis of De Niro.[5]

Regardless of this negative criticism, Robert De Niro wins an Oscar for his ineffable performance. There is an element of the daredevil that displeases people. The actor's body lifts the film to a meta-filmic level, where the rules of propriety are broken. De Niro is ill-mannered, injurious, cursing verbally and physically. The absence of professional gallantry is not well received, but it is the price of entry for the ethnic. Instead of the usual act of voyeurism attributed to film gazing, De Niro refuses to grant you the permission to "gaze" at his life unfolding. No easy familiarity here; hostility is used as a way to momentarily push the viewer off balance.

This being off-balance, in bilico, is the first criterium that makes *Raging Bull* ethnic. There is no scene of Italians eating spaghetti; there is no grandmother offering a slice of pizza; what we have is the afterlife of a world of stereotypical contents. The bodies are weighty in those well-tailored suits, and the words spat often vulgar. By pushing it all to disturbing bleakness what is shown through the pee-hole of the fourth wall prohibits the spectator of thinking of stereotypes. The violence forces the viewer to remain at a distance and, in so doing, prevents him/her from enjoying the pleasures normally associated to cinematic voyeurism.

What is presented on screen is something more than a quick visit into the world of Italians; Scorsese had gone through this experience in *Italianamericana*. In that film the spectator is taken by the hand and is introduced to his Southern Italian parents. *Raging Bull* does not provide an easy fix for the voyeur; this work demands respect and total commitment on the part of the visitor.

3. Episodic sequence. Int. Cleveland Arena. Night.
2-3=0. 4:07-7:43

A new title: "Jake LaMotta, 1941." Douglas Brode mentions how Scorsese had planned to "contrast the young and older Jake throughout" the film, but in the editing room he realized that the effect led to confusion. Scorsese chose to use the 1964 scenes as a framing device (128). An announcer repeats what is shown on screen: "LaMotta is undefeated, but well behind in points. The Bronx Bull has taken a lot of punishment in this bout." In the Cleveland Arena, Jake receives relentless punches from his African-American opponent. This is our introduction to Jake LaMotta. The perseverant boxer, the determined man from the Bronx, an Italian-American athlete, who makes a surprising comeback before this fight is over.

Under the guise of a continuous scene, this syntagma is made up of short scenes, finely edited together, to promote realism and vivaciousness. Each episode presented in this chapter belongs to a single mega-sequence, which itself takes the shape of a mega-episodic sequence. Indeed, mega-sequences often have the same shapes as the syntagmas suggested by Christian Metz. The sounds fake realism. Punches are louder than expected, and the photographers' cameras resonate exaggeratedly. The ring-bell is punch inside our head.

The word "Italian" is never pronounced in this film. This is a major step forward, a sign of maturity in the Italic culture. The spectator's knowledge of Italian Americans is taken for granted. No identification need be given; the cultural signals surpass stereotypes, and attain a universality normally reserved to nations. The ethnic is becoming global, regional and universal. Being Italian is not a strange thing out there; one asks to be defined in its every detail. Scorsese spreads these details throughout the film.

Jake and his brother Joey speak an excessive, geographically identifiable lingo; the Bronx is in the veins of these siblings. The LaMotta brothers are from New York; their words have different meanings in Cleveland.

In this scene, the fight seems to be fixed. Though Jake has knocked Reeves out, it means nothing. Jake loses (to Reeves' astonishment). The trait of "loser" is immediately attached to LaMotta. What is being announced is that victory can only come about if Jake works within the system. Which system this is we'll soon find out. Mayhem follows.

The organ player breaks into the U.S. national anthem, as if the nation could sanctify the good and the evil facets of the moment. The nation surrounds the ethnic, is more powerful than the ethnic. This is one reason why the family, friendship, and love are prerequisites to survival. The ethnic loner is doomed.

4. Sequence. Ext. Joey and Salvy. Day.
3-4=0. 7:44-8:28

Another title — "The Bronx, New York City, 1941" — delimits a geographical and temporal entity. We're back in the past. Joey LaMotta struts up the street beside mobster Salvy. They discuss Jake's attitude. The loss against Reeves was no coincidence. Success has its price tag. This theme will be explored to a greater extend in *Gangs of New York*, where the price for inclusion is the exclusion of ethnicity. The verbal references at the end of *Raging Bull* to *On the Waterfront* reiterate this point. Jake will be alone, and a failure unless he sells out to the Mob: "I could have been a contender": a contender to what? This is the Mac Guffin.

5. Scene. Int. The LaMotta's kitchen. Day.
4-5=0. 8:29-11:28

The Inciting Incident: we're in the LaMotta's apartment. Jake and his wife Irma quarrel over a burned steak. Three inserts (a complete scene) with Joey and Salvy are embedded in the kitchen scene. Unlike an alternating syntagma these edits do not bounce off another scene in order to stretch out its meaning. This specific way of embedding one scene inside another is a signature editing technique. Scorsese uses this filmic enjambment to move the story forward more rapidly. Linearity is avoided whenever possible, even though the sequence shot makes it presence felt. Scorsese rarely lingers on action; action necessarily grows out of the edit. Thelma Schoonmaker declares that "Marty has a very strong editing sense. He creates a great deal of what goes in his movies in the editing room, so we work very, very closely together. He's involved in every direction. Some directors don't work that way, but Marty does."[6] This is her first feature, for which she wins an Oscar.

Joey LaMotta arrives in the midst of an argument. Jake grabs Irma by the hair and threatens to have his neighbor's (Larry) dog for lunch. The chaos is violent, and yet when Jake sits at the table with his brother, he is smiling, asking Irma for a truce. What are we to make of this double-gesture: is it honesty or dishonesty? Jake is a prisoner of violence, but he can also be gentle at times.

Irma appears twice in the film; with no mention of a divorce, she will be replaced by the young Vickie. The next scene rises out of this scene. The justified and synchronized sounds seem realistic, but they are in truth hyper-realistic. Each sonorous detail is intelligently driven to its paroxysm. According to Thelma Schoonmaker, Frank Warner, the sound editor, built a sound tapestry "on which Marty kept laying down, little tiny details."[7] The sound editing took two months to complete.

>6. Scene. Int. Jake and Joey and Small Hands. Day.
>5-6=0. 11:29-15:05

At last, a proper introduction to Joey, Jake's younger brother, who has appeared in previous episodes. It becomes clear that Joey plays the role of the Sender: through him, Joey's life will change. He encourages Jake to leave his wife; there are many fights waiting still to be won, his words sound ominously symbolic. We know that Jake will fight many important bouts but will win very few. Jake complains about his hands: "I got these small hands. I got a little girl's hands... I ain't never gonna fight Joe Louis." Little girl's hands? A foreshadowing of the young girl who will take him down in Florida.

Jake orders Joey to hit him in the face which Joey reluctantly does. In the original draft of the script by Mardik Martin, Joey LaMotta did not exist. If he finally does in the film, it is thanks to Paul Schrader.

> My main contribution... was the character of Joey LaMotta. Jake didn't like his brother much, so he wasn't in the first draft and there was no drama there. I did some research, met Joe and he struck me as much more interesting. You had these two young boxers, the Fighting LaMotta's, and one was sort of shy while the other one had a lot of social tools, so Joey quit fighting and managed his brother. The only thing Jake was good at was taking a beating, he wasn't a terrific boxer but he could take a beating and meanwhile Joey was off managing and getting all the girls. So injecting that sibling relationship into the script made it a financeable film (Jackson, 131).

Unbeknownst to Schrader, what he had done was enable Scorsese to achieve that seesaw moment so essential to his creativity, without which the film would not have been made. Scorsese is quoted repeatedly as unwilling to do the film, despite De Niro's nonstop pleas. Scorsese thought something was missing in this story. What was lacking was precisely this sibling rivalry which elevates the project to another degree: the ethnic confrontation. To assimilate or not? And if so, at what cost? Incidentally, Mary Pat Kelly's chapter dedicated to *Raging Bull* has as title, "Blood on the Ropes" (a subtle reference to Bob Dylan's fifteen and major album, *Blood on the Tracks* (1975)? Scorsese would make a film on *Dylan, No Direction Home* (2005)).

This image of blood (for this is the price to pay) is mentioned in *Gangs of New York*, when Priest Vallon tells his son Amsterdam that he should never wipe the blood off of his knife. Culture is not free.

7. Scene. Int. Gleason's Gym. Day.
6-7=0. 15:06-17:15

From the kitchen scrimmage, we move on to Jake and Joey in the gym. It is warm up time. Jake is hitting Joey quite violently. Mobster Salvy and acolytes look on with disgust. Jake has no respect for these "good-for-nothing" come there to steal his hard-earned cash. Jake takes his frustration and anger on his brother. One of the wise guys mutters: "They look like two fags..." This is the second time homosexuality is hinted at in the film. The first time was in the previous scene, when Jake accused Joey of being a fag, and to "throw a punch like you take it up the ass". These homoerotic lines are expressed audibly. Scorsese deemed them important enough to leave them in the film. Such comments we will place in a semantic bag and see what we can make of them by the time the film comes to an end.

In an interview with Kevin Jackson, Paul Schrader speaks about the sexuality in the film, about "the kind of hidden sexual bond between the brothers, the sexuality of the siblings expresses itself by Jake being convinced that his brother has cheated him" (Jackson, 133). Schrader and Scorsese, he explains, believed that this sexual dimension is linked to what they coined "Deadly Sperm Backup".

Jake is obsessed about remaining celibate before fights. The topic comes up again in another Scorsese film, *The Last Temptation of Christ* (1988): "That's what happens when you don't sleep with women — your sperm goes up to your brain and makes you crazy" (Jackson, 133). Sexuality, we have noticed, entertains a spasmodic role in these films about "passing" from one status to another. Never innocent, sexuality is a promise that sometimes gets broken.

An interesting aside can be said about *Little Caesar* (1931) by Mervyn LeRoy, one of the first films to deal with the Italian Mafia. The writer, William R. Burnett, whose novel was the base for the film, which would turn Edward G. Robinson into a star, had complained to the producer Darryl F.

Zanuck about the homosexual subtext of the film. In fact, Enrico Bandello (Rico) has no use for women in his life; he is more than glad to have the sycophant Otero lie on his bed.

From the initial scenes, Rico demonstrates no interest whatsoever in women, whereas Joe Massara's main reason to get involved in the mob is to attract women; as soon as Joe meets Olga he sees no use in continuing a life of crime, a decision which infuriates Rico who becomes the boss.

This openly homosexual plot would be repeated in part in *Raging Bull*, though the homosexual (incestuous) relationship between men is not a main concern for Scorsese who simply lets it ride. Scorsese hints at homosexuality in *Mean Streets*, but again how much is conscious, how much is unconscious, is a matter of conjecture. Homosexuality appears in *Bread and Chocolate* and *A Pain in the Ass*.

Nino finds himself in the all-male barracks after all other ventures in finding work go array. When he is willing to participate in the cross-dressing celebration, it is however temporary. Nino is no homosexual. Yet the context is. The entire episode with his friend Gigi is riddled with homoerotic word-playing. It is too prevalent for it to be haphazard in intent. In *A Pain in the Ass*, Pignon actually pushes the situation with Milan; they end up sharing a prison cell together. In *Queen of Hearts,* homosexuality is never referred to. Danilo's relationship with Mario is never amorous, even when Mario brings Danilo back to his bed after the latter's failed suicide attempt, the rapport is non-sexual in intent. Friendship in this case, as with the friendship between Mario and Angelo in *The Mediterranean Forever* is firmly platonic. The attitude developed in the films seem to indicate that same-sex love is accepted as a way of life by Italian immigrants.

Chapter 2: Vickie
17:16-31:20

8. Scene. Ext. The swimming pool. Day.
7-8=0. 17:16-20:34

Jake inquires about fifteen-year-old Vickie sitting with Salvy and his wise guys. The conversation between the brother is explicitly sexual; it foreshadows the riff that will separate the brothers for many years.

Jake: "Did you bang her?"

Joey: "No."
Jake: "Tell me the truth."
Joey: "I just told you the truth. I tell you the truth the first time... You're a married man, it's all over. Leave the young girls for me."

"I tell you the truth the first time...": Joey means what he says. Later, Jake will question the soundness of Joey's character trait. Joey does not tell all the truth. He lies about his fight with Salvy. One mega-sequence ends and another begins.

9. Sequence. Jake and Joey go out.
8-9=0. 20:35-21:31

The brothers in dark suits gambol down the staircase while Irma, visibly upset, accuses them of being faggots. The brothers make their way to a dance hall. This is the last time we will see Irma. She yells: "Faggot. Go stick it up your ass." (Faggots? Does she really believe in what she said? Are Jake and Joey "faggots"? That homosexual subtext continues to raise its head.)

There are two inserts of a billboard (the second in the film; the first being the one introducing Jake LaMotta, the actor): "Holy Vance Society, Annual Summer Dance, August 6." Jake wants Vickie, but to have her he must go through the Sender — his brother.

10. Scene. Int. Dance Hall. Night.
9-10=0. 21:32-23:11

Joey and Jake in a dance hall. Jake is obsessively engrossed by Vickie's beauty. Subjective inserts of Jake staring in Vickie's direction, in slow motion, act more or less like an alternating syntagma. Very forceful is the contraction-separation of Jake and Vickie's worlds — a married mature man versus a fifteen-year-old girl. There is a similarity here to Lester's obsession with Angela in *America Beauty* (1999). This fascination for underage girls usually leads to disaster. It will not be different in this film.

11. Sequence. Int/Ext. Jake follows Vickie. Night.
10-11=0. 23:12-24:04

Vickie leaves with Salvy. Jake strides through a scuffle between patrons. From a distance Jake gazes at Vickie in Salvy's luxurious car moving out of the frame in slow motion. This is less about being a voyeur than about a man who must learn how to attract a young girl. The brawl inside makes its way outside, smashing Jake's transfixion. The dreamlike melody fades out.

Over the image of a closing door, Jake mutters condescendingly: "Go back where you come from." To go back where you come from? To whom is this question addressed? Its list of connotations is long, its messages not unheard of. Which immigrant has not heard this sentence before? Is Jake talking to himself? Is he telling himself to return to his wife? to his family? to Italy? How far back must Jake go before he realizes that there is no going back, just a moving forward. Much like Nino in *Bread and Chocolate*, there is no home to go back to. Here begins Jake's nomadism. The mega-sequence ends here.

12. Scene. Ext. Street in front of pool. Day.
11-12=0. 24:05-25:37

The chapter, built around short symbolic episodes, continues with this candid introduction to Vickie. This is a new mega-sequence. Acting as a proper Sender, Joey finally introduces Jake to Vickie, Jake's object of desire. Jake awkwardly caresses Vickie's fingers behind the fence grating which, as a physical divider, prevents the future lovers from being together. One thinks of Bresson's archetypal prison image in *Pickpocket* (1959), Michel separated from Jeanne. Both Paul Schrader (*American Gigolo*, 1980) and Jean-Luc Godard (*Je vous salue, Marie*, 1985) use this evocative scene to suggest the obligatory time to wait, the obstacles overcome before the lovers can meet: "Pour arriver jusqu'à toi, quel drôle de chemin j'ai dû prendre" ["To get to you, what a strange path I had to take"].

Such are the Bressonian words that bring together lovers imprisoned by their fate. On one hand, a married man, and, on the other, a fifteen-year-old virgin. Much more than Jake's infidelity what is brought to the foreground is the overpowering illicit desire. This crossing over into an unknown tryst ushers his breaking away from the Italian American family — if we are to accept Irma, Jake's first wife, as being Italian — her physical features superciliously comply to the olive-colored Mediterranean stereotype.

Vickie's skin, on the contrary, is ivory white, the color of something new. In Vickie, Jake recognizes his chance to change. She is not Jake's key, as some critics have explained, to getting to, or worse, at the mob. If there is a shameless message in *Raging Bull*, it is that one can never beat the Mob. Since the Mob (or if one were to be turgid about it, any organized criminal "fraternity") holds the key to success; trying to ignore it, as Jake swankily does, only spells failure. Jake is not there yet. He has taken the decision to divorce and marry this young "native" American girl. (The term "native" is used here in the way Scorsese defines it in Gangs of New York: he who pretends to be born from the ground of the American soil; the native opposes himself to the foreigner, the outsider, the immigrant, the ethnic.)

12. Autonomous shot. Ext. Car drive. Day.
11-12=0. 25:38-25:57

Jake and Vickie drive about in a convertible, with its synchronized motor hum, a country song barely audible in the background, coming out of the car radio. Jake asks Vickie to "Move over".

In *Mythologies* (1957), Roland Barthes suggests that "l'automobile est aujourd'hui l'équivalent assez exact des grandes cathédrales gothiques" (150). Tom Wolfe will push the analogy of cars-cathedrals further still: "Cars mean more to these kids than architecture did in Europe's great formal century, say, 1750 to 1850. They are freedom, style, sex, power, motion, color — everything is right there."[8] From syntagma 11 we know that Jake knows that Vickie is impressed by big cars; Jake is probably using the car as a phallic symbol to seduce the object of his desire.

13. Scene. Ext. Mini-pot golf. Day.
12-13=0. 25:58-26:52

After the ritualistic sex scene here is the couple playing a game of mini-pot golf. As with most of these scenettes, what is depicted on screen is a signifier for various connotations. Thanks to this game (which Vickie has never played before), the couple will walk into the house of the Lord. Over one of the holes stands erect a church. It is in this miniature church that the ball vanishes. "What does that mean?" asks naively Vickie looking for the ball. Jake on his knees, looking for the ball as well, bashfully replies: "That the game is over." Before it began the sex game is over. The couple have magically stumbled into the church of God where they receive grace. Michel Cieutat's explanation of this scene is revealing.

> When [Jake] plays golf with [Vickie] and their ball gets lost in a small church that houses the hole, Jake does not understand that it is a quasi-divine sign confiscating Vickie, in order to prevent him from further blindness, Jake is, like any Scorsesian character, alienated, that is, in the original sense of the term, alien to himself, which belongs to another (172).

Jake does not know who Jake is; he doesn't know if he loves men, if he loves women, if he is violent, if he is gentle. Jake is a stranger to himself. Most probably his self-loathing prevents him from loving anyone. The "small hands" syndrome he complains about is a metonymy of a troubling self-hatred that eventually destroys him. Vickie helps Jake, for a time, find insight to himself, by freeing himself of his sense of alienation. Jake makes his way out of the Italian-American ghetto and into the real world of the "native".

This moment is the first plot point in *Raging Bull*. Jake receives the key to another door through which he will have to walk — the door of love. What he doesn't know yet is that this door does not open up to heaven, but down to hell. The viewer is offered a genteel spectacle of statuary rape, while being charmed into a symbolic subterfuge. The fifteen-year-old virgin Vickie kindles the fire that will eventually destroy the abusive Jake LaMotta. Critics consider this attraction normal. Yet Jake LaMotta becomes a criminal, a crime he will have to pay for (but only at the end of the film, when he gets arrested for a similar crime): his love of underage girls.

14. Episodic sequence. Int. LaMotta's Parents' Apartment. Day.
13-14=0. 26:53-31:20

There is a knock on the door, but no one opens. After calling out "Daddy" Jake invites Vickie into his parents' apartment (there is no mention of a mother at all). The father absent ("Must have gone shopping. Sit down"), Jake can do as he pleases with this young girl. This syntagma is composed of short scenes of a symbolic geographic territory: the home of the mother and father. There are two mothers and fathers in the entire film: Jake and his wife Vickie, Joey and his wife Lenore.

These are not traditional couples, though they try to be: raising their children in proper homes. Vickie has questionable friends. The need for order is not simple. When violence erupts, the family unit caves in. The fathers are absent. They have been absent throughout this study. On such shaky ground, what foundation can possibly stand erect?

Jake and Vickie share a glass of water. "Salute". An Italian word is spoken by Jake in the security of his parents' habitat. A distinct clue of Italianness. Though Vickie might not be Italian, she seems to understand the language; she has spent time with Salvy and other wise guys. It is in the warmth of Jake's parents' abode that the mother tongue reveals itself. Jake wants to move away from his Italian-American reality, but he finds himself closer to that reality than ever before. Perhaps, this stop over is the last waving of the hand before embarking on this journey outside his milieu. Jake and Vickie share few words. In the kitchen, Jake mumbles: "Sit a little closer." Vickie sits on his lap. From the kitchen Jake take Vickie to the bedroom. Jake: "I bought the building."

Jake makes enough money as a boxer to purchase a house for his parents. This small detail, almost whispered, indicates how much economical stability LaMotta possesses. The gift also indicate the emotional attachment Jake has for his parents. He can afford a big car, a house for his parents, and a future for Vickie. Jake wants to be a family man, in spite of an impeding divorce.

Everything is not perfect though. In the dining room, Jake points to a bird cage: "There was a bird. It's dead." Vickie considers the proposition. What can such a phrase refer to — is it a hint to sex? After five years of marriage, Vickie will complain to Joey about how Jake does not have sex with her anymore.

On the walls, two holy images of the Virgin Mary and a female saint dressed in black. In the bedroom, a crucifix hangs over the bed and a statue of St Francis of Assisi stands on the dresser. Surrounded by such religiosity, Jake hopes for sex. The irony is too great for any spectator to miss. Vickie walks to a dresser, and studies a picture wrapped by a rosary. She gazes at the couple as Jake kisses her: "That's me and my brother, we were fooling around." Vickie compliments Jake on his good looks. Jake reacts : "Anybody ever tell you how beautiful you are. Yeah, they tell you all the time."

Jake lacks self-assurance. He is one of many men. This weakness gets bigger with time. It will be replaced by jealousy, the very kind of jealousy that will disrupt his respect for his brother.

At the thirty-minute mark the camera focuses on a triangle: Jake, Vickie, and the photograph of the brother in between the couple. An Italian melody fades in on this picture of the LaMotta brothers, their fists lift to their chest, ready to start a tussle.

Chapter 3: Jake, Vickie, and Sugar Ray
31:21-41:13

15. Episodic sequence. Int. Detroit Fight 1. Night.
14-15=0. 31:20-33:17

Over Sugar Ray's jumping boxer feet, a title: "LaMotta vs Sugar Ray Robinson, Detroit, 1943." Three main scenettes constitute this syntagma dedicated to Jake's career. Long takes, slow motion, travelling shots, Scorsese and Schoonmaker cover the gamut of camera movements and film editing procedures in order to skim over episodes of the fight between Jake LaMotta and Sugar Ray Robinson in Detroit.

The boxing announcer describes the fight as if it all were happening for a television audience. Television was not invented in 1943. This bout is covered for a radio audience. The episodes are presented, however, as if they were for newsreel. Everything is more real than real. The robust soundtrack is as lively as the fight detailed on screen. The highly stylized tracks flourish with hyper-realism. In many interviews Scorsese admits how he finds boxing boring, and it was this fear of shooting a boring film — *New York, New York* (1977) has been heavily criticized by reviewers – that pushed the director to transform a boxing film into a conceptually creative adventure. Every shot offers a revelation, every sound, a drop of grace falling from the heavens. The disappointment on Sugar Ray's face confirms a promise has been broken; this bout against LaMotta he should have won. Someone is not doing what he is being told to. Jake is doing as he wishes.

16. Scene. Int. LaMotta's Parents' Apartment. Day.
15-16=0. 33-18-38:00

Irma has disappeared from Jake's life. LaMotta is lying on the bed, feet in the middle ground. Vickie in a night gown comes out of the washroom, on the right a painting of the Virgin Mary on the wall. The couple kiss. Vickie says: "You said never to touch you before a fight." Jake insists she kiss his wounds. When the sensuality gets too hot, he rushes to the washroom sink and pours a bucket of ice-cold water on his pelvis. Religion, career, superstition, parents... everything in his life is forbidding this illicit desire. During this mega-sequence, Jake is not going to have sex with Vickie.

17. Episodic sequence. Int. Detroit Fight 2. Night.
16-17=0. 38:01-39:37

Jake LaMotta and Sugar Ray Robinson meet for the third time, and once again Robinson is knocked down by LaMotta, who, this time, comes out the loser of the bout. This syntagma presents itself, like many syntagmas in this film, as a block of short scenes linked together by a single action (a fight), one setting (the ring), one time period (an evening). In this new mega-sequence, the hyper-realist soundtrack is inauthentically loud, as furious as the images, but synchronized and justified.

18. Scene. Int. Dressing Room. Night.
17-18=0. 39:37-41-13

Joey throws a chair against the wall. Jake reveals his naivety: "I've done a lot of bad things, Joey. Maybe it's coming back to me. Who knows? I'm jinxed, maybe..." Vickie knocks at the door. Jake refuses to talk to her, and asks Joey to take Vickie home. Jake has total confidence in Joey. Jake stays alone, inspecting his wound in a mirror dividing his person in two. From Jake's reflection the camera tilts down to his hand in a bucket of ice-filled water. Silence on the soundtrack. For the first time Jake is alone, by himself, wounded, contemplating his "small" girl's hands in iced water. A "jinxed" fighter he is meditating, almost a Buddhist stance. If he wishes to win, he knows what to do; he has to separate himself from himself (sell himself to the mobsters). The chapter ends, and so does the mega-sequence.

Chapter 4: Jake Marries Vickie
41:14-43:48

19. Episodic sequence. Int. Fight. Detroit. Night.
18-19=0. 41:14-43:48

Operatic music on a black screen, a number of titles:

"LaMotta Vs Zivic, Detroit, January 14, 1944";
"LaMotta vs Basota, New York, August 1945";
"LaMotta vs Kochan, New York, September 17, 1945";
"LaMotta vs Edgar, Detroit, June 12, 1946";
"LaMotta vs Satterfield, Chicago, September 12, 1946";
"LaMotta vs Bell, New York, March 14, 1947"

followed by episodes of fights presented in black and white photographs interspersed with chronological yet discontinuous, color home-movie footage of Jake and Vickie getting married.

Honeymooning by a swimming pool; Joey getting married and the wedding reception; the arrival of children and wealth. Jake the married man, the father, the family man, the husband, with Vickie, their children, their house, their car, their wealth in color which stands in sharp contrast to black and white photographs of a victorious Jake LaMotta the boxer. The family life versus the professional side: there are two Jakes. In less than three minutes, the spectator learns that behind this veneer of prosperousness, Jake LaMotta has not spoken a word.

Robin Wood considers this sequence "virtually unclassifiable within the categories of Metz's *Grande syntagmatique* because "it combines certain defining characteristics of the bracket syntagma, the alternating syntagma and the episodic sequence" as well as it being the only time there is color in the film.[9]

Clearly, Wood suggests, the boxing scenes are an integral part of the "domestic happiness" in LaMotta's life. Family is not what it is made up to be. The film being in black and white, this color portion of the film presents itself, contrary to what is expected, as a mirage. Happiness lies outside the family.

Jake and Vickie, much like during the mini-golf ball, are living a fantasy, a graceful illusion perhaps, still an hallucination.

Chapter 5: First Signs of Jake Losing It
43:49-49:25

20. Scene. Int. LaMotta's New home kitchen. Day.
19-20=0. 43:49-48:53

Superimposed title: "Pelham Parkway, Bronx, New York 1947." Jake in his underwear and undershirt complains about his weight to Vickie, Joey and Lenore.

An undershirt has been used before to designate a particular Italian maleness-ness (for example, Sonny in *The Godfather*). Nino resorts to this non-verbal cliché in *Bread and Chocolate* when he seduces Elena; Danilo wears an undershirt during the birth of his children segment of *Queen of Hearts*. Dress codes are always significant. The dos and don'ts of what is worn in public are governed social rules. A specific garment can disclose respect or disrespect for others.

There is a familiarity about an undershirt that spells animality. There is a beastly unpredictability in Jake in his white undershirt. He was wearing an undershirt during the outrageous quarrel over the steak with Irma, his first wife. Comparably, the heat in the kitchen rises rather rapidly as soon as Vickie transgresses her domestic chores. Jake asks Vickie to make some coffee which never comes. Instead, Vickie willingly discusses Janiro's handsomeness. This mega-sequence leads to the Pinch-Point and Janiro represents the excuse for the first altercation between Jake and Vickie. Jake's sudden outburst of jealousy chisels a wedge between husband and wife. Jealousy is also responsible for the dispute between Jake and Joey. Jake is unstable. When Jake cuddles up to Vickie, begging for her forgiveness, there is something in the boxer that has snapped.

The weight, the coffee, Janiro, Janiro's good-looks, domestic chores are red herrings. Jake is cracking up, Joey is right. Why Jake would be falling apart is left unexplained. Are the hits on his head finally taking a toll on Jake? Is Jake feeding his paranoia? Most probably it is a combination of all of the aliments mentioned. Add to these the pressure of winning. The Janiro fight is fixed. At the center all of this commotion, Joey encapsulates Jake LaMotta political-cultural position: "There's no way you can lose, and you do it on your own, just the way you wanted to do it, without help from anybody."

Jake cannot do it on his own, this is the tragedy of this Italian-American athlete. To do it on his own, and on his own terms: this summarizes the "recurring theme" which Paola Casella believes, and rightly so, defines the "Italian Hollywood".

> And this is the vital point of Italian Hollywood, as well as the recurring theme in Hollywood films that deal directly with the theme of Italian life in the wider American context: How can such a reticent immigrant enter American society without sacrificing his ethnic identity? And how can the American melting pot welcome without mistrust an individual who refuses to be fully integrated? (17)

This dilemma between assimilation and separation, between success and failure, remains the cluster in which most Italian-outside-Italy individuals struggle to keep their dignity. The struggle is more vicious in the U.S.A. than anywhere else in the world, undoubtedly because the numbers at stake are higher. According to the National Italian American Foundation, one out of ten persons in the U.S.A. can trace his ancestry to Italy.

> There are nearly fifteen million people who have identified themselves as Italian American in the 1990 U.S. census, the Population Division of the U.S. Census Bureau reports. The Census Bureau estimates, however, that one out of ten Americans has some Italian connection, bringing the total number of Americans of Italian descent to 26 million. Italian Americans are the fifth largest ethnic group in the United States, according to the U.S. Census Bureau. The four larger groups are: the Germans, Irish, English, and African Americans.[10]

With such figures, the debate about who belongs and who does not belong influences every citizen's psychological, sociological, and cultural makeup. Jake's weight problem is more political than an issue about his vanity. It extends beyond Jake's physical appearance or a husband's duties. Jake is not being vain; he is denouncing the entire boxing cooperative. This Pinch Point plays on Jake's jealousy and his conceitedness, while raising a totally hidden and more pressing agenda (melting pot versus the individual's freedom). Should Jake play along with the system or not?

21. Scene. Int. Living room. Day.
20-21=0. 48:54-49:25
A short scene of three separate shots follows in which Jake cuddles up to

Vickie in front of Leonore and the children. This belongs to the same megasequence. In the background, as is often the case, music rises in volume as the scene comes to an end: Uplifting jazz on which Toots Thielemans whistles the melody. Once again, superficial signs of affection distract the audience from the gist of the action: obsession is on the rise. Jean-Claude Carrière, Buñuel's co-scriptwriter, extrapolates on what really happens in such cases.

> How many times could we say, of ourselves or of others, that a film has not been seen, or truly seen? For many reasons, some of which are unclear and some we cannot admit to, we see imperfectly. We refuse to see, or else we see something else. There is in every film a region of shadow, a stockpile of the "not-seen". It can be put there by its authors, knowingly and deliberately. And it can be brought there during a performance by a particular spectator (just one spectator who on that one day is unable or refuses to see everything), or else by that remarkably cohesive group whose reactions are collective even when unpredictable, the entity known as the audience (4-5).

Just as we think we are viewing one film, another film begins. Pinch Points do just that; they push the film in an unexpected direction, usually pitting the Sender against the object of desire.

Chapter 6: Jake's Jealousy
49:26-58:17

22. Autonomous shot. Ext. Sign. Night.
21-22=0. 49:26-49:30

From the living room scene, Jake, Vickie, Joey and Janet, Joey's date for the evening, sit at the Copacabana night club. (Joey is being unfaithful.) The stand-up comedian's voice bridges this scene to the following scene. An incredible amount of intertitles and signs pop up throughout this film which Scorsese uses as signposts, as used to done in the silent era.

23. Episodic sequence. Int. Restaurant. Night.
49:31-51:36

The stand-up comedian acknowledges Jake to the bar's patrons. We could consider all of these scenettes as separate scenes, but in truth one of their purposes is to introduce the capo of mobsters: Tommy Como. If the flunkies met along the way were minor devils, here is Satan. *Raging Bull*, not being a gangster genre, spares us the gruesome escapades into violence as elaborated in *Donnie Brasco* (1997).

Scorsese's film is about something else. From the mobsters (who praise Janiro) to Janiro in the ring ("He ain't pretty no more"), this section is superficially dedicated to Janiro and more specifically to Jake and his "cracking up". This action of first mega-sequence revolves around Jake's table. Jake sees and criticizes the mobsters. These are the people who holds the reins of Jake's success. Jake must deal with these people, against his will. Indicative of Jake's contempt for these men is manifest in Jake's effeminate handshake offered to Salvy. Jake spits when Joey mentions Salvy's fine suit. Clothes cannot conceal the person's insolence. Jake perceives the disrespect. When Vickie greets capo Tommy Como, the sequence shot is in slow motion. It is Jake inspecting his wife paying her respects to the people he scorns. Sitting beside Tommy Como, Salvy does not mince his words, "She's with that fuckin' gorilla." Jake the gorilla (in undershirt) versus the wise guys in suits. Beneath the expensive attire are dangerous hoodlums. The stand-up comic's one-liners are commentaries on the spectacle unfolding.

24. Scene. Int. Jake's table. Night.
23-24=0. 51:37-52:36

When Vickie returns to the table, an aggressive Jake drills her ("Don't start," she says.) She has received her share of abusive talk from Jake. Vickie has become an abused woman." Shut up, I will smack you in the face." Jake's bully-ness in uncontrollable. Whatever sympathy this man attracted has by now evaporated. Even the mobsters seem nicer persons in comparison. This film is not about depicting a nice loveable athlete. Tommy Como the outlaw sends drinks for Jake and his guests, appearing more gentlemanly than our law-abiding boxer.

25. Autonomous shot. Int. Stage. Night.
24-25=0. 52:37-52:42

The only reason why we mention this short sequence shot is because of its significant one-liner: "Hi, how are you, bald-headed fag?" This homoerotic one-liner introduces the next syntagma which centers around homosexuality and boxing.

26. Scene. Int. Tommy Como's Table. Night.
25-26=0. 52:43-55:16

Joey and Jake sit at Tommy Como's table, a single topic is discussed: Janiro. Jake speaks: "I got a problem — if I should fuck him or fight him." The homoerotic megatext will not go away. Jake offers to introduce Salvy to Janiro for sexual favors.

27. Autonomous shot. Int. Bedroom. Night.
26-27=0. 55-17-56:57

A new mega-sequence begins. Jake walks about the bedroom, scrutinizes Vickie sleeping under a crucifix. He wakes her up, asks: "You ever think of anybody else when we're in bed?" Janiro's face is once again alluded to. Jake's jealousy is a symptom of a more serious disorder.

28. Scene. Int. New York Ring.
27-28=montage with effect. 56:58-58:17

Episodes of the fight between LaMotta and Janiro makes up the final mega-sequence of this section. Juxtaposed on an overhead shot, the title: "LaMotta vs Janiro, New York, 1947."

On the hyper-realist soundtrack, the punches resonate louder and louder above the screaming audience. There are cries of a child. A proud Jake La-Motta literally massacres the opponent.

An insert of Tommy Como sneers, "He ain't pretty no more." Disfiguring Janiro is how Jake takes his revenge against his wife Vickie and the Mob. To see in this brutal episode hints of homosexuality is not an exaggeration. Jake's under the influence of his own obsession. Jake must prove his heterosexual masculinity to other males. A fixed idea: defining one's sexual identity.

Chapter 7: Joey Slaps Vickie
58:18-68:04

29. Scene. Int. Gym. Night.
28-29=0. 58:18-58:59

In a steamy gym Jake LaMotta is exercising. The assistant refuses to hand Jake a piece of ice; Jake must lose weight. On the soundtrack, operatic music. This short syntagma (also a mega-sequence) stands in opposition to the scenes that follow. What unfolds in this scene is pitted against what unfolds in the next scene. First, Jake is working out in a gym; second Vickie is out with Salvy and the boys. Is Jake's weight what pushes Vickie away? Sex is an issue, Vickie complains about it to Joey. The midpoint is next. The story takes a sharp turn.

30. Scene. Int. Copacabana. Night.
29-30=0. 59:00-60:14

At the midpoint, the second Turning Point, something major happens in this mega-sequence. Joey stands at the bar, sharing a drink with two men (one being Jackie Curite, played by Peter Savage, the co-writer of the Jake LaMotta autobiography).

Inserts of Vickie with Salvy are slipped into a rather ordinary scene. The conversation turns to the LaMotta-Janiro bout. In one such insert, Vickie reacts, "I'm not Italian, I don't care."

Distracted by Vickie's appearance, Joey bids the men farewell and walks straight up to his sister-in-law. The scene proper extends the "film stage". An upset Joey pulls Vickie aside.

31. Autonomous shot. Int. Salvy's table. Night.
60:15-60:20

This sequence shot, a cutaway, shows Joey and Vickie moving another corner of the bar. Though the Salvy and his colleagues are discussing about Vickie, the details of their conversation are muted.

32. Scene. Int. Cloakroom. Night.
31-32=0. 60:21-61:09

Joey reprimands Vickie for going out on a date with Salvy. Vickie counteracts: "I'm twenty years old… This guy don't even wanna fuck me." Vickie underplays the import of the rendezvous, Joey won't stand none of the alibis. An impetuous Vickie bickers over her husband's low sex drive. Five years have gone by since Jake and Vickie married, and already marital problems plague the couple. Boxing have deteriorated Jake's mind and body.

33. Scene. Int. Salvy's Table. Night.
32-33=0. 61:10-62:05

Defiantly, Vickie goes back to Salvy's table. Incensed, Joey orders Vickie to head on home, snarls: "You're making an asshole out of my brother, get your stuff." Salvy interjects, Joey fires off. An insert shows Vickie rushing out. The scuffle between the men is rowdy, leaving Salvy badly bruised.

34. Scene. Ext. Copacabana. Night.
33-34=0. 62:06-62:57

An insert back to the restaurant: bouncers and mobsters argue about rules of the game. ("Don't mention Tommy. You do what you do and we do what we gotta do.") The Mob might not be the Almighty. Or maybe it is: there is space for free will. Joey chooses to escape…

Synchronized, authentic, and justified sounds fade out, allowing an orchestral music to emerge. The second Plot Point of the film: Joey surprises Vickie with Salvy. Taking revenge on his brother Jake, Joey will break the rules. Salvy is hurt. The consequence of this brawl is two-fold: 1. Joey must negotiate with the Mob; 2. The scuffle will not go unnoticed by Jake, who sees in this brawl a mistaken justification for his jealousy.

35. Descriptive Syntagma. Ext./Int. Debonair Social Club. Day.
34-35=0. 62:58-63:17

Rain, the loud sound of raindrops. Establishing shots describe delineate the Debonair Social Club: writing, a certificate, coffee cups, men playing cards. In this mega-sequence Tommy Como has organized a secret meeting between Joey and Salvy. Orchestral music enhances the serene atmosphere in the café. Scorsese uses a similar syntagma at the end of the film. A common denominator links the contents of these two episodes semantically. We discuss this later.

36. Scene. Int. Table. Day.
35-36=0. 63:18-66:22

A scene full of realism, in the filming, in the acting, on the soundtrack. There is social camaraderie in the café, it may be the only moment of quietude in the entire film. Tommy Como calmly criticizes Jake for his stubbornness: "He thinks he can make it on his own." First, Tommy forces a bandaged Salvy and Joey to shake hands and reconcile their differences. "You guys have a lot of years between you." Salvy is asked to leave. Follows a most instructive dialogue between the two men. Tommy draws a remarkably accurate picture of Jake:

> The guy's an embarrassment… He comes to me, I make it easier for him… He thinks he's gonna walk in there and become champion on his own?… He's got no respect for nobody… He doesn't listen to nobody… He doesn't respect anybody… You tell him, I don't care how colorful he is, how great he is. He could beat all the Sugar Ray Robinsons and the Tony Janiros in the world. But he ain't gonna get a shot at that title, not without us, he ain't.

Here, explicitly detailed, directly, without a single moment's hesitation: the programme. The individual is nothing, the collectivity is everything. This study is not sociological, but if it were, it would have to deal with the very thorny topic about the individual's right versus the collective's rights? In this quagmire resides the essence of the ethnic versus nation knot. The laws in the U.S.A. favor the individual against the group. Nathan Glazer contends that

> the law is written so as to vindicate the rights of individuals... I believe the key principle that does in fact and should determine for a multiethnic state — including the United States — whether it elects the path of group rights or individual rights, is whether it sees the different groups as remaining permanent and distinct constituents of a federated society or whether it sees these groups as ideally integrating into, eventually assimilating into, a common society (268).

These considerations might seem to take us away from the film, however, they are expressly put forward themes Martin Scorsese slips into his discourse under the guise of organized crime. Of course, one would be amiss to utilize wise guys as both a symbol of capitalist behavior and an analogy for our political systems. *Raging Bull* is not a device for that kind of quandary. Scorsese is first and foremost an artist. Yet the autobiography of Jake LaMotta helps the filmmaker deal with his own personal complications while he is entertaining the world with the work. There is an entanglement of concerns that are being raised in this film.

A growing solitude is cutting Jake off from the community. Jake's physical and mental disorders have been brought to the fore. Scorsese explores the theme of madness more exhaustively in films like *Taxi Driver* (1976) and *Shutter Island* (2010), but at this point of his career, what concerns Scorsese seems to be what role, if any, an individual belonging to a minority group has, and what are the chances of this individual of coming out successful if he decides to move out of the minority ghetto.

37. Scene. Ext. Swimming pool. Day.
36-37=0. 66:23-68:04

In this new mega-sequence, Joey runs under the falling rain and joins his brother at the swimming pool where he first noticed Vickie. Devoured by jealousy and doubt, Jake states he is convinced Vickie is unfaithful. Joey suggests that he divorce his wife. Jake comes to the realization that he has no choice; he will have to have commerce with Tommy Como if he wishes to have a shot at the middle-weight title. This determining factor brings the chapter to a close. The plot switches lanes. If Jake has a self-made man up till, he must now sell himself.

Chapter 8: Jake Fakes It
68:05-73:32

38. Scene. Int. Gym. Day. 37-38=0.
68:05-68:18

This mega-sequence dedicated to the new Jake LaMotta has Jake and Billy Fox in a gym being weighed by the Colonel. A new fight has been announced.

39. Scene. Int. Corridor. Night.
38-39=0. 68:19-69:09

A long corridor, a handheld camera, Jake, Joey and the Colonel are talking about the fight. The voice of the Colonel links syntagma 38 to syntagma 39. The referee suspects the fight between LaMotta and Fox is fixed. Jake reassures the judge that he will not go down for anybody. The entire scene is made of two sequence shots: the first in the empty corridor with the Colonel's deep voice; the second depicts the three characters discussing in the corridor.

While the Colonel exits in one direction, Jake and Joey continue up the corridor without speaking. This image is used in various publicity ads of the film: the brothers walk in the corridor, toward the camera. These seconds are the last of happy moments the brothers share.

40. Autonomous shot. Ext. Street corner. Night.
39-40=0. 69:10-69:12

A title "LaMotta vs Fox, New York, 1947" appears on the Madison Square Garden at night. A bell sounds, and the judge's voice. The bout is about to start.

41. Episodic sequence. Int. The Fixed Fight. Night.
40-41=0. 69:13-71:23

Short scenes give the illusion of a uniform setting and temporal block. Which is far from the truth. Scorsese with Schoonmaker and Frank Warner have sown together the bits and pieces into a seamless entity. This is the first of many fixed fights, cameras' flash bulb burns into the screen. After four rounds, a bored LaMotta drops his arms; a winner is proclaimed, it is Billy Fox.

42. Scene. Int. Dressing room. Night.
41-42=0. 71:24-72:13

A realistic setting, LaMotta in his assistant's arm weeps: "What did I do?" Another assistant says: "It's a free country. Don't fight anymore."

The first mega-sequence ends with a clear message.
The price of selling out for the individual is shame.
The larger social network reacts violently.
The collective is jubilant.

The misunderstanding is at a higher level. What one surrenders has different meanings for different communities. The individual must choose his allegiance.

43. Autonomous shot. Front page of the Daily News.
42-43=0. 72:14-72:17

One headline: "Board suspends LaMotta." Underscored of LaMotta weeping carried over from the previous scene. Jake: "Tommy ain't going to forget you." A new mega-sequence begins.

44. Scene. Int. LaMotta House. Day.
43-44=montage with effect. 72:18-73:09

Jake throws the *Daily News* on the kitchen table. Joey discusses the bout, and how Jake should have taken a dive. Jake: "I ain't going down. I ain't going down for nobody... Look how they make me look. Like a bum, like a *mammalucco*." Basically, a fool, but the etymology of the word goes to the Arabic language: mamluk, meaning that one belongs to the king, is the king's property, in other words, one is a "slave". In contemporary usage, the term refers to a child in need cries out to his mommy. Branded as a misogynist strong-man, Jake LaMotta is now removing mask. He is Tommy Como's yes-man, his slave. "Slave" is a word that first appears in Medieval Latin, *sclavus*, around 1175. It was used to identify the people of the Balkan territory. After the Slavs were reduced to men and women without rights by the Germans and the Byzantines, the word's meaning expanded somewhat and began to encompass any man and woman who was not free. To live under the absolute dependency of a master, to become the property of another person, is to be a slave. Jake LaMotta is a slave.

If Jake LaMotta gave in, as he did, to the Mob he, in fact, lost his freedom. In this case, being a slave is made to seem a temporary strategy, for professional reasons, but, as we will notice, losing one's freedom is very much a permanent matter. Jake LaMotta has signed away his free will. And the responsibility of bring out the manacles falls entirely on his brother Joey. This is what the second Pinch Point, at the seventy-five minutes spot, reveals. Jake is another man; no longer Jake LaMotta, he is another person's puppet. He might play tough guy, but his actions are decided by Tommy Como.

In many respects, the kiss Tommy gives Vickie on the mouth should be viewed accordingly in this context; the master possesses privileges, one of which is the right to have sex with the slave's wife.

Tommy Como will not go as far as sleep with Vickie, but the possibility is undeniably there. The individual loses his authoritative dignity, his social pertinence, his cultural and social agency. Career ambition replaces pursuit of plenitude. The individual is assimilated into the collective. Success is collective. The contention, we must underline, is not the affiliation or dependency to the collective, but the freedom of chose to affiliate oneself or not that has been obliterated.

45. Autonomous shot. Int. Kitchen. Day.
73:10-73:32

The brothers are eating take-out food, drinking Cola. Joey ventures: "Tommy ain't gonna forget you. You're gonna get your shot, if he don't die." Why should Tommy die? Mobsters don't live forever, it is true, yet Jake is not naive enough to believe Joey's comment. How does what his brother say eliminate any wrongdoing of Jake's part? Joey is being untruthful, enigmatic. Ironically, if Tommy Como were to die, Jake would become a freeman. Tommy Como does not die, but if he were to die, another would take hold of the reins, and Jake become this other man's slave. Few slaves make it to freedom. The mega-sequence and the chapter ends on this sad note.

Chapter 9: Jake loses it
73:33-82:00

46. Autonomous shot. Ext. Detroit Ring. Day.
45-46=0. 73:33-73:35

A new mega-sequence begins. A sequence shot of the Detroit arena under the rain. A juxtaposed title: "Two years later, Detroit, June 15, 1949." On the soundtrack, the fading voices of Jake and Joey discussing Tommy's hypothetical death.

47. Autonomous shot . Int. Billboard. Day.
46-47=0. 73:36-73:44

Two inserts on a billboard: "Marcel Cerdan: Middleweight Campion. Jake LaMotta: Challenger." In the background, the hint of a song.

48. Scene. Int. Hotel room. Day.
47-48=0. 73:45-75:32

Jake LaMotta gets mentally ready to meet the French boxer Marcel Cerdan. Following Joey's suggestion, Vickie orders a cheeseburger. Jake flips. How dare she follow his brother's wishes? Slavery is contagious? Jake projects onto his wife an ailment that he himself is suffering from. Jake accuses Vickie of being a slave to Joey. In reality it is he, Jake, who has become a slave. Just as Joey is Como's slave.

Tommy Como the capo visits the LaMotta brothers at the hotel. An edgy Jake is divided in two: the real Jake and Jake's reflection in a large mirror. In truth, there is a reversal of roles at play. The reflection in the mirror is the real Jake, and the real Jake, an illusion.

Disgusted Jake spits (the second time, *vide* syntagma 23), pushes his weight on his wife, which only further alienates him from the woman he loves. Jake orders his brother around, but to no avail. What is left is Jake's vulgarity, which is omnipresent. Some critics

> like Neil Sinyard, read Raging Bull as "a militantly feminist film" in that it "presents men at their most pointlessly repulsive and destructive. The effect of the film is to aim a pulverizing blow at male values."[11]

A feminist film perhaps? Words Molly Haskell wrote in 1974, in From *Reverence to Rape*, might help us shed a little light on the Jake LaMotta's slavehood.

> It does indeed seem weird, not to say astonishing, that this privation [of sex] purveyed in fiction as the chief cause of misery among women, never seems to plague men, although if we are to believe their protestations of sexual need, legislated into double standard, they are biologically more sex-driven than women, and, it should follow, more anguished by the frustration of that need (338).

LaMotta suffers from the punches, the paranoia, the jealousy, the failure, from what Paul Schrader and Martin Scorsese called *Deadly Sperm Backup*, which might only worsen Jake's miserable condition. This DSP must also be taken metaphorically. Having lost his "soul", he fears that he will soon lose his wife. In reality, he might have already. What stands out in this scene is that Jake's freedom is totally gone. Jake tells Vickie that it is a free country, that she can order what she wants. And yet Jake knows by now that it is not a free country, that he cannot do what he likes. This dose of irony makes the scene more dramatic, more tragic. Jake is lying to himself, and preaches what is not true. There is no freedom for Jake.

49. Scene. Int. Room. Day.
48-49=0. 75:33-75:59

What appears next is an insert of Jake lying in bed. He is alone, away from the commotion in the living room. Joey and assistants discuss about the time it takes to stitch up a wound — an appropriate metaphor for a wound that might not heal — turns out to be the start of a new scene. A double-jointed shot overlaps the end of this scene and the beginning of the next. Tommy Como has come to pay his respect to LaMotta. Most to the point, Tommy Como has come to investigate that his subjects are acting according to plan.

Incidentally, Scorsese's father Charlie, is introduced officially as Tommy's friend — the first time we get a glimpse of Mr. Scorsese was at the Debonair Social Club. A moment of intimacy on the part of the director which translates as friendship and love of family, ingredients to the Italic that is badly needed in this episode about the killing of the Italic.

The director commits a gesture that stands at the opposite end of what is actually happening on screen. Collectivity is needed, but this collectivity is what disrupts Jake's freedom. The community that surrounds him is not different than the community that existed outside his post-immigrant past. This community of mobsters is equivalent to the community of the mainstream U.S.A. They want assimilation, integration, not individualism, liberty, ethnicity.

50. Scene. Int. Corridor. Day.
49-50=0. 76:00-77:01

Tommy inquires about Jake's spirit. Jake: "I gotta get in there and fight, then I'll know how I'm gonna feel." Suddenly, the film takes on the airs of a parable. Contrary to what Robin Wood suggests (that Tommy Como is a father-figure), Tommy is, in reality, Mephistopheles delivering the goods in exchange for the soul Jake had promised to hand over to him. In Christopher Marlowe's *Dr. Faustus*, Mephistopheles explains how the Prince of Hell is conjured:

> Therefore the shortest cut for conjuring
> Is stoutly to abjure the Trinity,
> And pray devoutly to the Prince of Hell.[12]

Scorsese becomes not the interpreter of this modern-day Faust but its messenger. Tommy might pronounce the word "God" ("God bless you"), but in his mouth the term holds no significance. For "there is no chief but only Belzebub".[13] Belzebub in subjective inserts, from Jake's point of view. Tommy kisses Vickie on the mouth ("Look at that face, as beautiful as ever"), and Joey, standing near by, wraps his arm across the Devil's shoulder. Jake's solitude could not be greater, he has been betrayed by the Mob, by his wife, by his brother. When scenes demand classical concentration Scorsese removes himself and delivers the goods. Robin Wood labelled the Scorsese of *Raging Bull* a "post-classical" filmmaker, that is, a representative of Classical Hollywood narrative as well as a divergence.[14]

Richard Combs considered *Raging Bull,* as the most Bressonian of Scorsese's films.[15] What is being said confirms what we believe: Scorsese refuses to break with tradition, even when dealing with subject matters only the most ascetic of filmmakers have dealt with: Bresson, Ozu, Dreyer. Scorsese, with the help of Schrader, performs the impossible, invigorates what classically has been sobriety itself.

Raging Bull is not comparable to René Clair's *La Beauté du diable* (1950), which also deals with the selling of one's soul to the Devil. Scorsese's film deals with the pact of ethnicity; Clair's with that of youth. But both works offer a sympathetic view of the devil: Michel Simon and Nicolas Colasanto are cuddly angels of darkness who can create a deadly havoc.

51. Scene. Int. Living room. Day.
50-51=0. 77:02-78:18

Viewed from Joey's point of view, his brother Jake, upset, slaps Vickie: "Don't you ever have disrespect for me." Jake warns Joey he will take care of him later. Is Jake losing his mind or simply expressing his lack of personal power? It appears that what he loses in personal power is transferred onto his professional power. This switch over becomes detrimental to the semantics involved. After the next fight, Jake will walk down the aisle of complete self-annihilation.

52. Autonomous shot. Int. Dressing room-ring. Night.
51-52=0. 78:19-79:50

This longest of sequence shots in the film begins symbolically with Jake practicing on Joey and then moves out of the dressing room and into the ring. Jake's falls hard on his brother, a foreshadowing of the real punch about to break their brotherly love. Majestic camera work takes the viewer from a middle shot to a crane shot above the screaming crowd around the ring, as though the high point of Jake's boxing career were brought about Scorsese's formal expertise. A fine example of how form and content marry one another magnificently in the hands of a master. The mega-sequence comes to an end.

53. Episodic sequence. Int. Ring. Night.
52-53=0. 79:51-82:00

In this new mega-sequence, Jake fights Marcel Cerdan for the Middle Weight Championship. Scorsese covers the bout by piecing together segments of the evening. At one point a title in juxtaposed over an overhead shot of the boxing gloves coming together at the opening of the fight: "LaMotta vs Middleweight Champion Marcel Cerdan, Detroit, 1949.' A number of fragments show Cerdan being pounced upon by LaMotta. This is the moment LaMotta has been waiting for. Bell ringing, announcement, photographers' cameras sounding like whiplashes on the soundtrack, the victor's belt. Success is his, wind instruments underscoring this moment of glory. Ends a major chapter (and a mega-sequence), Jake dancing in the hands of the Devil.

Chapter 10: Jake and Joey Quarrel
82:01-93:47

54. Scene. Int. Jake's Living room. Day.
53-54=0. 82:01-88:45

A new chapter and a new mega-sequence begin. A title is juxtaposed on Joey sitting, legs up on a coffee table: "Pelham Parkway, New York, 1950". The brothers converse in front a defective TV set (no image is seen on the set).

In full dress, Vickie comes home. Jake inquires, "Where have you been?" Joey and Vickie kiss on the mouth, then she runs up the stairs. No sound on the soundtrack.

Jake: "I don't even kiss Mom on the mouth the way you kiss her." This is the only time there is a mention of Jake and Joey's mother in the entire film.

Kissing one's mother is compared to kissing one's sister-in-law. Men must kiss women in a certain way. The kiss. The kiss of the traitor — for one; the kiss of respect — for the other. The image splits, cracks, spreads asunder.

The conversation between the brothers spins out of control. They discuss the fight between Joey and Salvy at the Copacabana. Joey is evasive, and in the discomfiture Jake asks if Salvy made love to Vickie, and finally if he, Joey, had made love as well to Vickie. Joey is taken aback, blurts: "How could you ask me a question like that?... I'm your brother... I'm not gonna answer that, it's stupid." Joey gets up, leaves. They will never speak again. Robin Wood suggests the idea that the two forms of violence presented in the film — violence against women and violence against men — need to be viewed as semantically connected. The fist, Wood advances, is a symbol for the phallus.

> Jake dowses his cock with cold water to prevent himself reaching orgasm, and in a subsequent moment marked by a close-up plunges his fist into an ice-bucket to cool it after a fight... if Jake behaves like an "animal" (violently, towards both men and women), it is because he is blocked from loving either; his insistence that Joey punch him in the face is answered by the embrace.[16]

Robin Wood spends the major part of his essay demonstrating quite interestingly the homoerotic subtext in *Raging Bull*, which one can or not agree with. As we have seen, however, in the previous films analyzed, this homoerotic element is far from being obvious, regardless of what Freud (who is quoted extensively by Wood) might have written on the subject. Though one could very well equate, as Wood does, the many images of the phallus or compare the mouth kiss between Joey and Vickie to the *in absentia* kiss Jake gives his mother, and come up with a homoerotic explanation of it all, we are not convinced that homosexuality, albeit its serious presence in the entire film, is the subtext of this film. It is a strong textual thread in this film, but something else is more important than homoeroticism is being repressed. *Raging Bull* is about the impossibility of making it on one's own. This film is also about how a brother (Joey) has to sell his brother (Jake) to the Mob in order for Jake to win the championship. And this exchange of favors mirrors the ethnic/nationalism argument that inextricably sustains a major portion of films by Italian outside Italy works. *Raging Bull* is not Little Caesar which can certainly be viewed as a homosexual film.

The episodic nature of the narrative remains too abstract and incoherent, as a psychological study of a boxer. Scorsese's film makes logical sense if read as the contract between a person in power and a person with no power. As with many men and women, emotional breakdown leads to alcoholism, suicide, and obsessive over-eating. Losing his soul, or if you prefer, having lost faith in himself is not sexual. Or if it is sexual in intent it would be more onanism than fantasy of another person. Such is the case with Edward G. Robinson's Rico.

A point of interest: in an interview with Kevin Jackson Paul Schrader reveals that he had initially included a masturbatory scene in prison — rejected by De Niro and Scorsese — a scene which would have brought us back to the "small hands" scene with Joey in Jake's kitchen (*Schrader*, 131). Jake's hands might be small, feminine, effeminate, but they are soiled with blood (the meaning of masturbation is "soiled hand"). Jake has soiled hands. Jake's hands are soiled by human liquid. Perhaps, not his own water, but that of another human. Self-love, self-destruction are not too far apart. An essential mega-sequence ends here.

55. Scene. Int. Bedroom-Washroom. Day.
54-55=0. 88:46-90:42

A new mega-sequence begins: dedicated to the abuse Vickie suffers in the hands of a lost Jake. On her knees before the bed, under a crucifix, Vickie is making the bed. Her going out has prevented her from performing household chores. This moment of independence comes with a price. Jake struts in, listens to the excuse Vickie offers for being out (she went to see a movie, Vincente Minnelli's *Father of the Bride* (1950). She refuses to speak about the incident that happened at the Copacabana. Jake slaps her across the face. Jake's interrogation continues: "Did you fuck my brother?" Vickie mutters "No."

Jake does not believe her. Under pressure, Vickie defiantly blares out that she made love with Joey and with all the mobsters. This scene leads far from the theme in Minnelli's film: a father worried about his daughter getting married. Vickie's parents are absent in *Raging Bull*, though they might not have agreed on this marriage with LaMotta which might be a big mistake for Vickie. Next is the third Plot Point. Jake has crossed over the threshold of no-return. If Jake possessed any redeeming factor, this scene cancels it for good. Jake has become a despicable madman.

56. Autonomous shot. Ext. Street. Day.
55-56=0. 90:43-90:55

One sequence shot, taken from across the street. Jake is rushing to Joey's house, Vickie is trying to stop him. A skirmish erupts behind a car.

57. Scene. Int. Joey's Kitchen. Day.
56-57=0. 90:56-91:43

On the soundtrack, jazz is heard in the background. An unrealistic scream has been juxtaposed on the realistic resounding mayhem. Joey and his family are seated at the kitchen table, having dinner. Joey reprimands his son, while the mother, silent, holds a daughter in her arms. The violence of the scene momentarily blurbs Jake entrance and rampage into the kitchen. Jake grabs Joey and brutally striking his brother who collapses. Then Jake turns around and punches Vickie in the face.

No visual adjective is added to these acts. The atrocity is barbaric. A displaced diegetic insert shows Joey's two children staring off screen at their parents, dumbfounded. No voyeurism here, except the sight of brutishness. The line between civility and inhumanity has been broken. Jake's hatred, directed at both, Joey and Vickie, the most important persons in his existence, leaves him empty. This is not repressed homosexuality, not self-punishment. The breakdown is psychological, familial, cultural, social, total. This Turning Point derails the plot as it was.

58. Scene. Int. LaMotta's Living room. Night.
57-58=0. 91:44-92:10

An explanatory insert of a blank TV screen glowing in the dark. Jake, alone in the dark, stares at it, blankly. Vickie limps into the house. The entire scene is made of two sequence shots: two lengthy takes of the TV set, and one of Jake in the foreground and Vickie climbing up to the bedroom. No word is spoken, the sound of Vickie's footsteps is heard, her shadow looming over a taciturn Jake LaMotta. Vickie has come back to leave.

59. Autonomous shot. Int. Bedroom. Night.
58-59=0. 92:11-93:47

Vickie, faced tumefied, is packing a suitcase. A wavering Jake begs her to stay. Vickie's reflection in the dresser's mirror reveals the crucifix over the couple's bed, almost like a blasphemous utterance. Jake in his unbuttoned shirt, undershirt and shorts, whispers the obvious: "I'm a bum without you and the kids. Don't go."

Vickie, powerless, let Jake embrace her. Vickie's departure is postponed but not forgotten. This entire scene in one sequence shot demonstrates once again the influence of neo-realism and *cinéma vérité* on Scorsese. The quest for realism, a respect for the actors' play, a need to capture "truth" of the moment on film, both on the diegetic and the formal level, are the directorial guidelines. Something is unleashed when film blends with live action. More than theatrics, it is the non-verbal essence of the body that blossoms between two splices. It is fiction, invention, but magic transpires in the game. This chapter and mega-sequence end on a drama note and great acting.

Chapter 11: Jake Loses His Title
93:48-101:27

60. Scene. Int. Detroit Ring. Night.
59-60=montage with effect. 93:48-94:56

A new mega-sequence begins. Jake LaMotta receives the violent punch Vickie should have given him. A juxtaposed title appears: "LaMotta vs Dauthuille, Detroit 1950." Back to the professional dimension of the protagonist. The audience appreciates the revenge punch given symbolically by Dauthuile for both Vickie and Joey. "Less than a minute to go, and LaMotta is losing the title that he won from the gallant Marcel Cerdan. After the tragic plane crash that took Cerdan's life, Laurent Dauthuile vowed to bring the title back to France." Dauthuille is taken by surprise. Jake LaMotta stuns everyone. After receiving a savage beating, Jake turns the bout around and comes out victorious ("One of the most remarkable comebacks in all boxing history").

Boxing is used in counterpoint to a defeat in Jake's private life. Joey, not by his brother's side, has reverted to voyeurism. The sort of anti-voyeurism experienced by his children. He is looking at his brother hurting on TV. Between Jake and Joey, the television set. No longer dialogue and touch, television separates and brings the brothers together, as it had done in Jake's living room.

61. Autonomous shot. Int. Arena Corridor. Night.
60-61=0. 94:57-97:00

In one sequence shot, walking out of the arena, a sympathetic and understanding Vickie offers to dial Joey's phone number. She encourages Jake to speak to his brother. Vickie: "He's your brother, you have to talk to him sooner or later."

Jake picks up the receiver, dials, but refuses to speak to Joey. The gesture, untrue, unfelt, forced, signals how final, decisive, the rupture between the brothers is. At the other end of the line Joey (in a displaced diegetic insert, a picture of a saint hangs on a wall) clamors against the silent listener he believes is Salvy. Jake listens, will not speak. One is tempted to conclude that Scorsese relies on the long sequence shot when he needs to capture a character's emotional state, and the short take he reserves for the expression professional sentiments. In the homes of these men, Catholic imagery abounds. The mega-sequence ends.

62. Alternating syntagma. Int. Ring. Night.
61-62=0. 97:01-101:27

A new mega-sequence begins. The TV transmission of Jake LaMotta's last fight (against Sugar Ray Robinson). Jake loses his championship title. Joey and his wife Leonore watch the match on TV. There is even a beer advertisement sneaked in. Water darkens like black blood on Jake's battered body. Exhausted, Jake refuses to fall. On the soundtrack strange (unjustified) noises enhance the fierceness of the spectacle. (Announcer: "No man can endure this pummelling.") Sugar Ray Robinson becomes the new World's Middleweight Boxing Champion.

As with all narrative sequences by Scorsese, nothing is clear cut and dry. This syntagma could easily have been called an ordinary scene inter-cut with displaced diegetic insert, yet when this portion of the story unfolds the action is presented more like a ping-pong match than an ordinary scene; from one location to another, from Joey and his wife in the comfort of their living room home to the pit of spectators getting splattered with Jake's blood. Vickie drops her face into the palms of her hands, refuses to look at the viciousness in the ring. Scorsese postpones his spectacle. Why else would he focus so much time on Robinson fixing LaMotta before he actually hits the opponent? Why show LaMotta dragging his feet up to Robinson, proudly muttering to his opponent that he was not knocked down?

Ruthlessness is in the suspense, not the strike. This final episode of Jake LaMotta's career as a boxer ends fiercely. Having sold his soul, Jake finds himself alone, with no one to succor him in his journey into Hell. His passion and love for Vickie is long gone. Lourdeaux is right in writing that Jake LaMotta "lands in a Florida jail where he beats his head against a wall", because he is "an Italian American furious about his willful pride and futile, isolating pursuit of mainstream success" (252). Casillo does not agree with Lourdeaux's position. In the former's eyes "Jake's abjection, whose career was devoted to obsessive-compulsive mimetic rivalry, is a masochistic syndrome of ascetic life-denial. He gradually rejects love, sex, and pleasure through an increasing preoccupation with his rivals" (246). Little wonder this obsession for otherness is mistaken for homoeroticism.

As we have seen, homoeroticism appears in *Bread and Chocolate* as a retreat when the community closes in on itself, or, on the contrary, when the only road left out *of sameness and madness is the love of a foreigner*. *Raging Bull*'s homosexuality, if existent, acts as a reminder of these two outcomes (closing in and sameness), but it is ridiculed because it is not being a serious choice. It is with other filmmakers *(A Pass in the Ass, The Cage of Madwomen (La cage aux folles),* and *Mambo Italiano)*, but it is not a choice for Jake. Schrader will visit homosexuality in *Auto Focus* (2002) about *Hogan's Heroes* star Bob Crane.

In *American Gigolo* (1980), the pimp Leon (Bill Duke) explains to Julian (Richard Gere) why he betrayed him. "It is because the other side will always have more money to offer" (a paraphrase). Jake LaMotta could never have expected to win against Sugar Ray Robinson who was protected by the Mob (at least so much is implied by *Raging Bull*). Tommy Como's deal was explicit: "Sign and you will have a chance at the championship." Jake had his chance and win; it is time to move on. Tommy Como has come to collect his share of the deal: LaMotta's soul. James Stuart Olson believes that

> There is a relationship between ethnicity and crime in American life, since crime was one route out of the slums... Struggling to make a living in Little Italy, some Italian immigrants turned to crime, but it was more difficult in the United States than in Sicily... Still, some Italians displaced the Irish and used gambling, narcotics, liquor, and prostitution as avenues to success... When crime did exist in Italian America, it was family oriented, decentralized, and involved only a tiny segment of the population (221).

What James Stuart Olson is suggesting is that crime might be a way out of the closed-in group. Is Jake LaMotta a criminal? Jake LaMotta violates every possible entente and rules of conduct. His defiant behavior turns him into an "animal", a "bum", a nobody. Jake is aware of his boorishness, his asking to be forgiven is a signal of his awareness; however, he is limited, and can appreciate the limits of the people around him and the wise guys. Jake at the pool, upon seeing Vickie for the first time, speaks of Salvy: "Big shot... Get him alone in the back room, smack him around, no more big shot...without his gun... real tough guys." Crime is the initiation test to entering a group. Everyone plays at being a boss, and yet everyone answers to someone else. The binding is almost fraternal, and deathly. Do the wise guys in *Raging Bull* frequent the same bars as the wise guys in portrayed *Donnie Brasco*? In *Donnie*

Brasco bodies are cut up; in *Raging Bull* men only talk about duty, but no one seems to be cutting up a traitor's corpse. Signing a "deal", via Joey, with Tommy (who liked Vickie) transforms Jake into a mobster who is now part of a family of friendly thugs. Jake is lost in their midst. Because he is lost (without a soul, to expound on the Faustian analogy), he roams about like a soul in search of a body, or, better still, to continue the analogy, it is the other way round: Jake is an empty body in search of his lost soul.

The body he owns does not suffice. He must alter himself, disfigure himself in order to win his way up to a level of spiritual decency. This spiritualness is not religious; it is more cultural than social. Unfortunately, seeking refuge in the sanctuary of cultural identity entraps Jake even more. Cultural allegiance is tenebrous. Its parameters are obscure, vague, open. Jake has no choice, he most leave New York. Olson writes that

> [o]lder Americans did not welcome the Italians. Calling them "black dagos" and "wops", many Americans considered them ignorant, inferior, and superstitious, lacking ambition and social taste. The size of the Italian immigration alarmed them, as did Italian Catholicism and concentration in urban ghettos. Italian immigrants often became scapegoats for the problems of crime, slums, and poverty (220).

Life in New York comes to an end with this chapter and mega-sequence. When we next see Jake, he is a different man living in Florida. Under the fifth president of the U.S.A., James Monroe, Spain ceded Florida to the United States in 1819 in exchange for the deletion of a $5 million debt. According to U.S. census figures, there were approximately 787,657 Italians (6.1% of the population) in 1990, and 1,003,977 Italians (6.3%) in 2000, which means that, by the late 1950s, Italians must have been a fairly large community. If one considers the negative effects the National Origin Act of 1924 had on Italian and immigration in general, we should not be surprised to find a cultural blackout omnipresent among Italians in the U.S.A. In the 1920s, there were 455,315 Italian emigrants to reach U.S. soil. After the Act their number is reduced to 68,028.

Even though, as James Stuart Olson rightly claims, Italians emigrated not so much to abandon traditional ways as to preserve them" (218), preservation depends, as displayed in *Queen of Hearts*, on vital replenishment for culture to flourish. Italians being cut off from a fresh supply of Italian culture from Italy faced tough times. They had to count on memory, and memory is a muscle that needs training. And there was not much of remembering happening in the U.S.A. after the 1930s. One can only image the state of Italian culture in 1950s. Moving south for Jake LaMotta is not always paradisiacal, well-known and famous as he is. Jake lacks social skills, which does not make him a likeable person. Reduced to being pretty much a man without friends, he relies on no one else but himself. He admits having no friends.

Chapter 12: Jake and Underage women
101:28-116:53

63. Scene. Ext. LaMotta residence in Florida. Day.
62-63=0. 101:28-102:44

A new chapter and a new mega-sequence begin with a superimposed title on two parked Cadillacs in a driveway: "Miami, 1956". (Incidentally, on the close-up of the license plates one reads 1954, and not 1956!) An overweight Jake LaMotta sits by the pool, surrounded by Vickie and the children, He smokes a cigar and answers a journalist's question. Jake: "Boxing is over for me." When the journalist probes Vickie on Jake's retirement, Jake remains quiet. He then politely asks Vickie if she has finished talking before he interjects. A change has come about in Jake. In New York, he would have spat out a blasphemous curse and ordered Vickie to shut up. (In the kitchen, while he discusses Janiro: "Since when are you an authority?").

In Miami, Jake seems cocksure, but dispassionate. Decent social manners have pacified him. Jake kindly tells Bob the photographer to take a shot of his family. The atmosphere is calm, people whisper when speaking, there is dialogue. The dark imagery of the Northern state scenes has been substituted by the lushness of the Southern state's bright light. Violin music accompanies this peaceful setting. The only element that stands out in the entire scene is the stylized, broken-up, mosaic-like photographing of the family. Instead of the simple one shot, one noise, one image scene photograph, Scorsese break up the action into a mosaic painting, as if to remind the viewer that what is shown is not as plain and as easy to understand as it all seems. Beneath the sheen, there is a tortuous maze. At the end of the interview, Jake discloses that he has opened a night club on Collins Avenue named Jake LaMotta's. A drum roll fades in that pulls in the next syntagma and a new mega-sequence.

64. Autonomous shot. Ext. Street. Night.
63-64=0. 102:45-102:51

The joyous jazz piece begun in the preceding sequence rises from inside the bar and over this establishing sequence shot of the bar, Jake LaMotta's. Here begins the new mega-sequence very much in the shape of an episodic sequence.

65. Autonomous shot. Int. Night Club. Night.
64-65=0. 102:52-102:21

Sitting at the bar in a whitish jacket, Jake holds a microphone which he passes over the young woman's body next to him. Over the feedback, Jake says, "Just wanted to see what the microphone on a sexy girl sounds like." The sound of a sexy girl, he will hear again, hours later, it will lead directly to prison. A sequence shot whose purpose is to introduce the viewer to LaMotta's new career, and his little vice: women.

From 1941 to 1956, fifteen years have elapsed. From boxer to stand-up comic, this is Jake LaMotta the bar owner. His body has expanded. In more sense than one. His single profession is to perform in front of people, first as a boxer, then as a comedian. "That's entertainment" were the words he pronounced in his dressing-room at the beginning of the film. The job might have changed, but the essence of the jobs remains basically unchanged.

Raging Bull could have been titled *The Entertainer*. The "stage" is a theme Scorsese developed in more detail in *New York, New York* (1977), *The Last Waltz* (1978), and *The King of Comedy* (1983).

66. Scene. Int. Stage. Night.
65-66=0. 103.:22-106:04

Jake on stage at the Jake LaMotta's. He brings a toast to the "losers" in the bar. Jake calls his patrons "losers" — a hard-boiled attitude for a speaker whose livelihood depends on listeners. "Salute" — the second time this Italian word is pronounced in the film. The first time was with Vickie when he invited her to his parents' apartment. The Italian language is rarely spoken by Italian Americans. Italian in this film is spoken only in the presence of liquid: water or alcohol. It is an act of sharing. The liquid and the language. Water, alcohol, the Italian language have a common denominator: it is the act of communion.

Now if communion is a parameter for this moment than it is logical we push the equivalence to the other portion of the equation. There is Jake, there is the sharing, and there is Vickie, on the one hand, and the "losers", on the other hand. Semantically, both Vickie and the "losers" stand on equal footing.

Casillo interprets this imagery of the fluid as purity and life-giving. If so, then this sharing is sincere, then the invitation made here is honest. A door is opened. LaMotta might speak English with Italians, but he remarkably speaks Italian with non-Italians only. The sharing is a call for circulation and association. No wonder Jake announces publicly that he and Vickie are celebrating their eleventh year of matrimony. He then recites the poem, "That's Entertainment", the viewer was introduced to in an earlier scene. Everything is entertainment for Jake. Yet beneath this bantering and chaffing, the stage is a serious call for comradeship.

67. Scene. Int. Guests' table. Night.
66-67=0. 106:05-107:21

Jake makes his way to the bar, and stops to greet State's Attorney Bronson and his wife. In trying to kiss the Attorney's wife, he accidentally spills alcohol on her. Connection is not easy for Jake.

68. Scene. Int. Night Club. Night.
67-68=0. 107:22-108:11

One of the waitresses refuses to serve alcohol to a young girl who claims to be twenty-one years old. Instead of asking for ID papers, Jake kisses the girl and her friend, the kiss being taken as proof of their age. In the background, Louis Prima's "Just a Gigolo". Jake's misogyny asserts itself in cheap womanizing. The truth is that we don't see much of Jake's sexual life. These episodes represent a day in the life of Jake LaMotta, but the puzzle is never complete, pieces are missing. These separate fragments belong to a larger episodic mega-syntagma; the entire film has the shape of one giant mega-episodic syntagma. Scenes 68, 69, 70, 71 contain the last Pinch Point of the film: Jake is arrested for serving alcohol to underage girls, and Vickie asks for a divorce.

69. Scene. Int. Night Club. Night.
68-69=0. 108:12-109:11

Jake performs a trick as he pours champagne in glasses stacked one upon another. On the soundtrack a R & B song, the lyrics of which are about a woman begging her man to come home. This "marvellously evocative image" (63), to quote Robin Wood, who suggests that the champagne-glass structure is a representation of Jake's penis that he pull out for the gaze of admiring women and men. Whether such is the intent of the structure is debatable. Accepting this imagist loquaciousness changes nothing to the plot.

Vickie is sitting in a car, waiting for her husband. While Jake is carousing, Vickie prepares to abandon him. There can no be doubt about Jake's drinking habit; when he was a boxer, he drank mostly cola. In Miami, his hold a drink in most of the shots. Is Jake a womanizer? Jake is playful with women (the microphone on the woman); he kisses two young girls. Do these events make him a womanizer? A more appropriate reading is Jake as an alcoholic loner. When the police arrest him, Jake is sleeping on a tiny cot, alone.

70. Scene. Ext. Parking lot. Day.
69-70=0. 109:12-110:24

Jake walks up to Vickie in a car. She asks him for a divorce, and wants the custody of the children. The mega-sequence dedicated to LaMotta the bar owner ends here on a sour note. Jake's solitude is total.

71. Scene. Int. Room. Day.
70-71=0. 110:25-112:01

A new mega-sequence begins with a new day. LaMotta is awakened by the D.A who produces pictures (shown as explanatory inserts) of the underage girl of the night before. The girl has accused LaMotta of introducing her to men. Jake says he would introduce the D.A. to men. It would be ridiculous to find a homoerotic reading of this line. The mega-sequence ends here.

72. Scene. Int. Vickie's home. Day.
71-72=0. 112:02-112:59

In the following mega-sequence Jake is looking for $10,000 bail money. Jake asks Vickie the permission to come and pick up his Championship belt.

Vickie: "Can't you get the money from your friends?"

Jake: "What friends?"

Friendless, Jake hammers the stones out of his Middleweight championship belt.

73. Scene. Int. Pawnshop. Day.
72-73=0. 113:00-113:32

The man behind the counter wants the belt. "The belt of a champion is a very rare item." Fame is meaningless outside its context. A belt has no value outside the ring. Jake has no value outside his environment. The Italic exists only if one wills it. Jake must will his excellence.

74. Autonomous shot. Ext. Phone booth. Day.
73-74=0. 113:33-113:51

Out the Mission Jewelry Store, Jake is in the phone booth. Without the bail money, Jake is heading for prison. The mega-sequence comes to an end.

75. Scene. Int. Prison. Day.
74-75=0. 113:52-116.53

This mega-sequence is about the prison. Jake struggles against two jail guards who try to push him into his cell. A title: "Dade County Stockade, Florida, 1957." After much swearing, breathing heavily, Jake sits on the cot in a dark cell. He bangs his head and fists against the wall. Light drops like grace from a window. A short maieutic monologue ensues: "Dummy, dummy, dummy. Why? Why? Why? You motherfucker! My hands! Why'd you do it? Why? You're so stupid.... They called me an animal. I'm not an animal. Why do they treat me like this? I'm not that bad. I'm not that bad. I'm not that guy." Lee Lourdeaux's reading of this penitential scene is accurate. LaMotta has much to repent.

> LaMotta's basic reason for betraying all sense of Italian family is his pursuit of success. Even more stubborn and proud an individualist than Charlie in *Mean Streets,* LaMotta wants the boxing title without having to feel he owes anyone. In the end, he lands in a Florida jail where he beats his head against a wall, an Italian American furious about his willful pride and futile, isolating pursuit of mainstream success (252).

If Jake was permitted to win a championship, he owes it, first, to his brother Joey, who intervened in favor of Jake with the Mob; second, to the Mob (via Salvy and Tommy Como); and third, to his wife Vickie, for knowing Salvy. Jake LaMotta is guilty of forgetting the deal he signed with Tommy Como. Robert Casillo could not have been more correct in suggesting that Jake repudiates "his former, violent self, as if he were a *doppelgänger* casting out its bad" (256). Some deeper power intrudes in this symbol-engendering machinery. It is the filmmaker Martin Scorsese who intervenes and lifts the experience at a higher level.

> If I said yes to Bobby, it was because unconsciously I found myself in Jake. I sensed that this character was a carrier of hope. It was for this hope that I made the film... The man facing the wall in the cell, that's me... What, at this moment, gives grace? That is the mystery. Something that allows him to say, "I am not that man." [17]

Scorsese and De Niro are partly responsible for this grace falling on Jake LaMotta who becomes the messenger of hope. By sandwiching the story proper in between the two scenes of Jake LaMotta in his dressing room, the narrative changes into a self-reflective *récit*. Jake LaMotta is an archetype to which a lesson has been attached. He is a messenger who returns from a journey in the underworld. He has a story to tell and the autobiographical tone of this story calls for a second reading. In *Transcendental Style,* Paul Schrader speaks of how grace is

> nonuniversal; it is a special gift and not everyone can receive it... If one accepts transcendental style, then all is grace, because it is grace which allows the protagonist and the viewer to be both captive and free... Consequently, the awareness of the Transcendental can only come after some degree of self-mortification, whether it be a foregoing of the "sins of the flesh" or death itself. Prison is the dominant metaphor... it is a two-faced metaphor: ... characters are both escaping from a prison of one sort and surrendering to prison of another (*Transcendental,* 92-93).

One can find grace in death; another, in a person or an object. Jake LaMotta finds grace in prison, in his own destruction. The man he longer is, the man who sold his soul to the Mob, to success, ends up in a prison cell. LaMotta is guilty for his rudeness, for his philandering, for desiring underage girls, for his violence, for his jealousy. He who stands at the margins of society, he who stands on the circumference, must learn the meaning of his situation. The discourse is two-fold: one is Faustian deal; and the other, redemption. He must understand what the selling of his soul entails, and he must learn to live with the decision that he is a man without a soul. Both paths converge into self-knowledge gained.

In prison, Jake is struck by light. The silence is broken by the sound of his own voice. He stands on stage, telling a joke about an unfaithful wife who is caught on the act by her husband. She says: "Look who's here — big mouth. Now the whole neighborhood will know." Vickie was never unfaithful. Why introduce this joke at all? Infidelity leads to entertainment. Entertainment is the outpouring of the private domain onto the public sphere. The role of the artist is to tell the world what he finds out alone. He is not a soothsayer. He does not foretell the future, but the present. Such is the role is given to Jake LaMotta. This mega-sequence and chapter end with an archetype: Jake as the messenger.

Chapter 13: Jake LaMotta as Terry Malloy
116:54-124:34

76. Scene. Int. Bar. Night.
75-76=0. 116:54-118:19

A new chapter and a new mega-sequence begin with Jake LaMotta on a different stage. The joke in the previous scene ends here. Juxtaposed title on Jake — "New York City, 1958". Jack is back in New York, in a small bar (he calls a "toilet"). His white jacket has been replaced by a dark jacket. The audience is unreceptive. LaMotta no longer attracts the large audience he did a year ago. If the artist tears the contract, he becomes a nobody. Jake the messenger is has-been, trying to make ends meet. The audience insult LaMotta. The threat of the boxer's comeback does not suffice to push away the onslaught of pettiness. Jake introduces Emma and applauds with the audience. The artist has the freedom of speech, but there is no one out there to listen to the speech.

77. Sequence. Ext. Street. Night.
76-77=0. 118:20-120:55

Jake notices his brother on the other side of the street. Jake politely directs Emma into the taxi; his roughness has been replaced by gentleness. A subjective insert shows Joey walking in slow motion. Joey comes out of the convenience store, Jake calls out but Joey who ignores his brother's plea. As Joey is about to step into his car, Jake begs for a truce. The call for a truce was heard in the kitchen, when he asked his first wife Irma for a truce after their violent spat. Jake speaks: "You gonna forgive and forget? It's a long time ago, forget about it. Just give me a kiss, come on. You're my brother. Come on." Joey softens up and let's his brother embrace him.

Jake: "Everything's all right? Family?"
Joey: "Yeah... You don't wanna do this here, come on. Let me call you. We'll get together in a couple of days."
Jake: "You'll call me?"
Joey: "I will."
Jake: "Don't forget."

More than "ironic inversion" of the kiss as the "construction of the heterosexual couple", to quote Robin Wood (65), this scene is about mending a broken family unit. An older brother wraps his bear-like arms around the younger brother wanting to keep a distance. Joey knows the punishment Jake can deliver, and he wants to avoid any further contact. Joey gives in. Joe Pesci explains how the scene had originally been planned. Jake would have said to Joey, " 'Go ahead, Joey. Hit me. I deserve it. Hit me. I deserve it.' Luckily, it did not end up that way during the filming... I had no reason to be mad at him except like "Come on, I don't want to do this'." [18]

"I don't want to do this" are the only words spoken by Joey, and they carry no sexual intent. A familial coming-together should be performed in front of the family. (Joey sarcastically insinuates this at the beginning of their meeting. Jake wants a kiss from his brother, but Joey refuses: "Wait, let me call my wife and kids. Don't you want them to see the kiss?")

Family reconciliation follows a strict logical pattern; the break up having occurred in front of his wife and children, it stands to reason that the concord should be done in the family. It is not a private but a communal agreement. Jake finds grace in his younger brother Joey when he least expected. The mega-sequence that began with Jake ends with Jake in the arms of his brother Joey.

78. Descriptive syntagma. Ext. Hotel. Night.
77-78=0. 120:56-121:20

A new mega-sequence closes the film. Here a sequence shot establishes the setting of the final scene. "Barbizon-Plaza" and another tilt over a signage announcing the event: "An Evening with Jake LaMotta, featuring the works of Paddy Chayefsky, Rod Serling, Shakespeare, Budd Schulber, Tennessee Williams." No Italian authors are quoted.

Jake LaMotta is the Italian representative figure. Jake LaMotta has climbed out of his hell; he is the messenger about to deliver his report to his audience. As a full-fledged Italian American, he interprets the world from his viewpoint.

This syntagma contains establishing shots of the dressing-room; it resembles the descriptive syntagma used in the Debonair Social Club, for the meeting with Joey, Salvy, and Tommy Como. The use of the same syntax should bring about a similar connotation.

In the first scene Joey betrays Jake by handing him over to Tommy Como (the Mob); in this one Jake recite the taxi speech spoken by Terry Malloy in Elia Kazan's *On the Waterfront* (1954). By placing the two incidents, in *Raging Bull*, one beside the other, we extract a common theme: the theme of brotherly love betrayed.

Just as Charlie (Rod Steiger) in the Kazan film betrays Terry Malloy

(Marlon Brando) by forcing him to take a fall, so too Joey betrays Jake by handing him over to the Mob, and thus forcing Jake to take a fall. The betrayal brings success to the brother who betrays. Joey is akin to Charlie; and Jake to Terry.

79. Autonomous shot. Int. Dressing Room. Night.
78-79=0. 121:21-123:46

In the artist's dressing room, cigar in his hand, sitting in front of a mirror, Jake LaMotta recites the "I could have been a contender" monologue, based on the Terry Malloy's (played by Marlon Brando) monologue in *On the Waterfront*. The entire scene is shot in one take. The soundtrack is synchronized, authentic and justified. There are no effects, there is no stylization. Jake delivers his final monologue to himself, to his double in the mirror, to the spectators.

> It wasn't him, Charley, it was you. You remember that night at the garden, you came to my dressing room and said, "Kid, this ain't your night. We're going for the price on Wilson." Remember that? "This ain't your night." "My night?" I could have taken Wilson apart that night. So what happens? He gets a title shot outdoors in the ballpark, and what do I get? A one-way ticket to Palookaville. I was never no good after that night, Charley. It was like a peak you reach, and then it's downhill. It was you, Charley. You was my brother. You should've looked out for me a little bit. You should have taken care of me just a little bit. Instead of making me take them dives for the short-end money. You don't understand — I could've had class. I could've been a contender. I could've been somebody, instead of a bum, which is what I am. Let's face it. It was you, Charley.

Jake speaks these lines to himself and to his reflection in the mirror. He is warming up before going on stage. He might be famous now, he might attract more people than he did in Miami or in New York as a stand-up comic. We are not privy to this detail. What is revealed in what we see and hear in this scene. What is beyond the screen is in abstentia. What is beyond the screen is the spectators in the theater. Jake enunciates the words authoritatively. He is talking to his doppelgänger. He is talking to us. There are no differences. The three entities (himself, his double, the spectators) for a single unit. The monologue is a dialogue is a conference.

Jake LaMotta has won the bout. No longer a loser, Jake is able to express himself, as an individual, as a companion, and as a messenger. Without violence straining his voice, Jake discloses his emotional and intellectual state. Not only has Jake mastered the tools of self-expression, he can saunter beyond the literal meaning of words, and use metaphors and the poetic dimensions of language. He explains the reasons why he punched Joey that day, many years ago, in front of his wife and his children. In his madness, for what else could it be, he let his obsessions (work, wives, success) blind him. He once believed that it was jealousy alone pushed him over the limit — he accused Joey of having had an affair with Vickie — but tonight he has a revelation. Having won the championship is equivalent to going to Palookaville.

The championship does not amount to much, except for the entertainment value the physical pain of the boxer can procure for the audience. Tonight he understands what he could not understand. Contrary to what he expected, Jake cut himself off from his brother Joey because he won the championship. His brother Joey willingly sold Jake's soul to the Mob, an ersatz of personal, cultural, and social success. All that led Jake nowhere. By a twist of faith, this new realization Jake wants to share with the world.

Jake does not need to excuse himself to his brother, but it is Joey who needs to excuse himself to Jake. Yet Jake must ask for forgiveness. By asking for forgiveness, he acquires the power to tell the truth about what happened that day in front of the broken TV in his living room. Winning, losing his soul, losing his wife to his brother, Salvy, Tommy Como – Jake understands that true victory is about never giving in. This illumination, this grace, this transcendental moment,

> this stasis… the quiescent, frozen, or hieratic scene which succeeds the decisive action and closes the film. It is a still re-view of the external world intended to suggest the oneness of all things… This static view represents the "new" world in which the spiritual and the physical can coexist, still in tension and unresolved, but as part of a larger scheme in which all phenomena are more or less expressive of a larger reality — the Transcendent (82-83)

this manifesto, what other name to call this perception, allows LaMotta to get up, cigar in his mouth, tap himself on the shoulder, and say, "Go get them, champ." When Scorsese as assistant comes into the dressing room and asks LaMotta if he needs anything, Jake replies that he needs nothing. At that moment, the film topples into a metalinguistic mode, a meta-filmic mode, whereby the shadow-boxing in front of the mirror becomes a major stepping out of the closest, not as homosexual — which would have been perfectly laudable, if samesex love was the essential outcome of self-worth, but it is not the case with Jake LaMotta — Jake comes out of ethnic repression and artistic ethnic suppression, and affirms his right to total expression of cultural and social self.

When Jake finally mutters, "I'm the boss, I'm the boss," he is assuming full responsibility of his future existence as a self-made ethnic. With his monologue, Jake LaMotta pays back in kind an upset Mephistopheles and rightfully reclaims his soul.

> Mephistopheles: "A soul pledged mine, by written scroll it gave,
> This have they robbed from me, adroitly snatched.
> To whom then shall I carry my complaint?" (Goethe, 278)

In *The Last Waltz,* Martin Scorsese asks Robbie Robertson, why he is putting an end to The Band. Robertson replies succinctly that, if he did not, he would surely die. To escape death, one must pull out of the game. Jake LaMotta had to stop fighting if he wanted to receive grace. The final mega-sequence and the final chapter end here. Follows an Epilogue.

> 80. Scene. Epilogue: Biblical text.
> 79-80=fade. 123:47-124:34

On a black screen, the following Biblical text fades in, one or two lines at time, each new line brighter than the previous, and then turn a shade darker.

> So, for the second time [the Pharisees] summoned the man who had been blind and said: "Speak the truth before God. We know this fellow is a sinner." "Whether or not he is a sinner, I do not know," the man replied. "All I know is this: once I was blind and now I can see."
> John IX, 24-26, *The New English Bible.*

> Remembering Haig R. Manoogian, teacher.
> May 23, 1916-May 26, 1980.
> With love and resolution, Marty.

The film is dedicated to Haig Manoogian "with love and resolution" who died before Scorsese finished the film. Manoogian had been Scorsese's film professor at New York University and the producer of Scorsese's first short film, *What's a Nice Girl Like You Doing in a Place Like This?* (1963), and his first feature, *Who's That Knocking at My Door? (*1969). After the failure of Scorsese's film, Haig Manoogian told Scorsese "that it would be advisable commercially not to make any more films about Italian Americans" (Casillo 61). These meaningful last words on the screen, according to Casillo, have baffled many reviewers, critics, and filmmakers; but they sustain our interpretation of the film as a cultural political statement.

After *Raging Bull*, Scorsese directed a number of films that carried an Italian-American content, each of these works bearing the stamp of metalinguistic/meta-filmic irony, almost with Bretchian/Godarian detachment. He also directed other films without an Italian-American content. These films still carry the imprint of an ethnic filmmaker. Precisely because he is an ethnic filmmaker, he can tap into other sources of inspiration, bringing to them his visions. *Raging Bull* does not indulge in playfulness. When he made the film, it seems Scorsese needed an autobiographical project that would permit him to flaunt his prowess of style. Producer Cid Corman asked him, "Why would you want to do a movie about this?"[19]

Regardless of the negative remarks written against this religious epilogue, one finds there Scorsese answer to Corman's question. As Martin Scorsese has repeated time and time again *Raging Bull* tells the story of a man who has everything, and then loses everything. Jake LaMotta loses his brother, his wives, Irma and Vickie, his children, his Cadillacs, his night club, his money, his dignity. When a disgruntled New York patron insults Jake for being a "funny man" (a clown), Jake smiles confidently, and replies: "That's why I'm here." The answer suggests a newfound maturity in Jake. This is August clown turned white clown.

In the Gospel according to John, the entire chapter 9, from which the quote of the Epilogue is extracted, revolves around the concept of blindness and evil. Jesus spits on the ground and turns the spittle into clay. He then takes the clay spreads on the blind man's eyes. Jesus tells the man to go and wash himself in the pool of Siloe. Siloe, according to interpreters of the Bible, represents Jesus.

Jesus says, "If a man believes in me, as the scripture says, fountains of living water shall flow from his bosom." The blind man washes himself and finds sight. Jesus reassures his disciples that "Neither he nor his parents were guilty, but that it was so that God's action might declare itself in him."

God's action should then be interpreted a manifestation of Schrader's concept of grace. Jake LaMotta, too, has washed himself with water soiled with blood before regaining his vision (the Dauthuille fight). He had to lose his dignity, before he could understand the world before him. He had to use spit (LaMotta spits a couple of times in the film) and mix it with clay (in the prison soil) before he could reclaim true victory. Jake LaMotta is a transformed man when he recites the final monologue.

Martin Scorsese changed our definition of the Italian outside Italy. In films such as *The Gangs of New York* and *Shutter Island*, Scorsese is able to transcend similar problematic of the individual in order to incorporate them at the collective level. Michel Cieutat believes that

> [through] Jake, an Italian-American of the second generation who experienced not only the integration into the U.S. system, while respecting the "via vecchia", but also the success and glory dear to the Calvinists, and who then lost everything in part through his fault, but especially those of the forces of evil, of which the Scorsesian and Dostoevskian man is metaphysically impregnated, through Jake Martin Scorsese understood that this story of a "man facing a wall" was his own (168).

Once the film finished, Martin Scorsese said, "That's it. Basically, this is the end of my career, this is it, this is the final one."[20] Luckily, that was not the case. Raging Bull, considered by many as one of the top ten films of all time, was the first in a string of films produced in the U.S.A. about Italian Americans. The protagonists of this Italian-American presence are many, and they do not always unite in a single political front. Difference of opinion and vision is be expected when dealing with individuals in deterritorialized collectivities.

Their names are Gregory La Cava, Frank Capra, Jimmy Durante, George Raft, Frank Sinatra, Victor Mature, Richard Conte, Vincente Minnelli, Ernest Borgnine, Sal Mineo, Anne Bancroft, Dean Martin, Ben Gazzara, Anthony Franciosa, Alan Alda, Francis Ford Coppola, Brian De Palma, Michael Cimino, Al Pacino, Robert De Niro, John Travolta, Liza Minnelli, Abel Ferrara, Sylvester Stallone, Madonna, Joe Mantegna, Danny De Vito, Joe Pesci, Danny Aiello, Nick Mancuso, John Turturro, Quentin Tarantino, Stanley Tucci, Annabella Sciora, Marisa Tomei, Leonardo DiCaprio. Their artistry has modified the meaning of the word Italian. Martin Scorsese elevates this tradition with craftsmanship and humanism, he has become a beacon for future generations of ethnic artists.

The structure

In 1980 filmmakers freed themselves of the stronghold of European cinema had on world cinema. With *American Gigolo,* Paul Schrader, whose contribution to the *Raging Bull* script is judicious, takes giant steps as a filmmaker by adapting the Bresson touch for American audiences. Nicholas Roeg, William Friedkin, Brian de Palma, David Lynch, Michael Cimino explore new contents and extend the golden rule of genres. John Cassavetes, François Truffaut, and Alain Renais assert their greatness. Reviewing some of the films released in 1980, one can see why a director like Martin Scorsese would feel unsure of himself. The wager he gave himself was serious, and fortunately he came out of the experience a better artist.

American Gigolo, by Paul Schrader
Bad Timing, by Nicholas Roeg
Cruising, by William Friedkin
Dressed to Kill, by Brian de Palma
The Elephant Man, by David Lynch
Fantastica, by Gilles Carle
Gloria, by John Cassavetes
Heaven's Gate, by Michael Cimino
La Cage aux Folles II, by Édouard Molinaro
Le dernier métro, by François Truffaut
Mon oncle d'Amérique, by Alain Renais

Raging Bull is divided into thirteen large narrative chapters. Much has been said about improvisation in the film, yet all of these bit and pieces of celluloid glued together make up a story that is far from being improvised. Certainly, Paul Schrader's introduction of Joey LaMotta provided a dimension to the boxer LaMotta's biography that worked in favor of Scorsese's need for character redemption, revelation, and resolution.[21]

Chapter 1 Jake and Joey LaMotta 0:00-17:15
Chapter 2 Vickie 17:16-31:19
Chapter 3 Jake, Vickie, and Sugar Ray 31:20-41:13
Chapter 4 Jake Marries Vickie 41:14-43:48
Chapter 5 First Signs of Jake Losing It 43:49-49:25
Chapter 6 Jake's Jealousy 49:26-58:17
Chapter 7 Joey Slaps Vickie 58:18-68:04
Chapter 8 Jake Fakes It 68:05-73:32
Chapter 9 Jake loses it 73:33-82:00
Chapter 10: Jake and Joey Quarrel: 82:01-93:47
Chapter 11: Jake Loses His Title: 93:48-101:27
Chapter 12: Jake and Underage women: 101:28-116:53
Chapter 13: Jake LaMotta as Terry Malloy 116:54-12-124:34

These thirteen chapters are divided into scenes (46), autonomous shots (19), episodic syntagmas (8), ordinary sequences (4), descriptive syntagmas (2), and alternating syntagma (1). Formally, Scorsese privileges the scene to any other syntagma; this is followed by a large number of autonomous shots (comprised mostly of sequence shots). This sort of syntax indicates the emphasis Scorsese puts on achieving the "realistic" effect. Whenever possible, the director and editor choose the semblance of realism over formal acrobatics. What does stand out is the appearance of syntagmas made up of fragments spliced together. The episodic syntagma is privileged as well: disparate scenettes edited in a sequence that give the illusion of time passing. The essential is favored, and the superfluous discarded.

Scorsese and Schoonmaker present a narrative block they have spliced into snippets of chronological actions which ultimately lead to symbolic parallelism. The same technique, also applicable to the sequence, the descriptive syntagma and the alternating syntagma, is used to enhance the momentum of the story. Inevitably, as we have pointed out, by using, for instance, the descriptive syntagma twice establishes a symbolically bond. Two descriptive syntagma introduce the topic of betrayal in Debonair Social Club and the Barbizon-Plaza scenes. The same hardware is put together to allow for the smooth running of a symbolic action. In both scenes, Joey plays a primordial role: it is Joey who by dealing with Tommy makes it possible for Jake to get to the championship bout. Jake alludes to this betrayal in his monologue.

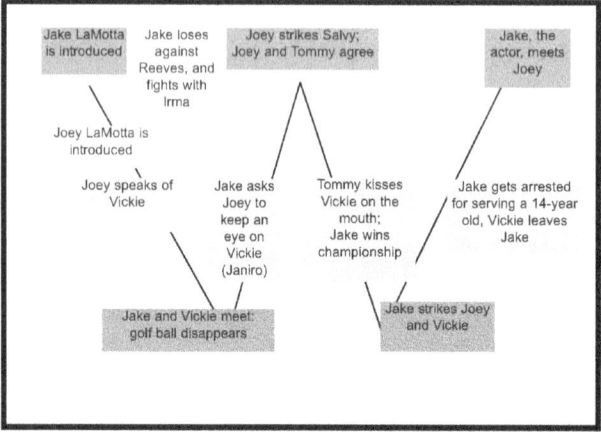

Figure 12

Thanks to the diagram (figure 12), we can notice how *Raging Bull* follows a traditional plot structure. Specific events develop at key moments and activate a chain of occurrences that converge and stabilize. If we look at the Plots Points, we notice that they are Turning Points (the bottom rectangles and the top rectangle at the midpoint) inform us of Jake's three objects of desire: 1. his marriage to Vickie, 2. the agreement between Joey and Tommy, and 3. finally the punches given to Joey and Vickie.

These are the main impetuses of the film. Jake is introduced to Vickie, whom he marries; Vickie is accused of being unfaithful; Jake accuses his brother of having had sex with Vickie. In the end Jake asks his brother for a truce. If one were to remain on this surface analysis, *Raging Bull* would basically reduce itself to the story of two brothers who love the same woman. This infidelity plot, however, does not yield further analysis. *Raging Bull* is not merely about infidelity. The engine that gets the narrative running is the betrayal scenario: Jake believes that he is betrayed by his brother Joey. The second Turning Point does encourage us to come up such a proposition. The ambiguity is rich in possibilities. Jake's conclusion is wrong. The betrayal exists, but not for the reasons he thinks.

Joey has betrayed Jake not because he sleeps with Vickie. Joey has betrayed Jake not because his buddy Salvy sleeps with Vickie. Vickie's betrayal is red herring. Joey has betrayed Jake because he sells Jake to the Mob. Cleverly, Tommy Como uses the spat between Joey and Salvy to pull out a contract. The moment he steps out of line, Jake comes under Tommy's control.

This is the revelation. The real betrayal is that Joey sold him to the Mob. Jake has been sold, and he discovers this only at the very end. What makes this film great is this reversal of fate. Jake does not wait for Joey to say "I am sorry" for having sold him to the Mob. It is Jake who asks Joey to forgive him. Jake knows the truth now, but Joey misjudges this gesture; he thinks Jake is asking for forgiveness for having punched him. Jake punched Joey many times, and Jacke would probably continue to punch his brother if a reconciliation was possible. One more punch from Jake would not create havoc.

It took years for Jake to come to this realization. When Jake runs into Joey, he is ready to offer his brother a gesture of magnanimity that Jake was up till then incapable of doing. He has to step outside of his own limits. This is the moment of grace De Niro spoke of no doubt. The narrative block that emerges from the Pinch Points (light shaded) deals with the presence of women in Jake's life. If we were to consider the Inciting Incident (involving Irma) as a variant of the Pinch Point, then this female motive permeates that entire dimension of the story. Whenever an action has begun, it automatically involves a woman (Irma, Vickie, the two underage girls).

Vickie is introduced to Jake thanks to the Sender, Joey. Without Joey, there would be no *Raging Bull* story to tell. More than a simple foil, Joey is responsible for the object of desires (Vickie, Salvy / Tommy Como, the breakup between Joey and Jake). All three Ojects of desire are directly and indirectly linked to Vickie.

From the moment Jake first sets eyes on her at the pool, Vickie is suspected of courting other men. Jake is quick to ask Joey if he or the wise guys have slept with her. When at the Copacabana, Vickie is ordered by Joey to leave, Joey starts a fight with his friend Salvy. By following his brother's orders ("keep on eye on her"), Joey suspects foul play. But no wrongdoing on Salvy and Vickie's part is ever proven. This undone deed, this unperformed act, nevertheless, is responsible for both Jake's success in his career. This error of judgement on the part of Joey lead Jake to Tommy Como.

The deal signed between Joey and Tommy, Tommy suddenly grants himself the right to kiss Vickie on the mouth. Joey repeats this prohibited gesture on that unforgettable day in Jake's living room. That Joey should perform a motion performed by Tommy places Joey, in Jake's eyes, on the same level as the mobster. Similitude of action positions the doers of this action on equal footing. The reasoning is simplistic, but logical. Tommy kisses Vickie, and Joey kisses Vickie, then Joey becomes Tommy. In other words, Joey is part of Tommy's mobster gang. Jake's jealousy prevents him from seeing the complete picture; it is only when the haze of jealousy vanishes that true understanding actually occurs.

The last Pinch Point is Jake getting arrested for serving alcohol to fourteen-year-old girls in his bar. Though Vickie is not directly responsible for this twist in the action, she does play a subtle role nonetheless. Jake has a weakness for underaged girls. Vickie is fifteen when Jake invites her to his parent's apartment. Vickie is present *in absentia* with the two young girls in the bar. Jake's kiss two fourteen-year-old girls recalls his kissing Vickie at the beginning of the tryst. That a mature man of his age does not notice the girls' real age indicates just how serious his craving for nymphets is. Moral judgment can be laid aside, but the not the law.

On the first level of the narrative (the top rectangles), Jake LaMotta is introduced as an Italian-American boxer. Jake is married to an Italian-American (Irma). Two Inciting Incidents appear in the first narrative block: the first, at the five-minute point, and the second at the end of the first mega-sequence, near the ten-minute mark. No matter how hard Jake LaMotta fights, he can never win a bout. When he does win, the fight (against Jimmy Reeves) is fixed. Success is possible only with the help of criminals.

Later, in the kitchen, Jake breaks out against his wife because she overcooks a steak. Both elements become the foundation upon which the rest of the story will grow: on the one hand, Jake will have to let go of some of his freedom in order to win a fight; and, on the other hand, as Joey suggests, Jake cannot possibly continue living with Irma (a woman) if he wishes to pursue a serious career in boxing. Professional success demands a sacrifice, both on the personal and inter-personal levels. This is where both ethnicity and sexuality converge. Just like Rico in *Little Caesar*, to be successful Jake must give up self-love and his love of women. What assimilation requires erases whatever qualities that constitutes a person.

At the mid-point, that is, at the second Plot Point, a major upset occurs. Upon noticing Vickie with mobsters, Joey loses himself and cruelly beats Salvy up. This murky episode is never openly elucidated by Joey when, at the third Plot Point, Jake demands an explanation on the "rumors" that have been circulating about. The audience is not privy to these rumors. Jake appears to suffer from paranoia. What Joey and the spectator know Jake is unaware of. No wonder the final monologue is also address to us the spectator who have betrayed Jake.

Jake gets to win the Middle-weight championship in directly because his wife, he believes, has slept with another man. This plot provides Jake with no satisfaction. Jake is necessarily redirected to Joey, whom he must accept as a necessary evil for his final enlightenment. Jake has to forgive Joey for having imparted the means for his temporary success, a moment of glory which blinded him to real personal success.

Jake's solitude is the ultimate reward for that awakening. What seems at first sight as Jake begging Joey for forgiveness turns out to be Jake having become so self-effacing, so honorable that he can embrace whatever harm done to him in the past. When in prison Jake screams that he is not the man who people think he is, he is tearing off the mask he willingly wore.

To achieve greatness in the mainstream was his greatest wish. But it turned out to be a false object of desire. Along the way Jake mistook "wanting to do it on his own" (words so often repeated in this film) for the various false objects of desire he found along the way. The virtual territory of becoming was always misconstrued for a tangible object. As Paul Schrader contends, "the means to an end, not to be confused with the end" (*Transcendental*, 97). Lourdeaux believes that this position is the opposite of what ethnic immanence is all about (14). One does not exclude the other.

Jake LaMotta describes this territory in his final monologue. Immanence is everywhere, but it is visible only after one is taught to recognize it. Comparable to Michel in *Pickpocket* or Julian in *American Gigolo*, Jake can say, "How long it has taken me to come to you" (Schrader is very present in *Raging Bull*). Jake LaMotta might quote Terry Malloy but he is a contender with collective insight. The conclusion is multifarious since Jake LaMotta's forgiveness encompasses the private, the professional and the interpersonal. This transformed Jake LaMotta, Martin Scorsese offers us as a model for ethnic magnanimity.

Notes

1. Robert Casillo, *Gangster Priest: The Italian American Cinema of Martin Scorsese*, Toronto: University of Toronto Press Inc., 2006.
2. Robert Casillo, *Gangster Priest*, p. 65-66.
3. Robert Casillo, *Gangster Priest*, p. 62. Here Casillo is paraphrasing Jerre Mangione of "American Artists of Italian Origin", in *Italy and United States*, edited by Humbert S. Nelli, all quoted by Casillo.
4. Robert Casillo, *Gangster Priest*, p. 65. A paraphrasing of Casillo's concept borrowed from Daniel Aaron.
5. Pauline Kael in *The New Yorker*, quoted in Douglas Brode, *The Films of Robert De Niro*, New York: Citadel Press, 1993, p. 132.
6. Quoted in Mary Pat Kelly, *Martin Scorsese: A Journey*, New York: Thunder's Mouth Press, 1991, p. 50.
7. Mary Pat Kelly, *Martin Scorsese: A Journey*, p. 147-48.
8. Tom Wolfe, in *The Kandy-Kolored Tangerine-Flake Streamline Baby*, quoted in Stephen Bayley, *Cars*, London: Conran Octupus, 2009, p. 13-14.
9. Robin Wood, "The Homosexual Subtext: *Raging Bull*", in *Australian Journal of Screen Theory* (Kensington, New South Wales), no. 15–16, 1983, p. 61
10. This document appears on the official Website of the NAIF (www.naif.org.).
11. Neil Sinyard in *Films Illustrated* (London), May 1981, quoted in Julian Petley, www.filmreference.com, 27 Feb 2008.
12. Christopher Marlowe, *Dr. Faustus*, New York: Dover Publications, Inc., 1994, p. 12-13.
13. Christopher Marlowe, *Dr. Faustus*, p. 13.
14. Robin Wood, *"The Homosexual Subtext: Raging Bull"*, in *Australian Journal of Screen Theory* (Kensington, New South Wales), no. 15–16, 1983.
15. Richard Combs in *Sight and Sound* (London), Spring 1981, quoted in Julian Petley, www.filmreference.com, 27 Feb 2008.
16. Robin Wood, "The Homosexual Subtext: Raging Bull", p. 62-65.
17. Scorsese quoted in Michel Cieutat, *Martin Scorsese*, p. 168; original source from Positif, no. 241, April 1981, p. 53: "I unconsciously found myself in Jake. I felt that his character was a bringer of hope." (Similar lines also quoted in Casillo, p. 265.)
18. Joe Pesci quoted in Mary Pat Kelly, *Martin Scorsese: A Journey*, p. 146.19. Martin Scorsese in Mary Pat Kelly, *Martin Scorsese: A Journey*, New York: Thunder's Mouth Press, 1991, p. 128.
20. Martin Scorsese in Mary Pat Kelly, *Martin Scorsese: A Journey*, New York: Thunder's Mouth Press, 1991, p. 150.
21. Quoted in Robert Casillo, *Gangster Priest*, p. 264.

CONCLUSION

Ethnicity is not a fad. When it subsides, it reappears moments later. A by-product of globalization of identity and philosophy, ethnicity alters every person's understanding of civil existence. Ethnicity has remodelled the cities and villages we live in, the fabric of communities we thought we had been woven so carefully. Ethnicity might skip a generation, but a person's age does not eliminate ethnicity. Israel Zangwill's notion of the *melting-pot* is as an invention as is pluriculturalism. Vocabulary changes, but the differences between the nomad and the sedentary remain. Nation-states fidget with their borders; plurality continues chafing on the laws. Where philosophers and politicians pause, the collectivity runs. If money can jump over fences, why shouldn't people?

Success is unattainable if fixed in an ideal; deterritorial ethnicity is not a tangible object, but a road taken. Ken Scambray calls this resurgence of ethnicity a North American Renaissance, a re-naissance, a re-birth, convenient metaphors, true enough, though we are not sure if re-birth can be applied to what does not die. Fulvio Caccia uses the image of the phoenix to explain ethnic re-emergence; ethnicity is what rises from the ashes; ethnicity is not something that can be to put on fire. Marshall McLuhan was correct in reminding us that the moment the vanishing point become multiple, horizons within and without multiplied. Ethnicity is baroque; nationalism, linear.

Wherever ethnicity appears, as it does in many countries, where cultural communities express their needs, it rarely is the revitalization of a ritual or belief once dead. Be it in music, film, art, literature, architecture, it is surely the continuation of a praxis already present in another location, in another domain. Artistic words generally appear in markets where achievements of another nature occurred first. If ethnic artists are able to produce their works, they did so to a certain extent because their lifestyle and customs have been favorably received by the society they live in. Business precedes art.

Loners have been the rule, but groups seem to be emerging. Italians seldom expressed them seldom as an ethnic group. Christina Rossetti wrote in the privacy of her London home. Frank Capra was alone in Hollywood. Tonino Caticchio wrote as a solitary poet in Montreal. The same can be said of artists of other cultural origins. The individual rarely feels or wishes to stand out from the majority voice. It is only when the individual is met by another individual that a sense of collectivity is felt. The immigrants and their offspring who form a cultural collectivity, willingly or unconsciously, which expresses itself as a social ethnic movement constitutes an extremely important event. The staircase to awareness is steep and difficult. But when the doors open, the perspective is broad.

The more appropriate metaphor to use when speaking of this process is the chameleon. The ethnic must adapt himself/herself to a myriad of environments. At any point in time, the individual must negotiate new definitions to define himself/herself and the group s/he belongs to. Empowerment and qualification are never easy.

I chose five films that might embody this transmutation. I began the analysis without any preconceived notions. I did not know if any of these films would in the end comply to my definition of the Italic, that is, an occurrence on things Italian that does not swerve back to Italy or disappear into assimilation, either in part or in total. This cultural phenomenon includes Italy, the Italic goes above and beyond the Italian proper. For Italian communities outside Italy this full-blown ethnicity can be called the Italic; each ethnic group defines itself, finding its specific beingness in a decentralized, non-territorial cultural network.

When such a deterritorial ethnicity spreads across the globe it takes on the appearance of the New Baroque. Coming from everywhere, one fragment at a time, and simultaneously, New Baroque dislodges the centralized culture. What was a circle develops into a spiral. Ethnicity is more than a question of margins and centers, as Anthony J. Tamburri, Paolo A. Giordano, and Fred Gardaphé advanced in their important anthology *From the Margins: Writings in Italian Americana*. Dimensions permutate constantly, altering both temporal and spatial entities.

Without this need for a center, ethnicity enables the distribution of works from one end of a territory to another, as well as from one country to another. Many confuse ethnicity with the promotion of mainstream establishment works of one country into another. Such a practice is not ethnicity, but common commercial free trade between nations. Ethnicity is the expression of a minority collective within a larger group, not necessarily a majority. Ethnicity is not the splintering from the majority. It is the emanation of a cultural pursuit that rises in different locations concurrently. Music from Italy distributed in Canada does not constitute ethnicity; music made by Italians in Canada, U.S.A., Germany, France, Britain, Argentina, Brazil does (for example, Marco Calliari who sings in Italian in French-speaking Quebec).

Many believe that *éloignement* from the ethnic environment hastens assimilation. Ethnicity is not a content, but an awareness, an authenticity. An ethnic content transposed in a non-Italic environment, if not enhanced by irony or cynicism, usually falls short of the target. Such narrations sound faulty, insincere, exploitative. Many non-Italian-outside-Italy subjects bear the similar traces of ethnicity, yet if they wish to grasp their full meanings they have to view their works in their own specific and authentic contexts.

Claude Lévi-Strauss has shown how narratives are myths society creates for itself. Why a story must be told is not easy to explain. Stories illustrate where society is going, and how a community copes with its transformations.

None of the films analyzed, surprisingly, promote assimilation into the mainstream culture. Some ethnic artists choose the path to assimilation; others choose the path less taken. Biography alone holds no deep significance in understanding a work of art. The narrative about being an Italian in Britain does not necessarily imply it has to be about being Italian nor about being British. Displacement from the ethnic environment (ghetto) might suggest disappearance (as in *Queen of Hearts*), but geographical stability does not mean preservation of culture. As long as a virtual territory can be found, assimilation will not result.

Displacement is inherent to the ethnic narrative. Giovanni Garofoli takes the train from Southern Italy to Switzerland *(Bread and Chocolate);* Ralf Milan flies in from Italy to France *(A Pain in the Ass)*; the Lucca take the boat from Northern Italy to London *(Queen of Hearts)*. Nicola Zavaglia shows how for centuries soldiers and ordinary men and women embarked on ships that left the Mediterranean to come to the shores of Montreal *(Forever the Mediterranean)*. Jake LaMotta drives from New York to Miami and back again *(Raging Bull)*.

Italians moved to Germany, Argentina, and Brazil. Does it matter if a filmmaker is Italian or not when narrating an Italian ethnic story? Does Delbert Mann (*Marty*, 1955) or Norman Jewison (*Moonstruck*, 1987) do less a fine job than Anthony Minghella in *The Talented Mr. Ripley* (1999) or *Breaking and Entering* (2006)? Distance from the subject matter adds a sprinkle of irony (stylization).

Perhaps any story can be told by any artist, yet appropriation of voice is a thorny subject when it comes to ethnicity. The younger Spike Lee attacks the great Steven Spielberg for *The Color Purple* (1985) and the fine Clint Eastwood for *Flags of Our Fathers* (2006), virulently. Considerations of this nature are serious, for they raise the issue of means of production.

Jon Amiel alone falls into the category of being a non-Italian. The script, however, is by an Italian-British writer. In *Queen of Hearts* the director's mise en scène relies heavily on if not stereotypes at least on irony and stylization; Amiel diligently erases himself and permits the delivery of lyricism prepared by Tony Grisoni, who supplied the director with an ideal Italic script. The same argument could be advanced for Édouard Molinaro who, probably of Italian origin, never openly confronts the Italian theme (not even in his autobiography); yet, when faced with the finished script, he strikes a balance when he chooses to use a "foreigner"— the hired gun is an Italian French — as the final object of desire. What *A Pain in the Ass* pushes to the fore is the unexpected (and comic) homoerotic subtext that Robin Wood noticed in *Raging Bull*.

Homosexuality finds its way into *Bread and Chocolate*. If *Queen of Hearts* and *The Mediterranean Forever* do not touch on the issue, it is because the filmmakers substituted it with friendship and the family unit. One could suggest the semantic binary pair homosexuality/family, but that would not be fully true; Molinaro removes the slash of the couplet and replaces it with an equal sign in *The Cage of Madwomen*, where homosexuals become a family. In *A Pain in the Ass*, Pignon leaves his wife to follow Milan, an Italian criminal, all the way to prison. Homosexuality, in most cases, is rarely analyzed, only hinted at, or vulgarly referred to. *Mambo Italiano* (2003), by Émile Gaudreault (written by Montrealer Steve Galluccio), a comedy that deserves to be studied, praises homosexuality in the Italian family.

A variety of themes arise with the ethnic narrative, one being the ethnic narrative as a genre in its own right. Ethnicity customarily juxtaposes itself on fixed genres (thriller, Mafia, romance), but after World War II ethnicity gains momentum and encompasses stylistic criteria that amount to what we associate with normally *genre*. Settings and characters are stressed in a selective manner which influence plot, mood, tone, and theme of a specific movie.

In the U.S.A. there are plenty of films that deal with love and a heavy dose of otherness. *Crossing Delancey* (1988) by Joan Micklin Silver is a romantic drama in which the Jewish culture plays a full role. Spike Lee's *Jungle Fever* (1991) is another romantic drama based on ethnicity. The initial spark for these films is the ethnic preoccupation; this is an *a priori* more than an *a posteriori* assumption. Ethnicity is the determining factor to the creative process behind a work of art. The ethnic component comes before the romantic story, and if it comes after its influence will condition the overall quality of the final work. And so we have a growing number of films that could be considered ethnic (in its widest of definition): Jewish, Irish, African-American, Hispanic, and Amerindian. What in the past would have been left unnamed and unstressed (like in music note) is in the ethnic genre underscored, accented, and italicized (pun intended).

The Italian ethnic film is one among many ethnic films that have come to the fore in the past decades. With the genre is attached a list of questions, however, that need to be answered. Does the filmmaker have to be an ethnic in order to be an ethnic film?

Does the filmmaker have to be of the same ethnic background as the ethnicity depicted on screen (appropriation of voice)?

Must the ethnic film limit itself to the lyrical voice (whereby the filmmaker speaks in his own voice)?

Must the ethnic subject matter be exclusively ethnic and headlined?

Is the ethnic family unit the sole haven for the social outsider?

What happens when this family unit breaks down?

Should ethnics marry only ethnics from the same group? from another group?

Does madness (or some variation of mental delusion or breakdown) have to be spotlighted?

What role does religion play here, if any?

How is sexuality expressed in an ethnic community?

If organized crime exists in this ethnic community, what role does it play?

Does the fact that ethnics entertain with non-ethnics (mainstream) — both on the inter-personal and professional levels — signify acculturation?

What constitutes the ethnic status?

Should the ethnic protagonist always be marginalized from mainstream society?

Do ethnic characters disappear if they leave their ghetto?

Must there a struggle between the minority and the majority collectivities for recognition of rights?

The main contention behind these questions — and there are plenty more in the hat from which these were pulled — is the relationship between the individual and the collectivity.

The ethnic is not a western hero who rides through a city, transforms its systems, and then gallops away on his horse into the sunset. The minority individual is the outsider who stays within a society that does not always want him.

In any democracy, a choice is given to the ethnic individual who can either choose to belong to one group or pass over to another group. Every option reflects a personal bias and a political attitude.

Preference is never trivial; details in appearance superfluous indicate directions the filmmaker believes ethnics should take.

Indecisions can embody fear whereby the only way out might be for our ethnic hero to dive into an "altered state". This parallel world inside one's mind becomes a virtual territory where the ethnic can escape to. This is where the timorous individual conciliates dilemmas.

This in-between state enables the frightened minority individual to be concurrently here and there, outside and inside. Martin Scorsese undertakes this voyage into madness in *Shutter Island*. On a certain plane, homoeroticism, when not integrally embraced, might represent such a virtual territory, but again a topic of this depth when not adequately addressed looks like an artistic quick fix which is as questionable as the appropriation of another's ethnic voice.

Imitation can be reliable if the creative act is invested with purpose. In *Shadows* (1959), the Greek-American filmmaker John Cassavetes dissects the African-American question with preeminent honesty; no one ever accused Cassavetes of appropriating the voice of African Americans. The ethnic genre surpasses subject matter. It is an attitude, an inclination, a philosophy. Much is at stake. Constant negotiation goes on when one decides to work in the ethnic genre. Artistic provisions are not up for hasty discussion. Averaging out content weakens the form. The pleasure for the viewer who receives the work depends on this honest performance.

Why then the punctilious reverting to criminals? Why the Wise Guys? The Sopranos? The Godfathers? Such contentious characters, when not studied for biographical purposes, act as a *modus vivendi* for the ethnic genre. There is no doubt that this concession will retract to the background when the ethnic genre acquires a stronger appreciation on the part of the conservative viewer. For the moment, ethnicity seems prisoner to these stereotypes. In collaboration with an associative genre, such as the gangster genre or the romance, the ethnic genre can more freely delve into darker moral geysers. In an optimistic way, Italians-outside-Italy should be thankful that such a "genre contract" has been made available to them. Quite possibly, without the gangster genre, in America at least, the ethnic content would never has evolved into its own genre.

We could surmise that the ethnic theme arose first out of the gangster; and gradually the Mafia narrative warranted sequences beyond action that would keep the audience holding on to its breath. These "narrative adjectives", these asides, communicated cultural observances that had not been dealt with before. The criminal agenda in film led the way to the creation of a subgenre. Even the Jewish-American Woody Allen reverts to organized crime in his film on Jewish culture, *Crimes and Misdemeanors* (1989) and *Small Time Crooks* (2000). In time crime stories give way to more general themes. Anthony Minghella's *Breaking and Entering* is certainly an ethnic film; yet the crime element is reduced to a minimum. In so doing, Minghella was free to explore the economic marginalization of Yugoslavian immigration in the United Kingdom.

When considering a film such as *Queen of Hearts* with its share of gangsterism, we know it is not a gangster film. Its mixture of romance and revenge obliterates even the tiniest presence of delinquency. This film is a fine example of the ethnic genre. Uncomplying to the rules of the gangster genre, the film plunges into a fairylike love tale, as told by a child. And from this tale emerges a romance of vengeance. It is also a *bildungsroman* that develops into a story of addiction — which is not as bleak as Blake Edwards' *Days of Wine and Roses* (1962). Amiel's film bounces in every direction, and the only way it can be understood fully is by putting it under the label of "ethnic film".

A number of gangster films are in truth ethnic films in the making. *The Sopranos* are more about ethnicity than they are about the workings of the Mafia. *The Godfather* trilogy, on the other hand, studies more closely the work of gangsters than their cultural heritage, albeit ethnicity solidifies its semantic structural framework. Many of Woody Allen's films belong to the ethnic genre. With *Annie Hall* (1977) and *Manhattan* (1979), Allen educates the viewer us on post-Holocaust Jewish culture in New York. The majority of Spike Lee's films fall in the ethnic genre, in his case, by exploring the rich and turbulent African-American history. *She's Gotta Have It* (1986), *Do the Right Thing* (1989), *Jungle Fever* (1991), and *Malcolm X (*1992) use stories of love, work and politics to promote ethnic understanding. *The Visitor* (2007), by Thomas McCarthy fits under the ethnic umbrella as well; here, a white American professor goes out of his way to help illegal immigrants.

Ethnic films have been around for decades, but there are still too few for critics to encapsulate them all into a genre. Blake Edward's comedy *The Party* (1968), with the hilarious Peter Sellers — is it or not an ethnic film? People see it solely as comedy, but behind the humor, Edwards is expanding our knowledge of pluriculturalism. As the size of the ethnic corpus grows, easier will become the task of defining the criteria of what makes up this treasury of contemporary nomadism.

Ethnicity, nevertheless, continues to displease. Ethnicity continues to be identified to displacement, homelessness, bohemianism, foreignness, superficiality, sedition, anarchy. For the sedentary nationalist — whose integrity is based on interrelatedness, sameness, assimilation – heterogeneity, multiplicity and discontinuity are incarnations of evil. Laughter facilitates the swallowing of a bitter syrup. Ethnic uses humor to conceal the tragedy of racism and irony to educate. Ethnic comedies like *Bread and Chocolate, A Pain in the Ass,* and *Queen of Hearts,* are more than what they appear.

By connecting different genres the ethnic filmmaker refines the modern sentiment of displacement and the forms utilized to depict these complex emotions of not belonging. The main purpose of ethnic films is to celebrate immigration and its extensions, not denigrate it. They do so by praising it as a transient phenomenon or as a perennial procession. North America, more than other continent, is by its very nature fertile soil for ethnicity to enrich itself and propagate itself.

Ethnicity can be tumultuous; many injustices are confronted; much ferocity against difference to be expected on all parts. Elsewhere the attempts seem fragile. France, for example, has opened its artistic door to the Jewish and Arabic artists on its soil. A film such as *L'Italien* (*The Italian*, 2010), by Olivier Baroux — starring Kad Merad, who plays Murad, an Algerian who passes for an Italian Maserati car salesman — blossoms with its lushness of "disturbing" cultural propositions.

Germany, with its large Turkish population, has opened its money coffers and helps ethnic filmmakers, such as Faith Akin, whose *The Edge of Heaven* (2010) raises cross-cultural issues that can no longer be ignored by European nations.

Filmmakers, writers, song writers, actors continue to produce at their rhythm works that will, if not sooner, at least later, attract the curious and the attention of the keen filmgoer. It is the eminence of the works produced that counts; quantity will satisfy the need for study. The biggest enemy of ethnicity is nationalism. The fear of treason prolapses.

In *Bread and Chocolate*, at the end of an inglorious journey, Nino gets off the train that was taking him back to Italy and walks into a No-Land, which exists only in his mind, and in the spectator's imagination. His is a virtual space that is neither Italy nor Switzerland. That symbolic space is called the *Italic*, that lies in between emigration and immigration.

In *A Pain in the Ass*, a jilted Pignon meets an Italian hired gunman who saves him from committing suicide. In the end, Pignon prefers sharing a prison cell with Milan, the gunman, than going back to his wife. What is offered here if not a No-Land instead of the cosy life of a shirt salesman? The interesting point that is raised in this film is the call for social change on the part of the host country.

This French film seems to be screaming, "Embrace the Italian foreigner, even if he is a criminal. Charity is better than violence."

This position can exist in an Atopia that is neither France nor Italy.

This is acceptance of the Italic: to be neither set in one country, nor erasing the place left behind.

In *Queen of Hearts*, Danilo must win back the woman he loves whom he had stolen from a criminal, Barbariccia, and comes out victorious thanks to the help of his son and his newly emigrated father. The journey, in this case, is on the surface different, yet the message remains the same. One can leave

Italy but one must remain connected to it via tradition which can then be passed on to the next generation. This fresh twist on the concept of emigration is positive. No hint of nostalgia here. The No-Land can exist, yes, but it must find a way to stay connected to another Italian source.

In *The Mediterranean Forever,* the voyage comes full circle. Because the narrative is founded on "real" events, the metaphors at work are more difficult to seize, but they can still be found. We are in the heart of the Italic. The fact that this film is situated in Montreal is significative. It is the triangulation of cultures that assists in the preservation of the Garden, which is a symbol for the No-Land of the Italic.

The filmmaker attacks racism and praises hard-working, life-loving Italians who integrate in the host country, yet maintain their cultural practices. Through familial ties and friendship, the Garden is the No-Land where the past meets the future. The grandfather who, like in *Queen of Hearts,* passes on culture to the grandchild. The Italic can work, as long as it is connected to its source, via fresh emigration. This call for fresh emigration is vital, and political.

In *Raging Bull,* the Italic is most complex, for it is hidden in a filmic rhetoric that often is dazzling. We are dealing with a master of the art form. Scorsese is the most visibly Italic without having let a character ever openly say so. This refusal to define oneself is intentional. Italians in the U.S.A. have been cut off from Italy for such a long time that they must vie for survival. The ways of survival are few: work, crime, art, and forgiveness. The attraction to assimilation is powerfully expressed in *Raging Bull.*

What is distressing (or, if you wish, fascinating) is the equivocalness of symbols. A single item can personify two distinct assimilatory forces: the Mob, for instance, is at once Italy and the U.S.A. What this does is erase the difference in countryhood but maintains the idea of assimilation untouched. Assimilation comes at a high cost: to achieve, one must lose one's dignity. Jake LaMotta has no choice. He must play by the rules of the game if he wishes to be a champion. Salvation is earned thanks to a brother's betrayal.

The Italic No-Land is a solitary place where we must learn to forgive those who betray us. The Italic, however, needs these "brothers" and "sisters" in order to integrate in their society. Of all the films, *Raging Bull* clearly states that success and assimilation are not worth the price you have to pay to buy them. These are things one must live with, and in a sense *Raging Bull* is a how-to book for all Italics.

Many artists do not venture into ethnicity because they are afraid of being accused of acting subversively, deceitfully, insubordinately, arrogantly, belligerently. The ethnic artist is neither a reactionary nor is he outdated. The ethnic enterprise is noble and will be remunerated, subsidized, acknowledged, honored, decorated for the humanism it restitutes to a century of moral embarrassment remembered for its xenophobia and solipsism.

Films Cited

Adieu Philippine, by Jacques Rozier, 1961
Alice Doesn't Live Here Anymore, by Martin Scorsese, 1974
Amarcord, by Federico Fellini, 1973
American Beauty, by Sam Mendes, 1999
American Gigolo, by Paul Schrader, 1980
American Graffiti, by George Lucas, 1973
Angel Makers, by Jon Amiel, 2010
Annie Hall, by Woody Allen, 1977
Auto Focus, by Paul Schrader, 2002
L'Aventure c'est l'aventure, by Claude Lelouch, 1972
Bad Timing, by Nicholas Roeg, 1980
Battleship Potemkin, by Sergei Eisenstein, 1925
Beau-masque, by Bernard Paul, 1972
La Beauté du diable, by René Clair, 1950
The Birds, Alfred Hitchcock, 1963
Blazing Saddles, by Mel Brooks, 1974
Borsalino, by Jacques Déray, 1970.
The Boston Strangler, by Richard Fleischer, 1968
Breaking and Entering, by Anthony Minghella, 2006
Buddy Buddy, by Billy Wilder, 1981
Caffè Italia-Montréal, by Paul Tana, 1985
La Cage aux folles, by Édouard Molinaro, 1978
La Cage aux Folles II, by Édouard Molinaro, 1980
Le Casque d'or, by Jacques Becker, 1952.
Le charme discret de la bourgeoisie, by Luis Buñuel, 1973
La Cecilia, by Jean-Louis Comolli, 1976
Chinatown, by Roman Polanski, 1974
The Color Purple, by Steven Spielberg, 1985
The Comfort of Strangers, by Paul Schrader, 1990
Les Compères, by Francis Veber, 1983
Concrete Angels, by Carlo Liconti, 1987
The Conversation, Francis Ford Coppola, 1974
Copycat, by Jon Amiel, 1995
Cries and Whispers, by Ingmar Bergman, 1973

Crimes and Misdemeanors, by Woody Allen, 1989
Crossing Delancey, by Joan Micklin Silver, 1988
Cruising, by William Friedkin, 1980
La déroute, by Paul Tana, 1998
Dersu Uzala, by Akira Kurosawa, 1974
Le dernier métro, by François Truffaut, 1980
Deux corniauds au régiment, by Nado Cicero, 1971
Le Dîner de cons, by Francis Veber, 1998
Dinner for Schmucks, by Jay Roach, 2010
Donnie Brasco, by Mike Newell, 1997
Don't Look Now, by Nicolas Roeg, 1973
Do the Right Thing, by Spike Lee, 1989
La Doublure, by Francis Veber, 2005
Dressed to Kill, by Brian de Palma, 1980
The Edge of Heaven, by Faith Akin, 2010
The Elephant Man, by David Lynch, 1980
L'Emmerdeur, by Francis Veber, 2008
En pays neuf, by Maurice Proulx, 1937
Entrapment, by Jon Amiel, 1999
L'exile est une longue insomnie, by Sabine Mamou, 1979
The Exorcist, by William Friedkin, 1973
Fantastica, by Gilles Carle, 1980
Father of the Bride, by Vincente Minnelli, 1950
F for Fake, by Orson Welles, 1974
Film d'amore e d'anarchia, by Lina Wertmüller, 1973
Fish Tank, by Andrea Arnold, 2009
Flags of Our Fathers, by Clint Eastwood, 2006
Flesh, by Paul Morrissey, 1968
Les Fugitifs, by Francis Veber, 1986
The Gangs of New York, by Martin Scorsese, 2002
The Garden of the Finzi-Contini, by Vittorio De Sica, 1971
Gare du Nord, by Jean Rouch, 1963
Gloria, by John Cassavetes, 1980
The Godfather, by Francis Ford Coppola, 1972
The Godfather II, by Francis Ford Coppola, 1974
The Godfather III, by Francis Ford Coppola, 1990
Gomorah, by Matteo Garrone, 2008
The Good, the Bad, and the Ugly, by Sergio Leone, 1966
Goodfellas, by Martin Scorsese, 1990
La grande bouffe, by Marco Ferreri, 1973

Green Pastures, by Marc Connelly and William Keighley, 1936
Heat, by Paul Morrissey, 1972
Heaven's Gate, by Michael Cimino, 1980
Hibernatus, by Édouard Molinaro, 1969
L'Invitation, by Claude Goretta, 1973
L'Ironie du sort, by Édouard Molinaro, 1974
It's a Wonderful World, by Frank Capra, 1946
L'Italien, by Olivier Baroux, 2010
Je vous salue, Marie, by Jean-Luc Godard, 1985
Jungle Fever, by Spike Lee, 1991
The King of Comedy, by Martin Scorsese, 1983
Lancelot du Lac, Robert Bresson, 1974
The Last Temptation of Christ, by Martin Scorsese, 1988
The Last Waltz, by Martin Scorsese, 1978
Light Sleeper, Paul Schrader, 1992
Little Caesar, by Mervyn LeRoy, 1931
Lucky Luciano, by Francesco Rosi, 1973
Ludwig, by Luchino Visconti, 1973
M, by Fritz Lang, 1931
La maman et la putain, by Jean Eustache, 1973
Malcolm X, by Spike Lee, 1992
Mambo Italiano, by Émile Gaudreault, 2003
Manhattan, by Woody Allen, 1979
Marty, by Delbert Mann, 1955
Match Point, by Woody Allen, 2005
The Mediterranean Forever, by Nicola Zavaglia, 2001
Mean Streets, by Martin Scorsese, 1973
Metropolis, by Fritz Lang, 1927
Mima, by Philomène Esposito, 1991
Miracle in Milan, by Vittorio De Sica, 1951
Mishima, by Paul Schrader, 1985
Moana, by Robert Flaherty, 1926
Modern Times, by Charles Chaplin, 1936
Mon oncle, by Jacques Tati, 1959
Mon oncle d'Amérique, by Alain Resnais, 1980
Mon oncle Benjamin, by Édouard Molinaro, 1969
Moonstruck, by Norman Jewison, 1987
La maman et la putain, by Jean Eustache, 1973
Nanook of the North, by Robert Flaherty, 1922
Ne touchez pas au grisbi, by Jacques Becker, 1953

No Direction Home, by Martin Scorsese, 2005
La nuit américaine, by François Truffaut, 1973
The Man Who Knew Too Little, by Jon Amiel, 1997
Mulholland Drive, by David Lynch, 2001
Notre Musique, by Jean-Luc Godard, 2004
Notorious, by Alfred Hitchcock, 1946
October, by Sergei Eisenstein, 1928
Once Upon a Time in America, by Sergio Leone, 1984
One plus One, by Jean-Luc Godard, 1968
On the Waterfront, by Elia Kazan, 1954
Les Ordres, by Michel Brault, 1974
Oscar, by Édouard Molinaro, 1967
Paisà, by Roberto Rossellini, 1946
Pane e cioccolata, by Franco Brusati, *1974*
Les Parapluies de Cherbourg, by Jacques Demy, 1964
Paris vu par..., by French New Wave Directors, 1963
The Party, by Blake Edwards, 1967
Persona, by Ingmar Bergman, 1966
Pickpocket, by Robert Bresson, 1959
Le Placard, by Francis Veber, 2001
La planète sauvage, by René Laloux, 1973
Play it Again, Sam, by Herbert Ross, 1973
Plein soleil, by René Clément, 1960
Pour la suite du monde, by Michel Brault and Pierre Perrault, 1963
Profumo di donna, by Dino Risi, 1974
Pulp Fiction, by Quentin Tarantino, 1994
Un prophète, by Jacques Audiard, 2010
Queen of Hearts, by Jon Amiel, 1989
Rabbi Jacob, by Gérard Oury, 1973
Raging Bull, by Martin Scorsese, 1981
Les Raquetteurs, by Michel Brault and Gilles Groulx, 1958
Le rôle économique des travailleurs étrangers, by Dominique Juliani, 1978
Rome Open City, by Roberto Rossellini, 1945
La Sarrasine, by Paul Tana, 1992
Satyricon, by Federico Fellini, 1969
Scenes from a Marriage, by Ingmar Bergman, 1973
Lo sceicco bianco, by Federico Fellini, 1952
Serpico, by Sidney Lumet, 1973
Shadows, by John Cassavetes, 1959
She Gotta Have It, by Spike Lee, 1986

Shutter Island, by Matin Scorsese, 2010
Small Time Crooks, by Woody Allen, 2000
La Société du spectacle, by Guy Debord, 1973
Soigne ta droite, by Jean-Luc Godard, 1987
Sommersby, by Jon Amiel, 1993
The Sopranos, created by David Chase, 1999-2007
Il sospetto, by Francesco Maselli, 1975
Stavisky, by Alain Resnais, 1974
The Sting, by George Roy Hill, 1973
The Suitors, by Ghasem Ebrahimian, 1988
The Talented Mr. Ripley, by Anthony Minghella, 1999
Taxi Driver, by Martin Scorsese, 1976
Teorema, by Pier Paolo Pasolini, 1968
Tetro, by Francis Ford Coppola, 2009
Toni, by Jean Renoir, 1935
Touchez pas au grisbi, by Jacques Becker, 1953
Three Fugitives, by Francis Veber, 1989
La trace, by Bernard Favre, 1983
Trash, by Paul Morrissey, 1970
Truly, Madly, Deeply, by Anthony Minghella, 1990
The Texas Chainsaw Massacre, by Tobe Hooper, 1974
Les vacances de monsieur Hulot, by Jacques Tati, 1953
La vallée des espoirs, by Jean-Pierre Marchand et Jean-Pierre Sinapi, 1987
Vertigo, by Alfred Hitchcock, 1958
Vie des travailleurs italiens en France, by Jean Grémillon, 1926
The Vikings, by Richard Fleischer, 1958
The Visitor, by Thomas McCarthy, 2007
What's a Nice Girl Like You Doing in a Place Like This?, by Martin Scorsese, 1963
White Like Me, by Eddy Murphy *(Saturday Night Live)*, 1984
Who's That Knocking at My Door?, by Martin Scorsese, 1969
A Woman Under the Influence, by John Cassavetes, 1974
Young Frankenstein, by Mel Brooks, 1974
Zabriskie Point, by Michelangelo Antonioni, 1970

Works Cited

Abrams, M.H. *A Glossary of Literary Terms*. 1957. New York: Holt, Rinehart and Winston, Inc., 1971.
Adamo, Maria Gabriella. "Méditerranée pour toujours: L'espace des origines, l'altérité, la langue migrante." *Langue-Culture méditerranéenes en contact*. Yannick Preumont and Régine Laugier, eds. Roma: Aracne editrice, 2007.
Adler, Alfred. *What Life Should Mean to You*. 1938. New York: Capricon Books, 1958.
Alba, Richard D. *Ethnic Identity: The Transformation of White America*. New Haven: Yale University, 1990.
Alberoni, Francesco. *L'amicizia*. Milano: Garzanti, 1984.
Allais, Maurice. *L'Europe face à son avenir: Que faire?* Paris: Robert Laffont/Clément Juglar, 1991.
Apel Willi, and Daniel, Ralph T. *The Harvard Brief Dictionary of Music*. New York: Washingston Square Press Book, 1960.
Armes, Roy. *Film and Reality: An Historical Survey*. London: Penguin Books, 1974.
Arnheim, Rudolf. *Film as Art*. (1957). Berkeley: University of California Press, 1974.
Aumont, Jacques. *Du visage au cinéma*. Paris: Cahiers du cinéma/Éditions de l'Étoile, 1992.
Aumont, Jacques et Michel Maire. *L'analyse des films*. 2nd ed. Paris: Armand Colin, 2004.
Aumont, Jacques, et al. *Esthétique du film*. 2nd ed. Paris: Nathan, 1983.
Bachy, Victor. *Notes de cours d'Esthétique du cinéma et de la télévision*. Centre des techniques de diffusion, Université Catholique de Louvain. In *Analyse structurale du récit filmique*. By Rogerio Luz, 1969.
Barthes, Roland. *Le bruisement de la langue*. Essais critiques IV. Paris: Éditions du Seuil, 1984.
—. *Le dégré zéro de l'écriture*. 1953. Paris: Éditions du Seuil, 1972.
—. *La chambre claire : Note sur la photographie*. Paris: Cahiers du cinéma/Gallimard/Éditions du Seuil, 1980.
—. "La mort de l'auteur." *Manteia*, 1968. *Le bruisement de la langue*. Paris: Éditions du Seuil, 1984.
—. *L'obvie et l'obtus*. Essais critiques III. Paris: Éditions du Seuil, 1982.
—. "Rhétorique et l'image." *Communications*. No. 4. Paris: Éditions du Seuil, 1964. *L'obvie et l'obtus*.
Barthes, Roland. "Le troisième sens." *Cahiers du cinéma*. No. 222. Paris, Éditions de l'Étoile, 1970. *L'obvie et l'obtus*.
—. *S/Z*. 1970. Paris: Éditions du Seuil, 1976.
Barzini, Luigi. *Gli italiani*. 1964. Milano: Mondadori, 1978.
Battistini, Matilde. *Symbols and Allegories in Arts*. Los Angeles: The J. Paul Getty Museum, 2005.

Bazin, André. *Le cinéma de la cruauté*. Paris: Flammarion, Champs/Contre-Champs, 1987.
—. *Qu'est-ce que le cinéma?* Paris: Éditions du Cerf, 1959.
Baudrillard, Jean. *Simulations*. Trans. Paul Foss, Paul Patton and Philip Beitchman. New York: Semiotext(e), 1983.
Bayley, Stephen. *Cars*. London: Conran Octupus, 2009.
Belluscio, Steven J. *To Be Suddenly White: Literary Realism and Racial Passing*. Columbia: University of Missouri Press, 2006.
Bennett, Andrew. *The Author*. London: Routledge, 2005.
Bergson, Henri. *Laughter*. New York: Double Anchor Book, 1956.
Bernardi, Sandro. *L'avventura del cinematografo: Storia di un'arte e di un linguaggio*. Venezia: Marsilio Editore, 2007.
—. *Il paesaggio nel cinema italiano*. Venezia: Marsilio editori, 2002.
Blanc-Chaléard, Marie-Claude, ed. *Les Italiens en France depuis 1945*. Rennes: Presses Universitaires de Rennes, 2003
Blanchard, Louise. "Mediterraneo sempre." *Le Journal de Montréal*. Tuesday, 6 June 2000.
Bondanella, Peter. *Italian Cinema: From Neorealism to the Present*. New York: Continuum, 2001.
Bonitzer, Pascal. *Le champ aveugle: Essais sur le réalisme au cinéma*. Paris: Cahiers du cinéma, 1999.
Brode, Douglas. *The Films of Robert De Niro*. New York: Citadel Press, 1993.
Bourne, Randolph. *The Radical Will: Selected Writings: 1911-1918*. Berkerley: University of California, 1977.
—. *War and the Intellectuals: Collected Essays: 1915-1919*. New York: Harper and Row Publishers, 1964.
Bremond, Claude. "La logique des possibles narratifs." *Communications*. No. 8. Paris: Éditions du Seuil, 1966.
—. *La logique du récit*. Paris: Éditions du Seuil, Collection "Poétique", 1973.
—. "Les bons récompensés et les méchants punis." In *Sémiotique narrative et textuelle*. Claude Chabrol, ed. Paris: Éditions Larousse, 1973
Brown, Joe. "Queen of Hearts." *Washington Post*, 13 October 1989.
Browne, Nick. "Rhétorique du texte spéculaire (À propos de *Stagecoach*)". *Communications*. No. 23. Paris: Éditions du Seuil, 1975.
Brunetta, Gian Piero. *Identikit del cinema italiano oggi*. Venezia: Marsilio editori, 2000.
—. *Storia del cinema italiano: Dal 1945 agli anni ottanta*. Roma: Editori Riuniti, 1982.
Caccia, Fulvio. *Republic Denied*. Trans. Dominic Cusmano and Daniel Sloate. Toronto: Guernica Editions, 2002.
—. *Sous le signe du Phénix: Entretiens avec quinze créateurs italo-québécois*. Montréal: Les éditions Guernica, 1985.
Canby, Vincent. "Four Movies, Two for Children and Two from Abroad, Open: Screen: *Bread and Chocolate*." *The New York Times*, 14 July 1978.
Canovi, Antonio. "La communauté italienne d'Argenteuil. Identité et mémoires en question." *Les Italiens en France depuis 1945*. By Marie-Claude Blanc-Chaléard. Rennes: Presses Universitaires de Rennes, 2003.

Carrière, Jean-Claude. *The Secret Language of Film.* New York: Random House, 1994.
Casella, Paola. *Hollywood Italian.* Milan: Baldini & Castoldi, 1998.
Caryn, James. "Queen of Hearts." *The Washington Post,* 20 September1989.
Casillo, Robert. *Gangster Priest: The Italian American Cinema of Martin Scorsese.* Toronto: University of Toronto Press, 2006.
Cavanna, François. *Les Rituals.* Paris: Belfond, 1978.
Chaplin, Charles. *My Autobiography.* 1964. Middlesex: Penguin Books, 1966.
Chandler, Charlotte. *Nobody's Perfect: Billy Wilder: A Personal Biograph.* New York, Simon & Schuster, 2002.
Chatman, Seymour. *Antonioni or The Surface of the World.* Berkerley: University of California, 1985.
Chauvet, Amélie. commeaucinema.com. December 2008.
Chesser, Eustache. *Why Suicide?* London: Arrow Books, 1968.
Chevalier, Jean, and Gheerbrant, Alain, eds. *Dictionnaire des Symboles.* Paris: Robert Lafont/Jupiter, 1982.
Chiellino, Gino. *Fremde.* Toronto: Guernica Editions, 1995.
Chion, Michel. *L'audio-vision: Son et image au cinéma.* 1990. Paris: Armand Colin/Cinéma, 2008.
—. *Écrire un scénario.* Paris: Cahiers du cinéma, 1985.
—. *La Voix au cinéma.* Paris: Éditions de l'Étoile/Cahiers du Cinéma, 1982.
Cieutat, Michel. *Martin Scorsese.* Paris: Rivages, 1986.
Coleridge, Samuel Taylor. *Selected Poetry and Prose.* New York: Holt, Rinhart and Winston, Inc, 1971.
Combs, Richard. "Raging Bull." *Sight and Sound.* London, Spring, 1981.
Cooper, David. *The Death of the Family.* London: Penguin Books, 1971.
D'Alfonso, Antonio. *In Italics.* Toronto: Guernica Editions, 1996.
—. *Gambling with Failure.* Toronto: Exile Editions, 2005.
Dalle Vacche, Angela. *The Body in the Mirror: Shapes of History in Italian Cinema.* Princeton: Princeton University Press, 1992.
Dante, Alighieri. *La Divina Commedia.* Milano: Bietti, 1974.
—. *Inferno.* Trans. John D. Sinclair. New York: Oxford Press, 1939.
Debord, Guy. *La Société du Spectacle.* 1967. Paris: Gallimard, 1992.
Deleuze, Gilles. *L'image-mouvement: Cinéma 1.* Paris: Éditions de Minuit, 1983.
—. *L'image-temps: Cinéma 2.* Paris: Éditions de Minuit, 1985.
Deleuze, Gilles, and Guattari, Felix. *On the Line (Rhizome and Politics).* Trans. John Johnston. New York: Semiotext(e), 1983.
De Mauro, Tullio. *Linguaggio e società nell'Italia d'oggi.* Torino: ERI, 1978.
Demoule, Jean-Paul. "Trois millions d'années d'immigration." *Émigrer immigrer: Le genre humain.* Olender, Maurice, ed. Paris: Le Seuil, 1989.
De Sanctis, Francesco. *Storia della letteratura italiana.* Italy: Bietti, 1973.
De Giorgio, Michela. *Le italiane dall'Unità ad oggi.* Bari: Laterza, 1992.
Durkheim, Émile. *Le suicide.* Étude de sociologie. 1897. Paris: PUF, 1981.
Ebert, Roger. "Buddy Buddy." *Chicago Sun-Times,* 1 January 1981.
Eco, Umberto. *L'oeuvre ouverte.* Trans. C. Roux de Bézieux and A. Boucourechliev. Paris: Éditions du Seuil, 1965

—. *La structure absente: Introduction à la recherche sémiotique.* 1968. Trans. Uccio-Esposito-Torrigiani. Paris: Mercure de France, 1972.
Faure, Elie. *Fonction du cinéma.* 1953. Paris: Éditions Gonthier, 1964.
Fellini, Federico. *Fare un film.* Turino: Einaudi, 1980.
Field, Syd. *Screenplay: The Foundations of Screenwriting.* 1984. New York: Dell, 2005.
—. *The Screenwriter's Workbook.* New York: Dell, 1984.
—. *The Screenwriter's Problem Solver.* New York: Dell, 1998.
Ferraro, Thomas J. *Ethnic Passages: Literary Immigrants in Twentieth-Century America.* Chicago: The University of Chicago Press, 1993.
Finkielkraut, Alain. *La défaite de la pensée.* Paris: Gallimard, 1987.
Foucault, Michel. "What Is an Author?" Trans. Donald F. Bouchard. *Screen.* Vol. 20. No. 1, Spring, 1979.
Friedman, Lester D. *Unspeakable Images: Ethnicity and the American Cinema.* Chicago: University of Illinois Press, 1991.
Fuchs, Lawrence H. *The American Kaleidoscope: Race, Ethnicity, and the Civic Culture.* Londons: Wesleyan University Press, 1990.
Gagliardi, Carole. *"Mediterraneo sempre." Le Journal de Montréal.* Saturday, 20 May 2000.
Gambino, Richard. *Blood of My Blood: The Dilemma of the Italian-Americans.* 1974. Toronto: Guernica, 1996.
Ganeri, Margherita. "La fine della letteratura italoamericana in Helen Barolini." *Italian Canadiana.* Vol. XXIV. University of Toronto, 2010.
Gardaphé, Fred. *Italian Signs, American Streets.* Madison, NJ: Fairleigh Dickinson University Press, 1996.
Genette, Gérard. "Frontières du récit." *Communications.* No. 8. Paris: Éditions du Seuil, 1966.
—. *Figures I.* Paris: Éditions du Seuil, 1966.
Gignac, Martin. "L'Emmerdeur porte bien son nom." *Le frelon vert,* 14 January 2011.
Gili, Jean A. *Le cinéma italien 2.* Paris: 10/18, 1982.
Glazer, Nathan. *Ethnic Dilemmas: 1964-1982.* Harvard: Harvard University, 1983.
Godard, Jean-Luc. *Histoire(s) du cinéma: Toutes les histoires, Une histoire seule.* Paris: Gallimard-Gaumont, 1998.
—. *Histoire(s) du cinéma: Seul le cinéma, Fatale beauté.* Paris: Gallimard-Gaumont, 1998.
—. *Histoire(s) du cinéma: La monnaie de l'absolu, Une vague nouvelle.* Paris: Gallimard-Gaumont, 1998.
—. *Histoire(s) du cinéma: Le contrôle de l'univers, Les signes parmi nous.* Paris: Gallimard-Gaumont, 1998.
—. *Jean-Luc Godard par Jean-Luc Godard: 1950-1984.* Paris: Cahiers du cinéma, 1998.
—. *Jean-Luc Godard par Jean-Luc Godard: 1984-1998.* Paris: Cahiers du cinéma, 1998.
Goethe, F.W. *Faust: Part Two.* Trans. Philip Wayne, London: Penguin, 1959.
Goliot-Lété, Anne, and Vanoye, Francis. *Précise d'analyse filmique.* 1992. Paris: Armand Colin, 2009.
Goldman, Annie. *Cinéma et société moderne.* Paris: Denoël/Gonthier, 1971.
Grazzini, Giovanni. *Cinema '78.* Roma-Bari: Editori Laterza, 1979.

Grazzini, Giovanni. *Gli anni Settanta in cento film.* Roma-Bari: Editori Laterza, 1977.
Greimas, A.J. *Du sens.* Paris: Éditions du Seuil, 1970.
—. Sémantique structurale. Paris: Larousse, 1966.
Grierson, John. *Grierson on Documentary.* Forsyth Hardy, ed. London: Faber and Faber, 1966.
Griffith Richard. "The Film Since Then." *The Film Till Now.* By Paul Rotha. Middlesex: The Hamlyn Publishing Group Ltd., 1967.
Guglielmo, Jennifer and Salerno, Salvatore. *Are Italians White? How Race is Made in America.* New York: Routledge, 2003.
Hansen, Marcus Lee. "The Third Generation in America." Originally with the title "The Problem of the Third Generation Immigrant." 1938. *Commentary.* No. 14, November, 1952.
Hawton K., and van Heeringen K. "Suicide." *Lancet,* 373 (9672): 1372–81, April 2009.
Hinson Hal. *"Queen of Hearts." Washington Post,* 11 October 1989.
Hobsbawn, E.J. *Nations and Nationalism Since 1780.* 1990. Cambridge (U.K.): Cambridge University Press, 1997.
Hontebeyrie, Isabelle. "J'ai eu trop de succès, j'ai été puni: Interview with Francis Veber." *7 jours,* 19 April 2009.
Iacovetta, Francesca, Perin, Roberto and Principe, Angelo, eds. *Enemies Within: Italian and Other Internees in Canada and Abroad.* Toronto: University of Toronto Press, 2000.
Jean, Marcel. *Le Cinéma québécois.* 1991. Montréal: Boréal, 2005.
Jackson, Kevin, ed. *Schrader on Schrader & Other Writings.* London: Faber and Faber, 1990.
Jacobson, Roman. *Essais de lingistique générale.* Translated by Nicolas Ruwet. Paris: Éditions de Minuit, Collection "Points," 1963.
—. *Questions de poétique.* Edited by Tzvetan Todorov. Paris: Éditions du Seuil, Collection "Poétique", 1973.
Jones, Ken. *L'Argent.* London: British Film Institute, 1999.
Jones, LeRoi. *Black Music.* New York: William Morrow and Company, 1970.
—. *Blues People.* New York: William Morrow and Company, 1963.
Jullier, Laurent. *Le son au cinéma.* Paris: Cahiers du cinéma, 2006.
Jullier, Laurent, and Michel Marie. *Lire les images de cinéma.* Paris: Larouse, 2009.
Jung, C.G. *Memories, Dreams, Reflections.* New York: Random House, 1965.
—. *Psychological Reflections: A New Anthology of His Writings, 1905-1961.* New York: Princeton University Press, 1978.
Kallen, Horace M. *Culture and Democracy in the United States.* 1924. New Brunswick (U.S.A.): Transaction Publishers, 1998.
Kay, Karyn, and Peary, Gerald, eds. *Women and the Cinema: A Critical Anthology.* New York: E.P. Dutton, 1977.
Kelly, Mary Pat. *Martin Scorsese: A Journey.* New York: Thunder's Mouth Press, 1991.
Kristeva, Julia. *Semanalysis: Recherchs pour une sémanalyse.* Paris: Éditions du Seuil, 1969.
—. *Étrangers à nous-mêmes.* Paris: Librairie Arthème Fayard, 1988.

Kuhlen, Merritt. *The Origin of Language: Tracing the Evolution of the Mother Tongue.* New York: John Wiley & Sons, 1994.
Landy, Marcia. *Italian Film.* Cambridge: Cambridge University, 2000.
La Vecchia, C., Lucchini, F., and Levi, F. "Worldwide trends in suicide mortality, 1955–1989." *Acta Psychiatr Scand.* 90 (1): 53–64, July 1994.
Leprohon, Pierre. *Le cinéma italien.* Paris: Éditions Seghers, 1966.
Lévi-Strauss, Claude. *Race et histoire.* Paris: Gallimard-FolioPlus, 2007.
Lizzani, Carlo. *Il cinéma italiano: Dalle origini agli anni ottanta.* 1979. Roma: Editori Riuniti, 1982.
Lotti, Gianfranco. *L'avventuroso storia della lingua italiana.* Milano: Bompiani, 2000.
Lourdeaux, Lee. *Italian and Irish Filmmakers in America.* Philadelphia: Temple University Press, 1990.
Luz, Rogerio. *Analyse structurale du récit filmique:* Le dieu noir et le diable blanc *de Glauber Rocha.* Université Catholique de Louvain, Centre des techniques de Diffusion, 1969.
Mackinnon, Kenneth. *Greek Tragedy into Film.* London: Croom Helm, 1986.
Magnusson, Linda. "Causes of the Italian mass emigration." http://library.thinkquest.org/26786/en/articles, 15 August 1999.
Mangin, Arnaud. FilmsActu.com, 9 December 2008.
Marcus, Millicent. *After Fellini: National Cinema in the Postmodern Age.* Baltimore-London, The John Hopkins University Press, 2002.
—. *Italian Film in the Light of Neorealism.* Princeton: Princeton University, 1986.
Marlowe, Christopher. *Dr. Faustus.* New York: Dover Publications, Inc., 1994.
Martellone, Anna Maria. "A Plea against the Deconstruction of Ethnicity and in Favor of Political History." *Altreitalie.* No. 6. Torino: Edizioni della Fondazione Giovanni Agnelli, November 1991.
Martinet, André. *Éléments de linguistique générale.* Paris: Armand Colin, 1967.
McKee, Robert. *Story: Substance, Structure, Style, and The Principles of Screenwriting.* ItBooks-HarperCollins Publishers, 1977.
McLuhan, Marshall. *Culture Is Our Business.* New York, Ballantine Books, 1970.
—. *The Gutenberg Galaxy.* Toronto: University of Toronto, 1965.
—. *The Medium Is the Massage.* New York: Bantam, 1967.
Menninger, Karl. *Man Against Himself.* New York: Harvest Books, 1938.
Merrell, Floyd. *Pierce, Signs, and Meaning.* Toronto: University of Toronto Press, 1997.
Metz, Christian. *L'Énonciation impersonnelle ou le site du film.* Paris: Méridiens-Klincksieck, 1991.
—. *Essais sur la signification au cinéma. Tome I.* Paris: Éditions Klincksieck, 1975.
—. *Essais sur la signification au cinéma. Tome II.* Paris: Éditions Klincksieck, 1972.
—. *Langage et cinéma.* Paris: Éditions Larousse, Collection "Langue et Langage", 1971.
—. *Le signifiant imaginaire.* 1977. Paris: Chrisian Bourgois, 2002.
—. *Film Language: A Semiotics of the cinema.* Trans. Michael Taylor. Chicago: University of Chicago, 1991.
Micciché, Lino. *Filmologia e filologia: Studi sul cinema italiano.* Venezia: Marsilio editori, 2002.

—. *La ragione e lo squardo.* Cosenza: Edistampa-Lerici, 1979.
—. ed. *Il bell'Antonio.* Torino: Philip Morris, 1996.
—. ed. *Il cinema del riflusso.* Venezia: Marsilio Ederitori, 1997.
Micone, Marco. *Le figuier enchanté.* Montréal: Boréal, 1992.
Molinaro, Édouard. *Intérieur soir.* Paris: Anne Carrière, 2009.
—. "Édouard Molinaro : Sans regret ou presque." Interview with Éric Clément, *La Presse,* 23 August 2010.
—. "Édouard Molinaro." *Le Parisien,* 15 December 2008.
Montagu, Ivor. *Film World.* 1964. London: Penguin Books 1967.
Montini, Franco, ed. *Il cinema italiano del terzo millennio.* Torino: Lindau, 2002.
Morin, Edgar. *Le cinéma ou l'homme imaginaire.* Paris: Édition de Minuit, 1958.
Negroponte, Nicholas. *Being Digital.* 1995. New York: Vintage, 1996.
Nöth, Winfried. *Handbook of Semiotics.* Indianapolis: Indiana University Press, 1990.
Novak, Michael. *The Rise of the Unmeltable Ethnics.* 1971. New York: The MacMillan Company, 1972.
Olson, James Stuart. *The Ethnic Dimension in American History.* New York: St. Martin's Press, 1979.
Olender, Maurice, ed. *Émigrer Immigrer.* Paris: Éditions du Seuil, 1989.
Ovid (Publius Ovidius Naso). *Le Metamorfosi.* Enrico Oddone, ed. Milano: Tascabili Bompiani, 1994.
Pasolini, Pier Paolo. *Empirismo erectico.* 1991. Milan: Garzanti, 2010.
—. *L'expérience hérétique.* Trans. Anna Rocchi Pullberg. Paris: Payot, 1976.
Petley, Julian. *"Raging Bull."* www.filmreference.com, 27 Feb 2008.
Perniola, Mario. *Enigmi: Il momento egizio nella società e nell'arte.* Genova: Costa & Nolan, 1990.
Petrella, Riccardo. *La Renaissance des cultures régionales en Europe.* Paris: Editions Entente, 1978.
Pettigrew, Thomas F. *Prejudice: Dimensions of Ethnicity.* Cambridge: Harvard University Press, 1980.
Pivato, Joseph. *Contrasts.* Montreal: Guernica Editions, 1985.
—. *Echo.* Toronto: Guernica Editions, 1994.
Principe, Angelo. *The Darkest Side of the Fascist Years.* Toronto: Guernica Editions, 1999.
Procacci, Giuliano. *History of the Italian People.* 1968. Trans. Anthony Paul. Middlesex: Penguin, 1978.
Propp, Vladimir. *Morphologie du conte.* Paris: Éditions du Seuil, 1970.
Queneau, Raymond. *Bâton, chiffres et lettres.* Paris: Gallimard, 1965.
Ramirez, Bruno, and Tana, Paul. *La Sarrazine.* Montréal: Boréal, 1992.
Realini, Michele. "Monsieur Milan." Radio svizzera italiana, 2 October, 2005.
Rieder, Jonathan. *Canarsie: The Jews and Italians of Brooklyn Against Liberalism.* Cambridge: Harvard University Press, 1985.
Rohmer, Éric. *Le goût de la beauté.* Paris: Cahiers du cinéma/Éditions de l'Étoile, 1984.
Rosoli, Gianfausto. "Le popolazioni di origine italiana oltreoceano." www.home-emigrati.it.com, 11 October 2011.
Rossellini, Roberto. *Fragments d'une autobiographie.* Paris: Ramsay, 1987.

—. *Un esprit libre ne doit rien apprendre en esclave.* Paris: Fayard, 1977.
Roy, André. *Dictionnaire général du cinéma: Du cinématographe à Internet.* Montréal: Fides, 2007.
Ruhlen, Merritt. *The Origin of Language: Tracing the Evolution of the Mother Tongue.* New York: John Wiley & Son, Inc. 1994.
Salvatore, Filippo. *Fascism and the Italian of Montreal.* Toronto: Guernica Editions, 1998.
Sand, Shlomo. *Comment le peuple juif fut inventé.* Paris: Flammarion, 2010.
Sapir, Edward. *Language.* 1921. New York: Harvest Books, 1949.
Scaruffi, Piero. "The History of Cinema: Franco Brusati." Trans. Judith Harris. www.scaruffi.com/director/brusati.html, 2009.
Scambray, Kenneth. *The North American Italian Renaissance.* Toronto: Guernica, 2000.
Scarpetta, Guy. *Éloge du cosmopolitisme.* Paris: Grasset, 1981.
—. *L'impureté.* Paris: Grasset, 1985.
Schrader, Paul. *Transcendental Style: Ozu, Bresson, Dreyer.* Berkeley: University of California Press, 1972.
Schifano, Laurence. *Le cinéma italien de 1945 à nos jours: Crise et création.* 2nd ed. Paris: Armand Colin, 2007.
Sebeok, Thomas A. *Signs: An Introduction to Semiotics.* Toronto: University of Toronto, 1994.
Seymour, Gene. *"Queen of Hearts."* EW.com (Entertainment Weekly), 16 March 1990.
Sinyard, Neil. *"Raging Bull." Films Illustrated.* London, May 1981.
Sollors, Werner. *Beyond Ethnicity: Consent and Descent in American Culture.* New York: Oxford University, 1986.
Steinberg, Stephen. *The Ethnic Myth: Race, Ethnicity, and Class in America.* Boston: Beacon Press, 1981.
Tamburri, Anthony Julian. *A Semiotic of Ethnicity.* New York: State of New York, 1998.
—. *To Hyphenate or Not to Hyphenate: The Italian/American Writer: An Other American.* Montreal: Guernica Editions, 1991.
Tamburri, Anthony Julian, Giodarno, Paolo A., Gardaphé, L. Fred, eds. *From the Margins: Writings in Italian Americana.* Lafayette: Purdue University, 1991.
Tirabassi, Maddalena. "Le emigrate italiane in prospettiva comparata." *Altreitalie.* No. 9. Torino: Edizioni della Fondazione Giovanni Agnelli, June-January 1993.
Truby, John. *The Anatomy of Story.* New York: Faber and Faber, 2007.
Truffaut, François. *Le plaisir des yeux.* Paris: Cahiers du cinéma, 1987.
Valéry, Paul. *Oeuvres II.* Paris: Bibliothèques de la Pléaide, 1960.
Valli, Sergio. *"Pane e cioccolata."* http://www.radioland.it/recensioni-films, 2009.
Verdicchio, Pasquale. *Devils in Paradise.* Toronto: Guernica, 1997.
Vegliante, Jean-Charles. "Cinema e presenza italiana in Francia." *Altreitalie.* No. 6. Torino: Edizioni della Fondazione Giovanni Agnelli, November 1991.
Voisard, Jacques, and Ducastelle, Christine. *La question immigrée dans la France d'aujourd'hui.* 1988. Paris: Calmann-Lévy/ Éditions du Seuil, 1990.
Walzer, Michael. "What Does It Mean to Be an "American"?' *Social Research.* Vol. 57. No. 3. Fall, 1990.

—. *What It Means to Be an American: Essays on the American Experience.* New York: Marsilio Publishers, 1996.

—. *On Toleration.* New Haven: Yale University Press, 1997.

West, Cornel. *Beyond Eurocentrism and Multiculturalism: Prophetic Reflections, Notes on Race and Power in America.* Vol. 2. Monroe, ME: Common Courage Press, 1993.

—. *Race Matters.* Boston: Beacon Press, 1993.

Wollen, Peter. *Signs and Meaning in the Cinema.* 1969. London: Indiana University Press and British Film Institute, 1972.

Wood, Robin. "The Homosexual Subtext: *Raging Bull.*" In *Australian Journal of Screen Theory.* No. 15-16. Kensington, New South Wales, 1983.

Wright, Will. *Six Gins and Society: A Structural Study of the Western.* Berkeley: University of California, 1975.

Zavatina, Cesare. "Some Ideas on the Cinema." *Vittorio De Sica: Contemporary Perspectives.* Howard Curle and Stepen Snyder, eds. Trans. Pier Luigi Lanza. Toronto: University of Toronto Press, 2000.

Index

Abbott, Bud 111
Adamo, Salvatore 28
Adamo, Maria Gabriella 221
Adler, Alfred 199
Aesop 147
Akin, Faith 337
Albanese, Vincenzo 218
Alberini, Filoteo 15
Alberoni, Francesco 130
Allen, Woody 106, 274, 335
Aloisio, Anita 30
Amandola, Vittorio 143-214
Amiel, Jon 11, 26, 143-214
Antonioni, Michelangelo 94, 258
Aristotle 129
Armes, Roy 30, 31
Arnheim, Rudolf 79, 84
Arnold, Andrea 154
Atkinson, Rowan 118
Aumont, Jacques 33, 42
Audiard, Jacques 154
Auteuil, Daniel 109, 110

Bachy, Victor 36
Barolini, Hélène 222
Baroux, Olivier 337
Barthes, Roland 16, 35, 41, 42, 60, 156, 283
Barzotti, Claude 139, 141 (n)
Baudrillard, Jean 19, 44 (n)
Bazin, André 32, 130, 139
Bechelloni, Antonio 139
Becker, Jacques 108
Bellour, Raymond 34
Bellocchio, Marco 218
Belluscio, Steven J. 147
Belmondo, Jean-Paul 29
Bergson, Henri 68, 96
Bergman, Ingmar 106, 135
Bergman, Ingrid 258
Bernardi, Sandro 31, 44 (n)
Berry, Richard 112
Bizet, Georges 91

Blanc-Chaléard, Marie-Claude 28, 139
Blanchard, Louise, 226
Bondanella, Peter 152
Bonitzer, Pascal 32
Bourdieu, Pierre 156
Bourne, Randolph 13, 18, 19, 42, 43 (n)
Brando, Marlon 9, 318
Brault, Michel 218
Brel, Jacques 29, 104-142, 191
Brassens, Georges 28
Bresson, Robert 148, 282
Brode, Douglas 276
Brown, Joe 148
Browning, Robert 27
Brusati, Franco 11, 20, 26, 31, 45-103, 145, 154
Buñuel, Luis 106
Burnett, William R. 279
Byron, Lord 27

Cabrel, Francis 28
Caccia, Fulvio 330
Calegero 28
Calise, Ugo 76
Calliari, Marco 30
Canby, Vincent 60
Canovi, Antonio 138
Capra, Frank 27, 146, 183
Cardile, Angela 104-142
Carell, Steve 109
Carle, Gilles 217
Carrière, Jean-Claude 290
Carrière, Marcel 218
Caruso, Frank 29
Casella, Paola 289
Casillo, Robert 270, 307, 314, 321
Cassavetes, John 27, 335
Castelnuovo, Nino 111
Caticchio, Tonino 330
Cavanna, François 28, 138
Chaplin, Charles 53, 64, 68, 86, 97, 160, 208
Chatman, Seymour 94, 257

Chesser, Eustace 210
Chichin, Fred 28
Chion, Michel 44 (n), 116, 158, 207, 257
Cicero, Nado 138
Cieutat, Michel 274, 275, 322
Clair, René 301
Clément, René 38
Clémenti, Pierre 105
Cocteau, Jean 28
Colasanto, Nicolas 301
Coleridge, Samuel Taylor 147
Combs, Richard 301
Comolli, Jean-Louis 138, 140
Connelly, Marc 12
Convertino, Michael 192
Cooper, David 79, 86, 103 (n), 140, 142 (n)
Coppola, Francis Ford 12, 20, 27, 65, 144
Cormon, Cid 321
Costello, Lou 111
Cotugno, Toto 139
Coutard, Raoul 114
Cowen, Paul S. 17
Curtis, Tony 167

D'Angelo, Frank 29
Dale, Cynthia 29
Dale, Jennifer 29
Dalida 28
Dalle Vacche, Angela 152
Darras, Jean-Pierre-104-142
Dante 71
Debord, Guy 106
De Curtis, Ernesto 100, 164, 204
De Curtis, G. B. 204
de Funès, Louis 105
de Gobineau, Arthur 14
de La Fontaine, Jean 147
Deleuze, Gilles 145
Demy, Jacques 111
De Niro, Robert 9, 270-329
Depardieu, Gérard 109, 110
Depraz, Xavier 104-142
De Sica, Vittorio 90
Di Capua, Eduardo 259
di Michele, Mary 215-269
Dorelli, Johnny 68
Douglas, Kirk 167
DuBois, W.E.B. 13
Durkheim, Émile 209
Duse, Vittorio, 141-214

Dylan, Bob 279

Ebrahimian, Ghasem 19
Edwards, Blake 67, 68, 336
Eastwood, Clint 107, 332
Ebert, Roger 148
Eisenstein, Sergei 94, 145
Eliot, T. S. 259
Ellwand, Toni 29
Elmaleh, Gad 109
Eustache, Jean 20, 106

Farrelly, Peter 147
Faure, Elie 151, 193, 213 (n)
Favre, Bernard 138
Field, Syd 37, 38, 39, 61, 72, 86, 99, 113
Fellini, Federico 20, 55, 67, 90, 106, 208
Ferrari, Marco 106
Ferraro, Thomas J. 19
Fiastri, Jaja 31, 45-103
Finaldi, Angelo 215-269
Finaldi, Carmine 215-269
Finaldi, Coco 215-269
Fiorelli, G. 98
Flaherty, Robert 30, 215
Fleischer, Richard 198
Fogliato, Patricia 29
Foucault, Michel 156, 157
Franken, Steven 67
Freud, Sigmund 89, 130, 199
Friedkin, William 106
Friedman, Lester D. 17

Gabin, Jean 108
Gagliardi, Carole 225
Galluccio, Steve 30, 333
Gambino, Richard 205
Gardaphé, Fred 331
Garrone, Matteo 15
Gaudreault, André 208
Gaudreault, Émile 333
Gere, Richard 308
Gignac, Martin 112
Gili, Jean A. 49, 76, 85, 103 (n)
Giordano, Paolo A 331
Glazer, Nathan 16, 295
Godard, Jean-Luc 145, 220, 282
Golio-Lété, Anne 143
Goretta, Claude 106
Goethe, Johann Wolfgang von 320

Grant, Cary 258
Greimas, A. J. 39, 40, 136
Grémillon, Jean 138
Grierson, John 30, 215, 216, 258
Grisoni, Tony 11, 28, 143-214, 148
Griffith, D.W. 145
Groulx, Gilles 218
Groulx, Sylvie 220
Guy, François 256

Hall, Rebecca 17
Hansen, Marcus Lee 155
Hardy, John 156
Hardy, Oliver 111
Haskell, Molly 299
Hawkes, Ian 143-214
Hayden, Joseph 48
Hitchcock, Alfred 158, 168, 177, 258
Hinson, Hal 148
Hobsbawn, E. J. 152
Hofstetter, Roman 48, 51, 60

Iacovetta, Francesca 261
Izzo, Jean-Claude 28

Jackson, Kevin 278
James, Caryn 148, 186
Jasprisot, Sébastien 29
Jean, Marcel 214 (n), 216, 217, 219
Jones, Kent 148
Jones, LeRoi 32
Juliani, Dominique 138

Kael, Pauline 146, 275
Kallen, Horace M. 13, 30, 83
Karina, Anna 45-103
Kazan, Elia 9, 42, 317
Keaton, Buster 132
Keighley, William 12
Kristeva, Julia 33, 89, 97
Kuntzel, Thierry 42
Kinski, Klaus 106, 107

Lambert, Jimmy 143-214
Lafleur, Louis-Roger 217
LaMotta, Jake 270-329
Landy, Marcia 152
Lang, Fritz, 42
Laroux, René 106
Laurel, Stan 111

Lavoie, Herménégilde 217
Lee, Spike 332, 333, 336
Lelouch, Claude 115
Lennon, Michael 9
Lemmon, Jack 106, 112
Leone, Sergio 54
LeRoy, Mervyn 279
Lévi-Strauss, Claude 14, 332
Lewis, Jerry 111
Liconti, Carlo 12, 29 , 219
Lipset, Seymour M. 222
Long, Joseph 143-214
Lourdeaux, Lee 18, 271, 272, 273, 314
Lucas, George 106
Luchini, Fabrice 29
Lumet, Sidney 106
Lynch, David 145

Mackinnon, Kenneth 54
Mailer, Norman 9
Mamou, Sabine 138
Mancuso, Nick 29
Manet, Edouard 68
Manfredi, Nino 31, 45-103
Mangione, Jerre 271
Manzoni, Alessandro 28
Marchand, Jean-Pierre 138
Marcus, Millicent 11, 43 (n), 152
Marie, Michel 33
Marinetti, F.T. 28
Marino, Giambattista 28
Marioni, Ray 143-214
Marlowe, Christopher 300, 301
Marsolais, Gilles 217
Martin, Dean 111
Martin, Mardick 270
Martinet, André 52
Mascagni, Pietro 273
Maselli, Francesco 138
Matthau, Walter 106, 107, 112
Mazzini, Giuseppe 28
McKee, Robert 39, 57, 61
McLuhan, Marshall 87, 330
Mendes, Sam 38
Menninger, Karl 95, 210
Metz, Christian 11, 16, 34, 41, 46, 49, 65, 93, 130, 144, 199, 207, 219, 276
Miccichè, Lino 34
Micone, Marco 221, 222, 223
Minghella, Anthony 28, 335

Minnelli, Vincente 304
Miron, Gaston 217
Montand, Yves 28, 29
Molinaro, Édouard 11, 20, 26, 27, 44 (n), 104-142
Moriarty, Cathy 270-329
Morra, Mario 63
Morris, Charles W. 15
Morrissey, Paul 111
Mortin, David 29
Moustaki, Georges 28
Mozart, Amadeus 70, 76, 83
Murphy, Eddy 92
Myrdal, Gunnar 147

Ninchieri, Guido 260, 261
Nolte, Nick 109
Nardi, Tony 29, 30
Nöth, Winfried 41
Novac, Michael 153, 200, 222, 223

Olson, James Stuart 308, 309
Oury, Gérard 12

Pasolini, Pier Paolo 30, 31, 33, 45, 103 (n), 154
Patucchi, Daniele 70
Paul, Bernand 138
Paulhan, Jean 32
Pernicci, Anna 143-214
Perreault, Pierre 31, 217, 218
Pesci, Joe 191, 270-329
Pierce, Charles Sanders 15
Portugais, Louis 217
Potter, Dennis 153
Prima, Louis 312
Principe, Angelo 261
Propp, Vladimir 39, 40
Proulx, Maurice 217
Provencher, Paul 217
Puzo, Mario 19

Queneau, Raymond 137

Ramirez, Bruno 30, 221, 222, 223
Reggiani, Serge 28, 29
Reisman, David 13
Resnais, Alain 260
Renoir, Jean 68, 138, 139
Richard, Pierre 109
Robertson, Robbie 320

Robinson, Edward G. 279
Rohmer, Éric 59
Rosi, Francesco 106, 152
Rosoli, Gianfausto 75
Rossetti, Christina 27, 331
Rossetti, Dante Gabriele 27
Rossellini, Roberto 15, 90, 257
Rossi, Vittorio 29
Rouch, Jean 218
Rozier, Jacques 35
Rudd, Paul 109
Ruhlen, Merritt 179, 206, 207
Russo, Vincenzo 259

Sacco and Vanzetti, 139
Sarris, Andrew 44 (n), 146
Sartre, Jean-Paul 130
Savage, Peter 270, 293
Scambray, Ken 330
Scarpetta, Guy 27
Schrader, Paul 27, 38, 270, 278, 279, 282, 299, 304, 308, 315, 319
Scorsese, Martin 9, 11, 20, 26, 27, 38, 106, 270-329
Sellers, Peter 67, 336
Seymour, Gene 148
Shelley, Percy 27
Schoonmaker, Thelma 277
Short, Martin 109
Silver, Joan Micklin 333
Simon, Michel 301
Sinapi, Jean-Pierre 138
Smith, Christopher 145
Sollors, Werner 12, 14, 18
Southon, Mike 165
Spielberg, Steven 332
Steiger, Rod 317
Stewart, James 183
Strasberg, Lee 155

Tamburri, A. J. 214 (n), 331
Tana, Paul 12, 30, 219, 221, 222, 223
Tarantino, Quentin 145
Tate, Richard 256
Tati, Jacques 53, 67, 68, 118, 158
Tessier, Albert 217
Thielemans, Toots 290
Timsit, Patrick 109, 112
Titian 68
Tognazzi, Ugo 105

Totò 7
Tovoli, Luciano 63
Travers, James 108
Truffaut, François 78, 131

Valente, N. 98
Valéry, Paul 16, 28
Valli, Sergio 100
Vanoye, Francis 143
Veber, Francis 104-142
Vegliante, Jean-Charles, 138
Ventresca, Robert 261
Ventura, Lino 29, 104-142
Verdicchio, Pasquale 151
Vice Versa 151
Villeret, Jacques 109
Visconti, Luchino 106

Walzer, Michael 14, 17
Warner, W. Lloyd 12
Way, Eileen, 143-214
Wenders, Wim 115
Wertmüller, Lina 106
West, Cornell 17
Whalley, Tat 143-214
Wilder, Billy 105, 106, 107, 112, 130
Wissler, Clark 95
Wollen, Peter 146
Wolfe, Tom 283
Wood, Robin 287, 301, 303, 312, 316
Wright, Will 39, 54

Zagaria, Anita 143-214
Zangwill, Israel 330
Zanuc, Darryl F. 279, 280
Zavaglia, Nicola 11, 26, 30, 31, 130, 145, 191, 215-269
Zavatini, Cesare 31, 218
Zola, Émile 28

Poet, novelist, essayist, translator, photographer, and filmmaker, Antonio D'Alfonso has published more than seventy books (including translations) and has made five feature films.

Born in 1953, he is the founder of Guernica Editions which he managed for thirty-three years before passing it on to new owners in 2010.

For his novels, he won the Trillium Award and the Bressani Award.

His film *Bruco* won the New York Independent Film Award.

His film, *Tata,* was released in July 2020, and Sono in June 2024.

The Two-Headed Man: Collected Poems 1970-2020 was published in 2020.

He has started on YouTube a series of Conversations with writers, musicians, and artists.

His essays of *In Italics: In Defense of Ethnicity* (1996), *Gambling With Failure* (2005), *Poetica del plurilinguismo* (2015), *The Italian Canadian Write*r (2023) offer a unique perspective on decentralized identities. His books have been translated in French, Italian, German, Spanish, Estonian, and Portuguese. He has published as part of his memoirs *Outside Looking In (Entries 1980-1981)* (2022) and *19th Avenue* (2025).

He holds a Ph.D. from the University of Toronto. In 2016, he received an Honorary Doctorate from Athabasca University.

About the Author

Poet, novelist, essayist, translator, ANTONIO D'ALFONSO has published more than sixty books (including translations) and has made five feature films. He is the founder of Guernica Editions which he managed for thirty-three years before passing it on to new owners in 2010. He is also a co-founder of *Vice Versa* and the Association of ltalian-Canadian Writers. For his writings, he won the Trillium Award, the Bressani Award. His film *Bruco* won the New York Independent Film Award.

He holds a Ph.D. from the University of Toronto. In 2016, he received an Honorary Doctorate from Athabasca University. His film, *Tata*, on fatherhood, was released in July 2020. *The Two-Headed Man: Collected Poems 1970-2020* was published in July 2020. He has started a series of *Conversations* with artists and producers on Youtube. *Outside Looking In (Entries 1980-1981)* appeared in 2022 with Ekstasis Editions, as well as, in 2024, his most recent book, *The Italian Canadian Writer*.

Diaspora

As *diaspora* is the dispersion or spread of people from their original homeland, this series takes its name in the intellectual spirit of willful dispersion of subject matter and thought. It is dedicated to publishing those studies and creative works that in various and sundry ways either speak to or offer new methods of analysis of the Italian diaspora.

Carmelo Fucarino. *Two Italian Geniuses in New York: Broken American Dreams*. ISBN 978-1-955995-05-4. 2023.

Anthony Julian Tamburri, ed. *Re-Thinking* The Godfather *50 Years Later*. ISBN 978-1-955995-06-1. 2024.

Anthony Socci. *United We Stand. Pre WW II-Chronicles of the Italian Colony of Stamford*. ISBN 978-1-955995-07-8. 2024

Casa Lago Press Editorial Group

David Aliano
William Boelhower
Leonardo Buonomo
Ryan Calabretta-Sajder
Nancy Carnevale
Stephen J. Cerulli
Donna Chirico
Fred Gardaphé
Paolo Giordano
Nicolas Grosso

Donatella Izzo
John Kirby
Chiara Mazzucchelli
Emanuele Pettener
Mark Pietralunga
Joseph Sciorra
Ilaria Serra
Anthony Julian Tamburri
Sabrina Vellucci
Leslie Wilson

www.ingramcontent.com/pod-product-compliance
Lightning Source LLC
Chambersburg PA
CBHW052044220426
43663CB00012B/2431